NEW WORLD ADAMS

NEW WORLD ADAMS

CONVERSATIONS WITH CONTEMPORARY
WEST INDIAN WRITERS

DARYL CUMBER DANCE

PEEPAL TREE

First published in Great Britain in 1992
Reprinted in 2008
Peepal Tree Press Ltd
17 King's Avenue
Leeds LS6 1QS
England

ISBN 13: 9781900715041

ARTS COUNCIL ENGLAND Peepal Tree gratefully acknowledges Arts Council support

For my own New Adams (and Eves)
Warren Carlton Dance, Jr., Tadelech Edjigu Dance,
Allen Cumber Dance, Daryl Lynn Dance, and
Yoseph Warren Dance

We were blest with a virginal, unpainted world
With Adam's task of giving things their names...

Derek Walcott, *Another Life*

...out of such timbers
came our first book, our profane Genesis
    whose Adam speaks that prose
which, blessing some sea-rock, startles itself
    with poetry's surprise,
in a green world, one without metaphors...

Derek Walcott, *The Castaway*

CONTENTS

ACKNOWLEDGEMENTS

This project was conceived in 1978 when I was doing folklore research in Jamaica funded by a Fulbright-Hays Grant from the Council for International Exchange of Scholars. Most of the interviews were conducted and transcribed during the 1979-80 school year with the support of a Robert R Moton Memorial Institute Grant. Much of the final transcribing and editing of the manuscript was completed during the summer of 1981 when I received a Virginia Commonwealth University Summer Grants-in-Aid. I am grateful for the support of all of these agencies.

I am especially indebted to the twenty-nine writers who graciously granted me the interviews, twenty-two of which follow. Most of them made other contributions to this project as well, some of which are noted within this volume. In addition I must express special thanks for their gracious hospitality and assistance to Mrs. Mervyn Morris, Mrs. Denis Williams, Mrs. Jan Carew, Mrs. Austin Clarke, Mrs. Kenneth Ramchand, and Mrs. Ismith Khan. Unfortunately, either for reasons of space or because of subsequent embargoes placed by two writers (Edward Brathwaite and Andrew Salkey), several of the interviews could not be included in this book.

During the six months that I spent in Jamaica on the Fulbright-Hays Grant and during the three later trips related to this project, innumerable friends assisted me in various ways. They advised me in planning for the trips, secured an apartment for me, provided me with draperies and kitchen utensils, stocked my refrigerator, furnished my bar, saw that I was supplied with difficult-to-obtain items, lent me typewriters, books, and various other supplies and equipment, babysat, chauffeured me, entertained me, and in every conceivable fashion facilitated my work on this project and made my stay in Jamaica one of the most pleasant experiences of my life. For such assistance I wish to thank Dr. and Mrs. Everett Allen, Mrs. Bailey, Dr. Malcolm Biddlestone, Mr. Eladio Bottier, Miss Erna Brodber, Dr. Vivinne Bryant, Mr. and Mrs. Dean Brown, Mr. Eddie Chang, Dr. Arthur Drayton, Dr. and Mrs. John Engledew, Dr. and Mrs. Carl Gibbs, Miss Joan Irving, Ambassador and Mrs. Frederick Irving, Mr. Donald Jackson, Dr. and Mrs. Ronald Lampart, Mr. and Mrs. Alstomi Lewis, Miss Rowena Lewis, Mrs. Ivy Marrett, Mr. and Mrs. Mervyn Morris, Mr. Harold Pierson, Mr. and Mrs. Cecil Phillips, Mrs. Velma Pollard, Mr. and Mrs. Asquith Reid, Dr. and Mrs. Ashok Sayney, Mrs. Beryl Thomas, Mrs. Jackie Turpin, and Mr. and Mrs. John Thompson.

I am grateful to the University of the West Indies for allowing me library privileges, furnishing me an office, and granting me membership privileges at the Senior Common Room. I also wish to express my appreciation to the Institute of Jamaica and the Kingston and St. Andrew Parish Library for allowing me the use of their facilities.

Among friends in the United States who kindly assisted me in preparing for the trip to Jamaica in numerous ways, including giving me letters of introduction to friends and relatives in Jamaica, I wish to thank Miss Ruth Richardson, Mrs. Frankie Hutton O'Meally, Mrs. Jennifer Royal, and Dr. and Mrs. Dennis Warner.

I wish to thank all of my fellow Moton scholars for providing the intellectual stimulation and encouragement that ultimately results from the kind of interaction afforded by the Moton Center for Independent Studies. I am particularly grateful for the very real contributions to my project made by Drs. Glenda D Smith, Edward A Robinson, Eunice Shaed-Newton, and Philip V White. I also wish to thank Dr. Broadus N Butler, President of the Moton Institute, and Dr. Blyden Jackson, Consultant to the Moton Institute, for their interest, encouragement, and helpful criticism.

I am indebted to the scholars and colleagues who recommended me for the grants that enabled me to pursue this project: Dr. JD Levenson, Dr. Richard Priebe, Dr. George Kent, Dr. Richard Dorson, Dr. Chester Hedgepeth, Dr. Paul Minton, and Dr. M Thomas Inge.

I am grateful to the many secretaries who assisted me in the preparation of this manuscript, especially Mrs. Elsa Estrick, who is not only one of the most efficient typists I have had the privilege to know, but who also has a keen ear for transcribing which was of inestimable value to me. Further she evinced an interest in and an enthusiasm for the project which was inspirational to me: when she sent me the last material on which she worked, she wrote: 'At long last we have come to the end of this, to me, fantastic work. Let me say that I have thoroughly enjoyed meeting all these people, and when next we meet hopefully with some time to spare, please describe them for me, in detail – my imagination has understandably run riot!'

I wish to thank my graduate assistant, Alison Workman, who assisted me in the updating of the bibliographies for this revised edition.

Finally, I am grateful to my mother, Mrs. Veronica B Cumber, who supported me throughout this project with her time, energy, money, and unflagging confidence and encouragement.

INTRODUCTION

In a 1971 Edgar Mittelholzer Memorial Lecture, Guyanese poet Martin Carter asserted, 'My contention is that it is almost impossible to take a piece of writing and understand it properly without having a fair idea of the circumstances which brought it into being or the circumstances which made its coming into being a reality' [*Man and Making – Victim and Vehicle*, Georgetown, 1972, p.14]. Richard Wright insisted that an author inevitably 'comes to the conclusion that to account for his book is to account for his life' ['How Bigger was Born', *Native Son*, (New York: Harper and Row, 1966; orig. publ. in 1940) p.viii]. Unquestionably, much of the insight into the circumstances which helped to create and to shape a particular piece of literature and ultimately insight into the text of the work itself can be gained from the author. Throughout my study and teaching of literature I have found a necessary component in the study of a work to be a consideration of what the author has to say about that work – even when his statement cannot be taken at face value. Despite the fact that William Faulkner, for example, consistently played the role of literary unsophisticate and unconscious author, I have found *Faulkner in the University* [FL Gwynn and JL Blotner, eds. (Charlotsville: University of Virginia Press, 1959)] and other interviews invaluable resources for the study of Faulkner. Although I have on occasions attempted to discredit some of Ralph Ellison's assertions in interviews, I believe that one of the best sources for beginning a study of *Invisible Man* is to be found in interviews with the author. John O'Brien's *Interviews with Black American Writers* [New York: Liveright, 1973] is, I think, an essential supplementary text to the study of Black American literature. The list of significant interviews could be expanded interminably.

   Thus fully convinced of the importance of this added perspective to the study of a work of literature, I began to conduct interviews with Caribbean writers in order to make readily available such a resource to students of Caribbean literature. I initially drew up a list of approximately twenty writers, whom, on the basis of their recognition in studies of Caribbean literature and their commendation by teachers in the field, I deemed the major writers in the area, and I set out to contact them. The success of this project has been overwhelming, even to me. Not only did I succeed in arranging interviews with all except one of those whom I initially hoped to include, [the exception is VS Naipaul] but along the way I 'discovered' other significant writers in the field who also granted me interviews. That I have within this volume interviews with most of the more prominent Anglo-Caribbean writers of today is reinforced by the fact that throughout these dialogues those whom the writers themselves cite as significant are almost inevitably represented in this study. Clearly, since these interviews were conducted in 1979-80, there is now a new generation of writers emerging, particularly women. There is the encouragement to a further volume.

A challenging aspect of this adventure has been the detective work involved in locating these authors and the logistics of arranging interviews with them. Their seemingly incessant movement from one place to the other was particularly frustrating for me, since for my purposes it was absolutely requisite that all the Jamaican writers stay put in Jamaica during the seven days of my trip there and that all the Trinidadian writers remain patiently in Trinidad for the next four days, while every one of the Guyanese writers steadfastly await my arrival in Guyana immediately thereafter for a three-day stay. At another time the writers in Canada, New York and the New England states were required to remain stationary during my four-day swing through that area. Despite their busy, even hectic lives, most of the writers went out of their way to accommodate their schedules to mine, and despite the fact that no trip was planned without numerous revisions, delays and threatening conflicts (not to mention exorbitant phone bills), each one was finally a resounding success. Even the disappointments, the embarrassments, the apparent catastrophes had happy endings. For example, my first planned interview with Vic Reid was thwarted when despite an hour of searching throughout Hope Gardens for his office on the afternoon before my departure for the United States, I never succeeded in finding him. When I made my second trip to Jamaica, however, he kindly volunteered to come to me for the interview. The tape of my first quite successful interview with the somewhat difficult to contact John Hearne was given to a secretary upon my return to Virginia Commonwealth University for assistance with transcribing, and it was promptly thrown out with the trash. I was happily able to arrange another interview on my second trip to Jamaica. On another occasion I planned to spend a peaceful night resting in the luxurious Upside-Down Hilton in Trinidad before conducting my first interview the next morning. Instead I spent the night in a hot plane grounded in Puerto Rico because of mechanical problems, accompanied by a plane load of American wrestlers whose already somewhat rowdy behaviour was further stimulated by the open bar that Eastern invariably provides during such emergencies. I did, however, arrive in Trinidad in time to shower and conduct the interview as scheduled.

There were the inevitable embarrassments, of course. My interview with Salkey suffered a most inauspicious beginning when, having been misled about the writer's identity by a friend, I rather unenthusiastically and impatiently made dull conversation with him for several minutes, thinking that he was someone else. I was somewhat embarrassed again after my rather formal letter to Earl Lovelace, which requested an interview and closed with, 'I am looking forward to meeting you and talking with you about your work,' to have him respond: 'I seem to remember very clearly meeting someone by the name of Dance...' How mortified I was to have to be reminded that not only had we met before many years ago when he was a student in the United States, but that we had indeed taught together.

There were also the innumerable fears inspired by several of the well-wishers who helped me to establish contact with the writers and to arrange my visits. Some of their warnings about the problems with violence, housing, food, travel, etc., within some of the islands were enough to alarm even the most stalwart adventurer. Others ominously predicted possible calamities arising from a host of individual aberrations of particular writers, ranging from alcoholism to lecherousness.

Luckily I found the writers to be surprisingly helpful and co-operative – and normal. They responded promptly and positively to my many letters; wrote or called immediately if any changes had to be made in our scheduled interviews; assisted me in making arrangements to travel to their homes and to contact other writers and scholars; met me at the airports; arranged to introduce me to key people in their countries who could assist me; took me to see certain significant attractions and sights; and frequently entertained me. In every island some of the writers made sure that I had the opportunity to learn and experience as much as possible about the cultural, the literary, and occasionally the political life of the area.

Only one writer stipulated a condition before he would agree to grant me an interview. In response to my first letter, Austin Clarke wrote: 'You have ranged far and wide to track me down. I received this note addressed to Yale University. It came this morning. You will have to provide me with two Virginia hams, one pepper-coated, the other sugar-coated, the cost of which I shall give you if your time and travel permit you to come here to Toronto. You'll be welcome if you brought the hams – COD!'

Before each interview I attempted to read everything written by and about the author. While this was at times an impossible goal, I was able to read all of the full-length published works by all except about three of the authors and most of the criticism done on their works. Often I was able to get manuscripts of unpublished works as well. During the interviews I talked with the writers about formative influences that helped them to develop as writers; their goals and concerns in their works; their views of the craft of writing and the role of the writer; controversies surrounding them and their work; their involvement in significant literary move-ments and activities at home and abroad, including festivals such as Carifesta; their founding of and contributions to significant journals; their views of the broad range of Caribbean and other literature; religious, economic, racial, sociological, and political events and problems in their homes and elsewhere; and a myriad of other subjects. Throughout each interview I attempted to pose questions that would elicit information that might be of interest and significance to the student of Caribbean literature. I avoided involving myself in any debates with the writers, though I did try to ask direct, pointed questions about controversial matters and to insist upon a response to contrary views.

The transcribing and preparing of the taped interviews for publication has been a long and tedious task. It was a primary goal of mine to retain as much of the flavour and tone and rhythm and content of the interview as is possible in a transcription. Therefore the editing has been kept to an absolute minimum in order to allow the reader to share the full portrait of the author that emerges from an extensive candid conversation. I have attempted to avoid any tampering that might in any way alter the actual speech of the authors or destroy the informal, conversational tone of the interview. Occasionally some of the authors crossed into patois. I have attempted to transcribe such passages as accurately as possible. Within the dialogue there are a few incomplete, broken, and mixed sentences, which have been retained because there is some idea which the author was communicating that I did not wish to delete and which I could not presume to complete. Very often there are comments or questions which I pose that are repetitious, naive or downright ridiculous. I have chosen to leave them in the final manuscript for various reasons: they often elicit the kind of clarifications and information that the reader may also find helpful; the writer's response presents important material which would appear incoherent without the question; and/or I thought the reader might enjoy a good laugh at my *faux pas* as I often did when listening to these tapes. Except in the few instances in which the writers instructed me not to do so, I sent copies of the transcriptions of the conversations to each writer for his own editing, with the request that he keep such editing at a minimum to avoid altering the conversational tone of the interviews. Several writers made no change; most made only a couple of actual corrections; a few did rather extensive editing. In almost every instance, whatever changes the writers suggested are reflected in this volume. Each interview is prefaced with a brief biographical sketch and a selective bibliography. More detailed bibliographical and critical materials can be found in what is almost a companion volume: *Fifty Caribbean Writers* published by Greenwood Press in 1986.

This project, to which I devoted most of my research time from 1978-1984 has been an exciting adventure, for it has included first of all the pleasure of discovering for me, a new world of literature during its most illustrious period. The quality of contemporary West Indian literature is suggested by CLR James's declaration, 'I do not know at the present time any country writing in English which is able to produce a trio of the literary capacity and effectiveness of Wilson Harris, George Lamming, and Vidia Naipaul' [Ian Munro and Reinhard Sanders, 'Interviews with Three Caribbean Writers in Texas', *Kas-Kas*, University of Texas, 1972]. There is something absolutely fascinating about studying the works of a 'nation' during its most productive and eminent period and at the same time meeting the authors, who have sense of themselves as, on the one hand, continuing a long literary and cultural tradition (largely Western and African) and, on the other hand, being a part of the beginning of an exciting new cultural development; writers who often view themselves as New Adams in a New World Eden, a fact that is symbolically reinforced by Walcott's insistence that 'there are so many places that are virginal, really primal, in the Caribbean... so many places in St. Lucia where there has never been a human footprint... and if one can lift one's foot up sharply and put it down on that place the resonances of that are the same as the resonances that it meant for Adam to put his foot down in Eden' [*New World Adams*, Interview with Walcott].

Daryl Cumber Dance

MICHAEL ANTHONY   1 5

CONVERSATION WITH

MICHAEL ANTHONY

Born in Mayaro, Trinidad, on February 10, 1932, Michael Anthony was educated at the primary school in his home town and the Junior Technical School of San Fernando. He worked as a moulder in an iron foundry in Pointe à Pierre, Trinidad, until 1954, when he went to England. There he worked in factories, on the railways, and as a telegraphist, and began his career as a novelist. After fourteen years in England, he left for Rio de Janeiro, Brazil, where he spent two years working at the Trinidad and Tobago Embassy. After returning to Trinidad and working for two years as a journalist, he served from 1972 to 1988 as a member of the National Cultural Council of Trinidad and Tobago, where he taught creative writing, conducted writing workshops and wrote youth-oriented books of a cultural nature. During 1975 to 1989, he also conducted broadcast historical radio programmes in Trinidad and Tobago. Since then, he has devoted himself to writing full-time and has done some visiting lectureships at varied universities, including the University of Richmond as teacher of creative writing (1990-1992), the University of the West Indies at St. Augustine, and the University of Miami.

Anthony's novels include *The Games were Coming* (1963); *The Year in San Fernando* (1965); *Green Days by the River* (1967); *Streets of Conflict* (1976); *All That Glitters* (1981); *In the Heat of the Day* (1996); *High Tide of Intrigue* (2001) and *Butler, Till the Final Bell* (2004). He has also done three collections of short stories: *Sandra Street and other Stories* (1973); *Cricket in the Road* (1973); and *The Chieftain's Carnival and Other Stories* (1993); a children's novel: *King of the Masquerade* (1974); a collection of tales: *Folk Tales and Fantasies* (1976); and many historical and non-fiction works: *Profile Trinidad (1498-1900)* (1973); *Glimpses of Trinidad and Tobago: With a Glance at the West Indies* (1974); *The Making of Port of Spain* (1978); *Bright Road To Eldorado* (1981); *Port of Spain in a World at War 1939-45* (1983); *First in Trinidad* (1985); *Heroes of the People of Trinidad and Tobago* (1986); *A Brighter and Better Day* (1987); *The History of Aviation in Trinidad and Tobago 1913-1962* (1987); *Towns and Villages of Trinidad and Tobago* (1988); *Parade of the Carnivals of Trinidad, 1939-1989* (1989); *The Golden Quest: The Four Voyages of Christopher Columbus* (1992); *Historical Dictionary of Trinidad and Tobago* (1992); *Anaparima* (2001) and *Historic Landmarks of Port of Spain* (2008). Individual short stories and essays appear in several anthologies and journals; whilst his editing work includes *David Frost Introduces Trinidad and Tobago* (1975). His works have been critically discussed by Kenneth Ramchand, Linda Flynn and Sally West amongst others.

Anthony received the Arts Council of Great Britain Literary Award in 1969; the Trinidad and Tobago National Award – the Hummingbird Gold Medal for Literature – in 1979; and the City of Port of Spain Award for History and Literature in 1988.

Michael Anthony lives in Port of Spain, Trinidad. The following interview was done at his home on Tuesday March 18, 1980.

DANCE: One of the things which strikes me in your stories is a very strong sense of family – very strong family units and particularly loving relationships between fathers and sons, at least in two of the novels – which is missing in a lot of West Indian novels… You are looking at me as if you hadn't even thought about that.

ANTHONY: No, really, I haven't thought about that. I do know that the thing about the relationship, the close family relationships, is something that I admire very much, and I think also it is a little bit of nostalgia because my father died when I was very young. I loved him very much and I really missed the fact that he wasn't there, and I thought that our relationship would have been a very meaningful one, and so I believe that I have projected this into my work, because to a great extent my work, particularly *Green Days by the River,* is autobiographical in a certain sense, in that there has always been this, this question of closeness between my father, mother, myself.

DANCE: Was your father ill for a long time as the father was in this novel?

ANTHONY: Well, he was. The question of time wasn't very faithful in my novel because my father died when I was ten, you know, but of course, as you know, it is not autobiography, so one just manipulates events to suit.

DANCE: Exactly. Speaking of autobiography, it's pretty much assumed, as a matter of fact I think you've said, that *The Year in San Fernando* is autobiographical.

ANTHONY: Yes, very much so. In fact you know I spent a year in San Fernando when I was very young, nine I think I was, and I have always been fascinated with this, looking back: I had always wanted to know if the way I saw things as a child was the way things were, you see, and so when I first started, first thought of writing a novel, I thought perhaps this theme would be the theme I would handle because I really wanted to look into the year and see myself as a little boy in that time, and try to see things objectively while I was interested in telling the story which I felt. Because I remembered it so well and because it meant so much to me, I wondered if I could make it into a story. But it really did happen. Several things though (this I suppose is the difference between autobiography and autobiographical novels, you know) several things in the novel I have placed there because it went towards making a story, but generally speaking, basically it's very factual.

DANCE: Were you in a home situation similar to that?

ANTHONY: Yes, very similar, very similar.

DANCE: Is the original of that family still living, Mr. Chandles?

ANTHONY: Well, I had always felt very embarrassed about it, you know, because one of the things is that when I first wrote the book I had the actual names, and I changed this afterwards. But anyway it was quite clear what I was talking about, but I had never thought the book would get published, let alone go to the people concerned, so when the book was published and especially when it got into the schools I thought at least they would hear about it and would be very annoyed with me, you see. So when I came back here in 1970 [from Brazil] I avoided being round there. But one day I met up with the person whom I called, I think, Marva…

DANCE: Oh, Marva. That's who he married, right?

ANTHONY: Yes. And she was very pleased about it, yes, and she was very happy to see me. So you know I was quite wrong about their reaction to it. Mr. Chandles (his real name was Mr. Sealey) died only two years ago. And the girl [Marva], she had the same sort of connections that I spoke of in the book you know; she came from Mayaro when she came there to marry him and the time she married him, you know, I was leaving, so I had always wanted to know how was their married life.

DANCE: Will that be another book? But you don't know enough about that?

ANTHONY: I don't think so. Well, I know enough really, I think, about it, because she had spoken to me at *length*, you know, about what happened.

DANCE: Two of the things that strike me very much about the young man in the book, Francis, is the sense of fear that he constantly feels. Did you live under…

ANTHONY: I think so. I think when I left Mayaro to go to live there, you know, I had always felt a little bit hurt about it. I have always been very sensitive to being at home and I didn't really like being anywhere else. There was of course, on the other hand, the fascination of being in San Fernando and being in a bright place with bright lights and so on, but I had always felt a bit rejected, although I knew my mother didn't mean it that way. In fact I wouldn't let my children go to live with *anybody*, you know, and so I felt a sense of fear too, because also I had a feeling like Mr. Chandles… he didn't really, I didn't feel that he treated me as he would treat his little child, and this sense of fear was something very real, and that was why long years afterwards I wondered, you know, to myself if this fear was justified. And I think it proved to be very helpful to me to write that book because when I was finished I had a very different impression as to what the year in San Fernando really was.

DANCE: And the other thing that struck me as being so significant there was the boy's need for love. I suppose this is a sort of outgrowth of his fear because it is partly a fear of loss of mother, of love and family.

ANTHONY: Yes, but somehow I feel that most young children are very much alike in this. I feel that especially where you come from a home in which things are very much rooted in a sort of unity, you do feel the need for having this bit of love. And I wasn't in a home where people cared very much about me as such.

DANCE: Or anybody else for that matter. Love seemed absolutely absent… OK. Kenneth Ramchand has talked a little bit about some of the symbolic suggestiveness of the situation of Francis in the novel when he suggests that Francis represents, he puts it, 'the condition of the modern West Indian' [*The West Indian Novel*, p.222] and then he goes on further to suggest that he represents the West Indian artist, operating in the shadow of the British nineteenth century novel. Did you have any such intentions?

ANTHONY: Well, since you yourself are a critic, I must be very careful how I handle the critic. … Now two things I want to say: the first is that when I wrote *The Year in San Fernando* this didn't occur to me at all. I was just telling a story as such. But a second thing I want to say is that it seems as though one can say a lot of things about certain things which a writer doesn't think about, and it could be just like how one's handwriting sometimes reveals one's character. I think certain things one says or does might reveal things beneath the surface, and the critics are always looking beneath the surface anyway. But I am not aware of this sort of thing at all. I remember one particular thing he said concerning the walking up and down on the pavement [p.215]. I don't know – I would have thought that was far-fetched, but perhaps there is some justification for the critic thinking like that, but certainly, at least I don't intend that the book be read in this particular way, because I didn't think of anything like symbols; I was just trying to tell a *straight* story.

DANCE: Well, let me ask you this. Do you see the situation, if we agreed to look at it in the way that Ramchand has suggested, do you see it as accurately reflecting your view of the West Indian writer, sort of there, under things, in the shadow of the British tradition and that sort of thing?

ANTHONY: Not really, I don't, not really.

DANCE: Like many other West Indian writers you've spent a great deal of time in Europe, I think I read somewhere fourteen years. And yet unlike most other West Indian writers who have spent a great deal of time in Europe, that's not a subject of your writing?

ANTHONY: No, no, it's not a subject of my writing at all and I don't know why, you see. Now I think some West Indian writers in the past have felt that they have to interpret a situation and in many cases – I can think of a certain book which I believe must have been written because they felt, or the writer felt this book ought to be written. But I don't think, particularly in fiction, I operate that way. I must want to write about something. You know, it must suggest itself to me, I must *feel* to tell the particular story to do it, so I've never really felt *that* writing about England. Most of my writing, well, a lot of it has been done in the Caribbean, a little bit has been done in England, but I never really *felt* – one of the things that happens quite a lot is that whenever I intend to write, whenever I write I tend to go back in a time which fascinates me. There is *nothing* about England so far that fascinates me. At least on that level. And strangely enough Brazil: I have been there two years and I really felt like writing about it. Not anymore now because you know I have been removed from the scene and it has gone out of my mind. Perhaps when I think of another novel, I don't know, but I don't think I will write about England somehow. But perhaps I ought to, but I don't know.

DANCE: ... As I read your works I become so involved in the characters and their motivations and their excitements that I find myself, without realising it, suspending my moral judgements. And this is very interesting to me and it's most disturbing because I find that I don't think about things in the way that I would ordinarily think about them because I get so involved... Take Leon, for example, in *The Games were Coming;* I get so involved with his efforts to prepare for the race that my only concern is that nothing go wrong and that he win the race. But a little bit later when I think about him in preparation for that race, I think he is a pretty selfish, cruel, young man.

ANTHONY: But he is... I think it is this sort of single-mindedness of purpose that most sportsmen have, and I think that certain times, of course, certain people are like that: they just want to prove a certain point to the exclusion of everything else...

DANCE: Do you see a world in which people are more or less completely motivated by their own selfish drives?

ANTHONY: Well, I don't think it's a good thing to be selfish, I don't think it is a good thing to be motivated by your own selfish drives, but no, I see a world of all different types of people. I don't know if in *The Games were Coming* I had that type. The point is that the whole focus of *The Games were Coming* was on Leon and his activities. And there are people like that in the world. But I certainly do not approve of a world in which everybody does this sort of thing. I certainly approved of Leon winning the race, but even so, I, myself, do not pass judgement; the fact is that for the purpose of the story he *was* that way...

DANCE: I want to ask you about another reaction that I have when I read your works. Your works are very compact; they are full and they are a whole. I can't argue that that's not true. Your *The Year in San Fernando*: the year is up and the story is over. *The Games were Coming*: the games have come and so the story is over. In *The Streets of Conflict*, the riot has occurred and so the story is over. But you have a very disturbing way of getting us interested in so many other issues, that somehow we are not quite willing to accept that the story is coming to an end even though…

ANTHONY: Yes, well, because so many things may come up after the climax.

DANCE: Exactly, exactly. I mean in *The Games were Coming*, for example, as excited as we are about the story and as focused as we are on it all the time, we begin to be concerned about the pregnancy of the girl, about the forthcoming marriage which I assume is to take place…

ANTHONY: Yes, but I wouldn't like to be there… [laughter]

DANCE: So maybe that's an easy way to avoid…

ANTHONY: … because afterwards I wouldn't like to be there till we know how things will work out.

DANCE: But that's interesting to me because I get so interested in them that I want to know what's going to happen. Do you ever plan sequels to some of these stories?

ANTHONY: No. I have never planned a sequel to any of them, but I see the point because a lot of people have said this to me. What would he do after that, or what would she do, and what would, what's the outcome? Of course, I just say that's another story and I wouldn't like to be there to find out.

DANCE: Well since the characters were based on real people, though this has actually nothing to do with the story, do you know the outcome of that situation? Or was the story based on real people?

ANTHONY: Well, the funny thing is, you know, that there is a very strange thing about this story: when the book was going to be published, just before it was published, and Deutch had a way of sending the book out to his friends and agents and so on to see if there is anything they could say before he goes into publication. And Naipaul's sister wrote to Deutch and said, 'Please stop it, don't publish that book yet, because there is something I want to tell you, that this situation actually happened with Sylvia and Jaggernauth.' Now actually, I can't remember now whether I called – in fact I haven't really read or even looked over these works since I wrote them, but the name of the store owner was Jaggernauth, Lakhan Jaggernauth. [In the novel his name is Imbal Mohansingh]. And well everybody who knows San Fernando and knows him would know where the store is and so on. But I did not know, I never knew that he had any relationship with a girl who worked in a store and so on. And Naipaul's sister told Deutch that this girl was called Sylvia; she worked in that store, and the selfsame thing I described happened between herself and Jaggernauth. So Deutch wrote to me frantically saying we'll have to change everything and postpone the publication date and so on, and it cost a great deal of money going through the whole thing and changing names; but so far as I know they were fictitious names. Sylvia was a fictitious name; Jaggernauth was just convenient because whenever I think of a shop on High Street I could think of Jaggernauth because he was so prominent… Now, but Leon was a fellow whom I, well I was thinking of a particular person called Lyons who lived at Marabella just by the Red Bridge… You know I knew him very well, a young fellow who used to work in the refinery, and he was not perhaps the best cyclist, but he was a very promising cyclist, and I just liked him, you know, liked the way he walked and his confidence and so on. So I had him in my mind and I called him Leon, because one other thing is that I usually have to, for myself, choose a name that is near to the person because I must believe in the person, and if it is too far, then you know, it is somebody different…

DANCE: Marisa in *Streets of Conflict* was very interesting to me… she is one of the few truly beautiful Black women I have met…

ANTHONY: … in West Indian fiction? Now one of the odd things is that I – now I don't make a point of doing this sort of thing, but, and other people tell me, because I am afraid I am not a very avid reader, particularly of West Indian fiction, because one tends to probably like, and then identify with them so much that you can easily imitate, you see. But people talk about this and say that West Indian writers always tend to look down on their women. I don't know how true that is in general. But Marisa herself was a, really a very beautiful Black girl; in fact, her name *was* Marisa… I think… that in writing, generally speaking, one tends to talk about the people that fascinate one, you see. So I think this would be a matter of coincidence, you know; if you really like somebody you talk about them.

DANCE: … I want to go back to one question I failed to ask you when we were talking about *Green Days by the River*. And it was about Mr. Gidharee's cruel treatment of Shellie. Again I think you prepared me for it and yet it seems so extreme.

ANTHONY: Well you thought so? Yes, I do not know if I can justify this, but it seemed to me at the time that this would have been his reaction. Perhaps it was extreme, perhaps you are quite right about it, I just seem to think that he would have acted that way. Perhaps the man himself – now again with Gidharee I was thinking of someone who lived just next to me. I have a story called 'Drunkard of the River'… That was another side of Mr. Gidharee; he was a man who would do things like that. He often drank in his real life, this man I am thinking of; he often drank rum and got on very unpredictably, and yet when he was his normal self he was such a *charming* man. So I don't really know if it was justifiable. A few people have mentioned this to me. Ken Ramchand thought it was a bit, you know, a violent sort of reaction. I suppose so, I suppose you are quite right about it.

DANCE: You've been making some comments about some reactions of other people, and I want to know how you feel about the critical response to your work.

ANTHONY: Well, I don't really feel very strongly about critical response. I suppose it's because, now you find in Trinidad, generally speaking, I have not really pleased the critics very much… but on the other hand I must say that I have got more than my fair share of attention through the schools; but so far as the critics are concerned, I haven't heard very much of them, but also I don't think I tend to bother too much with the critics in the sense that I feel I would write as I want to… One of the things you know when I first began writing short stories and sending them to the BBC, they had a lot of rules and regulations about you must write about local colour and the story must never be longer than 2,500 words and so on. I never really ever paid attention to that. It was not a very good thing to do, but I said they can only do one of two things – accept it or send it back. And I think I have tended to be like the cat who walks by himself, in very many ways, in very many things, and although of course everybody likes critical acclaim and all that, I haven't got that, I don't think I will ever get… well, I got some pretty good reviews, you know, here and there, but I got some pretty bad ones too. But I have not been too worried about that. I have felt a bit vindicated by the fact that almost all my books are used in schools now…

DANCE: OK. Well thank you very much, it's been interesting talking with you.

ANTHONY: It has been interesting talking with you too.

————————————

CONVERSATION WITH

LOUISE BENNETT

Louise Simone Bennett, better known as Miss Lou, was born in Kingston, Jamaica, on September 7, 1919. She was educated at St. Simon's College, after which she studied at the Royal Academy of Dramatic Art in England. Much of her life had been devoted to the study of Jamaican folklore, and her extensive collections of Anancy stories, folk songs, legends, proverbs, riddles and games. Her use of these folk materials, including the dialect, in her poetry and dramas have represented perhaps the single most significant contribution to the preservation and appreciation of Jamaican folk culture. Jamaica's most popular and best-loved *diseuse*, Miss Lou was much in demand as a performer, reader and lecturer throughout the Caribbean, the United States, Canada and Europe. At the time of the interview, she was living in Kingston with her husband, Eric Coverly, and many adopted children. Since that time, they moved to Fort Lauderdale, Florida in the early 1980s, then to Toronto in 1987. Miss Lou passed away in July 2006.

Bennett's many volumes of poetry include *Verses in Jamaican Dialect* (1942); *Jamaican Humour in Dialect* (1943); *Jamaican Dialect Poems* (1948); *Mi's' Lulu Sez: A Collection of Dialect Poems* (1949); *Lulu Says: Dialect Verses with Glossary* (1952); *Laugh with Louise: A Pot-Pourrie of Jamaican Folk-Lore, Stories, Songs and Verses* (1961); *Jamaican Labrish* (1966); and *Selected Poems* (1982). Miss Bennett also compiled or contributed to the following collections: *Anancy Stories and Poems in Dialect* (1944); *Anancy Stories and Dialect Verse* (1950); *Anancy Stories and Dialect Verse* (new series) (1957); *Laugh With Louise* (1961); *Anancy and Miss Lou* (1979); *Jamaica Maddah Goose* (1981); and *Aunty Roachy Seh* (1993). She has recorded twelve Anancy stories and some songs on Federal Records. Other recordings include *Yes M'Dear* (1980); *Miss Lou's Views* (1980); and *Children's Jamaican Songs and Games* (1980).

Miss Lou received numerous awards including the MBE for work in Jamaican literature and theatre; the Norman Manley Award for Excellence; the Order of Jamaica Award for work in the field of national culture; and the Gold Musgrave Medal for 1978 in recognition of her contribution to the development of the arts in Jamaica and the Caribbean. In 1998, she received the Honorary Degree of Doctor of Letters from York University, Toronto; whilst on Jamaica's Independence Day in 2001, she was appointed as a Member of the Order of Merit for her contribution to the arts.

Beside the official accolades, Bennett's dialectal approach to poetry has also been positively received by literary critics; in particular in H. K. Haagenson's monograph, *The Nonlinear Nature of Jamaican Women's Writing: Louise Bennett* (2002). Other studies include Carolyn Cooper, 'That cunny Jamma oman: female sensibility in the poetry of Louise Bennett', *Race and Class* (1988); Jahan Ramazani, 'Irony and Postcoloniality: Louise Bennett's Anancy Poetics' in *The Hybrid Muse: Postcolonial Poetry in English* (2001); and Denise de Caires Narain's 'The Lure of the Folk: Louise Bennett and the politics of Creole' in *Contemporary Caribbean Women's Poetry: Making Style* (2004).

My interview with Miss Lou was conducted before this book was conceived. I went to consult her about some work that I was doing in Jamaican folklore. Thus the focus was more on that subject than on her writings. The following interview took place on Friday, September 15, 1978, at Miss Bennett's home in Gordon Town.

DANCE: Your poetry reminds me a great deal of the work of Paul Laurence Dunbar in that it often deals with social problems but also reveals the humour in a situation. I notice too that the style – the verse form and rhyme scheme – in your poetry is similar to Dunbar's. Do you know his work? Did it influence you?

BENNETT: I know him, yes. I have read quite a lot of Paul Laurence Dunbar, and of Langston Hughes. In fact I knew Langston Hughes very well. Yes, he was a good friend.

DANCE: When did you know him?

BENNETT: I met Langston Hughes first in 1953, but I had known about him before and all that, but I met him personally and we became very good friends. I used to visit – whenever I would go to New York, Langston would have a sort of 'little thing' and have people, you know, people in the theatre come and that sort of thing, and I would do my verses and so. And I have even a picture inside with us doing a radio programme together, WWRM, with Alma John, you know. And he used to send me everything he wrote, he would send me, you know…

DANCE: Before he published it or after?

BENNETT: Well, no, no, after. He would always send me something, but we did talk a lot about what he was writing, and what he was doing and we had a lot of mutual friends, you know. I liked him.

DANCE: Yes, he was an interesting person. Let me ask you if you see yourself as a professional, polishing folk materials for a more sophisticated audience?

BENNETT: Never, never, NEVER-R! Never that! Oh no! [Laughter] No polishing, darling. I believe that the folk has such a lot to it to offer to people, and you know people just don't realise all the strength that is in this folk material, and when you polish you lose such a lot. I mean, I am not in the polishing at all. [Exuberant laughter].

DANCE: So no adapting, especially for television?

BENNETT: Well, no, I don't… Mek me tell you what happen: somehow I find it within the folk, you can always find something for your need. For instance, a lot of them are down to earth, very earthy, and all that. The folk themselves do not actually polish but they vary their expressions depending upon the occasion. For instance, a lot of these things came out of the old Jamaican functions and customs that we have: we used to have things like 'Pleasant Sunday Afternoon', in which they would perform certain things in a different way than they would do at the 'Dinky-Mini', which was a function to cheer up the family of a dead person, you know; therefore we can sing happy, and dance and things to keep the family cheerful. At that sort of Dinky, almost anything went; it was almost like a Digging Match. Like at the Digging Match, at the field days, 'Dig and tings…' a lot of things that were happening, topical things, but that sort of thing… But in Sunday's Pleasant Sunday Afternoons or at the Tea-Meetings, you would find that they have the same tunes, the same flavour, but different – maybe wording – put in a different way, and all that; and yet, it never lost any of the strength and the vitality, you know.

DANCE: What do you think about the folk tales, for example, of Philip Sherlock, where he retells them?

BENNETT: Well, Philip Sherlock retells them quite well, you know. Oh, yes. He tells them in a way, he tries to make them understandable. Now I am a language person in that I believe that my language is the best! [Laughter] But I don't believe nuttin wrong wid it! If you know what I mean. So I never compromise when it comes to the language, you know, I don't grovel, I say anything. You know I try to understand other people language; them could try to understand me too. Oh-h-h! [Laughter].

DANCE: That's very interesting. Of course, I am not particularly well-read in Jamaican literature, but it seems that you and Claude McKay and Vic Reid were among the early writers to insist upon writing in Jamaican dialect.

BENNETT: Well, I have been more consistent, in the dialect, in that I have never really compromised, but I feel if I have something to say, I say it in the language that people have been saying it around me for years, for hundreds of years, before they knew how to say it in any other language. [Laughter] You know what I mean? And this language is going on still; it is still the strongest thing that's happening around here; the people want to really express themselves – facts through the language, you know, and so, I mean, I can't really apologise for this thing at all.

DANCE: Have you ever felt the pressure to apologise?

BENNETT: Ah! Massa! Oi-i-i! From I start it till now, right now, at this moment! You asking! I have done a lot, within the forty years, ha-ha! But I tell you, still there are people, still you'll find this thing of almost patronising you, you know – [Mimicking] 'Oh, Miss Lou!' Ho-ho-ho! [Exuberant laughter] Well, of course, I don't bother with them because the people are understanding me and this is really what matters, and even the people who pretend sometimes, they do really know, they really understand, but they – you know. That's why, I don't like pretentiousness – the word *pretentiousness* – don't like that. I prefer you to be very natural, to be as natural as possible; I can't stand that business.

DANCE: Let me ask you something about Anancy. When I have collected tales here, usually when the people imitate Anancy they speak in a nasal tone and they lisp…

BENNETT: [Lisping] 'Im tawk wid a lisp tongue. 'Im tongue tie.

DANCE: Has that always been the way he has been portrayed?

BENNETT: Always been, yes.

DANCE: Do you have any idea why?

BENNETT: Because he tries – this is another thing, he makes himself ridiculous, because to cover up a lot of his trickery that he is carrying on; you see you'll find in one tale where he is really beating a man, and he has no right to because he was the thief really – Anancy went in and stole this thing and they caught another man, and he now starts to trounce this man and he should really be – I mean at that point, you should really feel vexed with this Anancy, you know, for doing this because after all the man was – he knows the thief, but the way in which he was beating him like [dramatising] 'shu-shu-booch yu!' and the stick that he was using, you can't help but laugh and all of a sudden the comedy overpowers the whole tragedy of the situation, and you are more taken up with the ridiculous situation than the plight of Brother Goat! Because of course, you know, it shows you what most of our Anancy stories show – because what Anancy is really trying to show you is that you can be tricked by your own stupidity and gr-e-e-d and pretentiousness.

DANCE: I don't know whether you are familiar with the collection of stories that's been done by Salkey in which Anancy appears as a more modern…

BENNETT: He uses some of my stories! Yes, we are good friends and he writes good. He says, 'Louise, I am going to use Anancy and Monkey.' He wrote me a letter asking my permission to use that because he liked that one especially, and I told him, 'Good, go ahead.' I have not seen what he has done with it.

DANCE: One of the most interesting things about that collection, different from any other I have seen, is that he modernises Anancy. Anancy is kind of a city slickster by this time, and in some instances, you know, he is a city creature who is going around fooling the women and this kind of thing. And you know Brer Rabbit in the States, and the animals in the States, have sort of moved to the city too. We have the pool-shooting Monkey now, and the sharp-dressers, and the hipsters, among the old animals, and what I want to know is: has Anancy become more modernised among the folk or is this just something that Salkey has done?

BENNETT: No, not more modernised but he *is* being – not as widely as Salkey has done. But what they *have* done is: they inject little things here like, you will notice that Anancy go to supermarket, rather than go to the 'grass-yard', you know, or something like that. Just little, here and there, but they have not completely modernised the stories, oh no, because those old things have a great deal of the strength of Anancy's character. This business of Anancy being *just* a trickster is, you know, this has been played up a great deal in Jamaica especially, saying [Mimicking], 'Oh, the Anancy mentality bad!' But the way I learnt Anancy, I knew Anancy as a child and it was a joy! We loved to listen to the stories, we loved to hear about this little trickify man, you know, and all that, and one thing we knew, that this man was magic, and we could never be like him. You know – he is a magic man. He could spin a web and become a spider whenever he wanted to. You can't do that, so you better not try the Anancy's tricks, you know, but it was fun!

DANCE: Let me ask you about something else. In one of your poems, 'Cuss-Cuss', there is a tracing match between two Jamaican women, and that reminds me of the Dozens in the States. Are you familiar with the Dozens, which is a kind of verbal match between two people? In the Dozens usually one insults the other one's mother. Do you know…

BENNETT: No, I have heard. I don't know too much about it.

DANCE: Is this called 'tracing' – somewhere I saw the term 'tracing match'.

BENNETT: Tracing, yes man, tracing match.

DANCE: OK. Is this a popular folk game?

BENNETT: Oh, child, oh yes. 'A bet a bax yuh!' They have a children game, that children play in this you know: 'A bet a bax yuh.' 'Yu couldn' vencha.' And, then they'll tell each other off, What? Yes, man. Yes. This is very strong.

DANCE: Does it have any special rules that…

BENNETT: And I tell you something. That's why a lot of the things that go on in Jamaica, you know – if you really understand the people you want to laugh, most of the time, because people just letting off steam and going on as if – that to that. And then all of a sudden you see them turn around, and if you watch them pulling, them quarrelling, and all of a sudden you see dem… blow off steam and come back and 'Awright', you know, different mood. [Laughter] If you only, if you know how to, to do this. Once we had for a little while, in Jamaica, was it '60s? Some little way there, I think towards the late '60s, they had this flare up of Chinese and Black people, you know. All of a sudden [Insolently] 'Chineyman, huh, Chineyman, hoo,' so all whole heap of things going on now, and next thing we hear them say, them say them having Chinese riot! [Laughter] So now, I went into a Chinese hardware store, you know, one day, and this woman, her husband is a full Chinese, she is a half-Chinese, and she is helping me; she say: 'Lawks, Miss Lou, you better buy quick yah, because I waan lock up di store because I hear say dem a beat up Chiney people, and ah lick down Chiney people.' Hear a man in the store: 'Cho, you a half-Chiney, you will only get a half-lick.' [Laughter] And everybody now dying with laugh. So my dear, little after we heard – do you know how that thing broke up? A Chinese boy, half-Chinese boy too, ride down on a thing down into the heart of a big crowd that had gathered on West Parade, West Queen Street, you know, right round Solas Market – big crowd out there were parking and talk 'bout Chiney people, and, and this boy ride down in the middle of them with a peaka-peow paper – peaka-peow, you see this is a lottery, which the Chinese have always run in Jamaica, very very popular, and mind you, it is illegal, unlawful you know, everybody buy this peaka-peow, you know, Wong Sam, and Hock Sun, whatever it is, all the different PP, all the different banks. So this Chinese fellow ride down on his S90, man, with the peaka-peow paper and says: 'What happen, bredder, nobody nah buy dis today, nobody buy dis… Wa happen? You are a foo'. Oonoo jus ah quarrel, oonoo nah buy?' Hear dem: 'Migod, mi did figat di ting.' See here, do you know that broke up the riot?

DANCE: But that's very interesting. Let me ask you about something else. In American, Black American folklore, we have a group of tales which explain how things came to be. In the Jamaican lore that I have come across you find a lot of animal tales that explain how animals got their characteristics. But in the Black American lore we have any number of tales that deal with races, and explain how the Black man got black, how his hair got kinky, why the Black man is on the bottom of the economic ladder and that kind of thing. And I have really been looking for those tales since I have been here and I have found only one. Are you familiar with any of those tales?

BENNETT: No, Sir.

DANCE: None?

BENNETT: No, because the funny thing is that we don't have a great deal of that in the folklore, and I mean to say I am talking from great experience in Jamaica, you know. We have [knocking on wood] – in fact this is the first time – I always hear about racial tensions and things and all that, and in Jamaica you knew that there was something, but it wasn't anything that you could, you know… I really never met, came up against any racial thing until the first time I travelled. When I went on a train in Miami and they told me that I couldn't go into the first class section (I had a first class ticket for I was going on a British Council scholarship), and they told me I couldn't go in the first class section until I passed the Mason-Dixie line! I said, 'I don't know what is a Mason-Dixie…' [Laughter] But this is the first time that I had really come up against something that was really tangible and hard. Because here, somehow, somebody always have a cousin or a bredder, or some distant cousin or somebody who white! [Laughter] So although the things that were black were not really given any great deal of prestige – or no prestige at all – you were not encouraged to – just stopped – you were discouraged. Yet among the Black people there was such a spirit and a belief in the little things that belong to them somehow it didn't – this didn't, because I know it did not deter me, and a lot of other people I know, and I am thinking of plenty people who I know, who just went on and did what they felt was right for them, you know, as a Black person. And though the things that were Black were not encouraged, they were done. The drums were still beating; Papa… is still jumping in villages you know, and you could always hear the drums at night. You know that there was a Papa… still in the village. And little things went on. So the culture lived, you know.

CONVERSATION WITH

JAN CAREW

Jan Rynveld Carew was born on September 24, 1925, in the village of Agricola on the East Bank of the Demerara River in British Guiana, now Guyana. After completing local primary schools, he attended Berbice High School in New Amsterdam. From 1940 to 1943 he worked as a customs officer in the British Colonial Civil Service and from 1943 to 1944 as a price control officer in the Government of Trinidad. In 1945 he came to the United States and continued his education at Howard University. He later studied at Western Reserve, Charles University (Prague, Czechoslovakia), and La Sorbonne.

Carew has worked as editor of *De Kim* poetry magazine (Amsterdam, Holland); editor of the *Kensington Post* (London); broadcaster on the BBC; lecturer at London University; Director of Culture for the Government of British Guiana; correspondent for the London *Observer*; reviewer for the *John O'London's Weekly*, the BBC, and the *Art News Review*; Publicity Secretariat for the Government of Ghana (1965-66); and editor of the *African Review*. He has also lectured and taught at Rutgers University, Princeton University, Northwestern University, George Mason University and Lincoln University.

Jan Carew's novels are *Black Midas* (1958; published in 1959 in the United States as *A Touch of Midas*); *The Wild Coast* (1958); *The Last Barbarian* (1961); *Moscow Is Not My Mecca* (1964; published in the United States in 1965 as *Green Winter*); and *Cry Black Power* (1970). He has a collection of short stories, *The Guyanese Wanderer* (2007). Among his children's books are *The Third Gift* (1975), *Children of the Sun* (1980) and *The Sisters and Manco's Stories* (2002). Carew's plays produced in Jamaica, Guyana, England, and Canada, include *Miracle in Lime Lane* (with Sylvia Wynter); *University of Hunger* and *Gentlemen Be Seated*. Several of his plays were produced by the BBC, and during 1963 and 1964 he wrote a series of nine plays for Associated Television in London. A collection of poetry, *Streets of Eternity*, was published in 1952 and *Sea Drums in My Blood* in 1981. Later historical and social studies include *Fulcrums of Change: Origin of Racism in the Americas and Other Essays* (1988); *Rape of Paradise: Columbus and the Origin of Western Racism* (1994); and *Ghosts in our Blood: With Malcolm X in Africa, England, and the Caribbean* (1994). Other short stories, poems, and scholarly articles have appeared in numerous journals and anthologies. Recordings of interest include a cassette, *The Legacy of Columbus* (1990), and a videocassette, *Columbus and the Origin of Racism in the Americas* (1991). Carew is also recognised as an accomplished painter.

In 1964 Carew's television play *The Big Pride* was selected by the London *Daily Mirror* as the best play of the year. In 1973 and 1974 he was awarded the Burton International Fellowship by the Harvard University Graduate School of Education. He won the Illinois Arts Council award for fiction in 1974. In the same year the American Institute of Graphic Arts awarded him their 'Certificate of Excellence' for *The Third Gift*. Princeton University's Afro-American Studies Program established the Jan Carew Annual Lectureship in 1974. He received the Casa de las Americas award for poetry in 1977. In 1980 his essay 'The Caribbean Writer and Exile' won a Pushcart Prize.

Jan Carew and his wife, Dr. Joy Carew, have resided in many locations in North America and Europe, and are now based in Louisville, Kentucky. Carew was appointed as Scholar-in-Residence at the Pan-African Studies department at the University of Louisville in 2000, where he continues his scholarly and creative writing. He also continues to serve occasionally as consultant and adviser to agencies and officials in the governments of Grenada and Jamaica. He has two sons by his first wife, novelist Sylvia Wynter, and a daughter by his present wife.

The following interview was conducted in Chicago on November 21, 1980.

DANCE: Could we talk a little bit about your education first? You went to college in Guyana?

CAREW: It wasn't really college. I happened to have been very sickly as a child, so I did not go to the leading school in Georgetown.

DANCE: Queen's College, perhaps?

CAREW: Quite. So I went to Berbice High School, which was one of the most fortunate things which could have happened to me. This was supposed to be a lesser school, but I really had remarkable teachers there. They were able to do the kind of experiments in education that suited my particular temperament, I can't think of any school I have seen anywhere that would have served me better – apart, perhaps, from Tolstoy's school, which he had started and run for the benefit of the children in and around his estate. My school sounded much like this. We were really allowed unusual freedoms, and I was not even required to attend classes all that regularly.

DANCE: Was it a school for exceptional students?

CAREW: No, just a school with exceptional teachers. The generation I grew up with in that school is now scattered all over the world in all kinds of fields and professions; and many of my schoolmates turned out to be remarkable people.

DANCE: Did it have any influence on your development as a writer?

CAREW: An enormous influence. The school I went to was really a remarkable one. The curriculum was remarkable; the teachers were remarkable. I did Latin, French, math, geography, literature, art, and general science. One was simply allowed to gallop along and do whatever one wanted to do.

DANCE: Were you trying your hand at writing, even then?

CAREW: Well, one of my masters, James Rodway, who, incidentally, was also Derek Walcott's teacher, encouraged me to write early in my school career.

DANCE: Not the painter?

CAREW: No, his father, who was a remarkable teacher. He is still in the Caribbean and I still have very close and fond contacts with him. He is descended from a very distinguished family in Guyana. The first historian in Guyana was a Rodway. JA Rodway brought to the school a kind of eclecticism, and imaginative force, and it was he, and several other teachers, who simply allowed you to express yourself. I mean, I remember doing translations of Virgil, Book 12, and I turned away from the set tradition and did a free translation which he praised highly, saying that I had entered into the spirit of the poem. He certainly encouraged me to write the kind of imaginative prose that was most unusual in school systems; so I wrote, and he was always extremely encouraging. He also gave me a wide range of classics to read.

DANCE: Queen's College was more traditional, I take it?

CAREW: Yes. I think Wilson Harris, Martin Carter [and some other Guyanese writers] were Queen's College graduates. But Wilson and Martin were both born in Berbice. That is my county. Berbice is called the ancient county, and it is a kind of backwater. It was an underdeveloped county of Guyana, but it had a remarkable texture, ambience and quality for the arts. Mittelholzer, in a profound sense, epitomises this. At one point, we lived on the same street – Coburg Street. And, in New Amsterdam many of us painted. I began painting in New Amsterdam, painting, writing poetry; and at Christmas time, painting Christmas cards with watercolours and selling them. Some people in Guyana, I imagine, still have cards that I painted as a boy.

DANCE: Did you know Mittelholzer when you were growing up?

CAREW: I knew him very well. He was an older person, you know. We treated him with the greatest kind of awe because he defied the philistine society, and lived his own life.

DANCE: When did you come to Howard?

CAREW: I came to Howard after working in the Civil Service. I worked as a Customs Officer; Burnham, the [late] President of Guyana, also worked in the customs.

DANCE: Oh, really.

CAREW: I had to break him in on the job, as it were. [Laughter]

DANCE: [Laughter] So you're close friends, then, I take it?

CAREW: We used to be. We are not any longer. And then I went to Trinidad. I lived in Trinidad for just over a year. And, then, from Trinidad, I went to Howard University. There was a question of raising the money to go abroad to study, because just about that time, the pound sterling had been devalued. I was determined to study in the United States, although I had taken the Cambridge University Entrance Exams.

DANCE: But you preferred Howard?

CAREW: I was absolutely against studying in England. I thought I would study in the United States where the system was a most eclectic one; and also there was a tradition of Guyanese who didn't have a great deal of money studying in the United States, so I began to do pre-med studies at Howard.

DANCE: Oh, when did you change your mind about medicine?

CAREW: Well, I think very early, I thought medicine in the United States was so corrupt and fraudulent. I really didn't see myself spending my life making money off of sick people. I'm sure if I had studied medicine I would have been an impoverished physician or non-practioner. I just had absolutely no interest in that kind of venal medicine. It seemed such a mercenary enterprise, gouging money out of the sick; I really couldn't have any part of that. The most vivid memories I have of Howard are of two professors, Mertz Tate, a historian, who was simply the most brilliant professor that I have ever met anywhere. She had an extraordinary intellectual influence on me. From the moment that I went into one of her classes, she just lit up the whole intellectual horizon of Howard for me, transforming it into an extraordinary place. The other professor was Arthur Davis – Arthur P Davis. And he published my first effort in the *Norfolk Journal and Guide*, which he wrote for regularly. [When I was in Trinidad before coming to Howard] I signed up to work on tankers, because they paid very well – it was very dangerous, but if you survived, you could accumulate a few thousand dollars after a single trip. One of my friends did this, and I was absolutely bent on following his example. I never told my family about these plans. I've always

had connections with the sea. My paternal grandfather was a smuggler, a very famous
one. He had a schooner that sailed between the islands and the coast of South America.
He was a gifted and able man. His schooner sank with all hands off the Guyana coast,
a very stormy coast in some seasons. My grandfathers, both of them, had a kind of
Ruskinian ethic and they made all their children learn trades. And the trade my father
learnt was to lacquer coaches and to paint designs on them. He was quite a gifted
painter, my father, he loved painting with an absolute passion and wanted to do
nothing else, but my mother compelled him to study dentistry, and he dutifully came
here [the United States] and did dentistry. He was also a tailor, and the only time he
really defied my mother was when he went back home with all the dental equipment
to practice, and he never did so for a single day. He became a tailor instead, and you
know [the difference in] status between a tailor and a dentist is enormous! [Laughter]
So my mother was absolutely mortified. He did this one defiant act and relapsed into
obedience once more. He was a fine tailor; he could design clothes beautifully.
DANCE: Was your mother from a family that would have looked upon tailoring as
not quite so acceptable?
CAREW: Oh, yes. The lowest common denominator of life. My father really didn't
care all that much about providing for the family. When my mother married him, he
was very wealthy, but he just let the money slip away because he never really had any
material interests at all… And then, after Howard – I got fed up with Howard – the
segregation in Washington, the terrible constricted life that one was compelled to live.
DANCE: So, it wasn't Howard so much as Washington that you got fed up with?
CAREW: Washington, yes. Howard was marvellous because at that time, really adult
students were coming in – Black ex-servicemen who had been all over the world.
They were a different kind of student, far more interesting people. And then I always
had much closer contacts with people from the South. Because the Southerners and
the Caribbean people have the same kind of rural ease about life, and the *mores* are
closer – deriving from the plantation society which we both know so well. I
transferred from Howard to Western Reserve. That was pure accident. I was fed up
with Washington. And a student at Howard, who came from Cleveland, told me that
I should visit him in Cleveland and look at the universities there. So, one day, I just
picked myself up, got on a Greyhound bus and went up to Cleveland. On the bus, I
met a young woman who was extremely pleasant and hospitable – her family took me
in because one of her brothers was abroad [and] I lived in his room. And then she, my
angel of mercy, told me about Western Reserve, so I went to Western Reserve. It was
a very segregated university. And I saw the Director of Admissions and just blazed out
in a passionate tirade to him for about a half an hour, about the offensiveness of
studying in a university where one has the nagging idea that one can't go certain places,
one can't go to a concert, one can't go to a cinema, and it obsesses one. It was not even
that I wanted to go to these places, but just the thought I couldn't go made life
absolutely intolerable! And he said, 'Well, why do you want to come here?' And I said,
'You have a concert hall nearby and I can go there, if I feel like going.' I thought the
fellow would throw me out; instead, he admitted me on the spot. He said, 'You can
come', and he didn't even have my transcripts – nothing. [He said,] 'We'll admit you
and it will be an honour to have you in this university.' I was the first student ever from
Guyana to attend Western Reserve. So, I had to fight against being a kind of zoological

curiosity and detaching myself from the Black struggle in America, saying that I was different. I lived in the ghetto in Cleveland for my first year at Western Reserve.

DANCE: I take it, then, that you always felt a close association with the Black community?

CAREW: I felt it immediately, and it wasn't even political; it was instinctive.

DANCE: That's not true of all West Indians who come to this country, you know.

CAREW: I know, I know, I know. It's a terrible thing with West Indians. I think it is the result of a lack of imagination. I went into the Black community and I lived in the house of a numbers-runner while I went to Western Reserve, and the whole street adopted me. I felt safe and nothing ever happened to me. I was always fascinated by the texture of African-American life. To go into a barber shop and to hear people talk – what I thought was the most beautiful language I'd ever heard – those chaps rapping, you know – I still enjoy it. [Laughter] I went into my barber shop in Evanston and heard an old fellow just a week ago talking about 1913 and journeying through the South – fascinating!

DANCE: Yes, it's an experience.

CAREW: And I don't think Afro-Americans understand how beautiful that language and experience and the totality of it is. Without it, the US language and culture would be dead as dirt. But in the Caribbean, you see, the man in the street is instinctively attracted to the Afro-American language, music, lifestyle. They think that the way Afro-Americans speak is almost magical, and it is! They take to it at once. That's the real authentic Black speech, not 'proper' language. At Western Reserve, I met a woman named Dr. Long, Dr. Fern Long. I was really unhappy and alienated in those days. The unhappiness stemmed from all kinds of things, some of which I wrote down in my novel, *The Last Barbarian*, but I really have to deal with it much more extensively. It was an unhappiness of not really knowing what I wanted to do, or knowing what I wanted to do but knowing that there were practical considerations and the shadow of my father's failure in life.

DANCE: What was it that you wanted to do at this time?

CAREW: I wanted to paint, to give up everything and just paint. I have been painting since boyhood, it had become a part of my life. So when the unhappiness increased, I turned to painting. I used to go to classes and that wasn't any great thing, because unlike Howard, at Western Reserve, I cannot remember a single professor… I think there was one Italian who taught me economics and a Dane who taught me geography.

DANCE: Now who was this Long? She was not a professor?

CAREW: No, she was the head of the library Adult Education Division. She was a very senior person in the library, and she was of Czech origin. She still kept connections with Czechoslovakia. Once she had asked me to come and to speak to her adult education class at the library. This was a way of singing for your supper – as a foreign student you were asked to speak. And so I went and I spoke, and then we chatted afterwards. I was a bit reserved, but I showed her some of my drawings. I had done the drawings for the people I lived with. They wanted to decorate their walls. I did some black and white drawings and framed them. She was taken aback and declared, 'I didn't know you painted!' and so on, and so then she greatly encouraged [me]. I then brought her some landscapes and portraits I painted with pastels – which I love. She said, 'Oh, God! You should have an exhibition and you should take part in the art competition in the museum.' So she commissioned me to do paintings for her as a way of encouraging me. She brought a whole lot of paints and pastels and paper and materials and I did a series of drawings. Some of them are still in the Cleveland Public Library. I last saw them about eight years ago.

DANCE: Do you illustrate your own children's books?

CAREW: No, no! I've never gone back to painting. But recently a kind of impulse to paint has been possessing me. The latest edition of *Black Midas*, which Longmans did for schools, has a painting of mine on the cover. When I went back – I am jumping ahead – when I went back to that Cleveland Library I saw in a way paintings that exactly paralleled my novels. For *Black Midas* was a Black man shouting, I did this painting from memory – just remembering a man on a street corner shouting, and the kind of light and shade and the life in the face – that is in the *Black Midas;* and then I have a painting that would be a perfect jacket for *The Wild Coast.* It is of rice fields and…

DANCE: Oh really! So in a sense you painted these stories first.

CAREW: I painted the stories first, and I never made the connection until I saw them (the paintings) again. But about Western Reserve, a series of accidents affected my life there. I went there – I had very little money – in my first semester, I could not afford to pay the fees. But I paid a deposit out of some money I had, and was racking my brains on how I could get a job. I took a course in the geopolitics of Latin America, and there was a Danish professor – and I talked to her after classes, and she said to me, 'You know so much about the subject; why don't you lecture the class?' So I gave a lecture to the class to which she had invited – I didn't know it – the Dean and the Vice President of the university. And after the lecture they came to me and said, 'Look, how did you get such a remarkable command of the English language? Where did you go to school? Are you here on a government scholarship?' And I wasn't, so they gave me a scholarship for the rest of my stay on the basis of that lecture. And so I was suddenly rescued from disaster. From Western Reserve, I went to Charles University in Prague. I got a scholarship to Prague because I was interested then in doing pure science – and going away from medicine. There was a student at Western Reserve whose father was the Czech Consulate General in Chicago. He put me in touch with the student union at Charles University; I wrote them and they offered me a scholarship. So I went home to Guyana for nine months – this was the longest period I was to stay at home for many years. And, you know, Wilson Harris is my brother-in-law… he was married to my sister, who is now dead. His children I practically inherited. They are very close to me.

DANCE: Did you and Wilson Harris grow up together in Guyana?

CAREW: When Wilson was courting my sister, I met him. Although we both had come from Berbice… I lived in Berbice, but he had moved to Georgetown. And he was a government surveyor. Wilson and I were as close as brothers then. And he made it possible for me to enter into the rain forest of Guyana. Whenever I went home I would go on expeditions with him. Because I couldn't afford the thousands and thousands it would have cost anyway, and it was a very stimulating business of being together; he was writing and I was writing, and Martin Carter was very close to us at the time. Wilson is an extraordinary person because he exercised enormous intellectual influences on people around him. The ordinary workers – those chaps who were just cutting lines – became intellectuals after years with Wilson. And I have a story I wrote for the BBC about going up the Canje River with Wilson and describing one night our having long and passionate discussions about Spengler's *Man and Technics* with all of the workers around him; they'd sit there, listening, absolutely enthralled.

DANCE: Well you know, this is very interesting to me because I heard somebody make the comment that people never knew what Wilson Harris was talking about when he talked. So that's not true, is it?

CAREW: Yes. In a curious way one has to really listen to understand it, and the men knew the codes to understand Wilson. You see, one of the problems with Wilson that people don't understand, one of the strengths and also a concern of what they think is a mystification, Wilson for seventeen years was in that rain forest by himself, talking to himself mostly. It's a kind of internalisation of the dialogue with oneself. The language that Wilson writes is a language inside his head alone in that immense unsettled forest when he had no one to communicate with really. Out of going with Wilson I began to write *Black Midas*. *Black Midas* was a story based on a story that one of the cooks in Wilson's party, Herbert Scotland, began to tell me about his life as a porkknocker. I was so fascinated by it that I took down big chunks of Scotland's life, but I couldn't use it because at the beginning I think writers who have someone else's story try to write the story exactly as it was told, and I'm a writer of fiction. So it took me years to untangle myself from the reality of Scotland's life and to write a fictional story which really had very little, at many points, very, very little to do with his life.

DANCE: But the kinds of adventures…

CAREW: They just gave you clues to reality and while we were there in the terrain you could see it bouncing off, so the original manuscript of *Black Midas* was, oh, it was about fifty-fifty Scotland's stories; then through five different sequences it ironed itself out because I was with Wilson and Wilson would talk, and Scotland would talk, and so I had to get these dissonances out of my brain and to write the story as my own story. Finally in London I began to do this. In the fifth version of *Black Midas* I worked out the correct balance of fiction and reality.

DANCE: OR Dathorne mentions the fact that your picture of the interior is different from Wilson Harris's picture of the interior of Guyana. He says, 'Jan Carew's Guyana is not Wilson Harris's – Carew sets the physical affirmation of individual struggle against a jungle wobbling before man's assertiveness; Harris, surrenders his community to the potency of myth and the will of landscape' [*Caribbean Narrative*, p.9]. Is that pretty much an assessment with which you agree?

CAREW: It is pretty much my assessment because our minds are totally different – Wilson's mind and mine are totally different. We both have Amerindian blood and have internalised some of the structures of Amerindian myth, but I would write it in children's stories – the myths. And my mind has to deal with harder realities. And in a curious way Wilson is a very fine mathematician. He is absolutely brilliant in math. You wouldn't know this from the kind of art he creates, and so he has a precise, mathematical dimension and then one that goes off into a metaphysical and intensely individual world. But my own thing is to write with a clarity to illuminate – the struggle – to give it the dimensions of great drama in which a man pits himself, his imagination, against unknowns.

DANCE: I've been interested in your use of folk materials in your stories, particularly one little myth that seems to be, I would imagine, one of your favourites, and that's the one that *The Third Gift* is based upon. In one story, I think it's *Black Midas*

– you use that story in *Black Midas*, don't you?

CAREW: Hmnn humnn.

DANCE: And you have the character say that he learned the story from their African ancestors. You first heard that story in Europe, right?

CAREW: I heard that story in England – fragments of it. The story is therefore largely invented, you know. Fragments of it I'd heard growing up as a boy in Berbice and the Canje River, and then I met an African from the Niger River, an Ejau artist, Loki Warridi, and he told me his versions of the story – I told him mine, and he said, 'Where did you get this story from because this is an Ejau story from the Niger River?' Afterwards, we used to swap stories. He'd tell me his stories and I'd tell him mine and they were so similar. So some of the people of Guyana must have been Ejaus from the Niger and they kept alive those stories. My growing up in Guyana, in the rural areas, gave to me a vast fount of myth and stories. It wasn't just one story. I was just fed endlessly with the vast range of stories that came into my consciousness. The consciousness of people in Guyana, Guyana in particular, and in the Caribbean generally, is quite different in the rural and the urban areas – there's an immense difference in the kind of consciousness they bring to bear in seeing the world around them.

DANCE: Let me ask you about Seymour. Did you know him when you were growing up in Guyana?

CAREW: I knew Seymour, yes. We all knew Seymour. He is a kind of institution. Slightly rambunctious, that Seymour, straddling all kinds of sides. And the good thing about Seymour was that he made a very profound contribution to keeping alive the spirit of literature in Guyana, the nation's literature. Some people criticise him because like JA Rogers, he wasn't very selective – he just published everything, good, bad, and indifferent. But that in retrospect wasn't a bad thing. At least it was an outlet, and how would you know what would eventually transpire? Then during all the political turmoil Seymour kept a kind of literary integrity – he published your works on its merits regardless of whether you are in favour politically or not. He's just published some poems of mine in a new anthology and I'm *persona non grata* with the present government of Guyana.

DANCE: I know you and your former wife, Sylvia Wynter, did one play together. Did you frequently collaborate?

CAREW: We frequently collaborated; it was a weird kind of thing at a certain point. When we were very close, it was difficult to separate things. I was exercising enormous influences on her and she on me. And, you know, her novel *The Hills of Hebron* is about half my own (I wrote about half – or more than half of it – which Andrew Salkey recognised instantly). But it was very difficult to disentangle my part and hers, and I find that kind of collaboration really disastrous on your work because it causes, eventually, a kind of tension. I think one can live with a writer, but you have to go completely separate ways. Sylvia was immensely talented – up to a certain point. Now, what she writes, I really can't make head or tail of. It's a whole mass of convoluted academic prose and…

DANCE: Are you speaking of her studies now – because I haven't read anything creative that she's written [recently]?

CAREW: Yes, her scholarly, academic writing, a whole hodgepodge of Marxist half truths which I don't think she's digested very well. But one of Sylvia's problems is that she was too talented, too early. She had everything, you know; she was bright academically, she could dance, she was a fantastic dancer. During the time she was doing graduate studies at London University she was dancing in leading clubs in London, she was a very fine choreographer, and she could act. She was acting on television. That's the period when I met her at a sort of turning point; we both had been in Europe for years, and it was refreshing to meet someone from home… And so the coming together was a very important event in my life, in my literary life, because she provided the kind of critical analysis not just of my work but of the kind of talent I had. I would spend a great deal of time praising other people. And she said, 'Why are you always worrying about people who have far less talent than you? You are constantly building them up into great beings.' And I mean this might seem to be a tiny thing, but it really was important… She gave me invaluable insights into my work. We actually met in the BBC one day, for the first time. She was reading poetry of West Indians, and she read a poem of mine. She just absolutely raved and said, 'Look this is the only genuine West Indian poem I read. It comes out of something, some spirit in it…' and she was going on and on. And I came in just as she was coming out of the studio, and someone said to me, 'You should have heard her, what she said about you, about your poem.'

DANCE: It was interesting to me just now when you spoke of meeting Sylvia Wynter as meeting someone from home. I take it you see the Caribbean as home, not just Guyana.

CAREW: Yes, the whole Caribbean, the whole Latin America. I think it's my Carib blood. I take the continent as mine – it's not just some little fragment of it, and home was a part of me – I am a real wanderer; this is a fact I have to admit to myself. I really need to travel the way people need food. Travel is perpetually stimulating to me. To go to the ends of the earth, I don't mind it; I actually need it. There have been compulsive periods where I say I must settle into one place; I must go and put down roots somewhere and stay there. And then that Carib wanderlust comes back and I go again, and I feel that I'm alive once more, and I'm in Siberia and in Asia and up in the Canadian North, and the whole world suddenly becomes more exciting.

DANCE: Yes that's very interesting. I want to ask you a question about *Black Midas* now. Indra's disdain for Shark and her warped sexual attraction to him when she calls him 'Black beast; Black brute', and so forth, suggests something of the frequent scenes in Black literature in which the white woman is pictured as desiring the Black man and yet feeling a kind of repulsion towards him. I was a little surprised to find it in an Indian woman. Historically there's a kind of explanation for the white woman having this kind of attitude…

CAREW: Well, it's just that they've patterned themselves after their colonial masters, and with Indra, it was a class thing, plus a Hindu thing. It's a Hindu exclusiveness. Now in Guyana that would not happen because the power arrangements have shifted…

DANCE: And the Blacks are in control?

CAREW: … and the Blacks are in control. So the terms of reference are different. But it was then – and Indra was not just Hindu. She did have some other blood. She was slightly Anglo-Indian.

DANCE: Oh, hmnn-humnn. I was a little surprised in your novels because the picture that you have of the racial relationships between Indians and Blacks is… well, there is so much racism in terms of the Indians' reactions to the Blacks, and when I'd read Mittelholzer and several of the Trinidadian writers I hadn't sensed that, and Selvon tells me in Trinidad it's a more recent kind of thing, that animosity…

CAREW: And this is a period thing because you see in Mittelholzer's time the Indian was still a coolie on the plantation. In my time the Indian began moving into the cities and to be very aggressive and to try to shed the stigmas that were put on them by [the] colonial divisions… Now it has gone to a further state with Rodney entering the arena in Guyana. He brings together the youths of the Indians and the Blacks and they shed these things, but it has been a – you know, you see it in terms of the evolution of events. In the early period the Blacks were very… my mother and aunts in Georgetown, were sort of the red middle-class.

DANCE: They were sort of what?

CAREW: The red middle class in Guyana… [Laughter] Red people are like myself; this is a term used in sociology in the West Indies now. Red people are the mulattoes really. My aunt would go to the market and then there would be an Indian – what you call a jobber. He would take an enormous load on his head and go all through that burning sun to take home my aunt's purchases at the market – just for a few pennies. So the Indians were just a lowly class. Outside of one or two families they were looked down on. So their aggressiveness in coming up is to make up… Now there's a whole class of rich Indians – it's very much like Kenya, in Trinidad and Guyana, you know, the Indians have moved up. Still, of course, the real situation is that the mass of Indians are still poor miserable peasants on the land. But the urban middle-class Indian is mostly the one with the prejudices.

DANCE: I see. What about the extreme colour prejudice among Blacks that we've experienced everywhere in the Diaspora and that you portray in your books…

CAREW: You know, it's less in Guyana for one reason. Our environment was so overpowering and our society was really backward in relation to, say, Jamaica or Trinidad; and there was more space. In Jamaica it's so enclosed. It has those rigid differences.

DANCE: Are you suggesting that there are greater differences in Jamaica because…

CAREW: Greater class difference, more inexorable class differences. Because there was more of an institutional structure to the differences, a structure which is possible on an island. In Guyana it is more difficult.

DANCE: But nobody could be more insistent upon class differences than that mother of the girl Shark was dating [*Black Midas*].

CAREW: Oh yes, that's true, but it's all relative. I would say in Jamaica it's ten times worse. You see, of course, time has shown, Guyana, since independence, has moved away more easily from that, whereas in Jamaica it is still very, very very strong. You could take the leaders, Manley and Seaga, both of them are upper class. In this country [the United States] Manley could be white. And Seaga *is* white. In Jamaica with 96% of the people Black, you would not find a Black to lead them after all of these years! It's a disgrace!

DANCE: Let me turn the subject to *Green Winter*. Is that very much an account of your own experiences?

CAREW: No. *Green Winter* came out of my cousin's – I had a young cousin who arrived on my doorstep in London, and so, as I said in the English edition, this fellow came one day. I hadn't known him in Guyana, (a) because I'd left a long time ago, and

(b) he belonged to a poorer branch of the family and the family tended to suppress news about poorer relatives. Dennis looked sort of acceptable; he had the right kind of colour, hair and features. He arrived and began working in London and living in my house. And when scholarships to Eastern Europe and the Soviet Union came up, at a time when I was a very close friend of Jagan's, I arranged a scholarship to East Germany for him. After one year he arrived back in London on my doorstep from the Soviet Union, saying that the quota to East Germany had been filled and he could go to the Soviet Union instead. So he went there.

DANCE: So you yourself did not study in Russia?

CAREW: I never studied in the Soviet Union… I studied in Czechoslovakia. I studied at Charles University. I studied in a communist society under a communist regime.

DANCE: Oh, I see. Is the view of communism that you portray in that book very much your view of communism?

CAREW: Well views change. My view of communism – you know that was looking at the inside – and now you know, I am a Marxist, and the kind of structural understanding of those societies, I would say, is now more profound and more advanced than it was then. Then I was a bit angry over the apparent manifestations of racism in the Soviet Union. But I also think that it is really fundamentally different to the United States because there is no structural base for it inside of the society. … There's an unwritten sequel to *Green Winter*. Dennis, my cousin, was expelled from Leningrad University as soon as the book came out. He went to Moscow, flew to Moscow from Leningrad, and insisted on seeing Kosygin or Brezhnev. He went to the Kremlin. He just spent hours there arguing with the guards, and finally he spoke to Kosygin on the telephone. He said, 'My cousin has written a book which you obviously don't agree with. I haven't even seen the book, but I have absolute faith in my cousin that what he says is the truth, and it's the kind of criticisms that you should pay attention to. So what worries me by this expulsion is that you are being very bad Marxists by expelling me and not dealing in a very objective and compassionate way with something that we really have to deal with. So I would like to come and see you.' Kosygin said, 'But look, I am very busy with the affairs of State,' and he gave him a letter to the Minister of Education, and he was reinstated. Then he stayed and finished his course in the Soviet Union, and he now works for the Ministry of Science in England, having done very brilliantly in the Soviet Union. It's a different kind of society, and it's a society that has such density to penetrate from the West. It takes a great deal to understand it, to take out the prejudices of communism, and to really look at the society. And I've been back since and have extremely cordial relationships with the Russians, which is not possible in the United States. Once you, say, take positions, they [the United States] never forgive you. You know my wife is a specialist in Russian. She's Afro-American. She was born in Chicago. She did Russian from high school, and did degrees in Russian. So going to the Soviet Union with her about two or three years ago was really quite pleasant.

DANCE: I see. In *The Wild Coast* there is a great mystery made of who Hector's mother is, and when it was finally revealed I couldn't decide whether the worse thing was that she was a mulatto, possibly, or that she was his father's sister-in-law.

CAREW: Yes. Well, that was the thing you see. *The Wild Coast* is more autobiographical than any of the other things I did… so far. That is the story of my own family, and it's the story of my great aunt, who had a child by one of the workers on the family plantation on the Corentyne Coast. That's where the family had extensive lands and homes. We practically owned villages. And then this child was raised and nobody was ever told who… The reigning story was that my great aunt was locked away in a room there in that old house for the rest of her life until she went insane. It was a very cruel and bigoted kind of society.

DANCE: And I suppose the really bad thing about that was that he was a hand on the farm, possibly Black.

CAREW: It wasn't so much that he was Black; he was what you call a brown man.

DANCE: Brown?

CAREW: A brown man. The Jamaicans say, 'brown man'. Just like yourself.

DANCE: That means dark?

CAREW: No, it means that you are not Black, that you are brown. And it is quite different because 'brown man' means your status is the status of the mulatto, creole, and you're the upper crust. So even though someone who might be lighter skin than you is a labourer, he calls you 'brown'; it's defining a class status. If this fellow had been educated and had his own carriage and so on, he would be perfectly acceptable as a suitor. [Laughter] But he just happened to be a labourer; he was working as a field hand… Did you see an essay of mine called 'The Caribbean Writer and Exile'?

DANCE: I don't think so.

CAREW: It's dealing with the whole [area of] Caribbean writing. But this gives insights into the kind of contemporary ferment in which I find myself. I am writing a novel too that I have been working on for years. It's called *Green Palaces of the Sun,* and it's about the journey into the hinterland, of going back into the Guyana hinterland. And that too has been going through transformations, and I must go back to it.

DANCE: In [Herdeck's *Caribbean Writers*] there's a sketch of you in which the editor describes you as a 'formidable adversary, but not without a great deal of charm'.

CAREW: Well I have been involved in political quarrels, and I don't make any differences between literature and politics. I think that that is an absolute fallacy, particularly with Blacks and Third World people. It is an utterly ridiculous postulate to separate them. So I am absolute about my political commitments and I involve myself in politics. I take an unequivocal stand on it, and I suppose my manner always surprises people; they think I am very gentle and nice, and then I can really, you know… advocating revolutions in a very calm voice when they…

DANCE: [Laughter] Have you ever participated in Carifesta or Guyfesta?

CAREW: Oh, yes. I have been in all of the Carifestas, I went to the one in Guyana, but my relationships with the government were so tenuous that although they had to invite me, they sort of played down my presence… But I didn't bother too much about that. And the one in Jamaica I took a fairly prominent part in that. My essay, 'The Caribbean Writer and Exile' was part of… the lecture I gave was the basis for the essay which I wrote. And then I went to the one in Cuba and again I have another essay called 'Fulcrums of Change'… In 'The Fusion of African and Amerindian Folk Myths', you see, I propound a thesis that the civilisation of this hemisphere is really based on the foundations of African and American Indian fusions – that the European civilisation – a third violent and powerful one – interacted with these. And that one has to look at the civilisation of the hemisphere from the African and the Indians first, because their cultures were the most complementary and they were the peoples who came closest, voluntarily, without anyone with guns behind their backs, and this is why I am so vitally interested in continuing the work that I have been doing, the research on the Columbian era. I am now finishing an essay for Van Sertima – you know we bring out a journal called *Journal of African Civilisations*. I am the Caribbean editor. I am writing a piece for Van Sertima about Este Vanico, the first African explorer in the United States. Este Vanico was the first explorer who crossed from the Atlantic to the Pacific. And Florida is a very interesting part of the United States, one that is very neglected in African-American studies for very obvious reasons: Florida was where the first Blacks came to the United States during the Columbian era; so Blacks had been there for nearly five centuries. In Florida, too, you had Blacks who after 1700 were never slaves. As Richard Hart says, they were slaves who abolished slavery. The war of liberation which Afro-Americans fought in Florida for 150 years is the most important resistance movement initiated by Afro-Americans in the whole history of this country. Nobody deals with it. They tell you [about] Denmark Vesey and Nat Turner. But not about the leaders who fought and won, like Kofi Abraham, Inti, Louis Pacheo, who literally had two-thirds of the United States armed forces fighting against them by the 1850s, but for obvious reasons this is an unpopular subject. So here again is the history that I'm writing. I have a manuscript; I've been working on it for years and years and years and I'm anxious that I get this work out, that I get the origins piece finished and then to finish my book on the Black Seminole Wars. Afro-Americans were not docile people beaten down by the system, they fought back. And then scattered groups from Florida went to Oklahoma, and some went to Mexico to the border state of Coahuila. I've been there to visit the descendants of these folk. And then one group went to the Bahamas. On Andros Island are Black Seminoles, who after the wars settled there. So you see, then, I feel, 'Should I write all this as novels or as history?' So I combine the two now into documentaries where I use dramatic forms. My interest is also in the theatre – in drama. I've written a number of plays.

DANCE: Let me ask you one last question before we end this interview. I'd like you to give me your assessment of West Indian literature – if you wish what's happening now generally in the field or your reactions to some of the writers who are writing now.

CAREW: Well, I think West Indian literature has now reached a kind of malaise, and things like music and ballads have taken over – Reggae is the most interesting, the most universal art form to come out of the modern Caribbean – because literature became too elitist and it could not meet the popular cultural demands. So it has got to transform itself, its meaning, it has got to politicise itself openly, not in any disguised fashion – not as political tracts, but as a genuine art form dealing with reality. And you know Andrew Salkey's *Come Home, Malcolm Heartland* is a step towards this goal; Neville Dawes's *Interim*; John Stewart's *Last Cool Days*, which I think is the finest of them because that penetrates into the heart of what the real new West Indies is; and the stunning novels of Roy Heath…

DANCE: Have you read Earl Lovelace's *The Dragon Can't Dance*?

CAREW: Yes, oh yes, yes.

DANCE: Is that anywhere near the…

CAREW: A fine writer, yes. That is moving and I'm sorry that I left that out. Lovelace is a brilliant [writer]. So I think we need to transform things. These are the important developments I see taking place. But… colonial hangovers. You take Walcott for example: Walcott is a colonial poet, really. Fine command of language, but events have by-passed him. Naipaul is an anachronism, and he's malicious and confused; he is simply held up by whites for us. Sort of popular, and that came about at some point before he wrote *A House for Mr. Biswas*. That fine short story of his, 'B. Wordsworth' had a real compassionate understanding of people. Then suddenly he went away from that…

DANCE: You don't think that that's shown in *A House for Mr. Biswas*?

CAREW: *Biswas* is an autobiographical work – a fine piece of autobiography – writing about that period. But Naipaul isn't genuinely creative. Naipaul feeds on real experiences and then distorts them. His going into Africa and Argentina. It's all a one-dimensional vision of a world.

DANCE: Well, thank you very much.

CONVERSATION WITH

MARTIN WILDE CARTER AND DENIS WILLIAMS

Martin Carter was born in Georgetown, Guyana, in 1927, and educated at Queen's College, Georgetown. Long active politically, Carter was a member of the People's Progressive Party, which under Cheddi Jagan came to power in 1953. When the British Government deposed Jagan's government a few months after its election, Martin Carter was one of the Guyanese who was arrested and imprisoned. Much of his best known poetry was written at this time. Martin Carter has held several political positions: including United Nations representative for Guyana and Minister of Information in the People's National Congress Government, from which post he resigned in disagreement with government policies.

Carter wrote several volumes of poetry, including *The Hill of Fire Glows Red* (1951); *To a Dead Slave* (1951); *The Hidden Man* (1952); *The Kind Eagle* (1952); *Returning* (1953); *Poems of Resistance from British Guiana* (1954; reissued in 1964 as *Poems of Resistance*); *Poems of Shape and Motion* (1955); *Jail Me Quickly* (1966); *Poems of Succession* (1977); *Poems of Affinity* (1980); *Poesia* (1988); *Selected Poems* (1989); Poesias Escogidas (1999). Two collections have been published posthumously: *University of Hunger: Collected Poems and Selected Prose* edited by Gemma Robinson (2006) and *Poems by Martin Carter* (2006) edited by Stewart Brown and Ian McDonald. His poetry also appears in practically every anthology of Caribbean poetry and in numerous journals. His work has been received critically in Rupert Roopnaraine's *Web of October: Rereading Martin Carter* (1987) and *All are Involved: The Art of Martin Carter* by Stewart Brown (2000).

The poet remained in Georgetown, Guyana with his wife, where he passed away in 1998.

Denis Joseph Ivan Williams was born in Georgetown, Guyana, in 1923, where he received his early education. He was granted a Cambridge Junior School Certificate in 1940 and a Cambridge Senior School Certificate in 1941. He later studied painting at the Camberwell School of Art in London (1946-48), but subsequently turned to archaeology, gaining a Master's degree from the University of Guyana in 1979.

Mr. Williams has held several teaching and lecturing positions in England and Africa, including the School of Fine Art in London; the Slade School of Fine Art, University of London; the School of Fine Art in Khartoum, Sudan; the University of Ife in Nigeria; Makerere University, Uganda and the University of Lagos. From 1967-74 Williams pursued research in Native American tribal art of Guyana, especially petroglyphs. Since 1974 Williams was the Director of Art and Archaeology with the Department of Culture, Ministry of Education and Culture in Guyana. He passed away in 1998.

Denis Williams is the author of two novels: *Other Leopards* (1963) and *The Third Temptation* (1968). Both are due for republication by Peepal Tree in 2008. He has also produced several works on West Indian and African art and anthropology: *Image and Idea in the Arts of Guyana* (1970); *Icon and Image: A Study of Sacred and Secular Forms of*

African Classical Art (1974); *Contemporary Art in Guyana* (1976); *Guyana, Colonial Art to Revolutionary Art, 1966-1976*; *Ancient Guyana* (1985); *Pages in Guyanese Prehistory* (1995); and *Prehistoric Guiana* (2003). He contributed numerous essays on art to several books and journals. Indeed, he was probably better known as an artist than as a novelist. Williams also edited several journals: *Odu* (University of Ife Journal of African studies); *Lagos Notes and Records*; and *Archaeology and Anthropology* (Journal of the Walter Roth Museum of Archaeology and Anthropology, Georgetown).

In addition to numerous prizes for his paintings, Williams was awarded The Golden Arrow of Achievement Award from the Government of Guyana in 1973. He has received several grants to subsidise his research in art and archaeology, including research grants from the University of Ife; the International African Institute, London; and the Smithsonian Institution.

On the morning of Thursday, March 20, 1980, I met Carter and Williams in the latter's office for our interviews. Neither of these voluble personalities could resist entering the interview with the other, so that what started out to be two interviews turned into one three-way conversation, which I found impossible to later separate into two individual pieces. This interesting variation to the standard plan of this book requires no apology, for the many interchanges that took place between the two writers make the following an exciting contribution to this collection.

————————————

DANCE: Shall we begin by pursuing an interesting topic which we were discussing last night regarding the ways in which Guyanese writers differ from other Caribbean writers?

WILLIAMS: I think by way of setting the background for looking at our individual Guyanese writers, that we have to see them against the background of the Caribbean as a whole. We very much feel that we *are* part of the Caribbean in this country, but there is something *else* that we are here, that we do not recognise in the remainder of the Caribbean. And I think that perhaps that might be because of our hinterland: our South American awareness. Not that we have all that many strong links with the rest of South America, but being born in Amazonia gives us a kind of backdrop in our thinking that I feel is lacking in the rest of the Caribbean. The ordinary person on the road has this feeling about the interior, the great mass of jungle behind him, and you can easily appeal to this. In fact take our National Anthem, the words of the National Anthem... I don't even remember the words of the National Anthem, but it has got all this 'Dear land of Guyana... of rivers and plains', and so on. And I think this is very much part of our definition of ourselves.

DANCE: Let me ask you if you are speaking more now of other Guyanese writers than yourself?

WILLIAMS: Not my own self. I have never myself personally tapped that area of experience in my work because I have written outside of this country. But certainly people like Martin Carter, Wilson Harris, Jan Carew, these are people who feel very strongly... and this man Ivan Forrester that I was talking about, par excellence, and for which reason you ought to see him or hear him. But you find very much this awareness of the vastness of physical existence behind us, in this...

CARTER: To borrow an expression from an American writer, somehow appropriate, it is a 'ghostly premise' that exists, you see, from which I think Guyanese writers
differ from Caribbean writers, in the sense that there *is* this premise – unspoken… but
it is present all the time. In other words, it is a *presence* that is not expressed literally,
not even symbolically. It *invades* what is written, without ever being articulated.
WILLIAMS: It's very real, it's very real.
CARTER: It's tangible almost.
DANCE: When you were talking about this last night I think you said something too
about the fact that there is a different racial outlook among Guyanese writers. Could
you talk about that a little bit?
WILLIAMS: Yes, well, but look here. When we spoke about this last night, specifically I meant that this Black consciousness movement, or Black consciousness
awareness, is not a very strong part or a motivating element in our writing. We have
got different racial polarisations, but they are political, it's not a definition of Black in
terms of white. We are completely, or nearly completely, free of this; and so therefore
the Black consciousness which arises out of the polarisation to the white world is not
a part of our mystique or our make-up here, and consequently people like this
Carmichael and so on who came down here a few years back on this kind of theme
fell dead; it fell completely dead.
CARTER: No response.
WILLIAMS: No, no, no! The people didn't understand what it was all about at all,
and as you wisely said, it is the experience of Europe that makes us know we are Black,
you know. When we go to Europe then for the first time you are made aware of Black
in that polarised sense.
DANCE: But the fact that so many of your writers have had the European experience,
suggests then that racial themes do enter your works as indeed they have yours after…
WILLIAMS: The English writers, our Guyanese writers who write in England, for
instance, very strongly – ER Braithwaite, *To Sir With Love*: that book could not have
been written in this country, could not have been! So that is something that, again,
ought to be taken into account when you try to read the motivations behind our sort
of writing. And I think that you are going to find a great difference between the work,
the ideational content of a person like Martin Carter and a person like Ted Braithwaite.
It's simply that Martin has written entirely in this country and Ted Braithwaite has
written entirely in the United Kingdom, and this makes a big difference though they
are both Guyanese writers. You will find that again also in Mittelholzer – beginning
of Guyana is Mittelholzer, not that he is our best writer by any means, but he is the
sort of panoramic background man who has looked at our present racial make-up in
terms of our history. And on a completely different level Wilson Harris does the same
thing. Where Mittelholzer is narrative and explanatory, Wilson Harris is again
ideational and philosophic.
DANCE: Mr. Carter, you seem to be a very political person, poet. Did you become a
poet because of the circumstances of your life and the need to address those conditions,
or did the conditions simply offer you a subject matter for your poetry?
CARTER: The first point I would like to raise very rapidly is the whole concept of
what politics *is*. You have the *realpolitiks,* in the sense of the organisation of the people
and you have politics, which is an idea of what people are and what people will

become. And, therefore, first of all I would like to discriminate between *realpolitiks* and politics *per se*. That will at least introduce the idea that everybody is political in the sense that they are involved in living. One can say that there is a politics of literature, just as one considers the politics of politics, if you like. Having said that I would like to go on, just make the point very rapidly, that I wrote poetry long before I got into politics, not necessarily good or bad, that is irrelevant. The point is that politics provided the platform really, or the framework – put it that way – in which one found oneself writing verse that appeared to be political in the sense of using 'political' symbolism, 'political' material (in inverted commas 'political', of course). And therefore what you get is an appearance of politics. I would like to suggest (and this is my own attitude to it) that it is related to the whole concept of what we call the public and the private. There is a tendency to describe poets, some poets (I am not speaking of myself) as public poets and others as private poets. But they seem to miss a very important point indeed, and that is that by definition it is impossible to be one without being the other, they both go together; and therefore what happens is an emphasis may be placed on the expression of one, but it doesn't mean the absence of the other. So that the most private poet (I use the word private not in the pejorative sense) but the most private poet could appear to be a political poet, while the most political poet could appear to be a private poet. It is a question of how you see it. Having said that, to return to your question. Politics is just accidental in the proceedings of practising, if you want to use that word, the art of the poet. It's incidental. I mean one can write about anything. It only provides the frame, as I said, for what you are doing. And one always takes what is readily at hand. One does not go out of his way to seek out something that is, inverted commas, 'poetical'. One must transform what is anything into what is poetry. So that that is the answer that I would like to give rather than saying that one is political or not political as the case may be. Secondly, there is (how to put it?) an apprehension among people over the word *politics*, and this of course is because there is a misunderstanding, I think, a misunderstanding which has come from a whole century of criticism, literary criticism, which in the Caribbean, particularly, has been an almost slavish reliance on… [and] an adoption of the critical principles that are dominant at a given period in England, particularly. The same thing happened with the English-Caribbean poetry; I can call a name out of my head: Egbert Martin, who was a semi-invalid, who wrote under the pen-name of Leo, and the incident that I am going to relate is much more telling in many ways than an analysis. He wrote an additional verse to the National Anthem of England… Can you imagine *that*?

WILLIAMS: Yes, give the date, give the date.

CARTER: Eighteen… the last decade of the nineteenth century. In addition to which he had published a little booklet of poems which Tennyson in England saw, and Tennyson said it was first-class; I think Tennyson said so because it resembled Tennyson's verse; Tennyson's attitude being, 'How is it possible that a creature living in that no-where could even be sensitive enough to realise that it is possible for him to be influenced by me!' It is the attitude I am getting at. Sartre in an introduction to…

DANCE: *Black Orpheus?*

CARTER: … *Black Orpheus,* where he said that the attitude of the European intellectual is one of 'interested contempt' of writers out of Europe. In other words, as far as he is concerned, why should these people want to write? And it is brought out very clearly by an interview with Claude McKay, who is a Jamaican writer, you know, Claude McKay.

DANCE: We call him an *American* poet too.

CARTER: Of course, because he went there when he was in his twenties... But he met Frank Harris in New York and he had been introduced, given a letter by a parson in Jamaica, a white parson who had sort of patronised him; so he went to Harris, who in turn gave him a letter to Bernard Shaw in England – I am coming to the point. When he went to England he sent the letter to Shaw. So Shaw wrote, 'Come and see me.' So he went to see Shaw and they were talking, and Shaw was watching this Black man in puzzlement! Then he said in effect, 'Tell me, young man, why do you want to write poetry? You should take up pugilism!' You see what I am getting at? 'What have you got to do with that? That is not your business, you should take up boxing like Jack Johnson, you know, not this sort of thing.' Now I reported that incident to a young poet at the University to give him an idea of what I am getting at – and what you think he told me? He reacted immediately. He said: 'You know what I would have done? I would have cuffed him!' I said: 'That's precisely what the man is saying.' That is an example of the profound sense of inferiority here vis-a-vis the outside world.

DANCE: A sense you mean of inferiority among the writers?

CARTER: No, the whole total atmosphere, psychological atmosphere of these countries. It is not an inferiority complex to the white man *per se*; it is an inferiority complex, a reflex inferiority then – put it that way – rather than a projective inferiority. And it finds its truth in the population, that people here (and I am speaking not only of writers who after all are part of the people), they dwarf themselves *before* they do anything else. So they start by dwarfing and *then* proceed to do what they have to do. So – put it this way – suppose you met someone and said, 'Look, man, so and so has done this.' For obvious reasons it may be something that he doesn't understand. It may be research into some field which is comparatively, you know, not everyday. And the only reaction you would get – it may not be put in the same words I am putting it – but I am translating for the sake of clarity; he would say, 'That is white people story, you know.' You see, in other words it is not for you to do it; you are presumptuous; how dare you even aspire to want to behave in that manner! That is not for you. And that relates throughout the society. I mean it is the whole basis upon which people operate and it vitiates the motivation of everybody. It affects everybody, the writers too, consciously or unconsciously. And therefore you may find that in the very assertiveness that you may come across, especially among the younger poets, and those who have got peculiar feelings about what literature is; they come to the conclusion that it *is* assertiveness, not because they are not possibly good writers, but because they are trying to fight this peculiar dwarfing that has occurred to them. Another thing you find too, is that among intelligent people in the Caribbean – let us speak of Guyana – you take an intelligent Guyanese who is familiar with ideas and writing and so on, and speak to him for a while and you discover that he has a prejudice against things like literature from Australia or Canada or New Zealand, because in his mind, unconsciously literature comes from England...

WILLIAMS: Or Europe.

CARTER: Europe, England, England, Europe, especially – I only said England to create a point of view – but as far as he is concerned those aren't real writers coming from

Australia and New Zealand. They, you know, they're not real. The real ones come from England. And now, this is a deep-seated thing in the English-speaking Caribbean, and I think all writers and all artists fight it, I expect, in their own way.

DANCE: Do you think there has been an over-reaction to it on the part of some contemporary writers, in some Caribbean nations, and particularly in the United States, who of necessity tried to create new forms? Do you consider that a kind of overreaction?

CARTER: Yes, I think that has happened. For instance, there is a volume edited by Clarence Major in which you will find a lot of the verse, which bears out the suggestion you are making, that is to say, in an effort to assert themselves against what they consider an imposition, now an oppression, they drop everything, you see, as though you're going to start all over again. But the point about that is it's impossible, and I'll give you an example of what I mean by that. Some years ago a young girl came to me with some verse and said to me: 'I've written these. Will you have a look at them?' So I looked at them and, I mean, they weren't very good, but I didn't want to upset her for obvious reasons – they are very sensitive, you know, the young. So I told her to come back and I told her, 'Let's leave it for a while, let's talk.' I said: 'What books do you read? What's the last book you read?' She replied that she doesn't read books. I said, 'You don't read books?' I said: 'Why?' She said she wants to be original. I said, 'Tell me something: how do you know there is a thing called verse as against what you see in the newspapers?' She said: 'Well, I have seen it.' I said, 'Good, that's precisely the point, and therefore what you're doing is cheating yourself. You most likely saw verse in the primary school, in a primary school textbook that has 'Mary had a little lamb, its fleece was white as snow', or one of the jingles, and those became your models. You're writing with that model which is the most elementary model you can possible get, so that you are not being original in the sense you mean. You're still making use of that which you have just picked up. The problem is that you have not picked up enough, and therefore by not reading you are really cheating yourself.' I think that that applies in a special sense to the American writer of the type that you find in the sort of verse of [name deleted] 'No! Shit!' with exclamation marks. I mean that could be brought in if you want; but that is not a poem in my opinion. I suspect that that is the sort of thing that is happening to them. Now, on the other hand, take a man like LeRoi Jones, who, no matter what you say of him, is an artist in my opinion and a good one too. He may be… I am not concerned about every thing, but he can write – there is no doubt about that at all: he has a commanding mind. You take Hayden…

DANCE: Robert Hayden?

CARTER: Robert Hayden, right. Now Hayden is traditional; he is more like our old-fashioned West Indian writers, better, much better. But Jones I think, he is on to it. Although I don't agree with what he is doing, I mean, I wouldn't try to criticise it: I wouldn't say that it's the writing that I would do. That's a totally different matter; that has nothing to do with me.

DANCE: You are not talking about politics now, you are talking about his poetry… What do you mean, the obscenities and that kind of thing?

CARTER: No, no, no, not at all, not at all.

DANCE: What do you mean?

CARTER: It is too intellectual.

DANCE: *Too* intellectual?

CARTER: In spite of the fact that the criticism we have against Jones is that he is the opposite, but he is a very intellectual poet.

DANCE: What do you mean by *too* intellectual?

CARTER: Precisely. What do I mean by intellectual?

DANCE: *Too* intellectual.

CARTER: Intellectual in this sense is the informing principle; it exists before the poem; in other words: in this way: I am going to write a poem about *this* rather than in the very writing of the poem you discover *what* you're writing about. This is what I mean by intellectual. An intellectual is a man (this is a bad description, but it approximates what I am trying to get at), he sets out to write a poem. I think a poem writes itself in the sense that as you write it, it suggests to you what you should write or how it should be written. That's what I mean when I say a poem writes itself. I think Jones leans more to the first proposition I gave you rather than to the second one, and that is why I say that it is intellectual. I don't mean that it is loaded with philosophical ideas taken from books or something like that. I don't mean that.

DANCE: I see. This whole discussion leads me to ask a question about something Denis Williams wrote about art, in which he said that even the word *art* itself and other such terms will not survive when a Eurocentric scholarship is replaced by an African one. He was talking about African art. And he went on to ask: 'For how could a critical terminology be applied indefinitely to a body of work from which it has not organically emerged – a terminology in any case laden with meaning, inflection and circumstance derived from quite another culture?' [*Icon and Image,* 1974]. Do you think there is even a problem with the matter of terminology in discussing literature. You spoke for example just now about talking to the girl about a poem: what is a poem?

CARTER: Well I will agree with that insofar as I think the terminology of art has been tremendously corrupted, in general. For instance, take poetry: there is a tendency, not a tendency, I mean a practice, for people to speak of poetry as art. I don't think poetry is an art in the sense that painting is an art or sculpture is an art.

DANCE: Is there anything else other than painting and sculpture that is an art?

CARTER: … Well, drama… Narrative – fiction or novel – that is an art.

DANCE: But not poetry?

CARTER: But not poetry.

DANCE: You'll have to tell me why.

WILLIAMS: Yes, because I feel the *absolute* opposite.

CARTER: I'll tell you why, and I'll start from a different direction and come back. I feel that an art is psychological in intent, intention, while poetry, to which I have not yet given a word, in the same way that you give the word art, (I haven't given it a word because I don't know it) is epistemological, as against psychological. Poetry particularly, I think, exposes or illuminates what I am trying to say. Now, the distinction that is made between what is known as the discursive and the presentational… Painting, sculpture, drama, just for the sake of argument, let us just limit ourselves to those. If we think long enough we may find other things. Now I am not being original here, these theories were advanced by Susanne Langer with whom I agree to a certain extent – everything has a limitation. While you get things like journalism, some kinds of novels, which I would say are discursive in contrast to the presentational – poetry I would say is neither discursive nor presentational but it makes use of both forms, and that is why you get, for instance, a poet like Rilke. But that is a different story. But to return to the immediate point that you are making, Denis's point about the terminology and so on. I would hesitate to, you know, give an opinion unless I examined what the proposition means, which I am not familiar with in *those* terms. I am familiar with them in *other* terms which are purely practical terms, in the sense of how it affects my practice. I am not interested in theorising about what art is or it isn't; what I am interested in is working out how to do it. What comes out, comes out as a by-product.

WILLIAMS: Yes, we are on this important theme about the self-diminishing, you called it by another word, self-dwarfing, as a function of the colonial experience and the kind of reactions it has engendered in various territories and in various artists. But don't you realise that on a certain level, there are artists in these areas, like I was saying to you about the Yoruba Singers last night, or Philip Moore and so on, to whom this is not a problem at all. Those are the people that I respect. They have no problem. They don't read. Those are the people who have not had to throw away a book.

DANCE: So they haven't had to discard any of these values they have accepted…

WILLIAMS: No, No.

DANCE: And yet you [indicating Carter] would argue I think…

CARTER: I'll tell you why I would argue it now, because it is not true.

WILLIAMS: He don't read! Philip Moore does not read!

CARTER: He reads! He doesn't read a book in the sense of opening a book and reading it, but he *is* reading. He is reading because he comes in contact with you or with people who have read; and therefore he may get it secondhand: but he *is* getting it. In other words, he [Williams] would tell Philip, 'Look, for instance, your thing on Cuffy's statue…' [National Monument commissioned to mark the 10th Anniversary of Independence of Guyana in honor of Guyana's National Hero, Cuffy, leader of the 1763 Berbice Slave Revolution.] in which you see things that Philip would not see and which the artist has not seen. There are many things in his work he doesn't see because he is concentrating on something else; he is concentrating on doing it, not seeing it – let us use that expression. You see. Good. So you look at it and say, 'Philip, you know this strikes me.' He has learnt from you what you have learnt from –

WILLIAMS: But that happens to all of us. Your wife tells you what you have done, your wife tells you what you have done.

CARTER: That's right. Precisely. So that's what I mean by he reads, that's what I mean by he reads.

WILLIAMS: I see, all right.

CARTER: For instance, suppose a man found (Ah, good example. He would know about this), when the statue went up, someone comes up and says, 'Man that thing too ugly,' you know. Well, Philip could hear that and therefore the concept of what is not ugly arises to him. In other words what is ugly for you is beautiful for me, and therefore there is a clash of ideas. And there is an idea of a thing which is ugly and an idea of a thing which is beauty…

DANCE: I am speculating about something I haven't seen. But may I assume that his idea of what is beautiful stems from the fact that he hasn't been exposed too much to the European standards that may have been accepted by you [Williams] for example?

WILLIAMS: Well, he has been exposed, but he is blind. They don't rub off on him. He has lived a lot of time in the United States and so on, but he just has no notion of

Greek beauty and the noble man on a horse as a symbol of heroism, national heritage and so on, he doesn't know – these symbols and images, just never affected him. So when he had to create the same thing for us, a hero, he created a hero of defiance, a stance that is just completely new in the history of art... In his imagery, the language that he speaks, is the broken, faltering language of the naive artist, but the thing that is remarkable about that monument is not the imagery, it is the concept. The man had to create a national hero; but immediately to all of us who had gone through the Greek and Roman thing, you would think of Donatello; you would think of a great horse and a noble rider, high up above your eye level, in some public square. Well Philip has been through all that. He has been to the countries where all of this is the image of their heritage, but Philip in exactly the same position, faced with the same proposition, came up with something so supremely simple. He conceived the shape of a man differently from anywhere in the pages of the history of art, and that is what is the great originality and lasting value of that work... And now that fellow, that Philip, he is so free because he looks at white people and doesn't see them. Or he looks at the Greek and Roman thing and doesn't see it. He stands up in front of Beethoven and doesn't hear it. It doesn't matter to him about Mozart; you cannot intimidate him with the grandeur of Europe. You can intimidate *me* any day with the grandeur of Europe.

CARTER: ... I would like to introduce this proposition that – let us assume that I go along with your argument – it is not that you *don't* see, it is rather that you subsume it... you subsume it by a principle which takes it in and gives it its proper place, relegates it in other words to its proper place in your practice. Now, in its appearance you may not see it, but my contention is that whatever has gone in comes out. He has seen it, but what he has done with it is to subsume it, put it at a level where it does not impinge on his practice.

DANCE: All right. Let me turn now to ask you [Carter] some specific questions about your own poetry. In many of your poems you treat imprisonment, touching upon the stifling impact of prison life, the loneliness for home and wife and child and comrade. Tell me something about your imprisonment...

CARTER: Quickly... I used to be a civil servant many years ago. Anyway there was a political movement and so on in which I got involved as an activist, not as an activist, an organiser, going around and interfering with people, interfering with things. Anyway, in 1953 the new movement, the People's Progressive Party, to which I belonged, won the elections. It was a popular movement. The British Government then abolished the Constitution and arrested five of us, of which I was one, and put us in a detention camp on the grounds that our liberty was a threat to the public safety – greatly exaggerated! Anyway, I stayed in the detention camp for three months. That is the first instance. The second instance – we came out and the next day we had some demonstrations on the road and so on; an emergency had been declared. You were prohibited from having demonstrations on the street and so on. One of our chaps got arrested for breaking some restriction and we demonstrated and we got locked up again; and then we were put in prison, which is a distinction. There are two things, detention camp and prison. Prison is the civil prison; detention camp is a political prison.

DANCE: Were your poems written while you were there in prison or afterwards?

CARTER: Some were written in both detention camp and in prison, but some, quite a few were written long before that.

DANCE: Was it then that the theme of freedom became so significant to your poetry?
CARTER: Freedom has always been significant. This was only a special condition
of freedom or non-freedom as the case may be; but whether in prison or out of prison,
the problem of freedom still exists, because all that the jail was was a prison within a
prison. It is like a hospital within a prison, a prison within a prison. You know a
hospital within a prison is a prison within a prison, just as a prison in this country is
a prison within a prison. And the country is a prison within mortality. And mortality
a prison within immortality. It's the whole interconnection all the time, so that the
prison is no different from a non-prison if you really push it to its extreme limits,
because it is not a question of the location or the barbed wire or the cell. It's a question
of your location within something. That is what makes it a prison or not a prison.
DANCE: 'Our prison of air is worse than one of iron.'
CARTER: Precisely. You can have a prison of air, and this can be worse than one of iron.
DANCE: OK. Though you usually write in the first person, the poems that I have
read are frequently…
CARTER: Well the first person, of course, is not I, the objective I. The 'I' is a fiction
made by the 'I', by the ego if you want to use different terms, so that the poem is an I-
making thing; in other words the 'I' doesn't exist until the poem is finished. …In other
words there is no 'I' that has gone in and said 'I'. The 'I' emerges as a consequence. And
therefore I call it a fictive 'I' in *that* sense only. … It's a made 'I' then, which can only
happen *after* the poem, it emerges out of the process of the poem. In other words, for the
writer himself in a completed work of art, it is as much a discovery to him as to the
onlooker. In other words he is just as much at a loss as anybody else until he has finished,
and when he is finished, he is as much astounded by what he has made.
DANCE: OK. Let me ask you about one other poem that begins 'I come from the
nigger yard of yesterday/ leaping from the oppressor's hate/ and the scorn of myself.'
[*Poems of Succession* p. 38] Let me ask you first if that's as racial as it sounds.
CARTER: No.
DANCE: I mean nigger is a very derogatory, racial word…
CARTER: No, no, no, no. No, no, no, no, no! No, no, no, no, no, no!
WILLIAMS: No, no, not here, no. A mother would call a boy a 'nigger man.'
CARTER: 'Nigger boy, come here.'
WILLIAMS: 'You nigger man, come here to me. You go and fetch something.' It is
not – and the nigger-yard is just the place 'where all-o-we' come out.
CARTER: It's a symbol.
DANCE: OK. It is a symbol of the poverty though, isn't it?
WILLIAMS: Yes, a symbol of poverty.
CARTER: But of reality, reality, what you see out here. For instance, I am going to
give you an example. Suppose I have a child (I, objective I), and I say, 'Boy, go to the
shop and buy a loaf of bread for ten cents.' The boy goes and being he is a smart boy,
he buys one for eight cents, right, so he gets some pennies for himself thinking his
mother wouldn't notice the difference in size. He brings it back and gives her, and she
obviously notices the difference. She says, 'Aiie, you nigger boy wha' you think you
cheating me!' In other words, he is no longer boy, he is a nigger-boy because – she is
using the word nigger boy as a whip; it is no longer a word of derogation; it is a way
of describing his behaviour. It is not describing him, it is describing his behaviour.

DANCE: But isn't it describing a behaviour which is derogatory?

CARTER: A behaviour only in relation to her.

WILLIAMS: Because a woman would call her husband, 'You nigger man – come here, you big nigger man, you big joker,' or, you know.

CARTER: Yes. It means 'you fool up'.

WILLIAMS: Yes. It hasn't got that sociological implication that you mean, not at all.

CARTER: Not at all.

DANCE: All right. Let me ask you one other thing about that line. Is the yard the yard of yesterday, because it is your yesterday which you have escaped or is the yard no longer a part of the world that you are viewing?

CARTER: It is yesterday in a symbolic sense, in [the sense] that yesterday, is here, and not here, at the same time; in the sense that today is impossible without yesterday, but being here today makes it possible for me to know yesterday from this position, so it's a conceptual thing rather than a descriptive thing. In other words, it is definitive rather than descriptive.

WILLIAMS: And that sort of thing is like a praise song. To talk about the nigger-yard in that way is to talk in a sacred sense almost, you know, it is grounding... for all of us.

CARTER: I mean, nobody as far as I know, from my experience here in this country at least, could ever take offence by telling him that he comes from a nigger-yard, because he has already conceived it or subsumed it. He started from there, so what? You're not telling me anything that is offensive to me.

WILLIAMS: Hmmn hummnn. All of us.

CARTER: All of us. I mean this is true to this country. It wouldn't mean the same in America; you call a man a nigger, I mean you looking for trouble!

DANCE: OK. Could we talk about *Other Leopards* for a while, Mr. Williams? Had you read *Invisible Man* when you wrote that novel?

WILLIAMS: I do not know when I read *Invisible Man*. I read *Invisible Man*, and I liked only the first bit of it, and then the other thing became what he calls intellectual.

DANCE: There are so many similarities...

WILLIAMS: Is that so?

DANCE: ... I think in terms of the hero, the protagonist of the book. Even to the actual development of plot and the ending...

WILLIAMS: Is that so? No, it never struck me. That book never hit me like that. The first part of the book as far as I remember (I read it a long time ago) was highly charged and somnambulist, which is what I liked about it. Well, *Other Leopards* was a situation in which I was successfully young in England. I was just about twenty-six or something like that, and I was in *Time* magazine and all this, you know, and I was absorbed completely in this whole English thing, and I was teaching at a very favoured college and so on, highly approved. But in the middle of all of that was the misgiving that I did not belong in that society, and I really had nothing very much in common with the people that were my comrades, as we call it. I remember looking out of the college window one morning – down – I was teaching at the top – fifth floor or something like that, and I was looking out of the window and looking down, and feeling that complete estrangement. And I thought to myself 'Any man down there could come up here and do the job that I am doing. I am not needed.' Though I was probably the first Black teaching in a college of art in England. Not probably; I was.

And that fact made it a little bit incongruous, you know, whether it is first or last, the fact of being a Black teacher of art. Art! Not mathematics. And I felt all the time a misfit, and consequently I was all the time needing to get out of England and into Africa as many of us feel the need to get back to what we call 'roots'. All right. The part of Africa that came up was, of all places, the Sudan. I sent out for two or three jobs and I got the one in the Sudan first. I went to the Sudan, there to find that I was among people like myself but who were completely strange. They were more strange to me than the people I had left behind. Now I was a painter. I am a painter. And the first thing I am, to this present time, is a painter, not a writer or a novelist. But in the Sudan, in the desert, you cannot paint! At least I could not because everything was this blinding glare. There was no colour; it was a desert, just khaki, camels, khaki. And this blasting sun – and so therefore I began to write. I wrote because of that particular context. I began to write simply because I could not paint.

DANCE: OK. Is Froad something of an autobiographical figure in his quest for identity.

WILLIAMS: Highly, highly, highly.

DANCE: What about the ambivalent reactions to race there? Is that autobiographical too?

WILLIAMS: Yes. To the present moment. It's autobiographical in that sense that one has got this thing that we were talking about earlier with Martin, this sense of self-diminish; and everything you know, at least me, personally, everything I know that is of value comes from my white ancestry, eh? and so on, and at the same time you feel the need to reject it, eh? But finding in Africa no base for this rejection (I think that is what everybody finds out, I think that's what they are doing, for I think everybody who goes to Africa finds he has no base for rejecting). The base for rejecting Europe is here, in our own environment, our own values and so on, which was very much to come when I wrote *Other Leopards*. All I could arrive at in the end of *Other Leopards* was just to try to shed all these plagues that Europe had put on me and to be just naked and cover myself in clay in order to treasure this anonymity, and anonymity is not a positive thing. It is a, a, a…

DANCE: It is a nothingness.

WILLIAMS: It is a nothingness, and this is what we… that's how *Other Leopards* came. It is not a book that I wrote easily, because I could not find the language. I could not find the exposition. I knew what I wanted to say and I kept writing English; I kept writing an English novel, I kept writing in sort of given phrases, given language, humnn?

DANCE: You *never* found the language you are saying?

WILLIAMS: No, it was not easy to write because I had to write it five times. It was only finally that I spoke in the book as I would speak in my own country.

DANCE: OK. Let me ask you about the relationships with Eve and Catherine which are so significant there. What are you suggesting, through those relationships? Is the dilemma being symbolised through the triangle with the women.

WILLIAMS: Yes, yes, yes.

DANCE: Would you elaborate on that a little bit?

WILLIAMS: There is a very ancient culture in the Sudan, which was very unknown at the time. I notice that people are talking about it a little bit more. The first culture of the Sudan took place at a place called Meröe and it was a real culture. In a sense it was a derivative culture insofar as it was highly derived from the Egyptian Pharaonic culture. Now these Meroitic people actually formed the twenty-sixth Egyptian dynasty. They conquered Egypt and ruled for about ninety years. The Black kings of the Sudan ruled in Egypt and so on. And this was the thing that I was discovering as I went out there. I did not know that Africa had such a noble history and all this kind of thing. Nobody knew and nobody paid any attention to it. I was very struck with this. And it is all in the desert; and there are temples, pyramids and so on. And there I discovered this queen, this queen of the Meroites, and this seemed to me a symbol of this great mother – this home, this womb that I was trying to return to. But I could not get there. The day-to-day flesh manifestation was this girl Eve, this beginning girl, but I could not get to her; she was closed to me. I could not get to her and that was the paradox, that in the end Froad chose the white girl because it was safer, it was known.

DANCE: Let me ask you why you selected to make the girl who represents the Black past, the noble queen, a Caribbean girl rather than an African girl?

WILLIAMS: It was fact. It was fact. She was Caribbean by blood, you know; she just was a Caribbean. She was born, you know, she was a Caribbean girl born in Africa and so therefore I could get to her, I could talk to her and so on.

DANCE: You are talking about – not in the book now, but in creating the character.

WILLIAMS: Yeah, the character that stood at the back of that fiction was a real person, but I could not contact – though this person came from my own country, she was born actually, her parents went to Africa and she was born in Africa and so on and that's the person, that's the Africa that I could not meet. Notwithstanding the fact that she shared my blood and ancestry, I could not meet this girl, and that was a predicament. There is no root, there is no – you've got to find yourself! You cannot find yourself in terms of any given, known thing, whether European or African. That is the thing that the West Indian writer has got to face, and I think that's what Brathwaite and Dathorne and Neville Dawes, those of us who went back to Africa I think all came out with that same realisation that there is nothing there to receive you. It is a complete fiction that you have made up. Eve is a creation of my own mind. That girl rejected my approach because I was approaching a mask. I was approaching something that I had made up. I was not approaching Eve.

DANCE: She doesn't so much reject you in the novel as you reject her.

WILLIAMS: That was the real situation. The real situation was that I could not get near to this girl, I could not – because I had come to her with a mask. And this led me, this experience led me to this great maternal Africa, this queen thing that I was trying to fuse with. It was not a possible thing. No.

DANCE: All right. Let's move now to *The Third Temptation* and tell me something about the book which you mentioned last night; that influenced you.

WILLIAMS: Well you see those books are very contrasting. *Other Leopards* is very much out of the trauma of self-discovery and so on. Now *The Third Temptation* was a different thing. It was written at a time (though I did not know it) of the break-up of my first marriage, and that was a personal sort of crisis that I was going through. But the actual exposition of the book, the actual way the book was made, resulted from reading Alain Robbe-Grillet, a book called *La Jalousie*. A tremendous book, at least I call it a tremendous book – only a little book – but I very much admired the clinical objectivity of those modern French writers. I very much admired the absence of any responsibility for the characters that you invent. You are not God. You are not omniscient. You observe. And Robbe was an observer, or is an observer. The whole beauty of those modern French novels is that they make no comment. It is a scientific exposition. It is purely clinical. This I admired greatly because there is a component in my make-up which very strongly admires reason, logic, order and so on. And this is what struck me about the limits to which the French had taken the novel. Coming from an English background with all that romantic stuff I found this terribly attractive, and that is what I tried to do in *The Third Temptation*.

DANCE: It impressed me as I was reading the novel that you were not so much writing a novel as painting a novel.

WILLIAMS: Oh yes? I did not know. I think somebody said that in some of the reviews.

DANCE: Oh, did I read this somewhere?

WILLIAMS: I don't know, I don't know, I believe… but I'm not aware of this. I was not aware of the painterly input into the novel, no, not at all, not at all!

DANCE: I mean each scene is so, so…

WILLIAMS: Visual.

DANCE: … so clearly painted!

WILLIAMS: Is that so?

DANCE: And you talk about that even. In the novel, I mean, you talk about introducing the aural aspects of things into the picture and you give us all these different views.

WILLIAMS: But you see – consciousness. Right! Now we are sitting down here and you are ruling out the noise of that traffic outside or a cock crowing or a dog barking. But I try to make a man who is standing in the high road just a few hours, three or four, (the whole time of the book covered two or three hours) and that everything goes through him, everything simultaneously – he is hearing the song of the seagulls on the beach, though the beach is not present, the beach is half a mile away, and so on; and I very much wanted to make that experiment of seeing things totally, not by selection as we all do, we are doing all the time. But… that experiment I owed purely to the French novel in which Robbe-Grillet starts by describing the passage of the shadows across the verandah as the sun rises. And he spends all the time talking about the precision with which those shadows move across the verandah and making you aware of the passage of time; incidentally. But it's purely objective, purely descriptive. And there is no 'I' that is doing this. That novel is so skilfully put together that there is no person present who is describing the passage of the sun, and the vision moves from the verandah rails across to the plantation over there and the banana trees are planted in such and such a style, just as you would take in everything, sitting on that verandah. And through a window someone is combing her hair endlessly, combing her hair endlessly. Now this absolutely removed, objective type of exposition is very attractive to me because then you are free of any responsibility for anything else beside what you state, what's there before your eyes, what you observe. You are not going to attribute motives to actions. Actions take place just as your eye sees them.

DANCE: You slow them down a bit though, so that as the reader views it, he might think for a while that he is really viewing a still picture.

WILLIAMS: Is that so?

DANCE: You don't do this intentionally either?

WILLIAMS: No, no, no.

DANCE: OK. Let me ask you about the matter of time which you mentioned just now. As you said, the whole action of the book takes place in just a few hours, I think it's three and a half hours if I followed it correctly. It must have been extremely significant to you, this matter of time, because you begin each section with an indication of the fifteen-minute or whatever period that section covers. But you did begin the novel some years earlier with the hanging. And then you make the rest of it extremely compact in this little three and a half-hour period – did you ever think about making the hanging a scene that you give in retrospection, as you do so many others?

WILLIAMS: It is not done in *that* novel as far as I remember.

DANCE: No, you begin with that.

WILLIAMS: Yes, it was begun as a memory, you know, somebody thinking. It set the scene for the troubled state of the mind of that man. The sense of guilt that you destroy somebody – which I was in the process of doing with my first wife.

DANCE: So this is autobiographical too?

WILLIAMS: Yes, yes.

DANCE: He seems obsessed by some sense of guilt, but he seems capable of such violence; he goes out and kills somebody else on that fine day without a great deal of thought.

WILLIAMS: No.

DANCE: Doesn't he push the man over into the…

WILLIAMS: Ah, yes, into the boiling lead. Yes.

DANCE: You forgot he did that?

WILLIAMS: Long time ago, that book was… 1968, I think.

DANCE: You minimise all of the violence in the work though. Is there any reason why the violence is… is so insignificant? For example, you might present it, then you back off from it and give us a view from a longer distance which makes it seem not quite so important.

WILLIAMS: I cannot explain the motive for that. I cannot explain. I do not know that I have a motive… I was more interested in that book purely with technique, and the book is unreadable because of this.

DANCE: So that character is really not so important then?

WILLIAMS: No. no, no, that's just what I was trying to get away from, this business of imputing meaning to people's actions. Actions are haphazard: you observe; somebody just kicked somebody else or whatever it is, and you have just seen it, you could never explain it, you can impute a meaning to that action, but it is not the truth.

DANCE: And the moment you do that you realise, I guess, that you could see it from another view?

WILLIAMS: Yes, exactly. Everything is relative. As I kept saying in the book, everything is relative… And so the business of the writer taking on the responsibility of explaining anything is powerless…

DANCE: OK. You mentioned the fact that this novel was written during the time that your marriage was breaking up and I suppose that has something to do with the kind of negative comments on women in that novel? That's reflecting your own…

WILLIAMS: Hmmn. Hmmn. Well what were the negative comments? What sort of... Well, bitch. Everybody's a bitch! Hmmnn-humnn.

DANCE: Yes all the time and, well, you see a little bit of it too in *Other Leopards* when Lobo thinks of his 'Dear old devoted, devouring, dead bitch of a mamma!' [p.41].

WILLIAMS: Hmmn-humnn. That's a predicament of us in this country. We are consumed by our mothers. It is, I think, probably the most striking thing about West Indian or Guyanese civilisation that the men are paralysed by love, they are paralysed! You know we have a most challenging country here, I mean a real man's country, but you don't get fellows going doing anything about the country. They don't want to go and break open the unknown and challenge and stand up to the unknown and tame nature and all this kind of image of what you know the male in Europe is. You don't have that at all, and I attribute that, right or otherwise, a good thing or a bad thing... We are full of love and we are very horizontal, you know, touch each other, but this business of pitting one's own mind or one's own intellect... I think the way in which men are trained in this country inhibits them, inhibits the functioning of some part of their manhood. I do not know. It is not a conversation I often have but it is a thing that I think about a lot. You can't help being aware in this country, that all the people live on the coast, all the people live on the coast-land, and 90% of the country is uninhabited and untamed, untamed because the men of the country have never gone out to do anything about taming it. That is something singular I think, because one hears all the time in literature of man pitting himself against nature and so we see in the films, we see the men with the problem, the film you know or the book, starts with the problem and the man has got to resolve that problem by the end of the book or by the end of the film and so on. We do not have that experience at all, and I do not know whether it is present in our literature.

DANCE: The people that Jan Carew treats are exceptions?

WILLIAMS: I briefly mentioned to you last night about the porkknockers. Now these are people who have left society; they have rejected society; they have nothing to do with society, and they live on their own terms, and I said to you in a sense they are comparable to the cowboys in the United States in that they live entirely on their own terms outside the law and so on. And they, they have made a world of their own, but it is not a part generally of *our* civilisation; we reject them too, and so they contribute nothing to our civilisation, or to our consciousness of ourselves or to our relationship to our environment. We've got a view of manhood that is, I do not know, I suppose purely mental. We see ourselves as man-minds, man-operators, but not very much as man-doers. We are not practical in that sense: a person's motor car breaks and he just leaves it on the road and goes away; he doesn't know a thing about it. Or his bicycle – when you are a small boy, your bicycle break and you just tote it into a little shop and so on. We are not man-doers and I think that's a serious comment on our kind of civilisation.

CARTER: Looking at the matter of preoccupation: now to say that the man tames nature, I am just using a phrase, you know... man presupposes that that is what a man does, a man tames nature, you see. In other words you are starting from a position of saying this is what a man does. And that this man here does not fit into that term of reference. He doesn't do that; therefore he is a different kind of man. The question I am asking is whether the idea that the man is a tamer, a nature-tamer, to use that expression, is not derived from a conditioning of let us say, Europe or industrial society...

WILLIAMS: No, no, no. No, no, no.

CARTER: Now having said that, the further thing is that the preoccupation, if you accept what you have said, the preoccupation then is not with natural relations but with human relations in the sense that the relation of mother to son, brother to sister –

WILLIAMS: And brother to brother, above all.

CARTER: Brother to brother, in other words that is the preoccupation in which nature becomes the background, so to speak, of those intimate and very, very per-intimate, that's the correct word, intimate relationships between creatures, you know, in other words, it is a creature-minded animal, rather than a nature-minded animal.

WILLIAMS: Yes. An anthropologist friend of mine while I was in the University of Ibadan, said to me, and this is an English anthropologist who had married an African girl, that (and I believe Dathorne made the same observation in conversation afterwards), that the European male, with his preoccupation with matter, isolates himself, distances matter, and operates on matter. The symbol is the man in the white coat in a laboratory, examining matter, ordering matter and finding out of it immutable laws, so that he can repeat the same experiment and predict. He defines himself in contradiction to matter, opposed to matter. The African man on the contrary has no control whatsoever over matter. He has witnessed epidemic, flood, disease, etc., fury, destroy human societies. He does not attempt to control matter; what he is certain of and what he seeks assurance from is his brother. And when I say that word 'horizontal', all African societies have got this horizontal relationship. It is brother-man that you have to be sure of, and they all have restrictions on the limits to which man can go vis-a-vis man. In the Sudan, the fellow carries a little thing on his shoulder, a little leather thing and in it is an amulet by which he swears that he will never draw his brother's blood. He must never draw his brother's blood. In Africa, the ultimate crime, the ultimate crime is to draw another person's blood. Blood must not be spilled on earth. The greatest supreme court in Yoruba belief, the Ogboni society, is there to regulate the relationship between human blood and the earth. If one drop of blood is spilled on earth – you read it in Césaire somewhere, this business of blood dropping on the earth. The relationship between man and man is paramount. *That* must be controlled!

CARTER: Allow me to interrupt, not to take it up, but as you were speaking, I was reminded very clearly of the *Oresteia*, when Orestes kills Clytemnestra and the Furies take over. He has spilled blood! Your family blood! I mean that is the maximum crime.

WILLIAMS: Now the relationship of man to nature now becomes mythological. He has got all manner of mechanisms in belief which explain drought, or smallpox, and explain these natural devastations, and he seeks through his cults to control nature in a mythological sense. It is not seen as matter – examinable, verifiable and predictable behaviour in matter. Now we have – this is our inheritance in the Caribbean – this is what we have inherited and we therefore, when I say confronting matter, I do not mean necessarily scaling mountains but also looking for microbes – My wife is a foreigner – she says: 'You are all juju men! You do not understand a thing!' You say, 'The door dunna want to open… me mind don't give me to do it.' She says that is the speech of a juju man, that is an obeah man. There is no relationship to matter, to find out why it is. We are in a truck (you know we lived for a long time in the jungle), I am there in a truck that goes off the road, because the roads had gone to porridge in the rain, soft mess, and the whole truck has gone off the road. And those fellows come out, those big strong chaps, come out to try to get this truck out of this mud. And they do every imaginable power thing they can do with big woods and all this kind of thing. So she stands there and she says, 'Don't you realise that it is only about fourteen inches of the back wheel that has gone into the mud; if you reverse, the truck will come out.' The drive is in the back wheel of the truck and – it's just partly in, all the rest is plenty foot of truck in the slush out there that they lifting and pushing and gouging. We reversed and it just come out. Because we think sensationally, we feel, we feel: 'Oh God, the truck gone! Lawd, Oh God, look at this thing!' It's feelings!

CARTER: The expression we use is: 'The truck gone in!' The truck is animated, you see. Not the truck was driven in: 'The truck gone in the fence.' That is what you hear if you go off the roads. A chap falls into a trench – or a mechanical instrument or something like that – that something is happening to somebody, 'It do it!'

WILLIAMS: 'This door don't want open.' You see. So that when I say that we have got this negative attitude to nature, it is, I could see the origin of it. I could see why it is present in our societies, and I do not know whether it is a good thing or a bad thing, but in the matter of dealing with the world, in the matter of earning foreign exchange and stop buying of traffic lights from other people, it is something that's got to be faced. Because right now the man is sitting down making plastic paper or something that abolishes your own wrapping paper, and that is what you going to have to rely on because he has got an electron microscope. And I say to my son all the time, 'You've got to go all the way; you can't sit down and hide underneath something called Blackness – you've got to go all the way. If you studying chemistry, you got to go all the way, my boy, all the way, because the next chap, fifteen years old in another country, is working chemistry with an electron microscope.' So that is a predicament. At any rate our writers ought to be aware of this kind of definition, of the Caribbean male, or at any rate to us here, the Guyanese male.

DANCE: Tell me something about the origin of Carifesta.

WILLIAMS: I think it just come about when these countries became independent. The best thing that can be said about Carifesta is that it filled a need at that time because the very first thing on becoming independent is that you do not know who your brothers are, you see… You have heard about Jamaicans, Trinidadians, Barbadians, but you never know how they live because the colonial situation had kept that knowledge from you. It was not necessary to the operation of colonialism that you had any affiliation with other people. And so therefore when we became independent, by way of defining your own self it was necessary to define yourself in terms of who your brother is. Huhn? And so the very first thing, we were all invited home, all of us who were scattered all over the place were invited home at the Government's expense to come and take part in Carifesta, and in the middle of Carifesta the Prime Minister called all these artists together and writers to ask, what are we going to do about defining the artist and getting the artist a place? That was one of the first meetings and so on. And these boys talked about this, that and that. But generally, what they said was that, 'Look, we had better first of all have some great big festival in which we can get all of the people of the Caribbean in to do what their thing is…' This Carifesta, I could see the need at that time as an instrument for getting to define oneself as Caribbean and to know what the Caribbean thing is and so on, but it has become a big political something or other since, a show window and sort of people bustling to outdo each other every two or three years, but very little regard for what happens to the artist. They don't give a damn about what is the artist doing in the three years interval. The artist is not supported – those countries have no machinery for maintaining the arts or for doing anything about the day-to-day reality of art, and it cost millions, it cost millions, and I think that that money could be better spent in feeding the artist and making him produce works that people would want to see. Instead of you know – right now the process has begun. Our administrators have just come back this last weekend from discussing Carifesta-Barbados. And why the hell Barbados wants to have Carifesta! Because Cuba had it and because Jamaica before that had it and Guyana and so on, so Barbados must…

CARTER: Nothing to do with art. Nothing to do with art.

WILLIAMS: Nothing whatsoever!

DANCE: You mentioned government support of the arts; will you discuss government support of arts in Guyana?

WILLIAMS: Well, as I said, we have got an administration and this consumes rather a lot of money; it has got a certain amount of expertise, that is hard to come by in the various fields, presiding over various aspects of the development of art in the country. I had on my desk this morning something about the next Lagos festival, Festac, which they are trying to operate as non-governmental. They are trying to operate this fiasco as non-governmental because they ran into the trouble that all over Africa or the Black world the governments send only approved people to represent these various arts, and not always the best people; and usually the very best people are at loggerheads with the governments and don't get represented. So by way of by-passing this very real predicament they have now institutionalised Festac as a non-governmental organisation which seeks the co-operation of governments and so on in holding these international Black festivals. Well, the predicament is in the end that they do have to come back to these governments… because it is the governments that pay these enormous air fares and send steel bands and great orchestras and such like. Those kinds of things could never be privately sponsored, so it is a predicament… If you by-pass the officials, well then you have no festival because the neglected artist, the person who is out of favour with the government, cannot afford himself to turn up at the festival to represent himself. It has got to be institutionalised. We've got the beginnings of an institution here that does that sort of thing and I am sure that it is not completely free from the point of view of affiliation, but that is a predicament all over the developing world. There is no private patronage of the arts in the developing world, it must be institutionalised.

DANCE: I would like for you to tell me about some of the new contemporary Guyanese writers.

CARTER: If I may. First of all, Ivan Forrester. He is about fifty, lived for a considerable time in the interior. He is a cousin of Philip Moore, by the way, comes from the country, in Corentyne, which is a coastal village. Black, very intelligent, naive in the best sense of the word. He would not be a person who would have read much poetry, so his method would be a naive method, that is to say, what he has picked up would serve as a model for what he has done, you see. Now one of the great dangers with that is that if you have only a few models, only a certain kind of material you can deal with. For instance, his best poem is called 'Mazaruni'; Mazaruni is a huge river; and it is written in very traditional form, but he manages to get into it, or out of it, a feeling of the river and of the immensity of space. Now there is another set of young men whose names, neither here nor there, who are like Zide – a young African boy. No doubt about it he has the temperament, and no doubt he means what he is up to, but he can't write, for a start; I mean he doesn't know how to write… He is not a student, he moves around with the chaps. [He has] that sort of assertiveness all the time which, on first reading – OK you're saying something. I mean what else have you done? But when you go on it is the same thing, he is stuck, more or less stuck. And that has happened to a lot of them… What is really interesting about this country is Arthur Seymour – he is bringing out an anthology of Guyanese poetry because a building society wants to celebrate some centenary and asked him to edit a collection. And I spoke to him a couple of days ago and he told me he has fifty-five poets – when I say poets – people who have written poetry. This country has a lot of poets you know.

WILLIAMS: Yes. Yes. Every police magazine has to have poetry you know, two or three poems. Yes, the police have uniform and guns and so on, but they write poetry.

CARTER: It is a fantastic phenomena – fifty-five! Now a lot of it is rubbish, I mean when I say rubbish, obviously not poetry, but nonetheless it has a poetic intention. The person would like to write poetry, which is good, I mean if it shows something, but that is the sort of general state of things. Another thing that happens here of course is – it is a very small society, so if a given person writes a poem and it becomes known, you are a poet, right. And you are put in a box. You are the poet, right, and everything starts from that foreign word. Nobody says, 'Isn't this a poet too?' You follow? No, this one is there and therefore nobody else, until they reach the absurdity of calling you national poets and all that sort of thing… And having said that you get another situation occurring among each of these groups, and that situation is the inarticulate resentment of what is considered the establishment. The establishment means a person whose name is known. For instance, suppose he writes something and he is mentioned in the newspaper or magazine or something, then you belong to the establishment by definition, and therefore there is a hidden resentment to that kind of creature.

WILLIAMS: That is true. That is true. A peculiar phenomenon.

CARTER: Yes. Resentment! And it's a block. A block occurs immediately. For instance, a chap come to me and shows me something. And I said, 'Show it to –' 'No, no, not show *him,* man.' And he wouldn't even show him! This is fantastic! He would not even show him.

WILLIAMS: I do not know why that is. It is very real, very real.

CARTER: Very real here. And it has a lot to do with messing up a lot of young people who can really move on. I mean they may not be poets, but at least they may be able to write something: a short story. You don't know what they may write. But here again as I said: they cheat themselves, you know. They cut their mouth to spite their face; and this is what they do all the time. And this is definitely very very strong here… You see another thing that is very interesting here is, for many years in this country – for the last thirty years I would say, the major art form, if you can call it that, is rhetoric, is rhetoric!

WILLIAMS: The preacher in the pulpit, that's their words, it is important to us.

CARTER: That is why somebody came to Guyana and said: 'Man, all you got is words!'

WILLIAMS: Yes, words.

CARTER: This is a country of words, par excellence!

WILLIAMS: Yes, a country of words.

CARTER: Yes… and the preacher is the same. I will give you an example, just to give you an idea. A journey at night, a journey to the sect, the religious sect, what you call a wayside church, an African-American church. Anyway, this chap that is preaching, he has a little boy over in the corner and so on, and he is talking, but what they do – they use excerpts from the Bible and they call on them, and have a sister sitting down. He say: 'Read out, Sister!' So the Sister go up and open the book or something and read a passage and he will comment on it. So she open the Bible and she says, 'We are the sheep of the Lawd.' So he says, 'Yes, we are the sheep of the Lawd! There shall be gnashing of teeth…' So, you know, you're waiting for the continuation, and hear the man now, again – 'And who no got teeth a so gum-gum!' Now I mean that is out of this world! But that is what I am talking about when I say these people have this sort of tremendous way with words. There is a tremendous tradition here of words… words, words, words. For instance I remember when I was in prison – issuing bread, you know, to the prisoners. And one of the prisoners was illiterate. So when he broke the bread – it was very dry – he said: 'You know something, they didn't put in the right ingreasements.' Changed the ingredient by the virtue of the inference of the lack of grease… That is what you up against here you see, and it's Joycean in a special sense, you know that kind of thing that Joyce would do, which I suppose is natural too.

WILLIAMS: The slaves, very early, they were not permitted to have religion, they were not permitted to be catechised and this began about probably around 1820 or so, and in the late '20s the first churches were built that admitted slaves, but slavery had not yet been abolished. Slavery was not abolished until 1834 to 1838, so therefore those fellows used to regard Sunday as their great day. Sunday was the only day that they're not working and they dress up like their masters in lovely clothes and so on and walk miles to go to church, and arrive at the church and spend (the church was in a big compound like this), they would live the whole day in the yard with their pots and babies, and nurse their baby and cook their food and so on to attend every single service of the day, and then at night they walk back, a total of ten miles to get back to their plantations. Words, a tradition of words.

CARTER: And when they reach back home they repeat the whole thing over again.

WILLIAMS: Yes, a tradition of words, they live for that. Yes, they were not a very visual people like the Mexicans you know.

CARTER: No, word-smiths. As a matter of fact we had an example here of a chap, well really you should know him – Prophet Wills.

WILLIAMS: Yes, I was thinking of him when you were speaking.

CARTER: Prophet Wills – he is a chap, an old schoolmaster, he used to wear a frock coat in the hot sun – walking about, but he never used a monosyllabic word when there was a polysyllabic word about. For instance, one day a man was driving a donkey cart. He was hitting the donkey and the donkey was recalcitrant. He wants to tell the man to release the donkey from the cart. So he says: 'Extricate that quadruped from the four-wheeled vehicle.' Just at which point a young boy riding a bicycle touched him. So he turned to the boy and he said: 'Why didn't you tintintabulate that metallic organ on your handlebars…' [Laughter] Well that is what you are up against and that is what you would find a couple of years ago; and there are still men like that walking about.

CONVERSATION WITH

AUSTIN CLARKE

Austin Chesterfield Clarke was born in Barbados on July 26, 1934, and was educated at Combermere and Harrison College there. He continued his education at the University of Toronto, Canada. He has taught at several American universities, including Yale, Indiana, Brandeis, Williams College, Duke, and the University of Texas, Austin. He has done several special documentaries and literary programmes on the Canadian Broadcasting Corporation. In 1974 he served as Cultural Officer in the Barbadian Embassy in Washington, and from 1975-6 he was Cultural Officer and Advisor to the Prime Minister in Barbados. Active politically in Toronto, he has run (unsuccessfully) for office there, and remains in the city to this day.

Clarke has written the following novels: *The Survivors of the Crossing* (1964); *Amongst Thistles and Thorns* (1965); *The Meeting Point* (1967); *Storm of Fortune* (1972); *The Bigger Light* (1975); *The Prime Minister* (1978); *Proud Empires* (1986); *The Origin of Waves* (1997); *The Question* (1999) and *The Polished Hoe* (2002). He has published six collections of short stories, *When He Was Free and Young and He Used to Wear Silks* (1971, 1974); *When Women Rule* (1985); *Nine Men Who Laughed* (1986); *In This City* (1992); *There Are No Elders* (1993) and *Choosing His Coffin* (2003). Other works include his various memoirs: *Growing Up Stupid Under the Union Jack* (1980); *Public Enemies: Police Violence and Black Youths* (1992); *A Passage Back Home: A Personal Reminiscence of Samuel Selvon* (1994); *Pigtails 'n' Breadfruit: The Rituals of Slave Food, A Barbadian Memoir* (2001) and *Love and Sweet Food: A Culinary Memoir* (2004). His theoretical essays include 'In the Semi-Colon of the North' (1982) and 'Some Speculations As to the Absence of Racialistic Vindictiveness in West Indian Literature.'

Clarke has received the President's Medal, University of Western Ontario (1966); the Belmont Short Story Award (1965); and the Canada Council Senior Arts Fellowship (1967 and 1970). More recently, he received the Rogers Communication Writers Trust Prize (1998) and the W. O. Mitchell Prize for an outstanding contribution to fiction in 1999. His ninth novel, *The Polished Hoe*, also won the Giller Prize for fiction in 2002, and the Regional Commonwealth Prize for best book in 2003.

Austin Clarke's writing has been discussed in Stella Algoo Baksh's monograph *Austin C. Clarke: A Biography* (1994) and various Canadian literary journals. The Caribbean-in-Canada identity pursued in his fiction has been discussed by Frank Birbalsingh in 'Austin Clarke: Caribbean-Canadians' (1996), Michel Fabre's 'Changing the Metropolis or Being Changed by It: Toronto West Indians in Austin Clarke's Trilogy.' (1991) and in 'The Immigrants' Pain: The Socio-Literary Context of Austin Clarke's Trilogy.' by Horace L. Goddard (1989). Beside these, Robert D. Hamner, Victor Ramraj and Leslie Sanders have also produced valuable studies.

This interivew was conducted in his home in Toronto on December 6, 1979.

DANCE: Tell me something about your family background.
CLARKE: What do you mean?
DANCE: What did your parents do?
CLARKE: Absolutely nothing.

DANCE: Oh, come on!

CLARKE: I was born in Barbados. My mother was at the time of my birth, I think, working in a hotel. My father was more or less unemployed, if he was a Barbadian in those days. As I grew up I found out that he was a bit of an artist; he used to paint and write poetry.

DANCE: You say as you grew up you found out. Did he live with the family?

CLARKE: No, as I grew up I found out that he was a painter. My mother didn't marry my father because it was said that he was from two or three social levels below her, so the family insisted that there should be no further contact.

DANCE: I see. This kind of social status was very important in those years?

CLARKE: Not only then, but it still is now.

DANCE: In Barbados?

CLARKE: In Barbados. Barbados is perhaps the most socially proper, or improper, country in the world.

DANCE: What is the basis for it mainly: education, finance, colour?

CLARKE: The basis was social, and to understand social you would have to understand family background and a little bit of economics because most of the people there were poor, and status of various kinds.

DANCE: There are several young men in your stories who grew up in basically fatherless homes, and a lot of the stories deal with the attempt to relate to the father later in life. Is that influenced by your own experience?

CLARKE: No, not by my own experience because I didn't miss my father. My mother was my mother *and* my father and my stepfather was my father, so I didn't miss my father. I was very glad, as a matter of fact, that I was growing up in that kind of circumstance because it meant that my family was larger, so I had three aspects of love. There was never any conflict and what in North America you would call any propensity for delinquency. But the point I want to make is that in Barbados when I was growing up there were lots of situations like this, situations that were not related to any one social group.

DANCE: The situation with the stepfather occurs in some instances and in some of the stories the mother very strongly encourages the son to relate to the stepfather and not to the real father. Was that based upon any of your own experiences?

CLARKE: That was based on my personal experience because when it was discovered that my real father was not of the social status to deserve this woman, this middle-class woman, the decision was final, so there could be no communication after that. In my own home my mother never once mentioned my father's name.

DANCE: Really? You left Barbados to attend college?

CLARKE: University. In Toronto.

DANCE: Scholarship, or…

CLARKE: No, I paid for myself.

DANCE: And you've been here basically since that time, except for short periods of time in the United States? Did you spend any time in Europe?

CLARKE: I was in England in '64 for two weeks, two terrible weeks; I don't like England.

DANCE: Only two weeks. And in the United States probably a total of about four or five years, on and off?

CLARKE: I would think more than that. I was at Yale from '68 to '71; I was at Williams College for half a year; I was at Duke for one year; and I was at Austin, Texas, for one year; and I spent one year as a diplomat at the Embassy of Barbados in Washington.

DANCE: Let me ask you a little bit about coming to Canada, because I think this is so important in your work since many of your works deal with Barbadians living here. I was, I must admit, a little bit surprised as I read your works at the extent of the racial problem that Black people face in Canada. I guess I'm still lost in the myth of Canada as the land of freedom to which we used to aspire to escape from America. But as I noted the problems in housing, employment, mixed couples, beatings of Black men by police, and so forth, it sounded very much like the racial situations that Blacks face in America. Is the situation as bad here or has it been as bad as the racial situation in…?

CLARKE: Qualitatively the situation is bad in the sense that if there is one ounce of racialism, then it is bad. I'm not the kind of person to say that the situation of Blacks and Whites in America is worse there than in other parts of the world because of the number of reported incidents. I would say if it exists, it exists. Then it's bad. Canada has been living with an unfair reputation for a very long time, and it probably started when Canada was referred to as the last stop in the underground railroad. But see, I understand this. It is a situation where a country, for whatever reasons, or in spite of itself, may quite genuinely harbour Blacks from another country in order to give the impression that it is a more liberal country. If you lived in a place like Toronto or if you spent some time in a place like Toronto, you'd soon find out that the moment you get to the backbone of relationships, you see the same reservations. It is not so ugly as it is in the States because there has not been what I would call the physical festering of this, but I'm talking about reservations.

DANCE: But no legalised kinds of racism, such as we have had?

CLARKE: No, no.

DANCE: You know, I remember in one of your novels in the trilogy, and you must forgive me because they all sort of come together as one story for me, Henry thinks about lynchings. You did not have lynchings, racial lynchings here? He was thinking about the States, I imagine.

CLARKE: No. The book you're referring to is *The Meeting Point*, the first book in the trilogy, and that idea came to Henry's mind because Canadians, white and Black, still regard America as a model.

DANCE: As a model?

CLARKE: As a model – in everything. In fashions, in money; etc., and so far as Henry is concerned, in Black consciousness. So if Henry, who was a Barbadian, is going to regard himself as a non-Canadian because of his alienation, then certainly the model that he has to accept, perhaps the only model he knows, is going to be a Black American model, and this model becomes acceptable to him because of the music, the jazz, the wealth of Black Americans, because of Marcus Garvey, because of DuBois and people like that. So Henry, coming from Barbados, could not rationally choose an African model since the model of Africa imported through the media to Barbados was one of a man running around in a state of savageness, grass skirt, etc. So the West Indian regarded himself all the time, even if not now, as superior to the African and in some cases superior to the Black American. This of course is based on ignorance of fact.

DANCE: OK. I want to ask you a little bit more about that later, but while we're on the matter of Canada, I want to ask you about your treatment of Canada in your works. In many of the works there's a suggestion that Canada kills, destroys West Indians, and one way it is suggested to me is through the fact that your West Indian characters in Canada do not procreate. Is this conscious?

CLARKE: Well, perhaps I may have been thinking, if at all I was, of procreation in a metaphorical sense. And I think that what you are referring to is the fact that for a long time in this country the West Indian population consisted mainly of students (men and women, but primarily men) and nurses, and in addition to those two groups, domestic servants. Now, a domestic servant (even though in cases some were middle-class in the sense of having finished high school, etc.) and nurses were not socially acceptable. When they came here they were despised by the other West Indians simply because of the class structure in the Caribbean. So these women spent very lonely lives.

DANCE: But I'm not talking just about the single women. It's very interesting to me that the couples, for example Dots and Boysie [in *The Meeting Point*], there's a great deal made of the fact that they're sterile.

CLARKE: There's a great deal made of the fact that Dots cannot have children, not because she's a West Indian, but because of her circumstance.

DANCE: That's exactly what I'm asking you. Is the situation in Canada destructive so that the West Indian cannot live, and continue, and…

CLARKE: Well, he can't be as careless about having children as he would tend to be in the West Indies because he finds himself in this country in a more strained economic and social circumstance.

DANCE: But it's not just that. For example, Dots and Boysie become relatively well-to-do, and they talk a lot about a child. You know, Boysie says he wants a child; Dots thinks he wants a cat; she goes out and gets a cat. Dots wants a child, but she wants a child who is crippled, who won't be able to walk, who is maimed. It just looks like if they have a child it's got to be…

CLARKE: No, I think you're reading a bit too much into that. Let me see if I can explain to you. Boysie is a strong, Black, not very educated Barbadian, who is accustomed, in Barbados, to ruling his women, as most West Indian men do or attempt to do. When he comes to this country he finds that he can't exert this influence over the woman because he is chronically unemployable. You know there are certain instances in Black American history which show that in a situation of acute racialism the woman gets the job quicker. It's not a very good job, but she gets the job. And she therefore is able to contribute, if not all, certainly most of the money to the family. Now if you come from a situation where a man regards himself as chauvinistic, though he may not be aware that he's chauvinistic, but does in fact behave chauvinistically towards his woman, and then finds himself in a situation where he can't get a job, it's going to do something to his mind, and this is exactly what happened in Boysie's case. So Boysie had lost that dominance, that natural dominance over his woman. Now Dots on the other hand had become so successful in a North American sense that she was agreeing with the *modus vivendi* that successful women, successful wives, have to be responsive to the percentage of children each family has. In other words if you have too many children, you are regarded as poor. You know, when one looks at the statistics of poor areas you tend to find that there are lots of children in a family and Dots was more or less reflecting the attitudes towards children of the people for whom she worked. And they had 2.1 or 2.5 children.

DANCE: Well, is there any significance to the fact that if she adopts a child, she wants to adopt a completely helpless, crippled…?

CLARKE: The significance there is that Dots had become so Canadian, Dots had become so conscious of her social responsibility, not in a Black sense, but in a North American sense, that she felt that all the problems she had suffered through her marriage and all the problems associated with her being successful, could be expiated if she adopted a child who would require love. Because, you see, in the relationship with her husband there was not much love and she felt she still had love in her and wanted to give love and that is why she felt it necessary to try to adopt a child who was crippled, a child whom she could in turn control; you see, that's the point. Because she could no longer control her husband.

DANCE: All right. Let me pursue the idea of death then in the fact that as the novel continues, you show Dots and Boysie, in a sense, dying, and you keep using the word dead. The music is 'dead', that they listen to. You call the bedroom a 'coffin' and so forth. You mention some of their problems, but these directly stem from being in Canada. Is that right?

CLARKE: Yes.

DANCE: Now, one thing that bothered me with that; it seemed to me that the problem with the relationship, the fact that they're dying metaphorically, is because they are Black in Canada. But then the same thing is true with the Burrmanns. He [Mr. Burrmann] can't get over the fact that he used to have to rely upon his wife. So is it more a male/female problem or a racial problem?

CLARKE: It is a male/female problem, but the ingredients are different. In the case of Boysie and Dots, they became dead because in order to adjust to this society they thought it was essential to destroy all the cultural appendages they knew in Barbados, and they knew when they first came. In other words, if you look around Toronto today, 1979, there are not many aspects of a Black culture, you see. Probably because there is no need, and if one may be permitted to be cynical, you would say there is no need because there is no ghetto or there's no oppression. I don't know whether it is essential for one to be oppressed before one can go inside oneself to dig out aspects of truth and personality. I don't know if that's possible. I don't know what is cause and what is effect. But I'm just saying in this country, and I would suggest in any European country, where there is no sizeable vibrant Black population and where there is no violent racialism, the tendency to be different tends to be less.

DANCE: You suggest early on that there are certainly West Indians who cling to each other and who find some sort of nourishment through that, but as we watch Dots and Boysie it's almost a ritualistic abandoning of things: he throws out his West Indian records, he stops speaking like a West Indian and so forth, and while we've been talking about what Dots and Boysie do, it seems to me that you make it quite clear that it's really Boysie (isn't it?) who is more concerned about losing his West Indian characteristics and becoming Canadian.

CLARKE: Boysie is a person who deliberately despises what he regards as despicable references to his past. I maintain that the Black woman is the more essential factor in the relationship. The Black woman is the receptacle of the culture; the Black woman is the stronger partner in the sense that she can withstand and has withstood more of the daily assaults on her personality, on her body, etc. What I find to be ironical is that she tends not to want to disclose this constant pressure even to the man with whom she shares her life. But she expects her man to be the leader. He can no longer be the leader because as I said, in this country he is refused the common possibility of success, he can't get a job, etc. So he abrogates this in a North American situation, and the woman then has got to carry the ball, as you would say in America. But she would prefer not to. If I was going to write more of that book, I would say that Dots probably would become a Christian in one of these Black fundamentalist churches.

DANCE: After Boysie left?

CLARKE: After he left. And she would be like Queen Mother.

DANCE: Have you read *The Amen Corner*? She would be like Margaret?

CLARKE: Yes, she would be like that.

DANCE: OK, OK. Now that we've gotten into the area of male/female relationships, let me move into one other thing. As I was reading *The Meeting Point* there's a scene that seems to me the most sympathetic male view I've ever read of the agony of the Black female as she watches her Black male pursue the white Canadian women, and that's the scene of the welcoming party for Bernice's sister when she comes to Canada... How did you decide to present that scene from the perspective of the women?

CLARKE: Since the injustice, since the social injustice or the bad manners was committed against the women, I thought it was more important to show how the women felt. The West Indian man wouldn't have any serious explanation to give to this. He would just simply say, 'Well, this is a new experience.' And in fact that experience or that action of his dancing with the white woman and neglecting the Black woman is not a very serious, I don't think, it's not a very serious comment on his attitude toward his women. I just consider it to be a newness and that is why I put it in the book from the point of view of the women. In other words, to show that in spite of the man's frivolous perception of their own behaviour, yet the hurt was more fundamental and more serious when it was looked at by the women.

DANCE: But isn't there a very clear preference for white women on their part?

CLARKE: No there's not. There's not.

DANCE: Oh? Well Henry says, you know, 'I've decided I'm a one-woman man and that woman's got to be a white woman' [p.83].

CLARKE: Henry is a man who has been knocked around; and kicked around all his life. No woman has ever loved Henry. I would suggest not even his mother loved him.

DANCE: You don't tell us about any of that in the novel.

CLARKE: I don't tell you about any of that but I mean, if I was going to be consistent, I would have to suggest that not even his mother loved him. He was what we used to call 'ugly' before we knew that Black is beautiful. And even in that context, even in that context, Henry would be an ugly man, ugly – morally, physically, intellectually – had no style. And all of a sudden a woman comes along and this woman is white. And this woman loves him. How then do you expect him to react?

DANCE: I thought Bernice would have loved him just as well.

CLARKE: Bernice could not love Henry because Bernice, because of her upbring-ing, wanted a man who was dependable, who had some ambition, who would come home every night, etc., etc. She wanted a Barbadian man similar to the one she had left in Barbados before she emigrated to Canada.

DANCE: OK. You sort of seem to be saying that this girl built his ego a little.

CLARKE: This woman gives him meaning.

DANCE: But now let me ask you – he's certainly all the things you said he is, but certainly he's not ignorant enough not to know that she's just loving the exotic Blackness in him.

CLARKE: He can't know that.

DANCE: Oh, yes. You tell us in that scene when she says, 'Oh I love you because you're black, you're so black, I wouldn't like you if you were lighter, you black beast.' [p.278] You mean he can't see that…?

CLARKE: No, he could not see before she said that, that her love for him was exploitative. And even though she says those words – and I don't want you to put too much meaning in that – it was her way of explaining her love for him. Now it is not a normal way in which a woman expresses her love for a man.

DANCE: Hardly! [Laughter]

CLARKE: But the point was made there with some amount of exaggeration because she was in anthropology and she saw in close quarters a specimen worthy of study. But what is important, I think, is that she, Agatha, did in fact, love Henry more than Henry loved her.

DANCE: I think that's true if we extend our definition of love.

CLARKE: Well, how would *you* extend it?

DANCE: I would say that she is probably more obsessed with what she thinks Henry is, because I find it hard to consider that love; she wants to make of him something Blacker than he is, she wants to make him appreciate Black art, she wants him to wear his hair a certain way. Obviously what's there with her is simply an obsession with Blackness.

CLARKE: No, I wouldn't say it's an obsession. I would say that here's a woman with a certain amount of enthusiasm.

DANCE: About…?

CLARKE: About a Black man who was a bit disappointing that he did not regard himself as a Black man in the terms in which she knew from her studies that a Black man ought to be. Now one really can't say that a white woman like Agatha *should* know more about being Black than a man like Henry who is a Barbadian. But see, Henry after a while had denied the whole idea of Blackness because when he looked around him, all the Black models were failures. This is not to say that Black models in Toronto at the time were failures, but his coterie of friends were failures. So in despising this Black model he thought that he could be better. It didn't mean, of course, that he wanted to be white, but it may mean that because the opposite of black is white and the models around him which were successful were white. So here you have Agatha who has come from one of the most successful situations, meeting this man and she is a bit appalled if not disappointed that he does not see himself as Black because that was the attraction. The only way that she could have a creative relationship with this man was because he was Black.

DANCE: That's quite clear, but the thing is that that, in and of itself, seems to me to be a derogatory approach to a relationship.

CLARKE: It is derogatory only when one is asked to comment on it. You see if these two people had been left alone, it is possible that the relationship could have been a normal relationship.

DANCE: How could it be normal? She is a woman from a successful family, a PhD candidate; he is, I don't want to use the word ignorant…

CLARKE: He's a bum!

DANCE: Yes. Yes, I mean, what is there to attract her to him normally? What can they relate on? What do they have in common?

CLARKE: Well, he's a man; she's a woman. I see it as simple as that. He is a man and she's a woman. You see what I'm saying is when the pressures come, in other words, when she is asked to, as you would say, articulate her association with this man, then she gets into trouble, because she is refusing to see the very basic truth. Here's a man who she thinks makes her happy in many ways. So I mean his status has nothing to do with it. But if the two people, the Black man and the White woman, are put in some kind of confined situation where they have to explain to others, I think that's where the problem begins.

DANCE: And it's a natural relationship until it gets to that point?

CLARKE: I would think so.

DANCE: OK. Let me move to something else. As I read many West Indian novels written by novelists who most often have gone to England, I notice a general dilemma seems to be the discovery that the Mother Country is not a mother to the individual novelist; that he cannot claim its culture as his own. This is very outstanding in Lamming and some others. England remains remote, distant, cold, and their literature stems from this fact. How similar is the situation for you having come to Canada and having lived in the United States for a while? In other words, do you face that same dilemma, were you as disturbed to discover that the Statue of Liberty is not yours as Lamming may have been to discover that Westminster Abbey was not his?

CLARKE: Let me say that I disagree with Lamming in regarding myself as an exile. Now I'm referring specifically to his book *The Pleasures of Exile*. I would say for what it's worth that I did not come to this country in order to be a writer. Before I came to this country I knew that Canada was a colony and still is a colony. Canada is really a third-rate country in all aspects of the word third-rate. So that I could be as happy living in Canada as I could be living in Barbados because they're both colonies and they're both subjected to the same self-doubts and paranoia. So I was not harnessed by any great disappointment; I am not harnessed by any disappointment, so my experience is not the same as Lamming's experience. You see what I found most interesting about England, when I went there for two weeks in 1964, was my great surprise that the Englishman I had met growing up in Barbados was not the same Englishman I met living in London or other parts of England. And I was most impressed by the disorganisation in England; the laziness of the Englishman, his parochialism; and I said to many of my friends and I think I said this to Salkey, I said, 'I don't understand how you, living in this country, could regard the Englishman as this great man!' So that I was able to see the Englishman in *that* sense, in *that* way, and I was able to think that way about him because my confronting him had been delayed by my presence in this country; and one thing about this country, Canada, is that it strips you of all if not most of the social stigmas that one gets in Barbados, the class structure. This country is, I would say, a plebeian society because it is made up primarily of immigrants who are all struggling to establish some status.

DANCE: Well, is the status situation in Barbados more real or imaginary?

CLARKE: Extremely real. I mean one could be as cynical and critical of it as one may wish, but it is a very real situation.

DANCE: Were you rejected as a young man in Barbados by a young lady because of her class? I ask you that because that situation occurs in a couple of novels.

CLARKE: No, I could not be personally rejected.

DANCE: Oh, you were of the upper-class?

CLARKE: I could not be because of the school I attended.

DANCE: Explain.

CLARKE: Well, in Barbados when I was growing up there were three important schools: Combermere, for men, I'm talking about the men's schools, Combermere, Harrison College, and Lodge. For women, there were St. Michael's, St. Winifred's and Queen's College. And if you attended any of those schools, then your status was assured.

DANCE: Well the attendance at that school was based on examination, wasn't it?

CLARKE: Yes.

DANCE: And there were some families who were willing to accept anybody who showed enough intelligence to pass the examination, despite what his parents did or what his colour was?

CLARKE: We had, (I stress had) a way of looking at things in Barbados which said if you were educated, your colour was not important, so that education crossed those lines, you see.

DANCE: So that a student in that school might well be of an acceptable class whereas his sister or brother might not be?

CLARKE: There are cases in Barbados where a boy who went to Harrison College, which was a top school, still is, and the girl went to Queen's College, which is a top school for girls, and a brother or sister went to what we call a lower school, and they belong to two different social classes outside the home. And in cases in the home, the treatment meted out to them by the parents will be different, will tend to be different. And even when they finished school and went for jobs you had... you see the situation. I mean, it is a comical situation, really, but it's a very real situation. In Barbados today the people who run the country have all, except for two percent, been to Harrison College. So you are assured a place in the country if you've gone to Harrison College.

DANCE: Speaking of people who run the country, let me ask you about your portrayal of the government in The Prime Minister. Certainly the government in Barbados is not as bad as it is in that novel.

CLARKE: In cases, worse.

DANCE: Oh, come on! People don't lose jobs of a lifetime for laughing too loud at a party?

CLARKE: Well, not exactly laughing but for behaving in an improper way, improper as defined by the people who run the country.

DANCE: And that standard for definition is as ludicrous as in The Prime Minister?

CLARKE: Well, it is ludicrous in The Prime Minister because I am making a point, a point of the absurdity of the situation. That is why in The Prime Minister the man loses his job because he laughs at a party. But the laughing at the party is nothing more than what is called inappropriate behaviour in a social situation. And men, if they have not lost their jobs, certainly have not got any more promotions for the rest of their tenure for having committed those social sins.

DANCE: Have you been back to live in Barbados?

CLARKE: I was back between '75 and '76, when I was working there.

DANCE: Were you on a government appointment?

CLARKE: Yes.

DANCE: Is there anything autobiographical about *The Prime Minister*?

CLARKE: Some things. John Moore may be regarded as Austin Clarke because I was in charge of radio and broadcasting and I was an Advisor to the Prime Minister at the time.

DANCE: Did you leave in quite the same circumstances as he did?

CLARKE: Qualitatively the exact circumstances.

DANCE: Explain.

CLARKE: Well I was fired from the job.

DANCE: But there was no fear for your life or anything?

CLARKE: Yeah.

DANCE: Oh, really?

CLARKE: There were threats against my life and I used to carry a .38 revolver. There were bomb threats at the place that I worked.

DANCE: You must have been very bitter about this?

CLARKE: No, I wasn't bitter.

DANCE: When did you write the novel in terms of relationship to this?

CLARKE: I wrote the novel the year after.

DANCE: The year after you came back? Are you sure there's no bitterness?

CLARKE: I don't think the novel is… as a matter of fact the novel, as it is published, is one-third the length of the manuscript. There were other parts in the manuscript which it was felt should be taken out because they were libellous and bitter.

DANCE: Ah, referring to people who quite clearly would have recognised themselves?

CLARKE: But it is said now that quite a lot of people *have* recognised themselves. That's not a difficult task in that kind of a setting.

DANCE: Where was your wife? Was she here in Canada?

CLARKE: Yeah, because it was only six months I was there.

DANCE: How did your wife react to stories like this where if you are read as John Moore (which it is difficult for you not to be) and it's a story of a relationship with another woman…? Does she think perhaps you are confessing some of your indiscretions?

CLARKE: No, because John Moore, the essence of John Moore is Austin Clarke, but not the details of John Moore. The point that I like to make about that is throughout the book the woman is the land, is the country, the soil, the earth: that is the metaphor, and that is the easiest way and perhaps the best way of doing it.

DANCE: So that in joining her, he is in essence returning to the land?

CLARKE: You see, throughout the book, the only positive thing, the only positive feeling John Moore has is towards the land, and technically speaking one couldn't go on and on saying let's look at the land and writing l-a-n-d. You see, one has got to use a metaphor. And another thing too that I think you ought to know is that the woman becomes two women and then becomes one woman and again becomes two women.

DANCE: You need to tell me who are the two women she becomes.

CLARKE: Well, there are some passages in italics which is another woman, a Black woman, by which I mean a woman of less sophistication than the powerful woman in the book, and so he is remembering that there are two kinds of women in Barbados, as there probably are in most societies: that woman who, you know, you go to when you want to hear some home truths, and the other woman you go to when you want to understand certain intricacies of diplomacy and things like that. But you put the two of them together and it should be just one woman.

DANCE: In your description of Barbados, you quite clearly suggest that it is paradise lost, since John Moore keeps recalling *Paradise Lost* and *Paradise Regained* and you emphasise the physical beauty of the land at the beginning and the end. I was trying to determine what the main problem is – and of course there's the Government and the tourists who have destroyed the paradise, or is it a combination of the two?

CLARKE: They both have destroyed the paradise.

DANCE: Is John Moore to any degree responsible for the fact that paradise is lost to him; has it just been destroyed by these aliens, or…?

CLARKE: It is lost to him because he has forgotten this country; he has forgotten the nuances; he has become arrogant in the sense that he could use a foreign acquired sensibility, which is Canadian, in order to describe and to solve and define certain problems, which had he not left for such a long time would have been at his fingertips.

DANCE: Did you have that problem?

CLARKE: Yeah.

DANCE: In a review of *When He Was Free and Young*, Keith Jeffers says that at your worst you come across 'as a West Indian who has been away too long' [*Black Images*, January, 1972, p.14]. Would you comment on that?

CLARKE: I don't remember that particular review, but it is a fact. You see, because, if you've been away from your country for as long as I have, for twenty-five years, and you persist in writing about the country, you can only write about the country from reminiscences, which is a very tricky thing. Now if you go back and attempt to perform any substantial or significant activity, your understanding of the people certainly is not based on any contemporary insight, you are like a blind man struggling. You are trying to ignore the intervening years. You're also refusing to admit to the attitude that Barbadians have of those who have left for a long time. A long time may be five years, certainly twenty-five years is a reasonably long time, so the attitude is one which says that the person who returns after that time is an expatriate and a foreigner and really has no right to come back. There is not much love for people who have left Barbados and who have come back.

DANCE: If your stories are representative, many Barbadians in Canada want to go back, even if they don't plan to go back, don't they?

CLARKE: Well, we all want to go back, not for any rational reasons, objective purpose. But we all want to go back tomorrow when we think we have come up against an unpalatable or distasteful incident in our lives. We all know we can go back at any time because we belong there. There are reasons, of course, which prevent us from going back. Some are economical, which I don't think are serious reasons. A more important reason why we can't go back would be psychological, that we had so-called outgrown our environment. You see, it's very easy to live in this country if you have not committed your psyche to the country; and if you have not done that, if you have not come to terms with the country, then you would continue to live on the fringes in a very creative way, in a very hustling way. The whole image of the hustler as you came across that concept in Malcolm X's *Autobiography*. The fact that he had retained that concept of the hustler helped him to proselytise the theology of Muslimism in America and to get lots of people to join the Muslims. Now in this situation here I can very easily consider myself as a long-winded tourist.

DANCE: But not in exile?

CLARKE: No, never in exile.

DANCE: You know, in one of my favourite stories, 'Bonanza 1972 in Toronto', this domestic is talking on the telephone through the whole story about having gone to this tourist show, and she's very bitter, of course, about the fact that she is ignored and the Canadians are entertained; the symbol of her anger is focused on that scene from the film in which she sees the white tourist with the sand from Barbados going through her hands, and it's the symbol of her having been robbed. She says at that point she felt like she had lost her baby. You have a lot of situations like that, and yet even with this strong desire to retain the homeland, which is Barbados, these people seem to actually work towards getting a house in Rosedale, and you force me to ask why don't they save and buy land in Barbados?

CLARKE: Some do, but not a large proportion.

DANCE: But I mean in your stories. Nobody does in your stories.

CLARKE: Oh, in the stories. I see, in the stories. The reason is that they are bombarded during their period of immigration by certain Canadian models of success and Rosedale happens to be one of them, and it therefore becomes an aspect of their ability to integrate (and they desire to be integrated) that they will aspire if only, you know, vicariously, to have this bastion of success. There are lots of West Indians who would like to live in Rosedale, symbolically speaking, and some of them have succeeded in living in Rosedale.

DANCE: And many of them would completely forget their parents as some of your characters do to achieve that?

CLARKE: Quite a lot would. Quite a lot would. I think that's a normal situation. I think that that situation applies not only to a West Indian but to many other immigrants.

DANCE: But does distance make it easier to do that?

CLARKE: The distance, yeah.

DANCE: Let me go back to something you touched upon a little bit earlier and that is relationships between West Indians and Americans. Now naturally quite a few West Indians have found it convenient to retain their West Indianness in America to keep from being confused with Black Americans, and that's a very practical thing, sometimes, like with Claude McKay, for example. [In his autobiography, McKay tells of being indiscriminately arrested as a draft dodger; however, he suffered only briefly the cruel indignities endured by so many American Black males seized under similar conditions, for the moment the judge noted his foreign accent he not only released him but reprimanded the detective who arrested him. McKay writes:'I flashed back

a smile of thanks at him and resolved henceforth to cultivate more my native accent.'
See *A Long Way from Home* (New York: Arno Press, 1937), p. 9.] In one of your stories
you have a character whose name is Goldie ['One Amongst Them'], and he enjoys
his Black American friends, but he is very careful to retain his accent, and one reason
for that of course is because it helps him with jobs and in relating to white people and
that sort of thing, but then it seems to me that it actually goes beyond those practical
reasons, that there's a real sense that Goldie has, quite clearly, of the inferiority of the
Black Americans. Could you comment on that?

CLARKE: Well, I think that this started a long time back with Marcus Garvey and
all the problems that he had with A Philip Randolph and DuBois and the chap who
wrote *Along This Way*… I can't think of his name…

DANCE: James Weldon Johnson.

CLARKE: Yeah. Now part of the responsibility must lie with the establishment's
structure in America.

DANCE: May I stop you one minute because this may have something to do with
it. Don't forget that Claude McKay rejected him too.

CLARKE: Claude McKay rejected Marcus Garvey on ideological grounds, which I
consider to be a rational rejection. The others that I mentioned tended to reject him
completely on grounds that were what people call nowadays geopolitical, that he had
come from this small place, which was not even independent and was coming into this
country to tell us Blacks what to do in order to gain independence and a positive
personality. Then too, the establishment structure would feel that it is safer to give a
job to a West Indian because he has no stake in the country; he has no dogma to grind.
He would tend to be less revolutionary. After all, his propensities are similar to ours
because all he wants to do is to make a good middle-class materialistic living. He
would not embarrass us by asking for too much. This is something that was grasped
very firmly by the intellectual establishment in the States during the sixties and I am
sorry to say that I was a part of that when I went to Yale, which had one of the first Black
Studies Departments anywhere. If there were ten professors in the programme, eight
were West Indian, and the chairman was West Indian. At the same time the chairman
at Harvard was a West Indian. When I went throughout the country teaching, the
majority of Blacks on Black Studies faculties was West Indian. The other reason for
this is that the American became aware of the fact that the West Indian intellectual was
well trained. I think the courting of the West Indian intellectual has been political and
it was used divisively against the Black man. That is one of the reasons that I stopped
teaching in the States.

DANCE: Was he indeed less inclined toward militancy? Could he be trusted to be
a safer…?

CLARKE: The West Indian was safer, as Malcolm would say in his very catching
metaphors, the West Indian was, if he is not still, the 'house nigger' and the Black
American the 'field nigger'. But you see, there is a swing, there is a revisionist's attitude
to that because some Black intellectuals nowadays are saying that it is important to
recruit the house nigger if you want your revolution to be successful, by which he
means that a revolution to be successful cannot be based only on enthusiasm and
emotionalism, but it must have some intellectual guidance.

DANCE: I've read only one story of yours in which there were no West Indian characters; that's 'Invitation to Join'. Do your other stories always have West Indian characters?

CLARKE: No, not all. There are very few stories that I've written which have no West Indian characters, and I would think that in all there would be five. I am writing a novel now which has no West Indian characters, a novel based on three very wealthy married ladies from Rosedale who carry on certain…

DANCE: Jewish?

CLARKE: No, only one is Jewish, but she is a fourth. She doesn't involve herself in these things. The others are all Anglo-Saxon, the three primary characters who carry on liaisons with certain men in a very high-class penthouse which they have rented.

DANCE: And the men are all Anglo-Saxon too?

CLARKE: Yes.

DANCE: Had you been reading a lot of Faulkner before you wrote the short story 'When He Was Free and Young and He Used to Wear Silks'? I ask you that because the style is so different [from your other works and so reminiscent of Faulkner].

CLARKE: No. It wasn't Faulkner who influenced me. I like Faulkner very much, and I don't think that I could imitate successfully… his famous book…

DANCE: *The Sound and the Fury*?

CLARKE: *The Sound and the Fury*, which I think is an excellent book, which goes into time.

DANCE: Well this is something you do in that story though.

CLARKE: But I *had* just read an excellent book, and I'm afraid that many people don't know about it, but I tried to mention it to every student of mine for three years at Yale and the other three years that I taught in the States. This book is called *African Education Philosophies*, I think, but it is written by a man called John Mbiti, and that book deals with time and philosophy; and then the other book [I'd read] which obviously influenced me was JP Donleavy's *The Ginger Man*; and of course my favourite poet [is] Dylan Thomas. And that's why the style of that short story.

DANCE: Did you consider yourself experimenting with style there or was it just a kind of natural way to tell that story?

CLARKE: That story is an experiment.

DANCE: You haven't done much similar to that, have you?

CLARKE: Not in such an obvious way.

DANCE: Are you pleased with it?

CLARKE: Yes, very pleased with it. I wish I could get myself in that mood again.

DANCE: OK. You were just telling me about a new novel, and you showed me its cover. Would you tell me something about…

CLARKE: Yeah, well, that novel – the working title and the title which I submitted it with to the publisher was *Amo (I Love) Amos, Amat,* the first thing you learn in Latin, first declension, first conjugation verb, *amo*, I love. It deals with Austin Clarke from the age of ten or eleven in a village and then he moves on, as one of the fortunate few in the village, to high school. The school is Combermere. And it ends when he leaves Combermere, which is a secondary high school, and he goes to Harrison College, which is a first grade high school.

DANCE: And it is strictly autobiographical.

CLARKE: It is a memoir in the strictest sense. But the title has been changed to *Growing Up Stupid Under the Union Jack*.

DANCE: Have you ever done any work in any other genres other than the short story and novel?

CLARKE: I have written two non-fiction things, both of which are unpublished. One is named *God and Mammon at Yale*, which deals with my three years teaching at Yale. And the other one is called *An American Dutchman*, which deals with my relationship with LeRoi Jones and my what I would call psycho-literary criticism of his famous play *The Dutchman*. In other words I'm trying to find myself in the hecticness of Black consciousness as an outsider being thrown into the midst...

DANCE: In your works, and in talking to a lot of other people, I find that many West Indians approach the Black militant movement with a little reluctance, fear, sarcasm, and so forth, and yet I think I see from our conversation today, and from many things that you've written, a great deal of sympathy...

CLARKE: No, no, no. Sympathy is not what I would call it. Respect. A great respect.

DANCE: Are you disturbed a bit by the extremes to which it is carried as you suggest in the short story where the soul brothers simply don't go to class and complain about the racism of the teachers ['Hammie and the Black Dean']?

CLARKE: No, I'm not, no, it's not that. It is really a caution that they should in fact have gone to classes and understood. I don't regret the extremes to which it's gone because I think that any movement has got to have extremes and it cannot be one thrust only. And that is why I really appreciated Malcolm...

DANCE: Is it mere coincidence that many of the examples of white racism in your novels are Jewish?

CLARKE: It is not. It is not a coincidence. It is very deliberate because I was stunned when I first went to Harlem and I did a programme for CBC; the Canadian Broadcasting Corporation, on discrimination in schools, and rents, etc., and housing and jobs in Harlem in 1963, and I was shocked because I'd been brainwashed by reading things about Richard Wright, who was helped during the communist years by Jewish intellectuals and the man Johnson, who wrote *Along This Way*, and all that; I was brainwashed that the Jew was the Negro's friend, if one can use that derogatory term, and I was even more nonplussed when I saw that most of the businesses, the big businesses, most of the apartments, which were run-down and dirty – I mean I've been into those apartments – and most of the teachers and principals in the schools in Harlem were Jewish. Now if they had nothing to do with it, you tell me who had something to do with it. So that my tendency to distrust Jews as the Negro's best friend is well founded in fact. And another thing too, one of the most dangerous men in America is a man Albert Shanker, who writes an advertised column in the *New York Times* every Sunday, because he was the man who messed up the whole situation in the States when they had the teachers' strike and all those problems. So what I'm saying about this situation is not based on my emotionalism, because I'm not emotional. It is based on my facts.

DANCE: OK. Is there anything you'd like to comment on regarding your works before we end this interview?

CLARKE: Nothing, nothing.

DANCE: Thank you very much.

CLARKE: I thereby close the interview. [Laughter]

CONVERSATION WITH

WILSON HARRIS

Theodore Wilson Harris was born on March 24, 1921, in New Amsterdam, British Guiana (Guyana). Educated at Queen's College in Georgetown, he later studied land-surveying in 1939, and after qualifying to practice he led many survey parties in the interior. He was Senior Surveyor for the Government of British Guiana from 1955-58. In 1959 he moved to London, which has since remained home to him until 1986 when he moved to Chelmsford. Harris has been writer-in-residence or guest lecturer at, amongst others, the University of the West Indies; the University of Toronto; the University of Leeds; the University of Texas at Austin; the University of Mysore; Yale University and the University of Newcastle, Australia.

A prolific novelist, poet and critic, Wilson Harris began his career with two volumes of poems, *Fetish* (1951) and *Eternity to Season* (1952) published under the pseudonym, Kona Waruk. Other collections of poetry include *The Well and the Land* (1952) and *Eternity to Season: Poems of Separation and Reunion* (1954). A revised edition appeared in 1978, published by New Beacon Books. Individual poems have appeared in numerous journals and anthologies.

A number of short stories appeared in *Kyk-over-Al*, the earliest appearing in 1947, and he wrote a number of unpublished novels. His first published novel, *Palace of the Peacock,* appeared in 1960. This has been followed by *The Far Journey of Oudin* (1961); *The Whole Armour* (1962); *The Secret Ladder* (1963); *Heartland* (1964); *The Eye of the Scarecrow* (1965); *The Waiting Room* (1967); *Tumatumari* (1968); *Ascent to Omai* (1970); *Black Marsden* (1972); *Companions of the Day and Night* (1975); *Da Silva da Silva's Cultivated Wilderness & Genesis of the Clowns* (1977); *The Tree of the Sun* (1978); *The Angel at the Gate* (1982); *Carnival* (1985); *The Infinite Rehearsal* (1987); *Four Banks of the River Space* (1990) – these last three novels make up a trilogy, collected and published as *The Carnival Trilogy* in 1993 – *Resurrection at Sorrow Hill* (1993); *Jonestown* (1996); *The Dark Jester* (2001); *The Mask of the Beggar* (2003); and *The Ghost of Memory* (2006).

Harris has also published two collections of short stories: *The Sleepers of Roraima: A Carib Trilogy* (1970) and *The Age of the Rain-makers* (1971).

His critical works include *Tradition and the West Indian Novel* (1965); *Tradition, the Writer and Society: Critical Essays* (1967); *History, Fable and Myth in the Caribbean and the Guianas* (1967); *The Womb of Space: The Cross-Cultural Imagination* (1983) and numerous other essays published in various journals and collections. Collections of his work include *Explorations: A Selection of Talks and Articles* (1981; ed. Hena Maes-Jelinek); and *The Radical Imagination: Lectures and Talks* (1992), a collection of talks by and an interview with Harris, edited by Alan Riach and Mark Williams. In 1999, Andrew Bundy edited *Wilson Harris: The Unfinished Genesis of Imagination* which includes a selection of Harris' essays.

Scholarship on Wilson Harris' work began with Michael Gilkes' *Wilson Harris and the Caribbean Novel* (1975) Other core studies include Hena Maes-Jelinek's *Wilson Harris* (1982); *Wilson Harris: The Uncompromising Imagination* (1991) and *The Labyrinth of Universality: Wilson Harris's Visionary Art of Fiction* (2006); Sandra E. Drake, *Wilson Harris and the Modern Tradition: A New Architecture of the World* (1986); ed. M. Gilkes, *The Literate Imagination: Essays on the Novels of Wilson Harris* (1989); Marco Fazzini,

Resisting Alterities: Wilson Harris and Other Avatars of Otherness (2004) and Sam Durrant, *Postcolonial Narrative and the Work of Mourning* (2003)and Joyce Sparer Adler, *Exploring Palace of the Peacock: Essays on Wilson Harris* (2003). However, for further reference, a full bibliographical catalogue which has been produced online at the Université de Liège, can be pursued.

Wilson Harris received the Arts Council Grant in 1968; a Guggenheim in 1973; a Southern Arts Writer's Fellowship in 1976; an honorary PhD from the University of the West Indies in 1984; the Guyana National Prize for Fiction in 1987; and an honorary doctorate from the University of Kent in 1988.

He is the father of three children born to his first marriage to Cecily Carew, the sister of the novelist Jan Carew. He and his second wife, Margaret, are presently living in Essex.

The following interview was conducted on May 13, 1980, in New York City, where I met the novelist, who was en route to London following a lecturing stint at the University of Texas.

DANCE: Mr. Harris, I know you're doing a critical study now, and I'd like you to tell me a little bit about your concerns there.

HARRIS: Yes, well, I think perhaps it may be helpful if I read a passage from this, and I left you to arrive at certain views:

'Since dread and loathing are clearly the soil of nihilism in that they are susceptible to hardcore extensions into inhuman emotion or eclipse of creative responsibility, their authentic ground or grounds of figuration in the human psyche, may offer some clues to the robot landscapes and structures of a nihilistic cosmos and also in doing so may expose a paradox, a complex capacity for the transformation of bias in hidden sacraments of fertility or regenerative force, which are little understood if at all regarded in society's addiction to mechanised environments. The very rigidity of bias and dread may be less natural than one suspects even though it appears and is in some degree genuinely natural. What is genuine, natural order, after all? Nature is composed of many natures or perceived orders. The desert is as natural as the sea. The Rocky Mountain as natural as the Rain Forest. Snow is as natural as fire. The atomic explosion is as natural in photographic particularity as the shadow of instantaneous death upon the pavement of cities. Nature in all its trickster garbs is inevitably a cultural phenomenon within the human species. As a consequence a transformation of bias may require a disruption of conditioned perception one equates with genuine or natural order…'

Now that is a draft passage which comes out of the critical book; and preceding that passage are cross-cultural probes into twentieth century fiction. I have been looking at a number of writers including Jean Toomer, Juan Rulfo, Ralph Ellison, Edgar Allan Poe, Paule Marshall, Jean Rhys, Faulkner, Jay Wright and others from the Caribbean, Europe and Asia. I think that one can perceive over the years, through the kind of expedition one has been making, illuminations in the work of other writers and artists, work that may have appeared at an earlier stage quite alien to one's basic concerns. Their work does remain different, but a new dialogue commences, a strange dialogue, because something discovered in one's own work helps one to see more deeply, even sympathetically into theirs.

DANCE: Will you elaborate a bit on your efforts to alter boundaries of perception?

HARRIS: My judgement is that it is vitally important for imaginative fictions to alter the boundaries of perception. Now one finds, I think, that this can be done when you discover intuitively – it's not simply an intellectual proposition – it comes out of deep-seated intuitive elements – that there are organic metaphors of painting and organic metaphors of music coming in a work of fiction, and bearing upon disruptions of bias, the transformations of bias and fear. Now in *The Palace of the Peacock*, at the end of the novel, one sees a tree walking, the walking tree. That is the uprooting of fear. A tree obviously has many associations. It has associations of joy, but it also has the association of something rooted in the soil, and when the rooted thing begins to walk, it is as if something that mirrors one's fear, if you like, begins to move, you see. At the same moment the painting comes into the tree. It is like a flower which comes out of the rocky landscape – the flower is a kind of painting. So when the tree moves there is a coincident painting in the tree, lightning flash, the peacock's eyes, etcetera, etcetera, and then, immediately after this, not long after, Carroll's music. The psyche sings as if the tree or rock were singing; so you have a coincidence, an organic metaphor you associate with music, an organic metaphor you associate with painting. And in *Da Silva da Silva's Cultivated Wilderness* one hears voices in da Silva's paintings, implicit human voices in 'painted' bird song; one 'hears' the sound of bells in a line of paint. Now all this, in my judgement, has to do with the intuitive alteration of boundaries of perception, and I was struck quite recently, when pondering on this, by a passage in *The Hidden Order of Art* by Anton Ehrenzweig, in which he points out that Beethoven in his late quartets – in his Ninth Symphony – was tormented by the notion that the instruments in the orchestra were mute, even though they were playing. How to make them sing? And eventually he couldn't do it. What he did was to disrupt conventional instrumentality with the human voice. It's always interesting, I think, in literature to look for correspondences elsewhere. I don't think that literature is simply a matter of the structure of the word – the word in my judgement has its roots in paintings, in hieroglyphic paintings and in gestures, long before 'the word'. The birth or genesis of the human imagination is more mysterious than one tends to think. It is impossible to say how the human eye was first amazed by the address of the canvas of the sky, the canvas of the sea.

DANCE: As you were talking about expansion of form and mentioning what da Silva does with art work, I wondered if you think Denis Williams has done something of the same thing with the novel when he makes it a sort of an art work, a painting. Is that the kind of thing you have in mind when you talk about expansion of form?

HARRIS: Denis Williams is a painter whom I greatly admire. I knew him extremely well in the early 1950s when I first went to London. In fact, in 1950 I stayed with him, and that was when he was working extremely hard on an exhibition which was to appear after I had left at the end of 1950. It was an exhibition which was seized upon by English critics. I don't know that in Denis Williams's novel – you're thinking *of Other Leopards*?

DANCE: Not *Other Leopards*, *The Third Temptation*.

HARRIS: It's a novel I've read but I don't know that this issue that I'm discussing applies to *The Third Temptation*. You may remember *Palace*, the end, where the tree walks. Now this looks like an irrational position, but note, as I said before, the subtle disruption of bias. You see, in the first passage I read, one is speaking of the psyche of nature in which nature has many faces and one tends to commit oneself to one face and then to think that is the truth of nature where it is merely one face of nature. I am suggesting that there is an untamed and untameable ecstasy in nature. In that sense nature overlaps with the Creator, with deity, whatever one means by that and people mean different things by that, but this is an untamed and untameable ecstasy – it's not simply a matter of hunting sensation for the sake of sensation – it's a matter that that flower, that song psyche, is something that has to do with some kind of immense joy one would associate with the Creator himself or herself or itself when the cosmos was created; that when some disruption occurred in some formidable, implacable element that denied life – when that disruption occurred and the flower, so to speak, came out of the rocky fastness, that there must have been an ecstatic cry of joy in the Creator himself or herself or itself. That ecstatic cry can never be tamed or domesticated. It will come home to us sometimes in various areas of sensibility that seem native to ourselves, that seem somehow capable of giving us... of playing with us gently, but it can never be tamed. When we think we have domesticated it, it could turn on us at times with terror just as a black hole of gravity could walk into the earth and consume it or the sun could send an arrow or the banal earthquake could demolish a whole city. Nature cannot be tamed, but the ecstasy that is there also cannot be tamed.

DANCE: As you talk about the diverse elements of nature, all of which are a part of the natural order of things, you almost always, it seems to me, come to the reassurance of song, of ecstasy. Is the writer's obligation then to remind the reader of these diverse elements of nature, but to remind him also of the ultimate beauty that will finally result?

HARRIS: You see, I think it is so vitally important to alter the boundaries of perception. One of the tragic things about the Caribbean is the way the Caribbean is locked into protest. Since I was a young man some of my close friends were Martin Carter and others who were genuinely radical figures; but one realises that there is an incessant round of protest which is not genuine radicalism. There are young people marching in the streets today [Harris is speaking of Guyana]; they are not protesting now against the British Empire. They're protesting now against their own leaders, who obviously, many of them, tend to be fascists – they rig elections and so on and so forth. They're right to protest, but what I'm saying is that to be simply locked in an order of things in which everything is reduced to the political slogan, to the political calculation, in my judgement is to freeze a boundary of perception. We need altered boundaries of perception if those communities are to deepen the whole measure of radical change, and this would involve something that has to do profoundly with the arts, with the sciences. I mean it is no use simply importing technology. There has to be that kind of eye which sees into the landscape and sees much deeper than what appears to be the real world. This is one of the issues that arise, in my judgement, with realism. Much realism in my judgement is realist fallacy. The more you mirror the world as it is, the more gaunt and barren the world becomes.

DANCE: When you were speaking then, I was reminded of a statement you made to the effect that many of the West Indians of your generation conceive of themselves as being radical politically, 'but their approach to art and literature [I'm quoting you now] is one which consolidates the most conventional and documentary techniques in the novel' (*Tradition, the Writer and Society*, p.45). You think radicalism, militance, must start with the arts and then carry over, I assume?

HARRIS: I think that science is so closely linked with the intuitive imagination in the arts that you cannot divorce them. Any kind of dynamic change would involve science, which would involve the spirit of science, involves the intuitive wealth of the psyche in terms of art, in terms of an imaginative awareness of the psyche of nature. I mean, you see what I'm saying with the psyche of nature: that all the various faces of nature, however real they seem, are merely parts, that nature is much deeper than nature appears to be, and that this subtle disruption allows one to perceive that even bias, which seems so entrenched, and fear, which seems so entrenched, are not as natural as they seem.

DANCE: In talking about some of these matters in nature, dread and loathing and so forth that you see in the modern nihilistic novel, are there any earlier influences on this? I think I've seen places where you've mentioned Melville...

HARRIS: Well, it's very interesting when one looks at 'Benito Cereno', which is undoubtedly a nineteenth century work of genius – it was written in the middle 1850s, and it exposes in a remarkable way the kinds of biases which existed within what one would have thought to be a liberal Protestant establishment symbolised by Delano. What, however, is striking about that novel, is that Melville, I feel, loses some of the possibilities which were available to him. For example, when he goes on the ship where the Black slaves have taken over, Delano encounters a chained presence – a man called Atufal, I think. Atufal is the kind of operatic presence which could have been sensed by Melville in terms of what I was speaking, the song of the psyche. He misses that. He also misses the song that these women, these Black women are singing; he sees this song as some sort of song which is hounding the men on to kill the Spaniards, whereas that song could have been construed slightly differently as a great lament, a great lament of soul as the women sensed that their men were destined to die. There would have been an alteration in the complex of the song. Thus what one finds in the end with Melville – though 'Benito Cereno' is one of the most remarkable fictions of the nineteenth century – is that the notion of fear and bias are absolutely entrenched in the figure of Babo. Babo eventually becomes mute. From the moment he's caught, the funeral procession starts. He has nothing more to say, and he becomes a mute figure. Benito Cereno follows his leader; the very skeleton at the bow of the ship is a mute, stifled song. It is stifled; it is lost; it's a mute funeral procession; and one goes on to see that this is something that gripped Melville's imagination – the notion of a world so polarised and so unable to alter that condition that eventually it mirrors a whole cosmos which seems invincibly polarised and invincibly evil, and Melville was haunted by this notion of evil, you see.

DANCE: Are you suggesting that he should have moved towards more of a resolution, that he cannot leave us there?

HARRIS: I think that if he had been able to disrupt those conditions which are symbolised in Babo, in 'Benito Cereno', if he had been able to disrupt those, well, then the psyche of nature would have become, not this posture of evil. Evil, after all, we know, is there. But the point I am making is that with Melville, after a time you begin to feel that he comes into a vision of things in which there is no way out of the trap. Even though he's done a formidable thing in exposing biases, he fails to go beyond these into another area of imaginative fiction in which the boundaries, which eventually settle so firmly in the novel, are altered. That kind of development does not occur in my judgement. He overlooked the potentialities in the chorus on the boat, the Black women who sing, Atufal, the chained operatic presence; buried in these potentials was a capacity for the song of psyche in the terms in which I have been discussing it – the disruption of 'landscape' (when I say 'landscape', I'm using landscape as a metaphor – the rock mirrors our bias or the rooted tree mirrors our fear; I am using it in that sense); the whole vessel is a kind of landscape and at a certain moment it seemed to congeal into a mute song and a confession of incorrigible bias or evil.

DANCE: OK. Let me ask you one other question. Is it possible that choosing to limit himself to Delano's perception made it difficult for him to go further – to achieve some of the things that you would have liked for him to…

HARRIS: But you know that in an imaginative writer there is an intuitive element that breaks up his ego position. I use the term *ego* to suggest the way in which one is conditioned by history, by the way one has been educated, by one's family and so on, but there's an intuitive thing which comes up and in some degree alters that ego. This intuitive thing is much deeper, it's much older, it's a strange unfathomable source that informs the imagination; and this was clearly at work in Melville in that the Delano position was being demolished, but he needed to go even beyond that. Eventually, as you know, Babo is consolidated as a figure of dread, and nothing more. Babo becomes a silent figure. Now to give you an illustration of how this has been treated a little differently. If you look at Wole Soyinka's play, *The Road*, there's a mute figure there called Murano. Murano is in some ways as mute as Babo. The difference with Murano is that Murano begins to dissolve – it's as if a mask begins to dissolve – and one has a sense that the mask has its roots in some fertile soil where as it dissolves it becomes the seed of a new tree of life, implicitly. Now, in other words, Murano seems to stand between the root of experience and the not yet born flower of experience, some kind of unstructured element seems to stand between the seed that falls into the soil to dissolve and the flower that is to come at some stage, which has not yet appeared, so that Murano's muteness has the 'singing' seed. This is not the case with Babo. This is not to dispute Melville's genius, not for one moment, but I'm saying that his novel, and the whole ground of nihilism, has in some degree sprung from this failure of the nineteenth and twentieth century imaginations to alter the boundaries which seem so implacable, so implacable that in fact we live in a world that is hideously polarised – between the United States and the Soviet Union – you could go on and on and on for ever working out these polarisations – the dread on either side of the fence – the fears that each group has of the other. It is no use protesting against the Russian actions. I disapprove immensely of the invasion of Afghanistan. But to mount a protest is invalid in the final analysis. Something much more creative and complex has to happen within twentieth century civilisation – some alteration in these boundaries that are so implacable. And this is where one comes back to the psyche of nature and to incredible fictions in which you can perceive organic metaphors of music, organic metaphors of painting, the 'voice that sings', which manifests the song of the psyche. And when I say 'organic metaphors' I say this deliberately because I am not speaking of music in fiction as an imitation of sound, but of organic metaphors.

DANCE: Yes. As we've been talking about your philosophy of the novel, I'm reminded of the fact that it seems to me that you and Denis Williams are perhaps the most innovative, experimental novelists in the Caribbean, and you've suggested yourself that most Caribbean writers do not alter, experiment, innovate in terms of art, and I want to know if this is mere coincidence, or were your experiences and education and acquaintance growing up in Guyana in any way contributing factors to your tendency, the two of you, to explore new forms?

HARRIS: I think Denis Williams would have to answer for himself. As I was saying earlier, I greatly admire the work he was doing as a painter in the 1950s. I thought him one of the first formidable painters to come out of the Caribbean (Aubrey Williams, incidentally, is another exceptional painter), and Denis moved on after that to write impressive novels. What we may have in common perhaps, is faith in the depth-mind of cultures and a distrust in realist fallacy… The 'real' world appears to be a world of violence. I am not denying that violence is very much in evidence, but I am convinced that many other subtle and marvellous things are occurring which do not appear in the newspapers, so we live in a world where the symmetries are symmetries of violence, and all symmetries tend to be self-defeating in the final analysis. I must be very careful here – you see this does not mean that one does not admire symmetry – but I believe that one has to see that there are strange and curious distortions within the world that confront one, and that those distortions are much more subtle and peculiar than one imagines. And there has to be some ground which allows these distortions to flourish in terms that address us so deeply that we're able to move out of this narrow realism that seems absolute, that seems to be the real world.

DANCE: Your style of writing, several of your works have been confusing to many people. Of course you've received high critical acclaim; but then so many people claim to be unable to understand your work. Sylvia Wynter described your novels as 'a highbrow consumer product, accessible only to the initiated' (*Jamaica Journal* III, p.40). Andrew Salkey quotes a friend of yours as saying, 'He's become wilfully obscurantist. He's moved… to a forced complexity' (*Georgetown Journal*, p.155). Salkey also quotes a Georgetown official who had invited you to give some lectures and observed, 'but we're sure that nobody will understand them' (*ibid.*, p.169). Even CLR James, who praises your work highly, characterises you as 'one of the strangest of living novelists' and says your 'latest books are stranger than ever' ('Interview with Three Caribbean Writers,' *KasKas*, 1972, p.28). Does it bother you that so many consider your work so complex and erudite and enigmatic?

HARRIS: Andrew Salkey and the others are obviously entitled to their own judgements. I suppose in that sense, perhaps, one is strangely close to Europe because it does seem to me that in Europe you are aware of certain kinds of thrusts whether coming from music, from painting, from imaginative writing. I mean if one were to, for example, look at the work of Rimbaud or Claude Simon, to give just two examples; I suppose in a sense – this has never been a design, I've never designed it in that way, but I would think that the emphasis on art, the emphasis on the creative imagination which one finds in Europe, is an emphasis which sees art as a valid pursuit, as valid as science; art is not simply entertainment, nor is it simply political protest, nor is it simply realist fallacy. It is much more concerned with the alchemy of possibilities, the alchemy of change. In some degree in Europe there is a stultification because of the growth of nihilism and the loss of complex faith. We can see that even a formidable playwright like Beckett is involved in parody, and parody has become more and more pertinent to the European imagination. Now this is where I diverge from Europe because I do have a profound and deep-seated faith in the psyche of nature. I believe that nature is not ultimately tragic; it is not a field of ultimate tragedy. Tragedy, however noble it may be, is a manifestation that signifies ultimate defeat within a decadent or hollow nature, whereas I believe that the risks one takes in nature are meaningful risks and that though one may be defeated and will be defeated in the end because one is mortal, that through that defeat lies some kind of embrace, some ultimate embrace, in which one is taken up by what cannot be tamed or domesticated in nature and taken through into other dimensions. This is where I diverge from the European position at the moment, though I admire it enormously for its innovative skills and because it still persists with the view that art is a valid way of looking deeply into possibilities, just as science is, and that there is a connection between the two, you see; but parody will always arise where one loses complex faith, and Europe has been overshadowed by this notion of the death of God, indeed the 'death of man' as the French philosopher Michel Foucault portrays it. Many of the great European writers are involved in parody. Parody may cut to the bone and heart of liberal complacency, but it does not seem to go beyond that, and it is here that this whole notion of the alteration of boundaries of perception becomes profoundly active.

DANCE: In your works you seem to suggest that, even though there is a great deal of death, there's really no such thing as death?

HARRIS: I do believe that death is real, that one's mortality is real, but that one's mortality is one of the ways in which, when one becomes aware of the ecstasy that lies at the heart of creation, the untamed and untamable ecstasy, one knows in fact that the shell which one wears is not equal to the burden of that ecstasy and thus one knows that one is destined to perish; but the paradox is that because one is part of that untamed ecstasy, what one carries is also partial. How this will dissolve and melt into what lies ahead of us, of course, is something that no one can see, but throughout, the whole thrust of imagination, it seems to me, in art, can be a very serious thrust. This I take from Europe. I mean I find that the European imagination with its obsession with the significance and importance of art is very valuable. It is not simply a static drum beat in Jamaica or Trinidad or writing sort of realist fallacies, which most West Indian writers seem to me to do. I can understand why they are trapped that way. I was listening to a BBC broadcast in which there was a young Black West Indian poet – I can't remember his name – but he was pointing out that in his judgement art has no significance except as entertainment or political protest. Now those are popular views in the Caribbean and they're views which show how bankrupt the Caribbean is. But I do not take the view that Naipaul takes, that the Caribbean is totally bankrupt. I believe that there are immense resources in the Caribbean if one looks at the pre-Columbian legacies and myths – now many of these pre-Columbian peoples have vanished – yet there are the Arekunas, the Arawaks, the Macusis, and so on, and that's a marvellous heritage. What seems to me immensely important about the tradition in the Caribbean, indeed in the Americas, is that these strange myths coming out of the pre-Columbian past have survived, though these people in their political format have vanished; and this is where I think lies the seed of supportive tradition for the native

Caribbean and the Americas, because the fictions that are now being written have therefore some kind of deep-seated companionship, deep-seated support, sustenance, coming out of the past. A tradition of native survival of complex forms of art exists in the soil of the Americas to enter into cross-cultural being with Africa, Europe and Asia.

DANCE: Let me ask you something about those myths you treat in *The Sleepers of Roraima*. How did you become familiar with them?

HARRIS: Well, I think that intuitively for a long time I have had the sensation that in the Caribbean and the South Americas, indeed the North Americas, the pre-Columbian legacies are immensely important because, much as I admire Europe in the way I've said, I do feel that this quest for tradition is vitally important in all areas of imaginative pursuit, and that we do have in this strange surviving realm of myth the seeds of native tradition. By tradition I'm not speaking of something static or something fixed. In terms of the Caribbean and the Americas, South Americas, North Americas, I believe the tradition should be a cross-cultural phenomenon, not a phenomenon of assimilation. I mean I would go along with Aimé Césaire in his repudiation of assimilation. Because assimilation is grounded in conquest – one culture overpowers the other, consumes it, assimilates it, you see, whereas the cross-cultural phenomenon is not grounded on conquest – it is grounded on a deep-seated sensation that where one stands is always a partial reality, that one has roots that go deep, and deep in all sorts of directions and you cannot take images for granted, so that one's roots relate to another set of roots elsewhere which may seem almost incompatible, but the relationship is there and that quest, that sensation of the way roots relate, alters the whole shape of imaginative fiction: the way you would read it, the strategies of reading it, the strategies of entering into that kind of sensation that all images are partial, is quite different from the strategies set up by the comedy-of-manners novelists in which you have a total sovereign conviction lying behind the apparatus of fiction, you see, because there is no such sovereign institution in the kind of heterogeneous world that I'm discussing. All institutions are partial and therefore you cannot take them for granted. It is in this sense that one has to seek for a tradition in the Americas, and that kind of tradition, in my judgement, is fostered by the ground of myth, because myth has in it an element that cannot be tamed or domesticated, you see. And therefore, to come back to your thing about *Sleepers of Roraima*: in each case I have taken a particular reality through which to explore and to descend into elements long eclipsed by models of conquest. 'Couvade' involves a dance and masculine/feminine balance of selves. 'Yurokon' is the bone flute associated with cannibalism. Yurokon is a distant cousin of Quetzalcoatl as I discovered after I wrote that story. You will find this in Roth, Walter Roth; you may not agree with Walter Roth's philosophical views, but he is undoubtedly a very important anthropologist for the Americas. And you'll find Levi-Strauss has quoted from Walter Roth. My intuitive interpretation of the Yurokon flute, bone flute, is that it points to a 'magical corpse' which seems both dead and alive. The music exists in two worlds. It descends into apparent oblivion and yet it sends out concentric ripples. It is like a stone that falls into a pool and sends out concentric ripples. On the first ripple appears Quetzalcoatl. In other words the institutions of Quetzalcoatl's day were dressed up in a kind of marvellous investiture involving the marriage of heaven and earth, of the quetzal bird and the snake, you see.

But that posture hardened and became so adamant that eventually it split into a catastrophe. Quetzalcoatl vanished in the sea. On the next horizon appeared what is known as Kukulcan. This was followed by Huracan. After that came the Caribbean Yorokon. On each concentric horizon it's as if a painted mask or investiture appears and sings through the bone flute. That's how – to put it as briefly and graphically as I can – I found myself involved half-consciously, half-unconsciously, in a body of myth I found existing in the work I was doing before I became intellectually aware of it.

DANCE: There's one motif that I noticed in, I'm sure, two of the stories, and that was the quest for a mother – the mother is missing and the son… [My question was intended in reference to *The Sleepers of Roraima*, which we had been discussing, but I did not make that clear, and Harris responded regarding women in his work generally, a subject which I intended to ask about anyway.]

HARRIS: I wouldn't say 'missing'. For example, in *Palace of the Peacock*, the woman Mariella appears at the outset in a rather debased posture. She's been beaten by Donne. There are stripes on her legs. But later, on the mission of Mariella, you enter another dimension of Mariella. The seed of the past is there, as if Mariella is now dressed in the land, and then out of the land or mission comes the old crumpled Arawak woman who's taken into the boat and forced to be a guide, and that crumpled woman suddenly metamorphoses into a gigantic figure, muse figure, when the boat seems to be on the lip of the abyss, is going to fall into hell, as it were. The crew is afraid the boat will be crushed on the rocks. At that moment, the aged Arawak woman metamorphoses into a vision that recalls the Behring Straits, the long epic journey that the people had made through North America, Central America, South America; the metamorphosis of muse figures is necessary and extremely important, I think. That necessity appears in some of the black Magdalen figures, Magda in *The Whole Armour*, for example, who is half-African and half-Chinese, and the black Magdalen figure in *Ascent to Omai*. I know it is a difficult matter for people to understand the complications in metamorphosis in an age of realism such as ours where the tendency is not only to exploit women-figures, but to debase landscape because one thinks the landscapes are there simply to gratify one's lusts or pleasures. It is apparently natural for the male ego to perceive women-figures and property as synonymous. Reason is a marvellous thing until it becomes hubris; then it becomes a kind of violence. We use reason to build the most fantastic war machines. We use reason to justify coercion, possession, and even to beat into the soil everything we do not like. The Nazis would have regarded themselves as eminently reasonable because they saw themselves as pure, incorruptible. Thus they could beat the Jews into the soil. There are resources of imagination which alert us not to invest in reason as a tool or weapon, and to plant in reason a luminous, compassionate and creative vision. When one goes back and looks at ancient Greek myth, one understands at a deeper level than reason Pygmalion's irrational sensation that the sculpture of Galatea had come alive. The same phenomenon occurs in savage pre-Columbian myth. The cherry tree is cut and becomes the daughter of the Chief, the sculptured tree comes alive. That strange kind of inner necessity is what makes it possible for us to enter into the living psyche of nature which cannot be tamed but may confer rich blessings.

DANCE: You were talking a little earlier about roots and about your interest in the Amerindian myths as part of the tradition certainly of the New World, and the discussion of roots made me think about Poseidon of *The Secret Ladder*, who is a very important symbol, a representative of, may I say, African roots?

HARRIS: Well, Poseidon is a figure in whom there's a cross-cultural element. Poseidon is an African figure but also seems to have some Greek momentum in him – Poseidon, the very name Poseidon, and as you know, Black Americans and people in the Caribbean have all sorts of names, names that come from Europe, from Greece, from elsewhere. I believe that in the Caribbean the Greek myths are very important, but then they must not have the kind of monolithic position which they once had when the conquistador ruled the Americas and simply established his myths as some absolutely sovereign ego condition and everything else was beaten into the ground. I think that once European myth secretes itself in the soil of the Americas as a genuine kind of fertile enterprise, partial and therefore susceptible to other strange parts which come from Africa, from India, from the pre-Columbian past, once it does that, then one has a rich fabric, a rich tradition, building all the time in various kinds of ways, not in one way at all, in all sorts of contrary ways and types but building nevertheless. This came home to me when I travelled in the Canje as a surveyor and I remember coming across a very old man. It was said that some of the Black people who lived in the Canje were the descendants of the escaped slaves in the eighteenth century who had run across from New Amsterdam, across the Canje, which is a very complex landscape. If one conceals oneself in the Canje it's very difficult to be caught because the place is so cut up, you know, into ridges of high land with great moats of water around these ridges that you could hide there and few people could really get in. Now these people may have concealed themselves successfully there. At least this is part of the legend; I don't know how absolutely true it is, but one had the sensation therefore of a figure who is *in* the landscape, and I think landscape is an immensely important feature because landscape is a muse apparition. Poseidon was *in* the land; yet his roots ran into rivers and seas. The rivers are as much muses as the woman apparition is to the man, as the man apparition is to the woman, so that Poseidon is a figure strangely rooted in the past in the way he was able to secrete himself in that kind of world. He has therefore these deep roots, but he also has the myth, the mutated myth of Africa in him, a mutation occurs, changes occur, and the mutated myth of Europe in him – Poseidon – so that in fact the whole notion of this Poseidon figure with his roots in the sea and the land – that whole notion undergoes a strange change in the Americas – it relates to the past but becomes something new.

DANCE: As you were talking about your reaction to the man you met who obviously was the basis for this character, you sounded a little bit like Fenwick [in *The Secret Ladder*] – I guess that's a slightly autobiographical sketch?

HARRIS: Fenwick? Well, nothing in my judgement in one's fiction is absolutely autobiographical, but what happens is that one senses some element in oneself which comes alive, but that element that comes alive is an imaginative element. But I take your point because I travelled in that area, and it was an area which signified a great deal to me because of events that occurred there. One of my predecessors, a young land surveyor, was killed there by one of the men who more or less went berserk at a certain point and shot him to death. I had left there about two weeks before, and it could have happened to me. [Author's note: there is, of course, the scene in *The Secret Ladder* when Chiung, wearing Fenwick's jacket, is attacked by Poseidon's men who assume he is

Fenwick.] And that's how the whole fiction grew up, you see. It grew out of all that, but if you examine the fiction closely you will see that none of the figures are biographical. They're all mutated and changed.

DANCE: I don't really know much about your life. Was your family background at all similar to Fenwick's?

HARRIS: In some degree. In some degree similar.

DANCE: What about racial background?

HARRIS: In some degree, yes. Because I'm mixed.

DANCE: Your parents?

HARRIS: Well, yes, I mean many Guyanese are…

DANCE: Yes, but are your parents – is your mother white like Fenwick's mother?

HARRIS: Well, Fenwick's mother wasn't supposed to be white, but she was a woman who was, now let me try and remember, she was supposed to be part European, part Arawak, part… and even there was a suggestion that there was East Indian in her, but her husband was virtually Black. Well that kind of thing is very true of many Guyanese. I suppose it's true of Americans as well. A man like Jean Toomer was very mixed, and at one stage it is said that, to use the horrible American term, he 'passed' for white, and yet he is one of the profound agents in this enterprise of Black fiction and so on. In 1923 he published a book which had elements of stream of consciousness in it, elements of drama in it, elements of poetry in it. I think that was really astonishing.

DANCE: Yes the point I was getting to was that the racial mixture with Toomer as with Fenwick here is a very crucial element in his sense of himself.

HARRIS: Yes, yes. But I don't feel that in myself, really, because my antecedents are rather like that in a more spread out way, you know. I couldn't trap it precisely, but in a more spread out way it's like that, and therefore I have never been able to feel really confined by the necessity to chart any one particular course. I believe the cross-cultural thing is immensely important because through the cross-cultural thing one could begin to disrupt the legacies of conquest, you see, and wrong-headed assimilation. The legacies of conquest are very formidable in the Caribbean, and one of the fears I have is that this is going to get out of hand and you may have Black men seeking to overpower others without realising what they are doing, or Indians from India seeking to overpower others, or some group that is strong enough to assert itself in some way. I mean one must have fears about the authoritarian spectre in the Caribbean. I see 60,000 Cubans have left Cuba. Now bear in mind that Cuba is one of the few revolutions in which there were genuine romantic revolutionaries – Che Guevara was a man who in Bolivia, arrived at a place (he suffered from asthma), and needed medicine. He could have blown up the hospital and taken what he needed, which is what most so-called revolutionaries would do now – these people who seize on people in embassies and so on and so forth, and in an absolutely ruthless way would kill, kill. But what did Guevara do? He went in and bought this like an ordinary person, said he couldn't interfere with these people: it was needed by the people, these drugs. And that's how he revealed himself to the authorities. Now Cuba, therefore, is one of the few revolutions which came out of that kind of deep-seated romantic vision which has in it a kind of poetry Blake, indeed Byron, would have understood – a kind of – you know – beauty. And look what is happening because of the insistence,

I think, in the Castro regime to make a cult of personality – the one-party state. There are no free elections in Cuba as far as I know – this tendency is seeping all over the Caribbean. These so-called Marxist parties are basically fascist and totalitarian parties. Few of them have any grasp of Marx; few of them have read *Das Kapital*: they find it too complex and difficult to read. They read little pamphlets based on Marx and these people are coming up with the notion of revenge you see, how to overturn those whom they regard as their exploiters. The tragic thing is that their so-called exploiters have long left and the people on whom they are going to reap havoc are people like themselves, but people of a different ethnic background. Now that is one of the dangers one faces, and quite frankly I think these dangers have come out of the ground of realism, the way people pursue patterns that seem to them the only real patterns; the only real patterns they seem to see are patterns of power, establishing themselves as lifetime presidents and lifetime prime ministers – these seem to be the only real things. It is the bankruptcy of realism, which we have discussed before, coming home to us in power politics, despite the fact that you do have in the Americas redemptive possibilities. The heterogeneity of the Americas, I would have thought, is a marvellous redemptive capacity for peoples to relate to each other within a cross-cultural thing in which they are not brutalising each other, and yet out of that complex could come a new kind of passion, a new kind of beauty, which indeed would be a phenomenon of sensibility.

DANCE: But that's not happening anywhere?

HARRIS: It could happen. It's not happening now, unfortunately, anywhere, on the scene as it is.

DANCE: Let me ask you a little bit about Caribbean literature in general. I know that in one of the courses that you taught when you were at the University of Texas before, 'Contrasts in Modern Fiction', that you used works by two West Indian novelists other than yourself, and they were Denis Williams and George Lamming. I want to know if you selected their novels simply because they fitted into the thematic interest of the course or if you considered them the most important…

HARRIS: Well, they did fit in. Let's take Denis Williams first of all. The novel I had there was *Other Leopards*. What I admire about that novel is that there is a shamanistic thrust. A shamanistic thrust, as you know, is a thrust where at a certain point in the novel the sort of hero, if you like, disappears into the wilderness and he could be fed and protected by the creatures and agents of psyche in the wilderness and could return imbued with a new kind of wisdom. Now Denis Williams, I thought, wrote a remarkable novel there in which first of all you have this shamanistic thrust, but it becomes abortive, I must confess, in that the hero never returns. Nevertheless the important thing is there… The other thing that I admire about *Other Leopards* was that Denis Williams did not take Africa for granted. He saw Africa as a formidable proposition in which it was no use hiding behind all sorts of slogans and all sorts of idealisms – that one would have to encounter formidable realities. For example, the Queen figure who appears there is a figure who seems very implacable, and it raises the whole question of the muse, of the muse figure, and how this muse figure could be metamorphosed. Now Denis doesn't metamorphose the muse figure, but what he brings home is that the necessity is there for this metamorphosis, and those were some of the issues I sensed. It is a novel, therefore, which it seems to me – you know the

African writer Armah – Armah is greatly admired – but I would have thought that *Other Leopards* had already moved into that kind of ground. It is a ground in which you ask yourself important questions about the nature of the imaginative thrust, its complexity, and not to take for granted what many Africanists take for granted, without any sort of exposure to the bewilderment that could fall upon them when they confront certain patterns that may have become rather monolithic in Africa itself. The Queen figure, this Queen with all the necklaces around her neck, is a formidable African monument, a woman who becomes a strange kind of tyrant in that she can press the male figures into the ground. And I thought that what Denis was doing there, in some degree, was to bring home to us how formidable Africa is – that one may come up against monoliths in Africa which are not really consistent with one's vision of the kinds of changes one seeks in the New World, and that was a courageous thing to do because the tendency is to go to Africa overboard, as if Africa is some utopian construct in which you simply walk into paradise. Now this is not the case, and I think Denis Williams was making this brilliantly clear in *Other Leopards*. It is not that his sympathies were not there in Africa and his judgement of African art and African masks is a fine judgement in his book, his critical book, *Icon and Image*, but even there you get lurking in it this notion that there was a tendency in Africa to go for a rather monolithic position, whereas I myself do not accept these monoliths. I look for distortions, meaningful distortions in all assumptions of absolute sovereignty.

DANCE: And George Lamming?

HARRIS: Well, George Lamming's *In the Castle of My Skin* is undoubtedly a Caribbean classic. What interested me there was the sense I had in that novel that George Lamming was not satisfied with realism, that there was a deep-seated distress about the world. In mirroring the world, there was a deep-seated distress, a necessity to thrust away from that world, you see, and you find this in the way the boy is presented in a number of scenes with the archetypal fisherman. There are the beginnings in *In the Castle of My Skin* of a disintegration of the personality which is to become more manifest, I think, in his later novels. I think this disintegration of personality has to do with some deep-seated necessity that Lamming perceives, to alter the fabric of the realist posture and, in altering it, to experience the breakdown of certain conventions of personality which after all underpin what we call character. Now I don't know when one looks at his novels that he has been able to bring into play a novel form that would set up this matter of alteration of boundaries, but I don't want to be sharp on this because I don't know what his deep-seated intentions are and I may be reading something into his novels which springs from my own thing. But put that aside. The point is that in dealing with *In the Castle of My Skin*, you can see these tendencies at work, I think, in a remarkable way. I mean you can read it simply as a novel of childhood if you like, but you also have this thrust, the beginning of this disintegration of personality in a number of figures which appear, and I would have thought that this disintegration is one of the ways of assessing the nature of reality as not conforming to rigid expectations.

DANCE: You know, when you were talking about Denis Williams's *Other Leopards*, you mentioned that you saw as one of the shortcomings of the novel the fact that the shamanistic thrust was aborted and that the hero does not return. Do you have the same criticism of Ellison's *Invisible Man*?

HARRIS: Well, *Invisible Man* raises another kind of question. I think *Invisible Man* is a major American novel. Where its defect lies is in the debased muses. There is only one muse figure that seems to get out of this debasement. That is the woman, Mary, but even she is defeated by the debased Harlem landscape in which she lives.

DANCE: Is she defeated?

HARRIS: When I say 'defeated', she isn't herself defeated, but the Invisible Man has to leave. He can't find the solace which he had hoped to find. You see, if you look closely at Ellison's novel, you can see this notion that I was speaking of before – the stone that falls into the pool, concentric horizon. On the very first horizon, more or less, is the boxing ring, where the student dies metaphorically; his awakening is bleak, but he sees how hollow have been the shapes and pretensions of the past. Now he is surrounded by some muse figures there; there is the blonde woman who is a terrified creature; now that's a debased white goddess figure; but even the old woman in the blues music when he descends there cannot help him because her sons would have beaten him; and the next one is, of course, Bledsoe's college and there you have another grouping of muse figures; there is the woman with whom Trueblood commits incest, his daughter, involuntary incest, and, of course, you have accompanying that the surreal dream of going into this plantation house, where the Invisible Man runs into a clock. Now those muse figures are also violated muse figures. Now you go into the paint factory and Tiresias appears there, who is – I say he is Tiresias – the man who sets off the bomb, because you know you have the Greek thing in Ellison's world. Really the Invisible Man is an Odysseus figure, half Anancy, half Odysseus, you see. And this is pointed up by curious clues. I mean, for example, there is the one-eyed giant, the Cyclopean giant, Jack is a part of this, there is the doctor in the hospital, and even the Invisible Man very early in the first phase of the book wears the Cyclopean mask when his eyes seem to pop out of his skull. What I find astonishing about this novel is that all the way through, on each horizon, this dying god apparition appears surrounded by his muse figures. The muse figures basically do not possess the seeds of metamorphosis, you see, thus the bleak awakenings Invisible Man undergoes.

DANCE: So they're only possible muse figures?

HARRIS: They've made Invisible Man's awakening increasingly bleak, but what strikes me as amazing about that novel is the formidable implications of complex myths which I have outlined very briefly.

DANCE: You mean you are amazed at that kind of use of myth by an American writer?

HARRIS: Perhaps it does exist in other American writers. We haven't time to go into that.

DANCE: What about Toomer's muse figures?

HARRIS: Well, Toomer is a very interesting figure, but it works a little differently there. Let us take the case of Fern. Fern is the virgin whore. She has these men, but she feels nothing. She feels something at the end when in a state of confused emotion she sings, she suddenly sings, and her voice seems both old and young. After that she returns to this posture of insensibility, but at that very moment the disruption occurs, and it is a disruption because you may remember that Fern is described as a woman in whose eyes flow all these landscapes. The landscapes disrupt and sing, but Toomer loses it after that and it settles back again to this dumbfounded, insensible posture – this is why I'm saying that when I look at these novels I find traces of things. To what extent these novelists were consciously aware, I do not know.

DANCE: You consider *Cane* a novel?

HARRIS: No it's not a novel; it's a series of impressive sketches, some of which I would call short novels. I regard Toomer as a kind of asymmetric writer in that there are no symmetries – by asymmetric I mean you can find stream of consciousness; you can find the play device, sort of poems; this asymmetric position is what makes Toomer a curiously original sensibility because asymmetry rests on the notion that connections between various features of the world are not necessarily symmetric connections. In that way the world opens up to an infinity of possibilities, because connections exist where you least suspect them to exist. Asymmetric position therefore is one which lends itself to all sorts of perspectives of metaphor in which there is an unnamable centre, if you like, of light. I mean if one were to say, for example, that the sun is a rose, one doesn't mean that literally, but one means that between the sun and the rose exists an unnamable centre of light, which you can't structure. The sun is a partial signature of that unnamable centre of light. So is the rose. Thus you could go on into infinity. Not only is the sun a rose, it is something else, and something else, and something else that could take you into areas which would seem remote from the sun, and yet you deepen your apprehension of the nature of light; and asymmetric fiction works like that. Now I think there is an intuitive asymmetry in Toomer that is remarkable.

DANCE: Let me ask you about one other American author of whom your work frequently reminds me, and that's Edgar Allan Poe. And the reason I particularly want to ask you about him is that in your commentaries you frequently mention other writers whose philosophy and whose style and so forth have appealed to you, but I don't remember you saying very much about Poe, and yet it seems to me that there are a lot of similarities between your work and Poe's, particularly, in your deranged narrators and the dreamlike world fluctuating between dream and reality, and the dead returning in the bodies of others. I particularly thought about Poe when I was reading *Companions of the Day and Night*. That dark, Mexican, goddess-like girl, and the descriptions you use, remind me so much of Poe's *Ligeia*.

HARRIS: Yes. Let me say two things quickly about this. *Companions of the Day and Night* is really a vertical novel; the linear shape of the novel is a kind of deception. I mean, if you read it closely you will see that there are a number of motifs that relate to the descent – in other words the idiot who is falling from the top of the 'pyramid of the sun' is ceaselessly falling, so the man you meet at the very outset of the novel you could view as this ceaselessly falling body, falling through the very streets and pavements of Mexico into the ancient lakes on which Montezuma moved; and in New York City for example when the great billowing curtain comes up on his head that has the drawing of the Pyramid, it strikes his head, his head seems to dissolve, becomes the bone and the rose; the bone and the rose relate to the nuns in the room, and all the way through you find these motifs relating to this falling 'body' that re-dresses itself, unravels the investitures it wears. Just to say that quickly. Now with Poe. Poe is, I would judge, a very important American novelist. Now Poe had a pathological hatred of Black people.

DANCE: Yes, but I'm not talking about the racial issue at all.

HARRIS: But Poe had an intuitive thrust that seemed to defeat his own intentions. I mean, take *Arthur Gordon Pym*, which is a horrendous novel, but Poe was intent there on building a world which would have an absolute order, an order that would be invincible. And he also had some notion that slavery was ordained by God – all these curious notions flourished in Poe.

DANCE: Rather typical for his time and background.

HARRIS: But there were other people at that time who were working against this and other people who were protesting against the ground of – but Poe somehow decided, 'Well I have to defend it.' What is strange about *Arthur Gordon Pym* is that the whole novel eventually is a revelation of how obsolescent and decaying that world was, and thus you get these corpses on the ship. The ship is manned by corpses, and the corpse becomes a symbol of a decaying world in which the world is run by robots, the order of things is dying, you know; but there's another thing about Poe – the psychical kinships between the white and black characters. For example, the black cook Seymour, who takes the axe (the mutineer), disguises, conceals within himself, the grandfather, Pym's grandfather, who would have struck him down with an umbrella. Poe can't be too sharp with the conventional grandfather; he has somehow to attack him and pull him down, but he's at liberty to take the black figure and treat him as he likes. But when you look closely, all of this seems to come out of some schizophrenic position in which Poe had begun to move into some ground of being in which he was demolishing the very world he thought he was shoring up. Strangely enough, you find references to Poe running right through Black American literature, even when they are disparaging references, because Poe is at the beginnings of a changed tradition in American fiction which was to be fantastically deepened, of course, by writers who came after, like Toomer and Faulkner and Ellison and so on, but Poe was at the beginnings. Melville was influenced by Poe clearly. I mean the end of *Moby Dick*, the man who is chained when the boat turns over; this of course may have been influenced by *Pym* when the *Ariel* overturns, sinks. But where I differ… I mean I don't know. The point is this, that Poe was a writer who sought to deceive people by attempting to write a lucid kind of narrative that was a deception. His lucidity was deceiving because the thrust of his narrative had to do more with a world in which there were spectres arising from the very abyss of history, but he wanted to present this in a manner that would make it appear almost journalistic. The kind of fiction that I think I write is a fiction which is much more prepared to see the fragmentation of the world and to sense that within that fragmentation lies a kind of creation myth. Now this I don't design for. The decay of the world seems, becomes in the end, absolute in Poe – everything is falling, whereas I believe that creation myths are rooted in catastrophe. One of the marvellous creation myths is the one where the Caribs pursue the Arawaks. The Arawaks run up the food-bearing tree and the Caribs set fire to that tree. The sparks fly up into the sky and become the Pleiades. Now at that moment when the whole world seems to be burning, the world is recreated new, and I think that creation myths have to do with this. When we fall into the trap of taking nature for granted and debasing it, it seems to be pulled out of our grasp as if everything has come to an end, and then at the last moment handed back to us because then we see how marvellous and strange is the world in which we live and how intensely beautiful it is.

DANCE: Are there any other West Indian writers on whose works you would like to comment?

HARRIS: Perhaps I should say something briefly about CLR James. I think that

CLR James is a great West Indian. I am immensely struck by the way he has been able to hold together so many differing philosophies. It is well known that he is a Marxist: he's one of the most astonishing Marxists I have met because he has a vision of European art, of existentialism; he has a deep-seated apprehension of the ancient world; he seems to me someone who has that profound capacity for humanism. In terms of his work, the book on which I have commented and which I admire is *The Black Jacobins* for a number of reasons, some of which have to do with the ways in which one senses that Toussaint is not a figure that can be easily structured. His sympathies and his kind of genius clearly were something that set him apart from most of the people with whom he lived, and it was a tragedy that at that time the whole scene in France was hardening in such a desperate way that they didn't realise how important Toussaint was in the Caribbean. And that book also is a book which brings home to me a very strange portent, and it has to do with the imprisonment of Toussaint and the sense in which one begins to feel that mirrored there in a shadowy way are some of the coming evils that one associates with the concentration camp. I find it astonishing that Toussaint, who was a slave in the Caribbean, is a figure therefore who is pertinent to European history because he manifests in a shadowy way that coming evil – within 'revolutionary' France of all times and places – and brings home to us that the apparent desolation in the Caribbean is much stranger than one thinks; it has strands and threads in it which run into the future in a peculiar way; it's not just a finished story; it's not just something that one could see as a total loss because even there in the figure of the slave, one begins curiously to anticipate something of the events that were to torment the European imagination in the later stage. And in that sense one sees that nothing really is finally and absolutely lost in the psyche of the human imagination. There is the potential for regenerative beauty and there is the potential for nemesis.

CONVERSATION WITH

JOHN HEARNE

John Hearne was born on February 4, 1926, in Montreal, Canada, to Jamaican parents, who returned with him to Jamaica when he was two years old. He grew up and received his early education in Jamaica, leaving at the age of seventeen to serve in the Royal Air Force as an Air Gunner. From 1947 to 1950, he studied in the United Kingdom, first at Edinburgh University and then at London University. Hearne taught at the University of the West Indies since 1962. He was a visiting fellow in Commonwealth Literature at the University of Leeds in 1967, and O'Connor Professor in Literature at Colgate University in Hamilton, New York, in 1969.

His novels include *Voices Under the Window* (1955); *The Faces of Love* (1957); published as *The Eye of the Storm* (1958); *A Stranger at the Gate* (1956); *The Autumn Equinox* (1959); *The Land of the Living* (1961); and *The Sure Salvation* (1981). Using the pseudonym John Morris, Hearne collaborated with Morris Cargill on *Fever Grass* (1969) and *The Candywine Development* (1970). Hearne's short stories have appeared in numerous anthologies of West Indian literature. His play, *Freedom Man*, was produced in Jamaica in 1957, and *The Golden Savage* in London in 1968. He edited *Carifesta Forum: An Anthology of 20 Caribbean Voices* in 1976. An important critic of West Indian literature, he also wrote one of the earliest pieces acclaiming the talent of Derek Walcott *(Focus,* 1960) and one of the first studies of Wilson Harris ('The Fugitive in the Forest', *Journal of Commonwealth Literature*, IV, Dec 1967, pp.99-112). With Rex Nettleford, Hearne co-authored *Our Heritage* (1963), in which Hearne focuses on European and Asian influences in Jamaica. He was at the time of the interview also a regular contributor to the *Gleaner*, where his often acerbic political commentaries have not only sparked heated controversy, but also apparently provoked assassination attempts. Until recently all his fiction has been out of print, until Peepal Tree Press reprinted *Voices Under the Window* in 2005.

John Hearne was awarded the John Llewllyn Rhys Memorial Prize in 1956 and the Institute of Jamaica's Silver Musgrave Medal in 1964.

This interview took place on March 10, 1980. It was the second attempt to interview Mr. Hearne; the tapes of the first interview were unfortunately and inadvertently destroyed.

John Hearne died on December 12, 1994.

DANCE: Will you tell me something about your family background.

HEARNE: Well, both sides (my grandfather's side were planters) came somewhere in the middle eighteenth century; my mother's side were merchants really. They came, again, from the middle of the eighteenth century – except that on my mother's side, they were really journalists, émigrés, Jewish émigrés – from France towards the end of the eighteenth century. They left France just before the Revolution, and they were among a group of free thinkers and the like; I think that's where the writing side comes in.

DANCE: I see. So French…

HEARNE: Well, Jewish, and the usual West Indian mixture: Jewish, Irish, English, and whatever you like.

DANCE: I see. OK, what about the Black heritage?

HEARNE: When that came in one doesn't know. I mean, I have records of my great-great grandfather marrying a free woman of colour about 1820 or thereabouts, and after that, well, it was just the usual [case] of a plantocracy marrying into an ex-landed plantocracy, marrying into a merchant class, gradually, I mean until – my grandfather had the plantation until, oh, I was five or six, and then he sold it and tried to go into business and he didn't do very well; he lost everything.

DANCE: Andrew Fabricus is not something of you, is he? The father there, as I thought about it, and the experiences...

HEARNE: Probably unconsciously, I am not sure.

DANCE: Well, the thing that I was thinking was that his own family background and his family status and that kind of thing sort of parallels, I assume from what you are saying, yours?

HEARNE: Something like, I should imagine. It wasn't certainly a conscious basing on it; it was the background that I knew.

DANCE: Umn-humn. When did you begin writing?

HEARNE: Seriously, I suppose I began at about seven. I always was writing, but in any real terms, I mean that are not just said in fun, when I went to Edinburgh after the War and I became assistant editor of *The Student*.

DANCE: But Jamaica College you attended here? Right?

HEARNE: Yes.

DANCE: There you wrote short stories and that kind of...

HEARNE: Well, towards the end of my time at Jamaica College, before I went off to the War, I found that increasingly my English essays in the senior year were no longer essays but were taking more and more a fictional form in which, whatever the theme was, I would attempt, instead of dealing with it as an essay, to turn it into fiction.

DANCE: Were there any particular instructors who might have encouraged you along these lines there?

HEARNE: Oh yes, yes. There was no question that the atmosphere of Jamaica College at the time – this was back in 1941, '42, '43 – there was an exceptionally imaginative group of teachers in the humane studies, in English and history, who actively encouraged, not only one's writing in that fashion, although you know I was warned that for the purposes of passing exams you would have to write in the conventional fashion – for class work I was encouraged; and, of course, I was given almost endless freedom to read. As one became an older boy, after fifteen, sixteen, there were whole periods when I was just allowed to slope off into the library and read as I pleased.

DANCE: Yes. Were there any major influences that you are aware of on your own development as a writer, in terms of other writers perhaps, that you could tell me something about?

HEARNE: Again, one has to sound a little pretentious, or a little imitative of the only answer there is to that, or the only two answers I know that are really satisfying. Faulkner, who is the American writer with whom I feel the greatest affinity, said that, 'Writers don't learn from life; they learn from other writers.' And Hemingway, who began a list once for an interview and then suddenly said, 'Well, where do I stop?' And then I realised also that Hemingway was right when he said, you know, 'I have learnt as much from the great painters, as I have learnt from the great writers' – not as much, but certainly learned invaluable lessons. For structure I have learnt, I think, from Mozart and Beethoven and Bach, how to fit that iron frame out to the scale around your idea. But influences, direct influences: let's say, Defoe when I was young, when I was about twelve; Jane Austen, oddly enough, when I was about sixteen; and then the discovery of Hemingway when I was about eighteen; Eliot when I was about eighteen; and then the many important discoveries of Conrad and Faulkner when I was a little older, but I think that perhaps the real, insofar as any writer can trace an influence, the discovery of Flaubert, Stendhal, and Tolstoy when I was about twenty-one or twenty-two.

DANCE: Let me ask you another question. George Lamming, who like most critics, recognises that you are 'a first-class technician' (I am quoting here)... has attacked you for your failure to picture and appreciate the peasant sensibility [*The Pleasures of Exile*]. He somewhat modified that comment incidentally when I interviewed him, but it is a fairly representative comment of several reactions to your work. What is your response to that?

HEARNE: Well, what can one respond to that? I think that it's a false comment. When I say false, I don't mean it is a deliberate lie; I think that it's a failure of appreciation. I think that I am pretty good at the peasant sensibility. I will admit that I have never done, except for a couple of short stories, sustained work from the peasant point of view. George did a lecture up here once, a very good one, several years ago, in which he compared his handling of a riot and mine: his in *Castle* and mine in *Voices*, in which he said the point of view was different. That is quite accurate, and in point of fact it was very useful to me. But I am not going to pretend that I can see into the world through a peasant's eye any more than any man of my background could. I can relate and I hope I can portray him with truth. I hope I can – let me put it this way – lie with sufficient integrity that when the world has to be seen from his point of view that I am lying with truth. But I am not interested in portraying the world from a peasant's point of view.

DANCE: OK. Is there even a slight reservation, such as I think I noticed in *Land of the Living*, when you choose to see Beatrice and Heneky through the eyes of the narrator? You know it strikes me immediately as a rather unusual choice because the narrator is a world removed from them because of the racial and the class situation; and he is, I think, a rather weak character where they are very strong characters, and we somehow feel that he is not capable of telling us everything there is to tell us about those strong people; and yet you give those people to us through him.

HEARNE: Well, the reason for that was that Mahler, Heneky and Bernice in *The Land of the Living* are all, in their particular way, the dispossessed. Mahler because he was a Jew, a late '30s Jew; Heneky because he is a bewildered man looking for cultural assurance; and Bernice because she is a woman of great strength of – and I think, goodness of – moral foundation, and she is a woman in a society that has no place for somebody with her intelligence and her morality because of her sex.

DANCE: But also because of the colour?

HEARNE: To a much lesser extent... Because if she had had the ruthlessness, the self-seeking and utter selfishness of say Rachel Ascom in *The Faces of Love*, she would have been a very big woman. Her colour I don't think has much to do with it at all. It is because she is – she wants to be a decent person and she is dispossessed because of her sex.

DANCE: But – I don't want to argue the point with you – but it did seem to me that that was one reason that Stefan couldn't consider a permanent relationship with her.

HEARNE: No. I don't think it was to do with colour at all; it wouldn't have mattered to Stefan at all. What separates them there, of course, is her lack of education.

DANCE: OK. Perhaps it is more significant.

HEARNE: Very significant, because Stefan is bright enough to know that, what do you talk about five years after they are married? There is no way that Bernice can ever be the companion that he needs. After five years of loving is over and he would now have to establish that parity of intellectual companionship which she can never learn in time...

DANCE: Well he selects a mate who seems to me even weaker. She may be able to talk if she is sober enough to talk, but I mean, is that a very wise selection?

HEARNE: I don't think it is a terribly wise selection and I don't know – that may end in disaster too. He probably will leave her for somebody like you, somebody who would be able to talk to him on equal terms. Because you are quite right, in five years the woman that he does select is going to be something of a bore.

DANCE: OK. Let me ask you about the place where you set many of your novels, Cayuna. Why did you decide not to call it Jamaica since it becomes pretty obviously Jamaica?

HEARNE: Really because – a function of size. If you are writing about a place this size you tend to inhibit the imagination by sticking strictly to the geographical fact. By creating a Cayuna I could import from other West Indian islands certain aspects of life. I could in a sense make my own Yoknapatawpha, where I could play around certain characters, certain geographical features and the like, which gave me not so much a license, but it gave me a frame that I could fill in.

DANCE: But yet within that frame you, like Faulkner, in Yoknapatawpha, stuck pretty closely, didn't you, to the actual geographical...

HEARNE: Yes, one keeps fairly closely to a picture, but I liked the idea of a place that was of the place, was of the region, but was purely of my imagination. In point of fact, I was the first one to do it. Vidia did it afterwards in creating... What was it? San Cristobal? Or George did it...

DANCE: Lamming who does it, yes.

HEARNE: But he did it after me. Nobody else had thought of an imaginary West Indian island, and then all of a sudden I saw everybody was creating imaginary West Indian islands. Wilson Harris doesn't have to do it because he is dealing with what is pretty well a continent. He has two million square miles of jungle to float around in. I don't.

DANCE: Let me get back to Rachel Ascom whom you mentioned a little while ago. She is a real vixen, but as a woman reader I was really impressed to see a female wielding the kind of power that she wields in that novel, a kind of economic and political and sexual domination of the males which is most unusual. How did you happen to create this kind of woman character? You don't find many in West Indian literature written by males.

HEARNE: Well Rachel Ascom really was created out of me. I mean I imagined what I – since all of us have a lot of male and certainly any male that writes has a lot of woman in him – I said to myself, what if I were Black and a woman and clawing my way up in a society dominated by male whites of, well, an education; how would I have done it? Particularly if I were a handsome woman who liked making love; and I just sort of dug her straight out of me.

DANCE: So she comes straight out of a male sensibility? I know, obviously, she is your creation and yet even as you are creating her you see her as coming out of the male sensibility rather than some effort at a female sensibility?

HEARNE: Well, I don't know how much she sounds male. I tried to write myself, the male part of me, out of her.

DANCE: Is she a woman such as any woman you have ever known?

HEARNE: I know dozens of her.

DANCE: Really?

HEARNE: Any higgler down King Street. Any higgler that you see on King Street that is keeping a man and twelve children on her capacity for enterprise, entrepreneurship and the like, is – there is a lot of Rachel Ascom in them.

DANCE: OK but that's on a different level, and generally a woman moving in a professional field dominated by men would have to – could not assert those kinds of drives; she would have to use her femininity. But Rachel manages…

HEARNE: She manages, yes, because she is more ruthless than most. And she just happens to have an exceptionally high IQ. And she makes it, I think, largely because she is the first one that has risked it, and it's the element of surprise I think, as much as anything, by which she takes her society. But I don't know what would have happened if there had been two Ascoms competing for the same position at the same time. They probably would have both got clobbered. But because she was the only one, then she made it.

DANCE: Did you expect that she would be viewed by your readers as an exceptionally unattractive person because of her ruthlessness? I tended to think as I read the novel that I liked her more than you intended me to like her?

HEARNE: I like – no, well I am very fond of Rachel. Again, most of my themes are the themes of the dispossessed or… those seeking a sort of justice that history has denied them – one way or another. And it is impossible for me not to sympathise with Rachel. Her ending made me a little hesitant; it may have been sentimental, and yet in a way I hoped that it was not so much a self-sacrifice as a final assertion that she could do that too – when she puts herself between a lover's bullet and another lover's body, I mean, she is really a very – she is a desperately lonely woman and she is, I suppose, you know, in a philosophic sense, an existential character, who has come without knowing it to the end of a meaning of her life. She has done all the things that she set out to do and ultimately they are not terribly satisfactory. I suppose the self-sacrifice at the end is really a proof that she can do anything that a man can do or that a person can do, just as well as any other person.

DANCE: But you make it seem so deliberate when you talk about it rather than almost instinctive as it must have been.

HEARNE: I don't know how instinctive…

DANCE: I guess with her any act would be to a degree deliberate.

HEARNE: I think so. I don't think that Rachel ever made a totally instinctive act in her life, except to know, except the instinctive act of knowing that she was not going to remain a country girl and bear eight children for some slob of a farmer.

DANCE: With her I had something of the same reaction that I had to Beatrice and Heneky. She seems such a strong woman to be viewed through the eyes of a jealous lover whose view I think we must instinctively distrust.

HEARNE: Umn-Humn. Yes. Quite.

DANCE: Again, I suppose even his name Fabricus, might have suggested it. Did it consciously suggest that he might be fabricating?

HEARNE: No. Although – I don't know. You may be right, unconsciously I may have just picked that fact; it may have just occurred to me. Now that you say it, it makes sense.

DANCE: But undoubtedly he is jealous, he is rejected and he is hurt. He doesn't seem, you know, a small, bitter character, but yet I think we must believe that he could not give her full justice. So why do we see her through him? Why did you choose to have him show us Rachel when his vision cannot do justice completely to her?

HEARNE: Because he is in a position to know her better than anyone else. He has the knowledge of her, where she began; he is not as possessed with her need for self-promotion. Fabricus wants to restore a lost position which his kind have inherited, or had inheritance of over two hundred years, which the family of his father has lost. But it is in many ways a modest ambition. The other lover, Rygin, although without Rachel's total disregard for other human beings, is too much like her; he couldn't see her.

DANCE: He couldn't see her. He couldn't see her for what she really was?

HEARNE: No, because he would have to be looking at himself. Fabricus can see, I think, with sufficient detachment despite his jealousy, despite his sense of betrayal. He can see a human being in the round, in the way that Rygin can't see and which the Englishman, the English editor that comes out, can't see because he is mesmerised. He is a weak, not a weak, but a gentle character who is not prepared for that sort of raw emotional power and he can only see that he has found a protector.

DANCE: Does Rygin have a meaning – the name?

HEARNE: That was chosen purely from a famous gunman that we had here many many years ago. I was away at the War at the time.

DANCE: The subject of *The Harder They Come*.

HEARNE: No. He, well, he was something a bit more than that. He was a bit more of a Mafia type. He was a real toughie. Mark you, Perry Henzell did base a lot of the events of *The Harder They Come* on the way that Rygin died.

DANCE: And you actually were thinking of him when you selected the…

HEARNE: No, no, I just selected the name, because it seemed a nice name. And also in a way because the Rygin of my book could have become a Rygin, the sort of Rygin that shot God knows how many policemen and who got himself finally shot to death on one of the quays off the harbour there. Had he not had that creative streak in him that he wanted to be a builder instead of a taker.

DANCE: Barrie Davies in an essay on your novels, which was published in *The Islands in Between*, calls your scene of the hurricane in *Faces of Love*, quote, 'one of the most powerful scenes in Caribbean fiction' [p.115]. And I certainly agree with him, though sometimes I felt that the scene was not central to the story. Did the scene grow out of any personal experience? It's beautifully done, and it's hard to believe it's fully imaginative.

HEARNE: Well that is a scene that oddly enough did come out of an adult experience. We had that monster hurricane in 1951. In 1951 we had a terrific hurricane and I used a lot of it.

DANCE: Were you in danger? Were you caught in any situation that...

HEARNE: Well, my entire roof went in one second and zinc was flying around. I was in the country and I had a house down in town, an old-fashioned house, and every shingle went with one – in a split second – when that wind just fell on the house and you could hear the nails scream as they were pulled out of the shingles, and all of a sudden I was just looking up at a black sky and a lot of rain, and I could see zinc flying across the yard by the lightning flashes and I could see an enormous tree that was suddenly turned upside down before I got the family down into – luckily it was a two storey house, and we went under a table – in point of fact, it was a large mahogany table, in the dining room, and just figured that the walls would stand and that we were going to get very wet. Well, we didn't as a matter of fact, because the table was big enough that it was a roof. The wind was fickle and it didn't – although it grew steadily – it didn't after that first monumental gust, it didn't do more than just blow rain across the roofless house and drip water through the upstairs floor.

DANCE: I wanted to ask you about Walcott. I notice *O Babylon* mentions that you contributed to the text of the play.

HEARNE: No, I didn't contribute to the text.

DANCE: Maybe it wasn't contributed, but he says something about your influence.

HEARNE: No, that was... we are very close friends, Walcott and I. He wanted to know something about (what shall I say?) the ethos, the vision of the Rastafari movement and we had a very long talk on a Saturday morning, about two or three hours and then another long talk, and then another long talk, in which I gave him my version of what lay behind the social, cultural pressures that had – I wouldn't say forced – but had generated the Rastafari movement from the '30s on. So much for Lamming's concept that I don't have a peasant's vision. Because although it isn't strictly speaking a peasant's vision, because the Rastafari movement was essentially an urban lower class. It wasn't big, when it started, you could hardly call it a proletariat, it was the first of the dispossessed peasants.

DANCE: And how did you come to know so much about the movement?

HEARNE: Well, I don't know a great deal; I mean I have met them. They come to see me and I chat. I go to some of their meetings. I am not as knowledgeable on it in an academic sense, as say Rex Nettleford, but I did have I suppose certain intuitions about it in a parable sense you know – a fable sense, in a mythic sense, that Derek must have found useful.

DANCE: I see. When did you meet him? When he was a student here?

HEARNE: I had come back from the War and from University in Scotland and England, 1950, and he was then – I was teaching for a couple of years across at Jamaica College, and he was a student and I met him then.

DANCE: Was he then writing?

HEARNE: Oh yes.

DANCE: And did you have any kind of association with him as a writer, I mean did he bring you manuscripts? I think I saw something about your encouraging him as a developing writer or your recognising his talent early or something like that?

HEARNE: Well, I certainly was the first one to put on record that he was the only poet that had yet emerged from the English-speaking Caribbean, and up to a few years ago he was the only poet that I really considered worth writing about. I wrote that, you know.

DANCE: When did you make this judgement – after how many works of his?

HEARNE: I think it must have been in '59. I did it for one of the Edna Manley's *Focus* magazines. And I said that he is the only authentic poetic voice that had yet emerged, because the others I consider… I mean the rest, I consider quite tasteless, including Claude McKay.

DANCE: Including Martin Carter?

HEARNE: Martin Carter is a good protest writer in the Mayakovsky tradition. I don't consider him a poet in Derek's class. And now, on the other hand, obviously Brathwaite and Morris are authentic poets.

DANCE: But had they published very much in…

HEARNE: No they hadn't published at all then, or hardly, I had hardly seen anything of them.

DANCE: You wrote a highly critical review of the works of one of your former colleagues, Orlando Patterson?

HEARNE: Orlando is a brilliant sociologist, there is no question; he is one of the top minds in an extremely difficult discipline. And Orlando should stick to *sociology*. As a novelist, I wouldn't even – I only wrote it, really I would never write another review like that because I only review books that I like or that I think are worthy of the real rigour that one should bring to another man's work. And I don't think that he is a novelist at all.

DANCE: Do you think his works can be considered important sociological novels?

HEARNE: I don't know what you mean by the sociological novel, I honestly don't. I mean you have a novel or you have a work of sociology. Now why on earth Orlando wastes that brilliant talent that he has in writing fiction that is embarrassingly bad when he could put all that knowledge, all that talent, all that energy, all that magnificent mind to making a really first rate sociological monograph. I am not even asking for a big fat book. But it's read because it is exotic, I suppose. I don't consider it, any of Orlando's novels, any more of a novel than that fellow who wrote *To Sir With Love*.

DANCE: Braithwaite.

HEARNE: The other Braithwaite. Yes. It has dialogue and it has what passes for characters, but I can't consider it a work of art.

DANCE: What [Caribbean] writers/novelists do you consider as making significant contributions these days? Who are the more important ones? You mentioned Naipaul I think.

HEARNE: Naipaul is probably the most important except that I would – probably in terms of sheer volume – Jean Rhys, I think, wrote the best West Indian novel.

DANCE: Really, which one is that? *Wide Sargasso Sea*?

HEARNE: *Wide Sargasso Sea*. Yes. Wilson Harris… invaluable. Lamming, if he never writes another but *In the Castle of My Skin* will be read a hundred years from now. That is the most beautiful…

DANCE: May I assume that you think his later works are not as good?

HEARNE: I think that they are not as good.

DANCE: OK. Others?

HEARNE: Who am I naming?

DANCE: Selvon?

HEARNE: Selvon I find a deeply tender, a deeply truthful minor writer.

DANCE: Reid?

HEARNE: Reid. Well, you know he tried a thing which was a very brave thing to do in *New Day*. Nobody else had tried it and it's all right in the sense that it is a very scrupulous and conscientious work, but it's hardly a work of art. I think that his *The Leopard* is one of the most vastly overrated books. I can't find a single redeeming feature in it.

DANCE: Have you read *The Jamaicans*?

HEARNE: Yes [breathlessl! And the less said about that the better.

DANCE: O.K. The other writers you…

HEARNE: Let's see. Let's start with Guyana. Harris and the other Williams who wrote *Other Leopards*.

DANCE: You like his work? Have you read *The Third Temptation*?

HEARNE: No, I haven't. Naipaul. Michael Anthony.

DANCE: Ah, you like Michael Anthony. Have you read Earl Lovelace?

HEARNE: Earl Lovelace, yes. Well I think that Michael Anthony, his studies of childhood, are quite beautiful. They are not as profound as George Lamming's. George's singular contribution to the fiction of the West Indies is that he is the only one of us that has really come to terms with childhood, and for that alone George deserves you know a place at the top table.

DANCE: Michael has not?

HEARNE: Michael, yes, but not as deeply as George. Tender, yes, beautifully done, *Green Days By The River* and *The Games Were Coming*. Yes, beautifully done but for sheer weight of observation, for a society seen through the camera eye of a child, George is beyond compare and he is the only one that has taken the risk.

DANCE: Have you read Merle Hodge's *Crick Crack Monkey*?

HEARNE: Yes, and it's, you know, it's competent and the like, but if I hadn't read it I wouldn't have missed anything. Then who else? Jean Rhys, of course; Wilson as the true original, you know, Wilson is so difficult a man to come to grips with, and I was very glad that I was the first to do a serious critical study on him, in a short essay.

DANCE: Did you want to comment on Salkey?

HEARNE: Salkey began well. His *Escape to an Autumn Pavement* was a fine beginning.

DANCE: *A Quality of Violence*, I think [was his first novel].

HEARNE: *A Quality of Violence*? I think *Escape to an Autumn Pavement* was a better book. When I say a fine beginning, I think that that was Salkey coming into a splendid maturity. And then God knows what happened to him, as he has gone all political on us. But a considerable book. There were some good short stories written by the early ones like James and Alfred Mendes. But what I am talking about now, I consider the real novelists. Claude McKay, for my money, wrote two good books. *Home to Harlem* and *Banjo*. I think that *Banana Bottom* – that is a book I won't even teach. I refuse.

DANCE: Is it too sentimental?

HEARNE: I think it is a disastrous book. I don't know why Kenneth Ramchand gives it the place he does in his study. And they still teach it over here and I just – if they ever ask me to reflect on it, I say, 'No, why should I have to say unpleasant things about a man whom I respect so profoundly for a major talent.' The most neglected and unknown writer from the West Indies of course was Eric Walrond whose *Tropic Death* was republished the other day, and who I think had he not gone off into that mysterious private pilgrimage in the mid 1920s when he just lit out on a Guggenheim scholarship from New York and was never seen again.

DANCE: That volume that has just been republished is the only one that I know of his. Did he do another?

HEARNE: I understand there are other manuscripts, but I have seen critical pieces by him, but something – I don't know what – happened to Walrond. He vanished into the Cartier-Bresson, Picasso, Cocteau crowd; he was in the French Resistance, in point of fact, and only surfaced after the War in England when he suddenly was introduced to his daughter, who had never seen him. I believe there are some manuscripts that the widow has, which she won't release.

DANCE: How do you know this? I have never read any of what you are telling me about, meeting the daughter in England and all that kind of thing?

HEARNE: No, it's never been published. I know that because when the daughter, who was a colleague of mine here... Who were the successors to Boni and Liveright, the publishers? And when they wanted to bring out *Tropic Death* again, she had the only known copy of the original, because her mother in a fit of rage had burned about a hundred copies years and years before, and she brought me this literally worm-eaten copy from 1926 or 1925 when it was published. I had never heard of the man. And when I read this, I said, 'Well,' I said, 'this is astonishing!' ... he could have been perhaps the considerable figure, first figure of... he certainly is as an artist so far ahead of McKay. McKay is a brilliant and courageous pioneer; *Banjo*, as I say, and *Home to Harlem* are works of considerable merit, but the rage and troubling quality of Walrond's imagination – we are dealing with a very different level of artist. And God knows why he disappeared. Perhaps he just couldn't let that imagination loose in the sort of society that he inherited in 1936. I don't know. Nobody has heard anything definite about him; all I know about him is what I picked up from word of mouth.

DANCE: I see. That's very interesting because it certainly adds to what little I knew about him, though I appreciate that one volume very much too. Speaking of writers in exile, that's often an issue of great import to many Caribbean writers since many of them do go into exile and many of them used to apologise for it. But recently, it's been interesting to me that as I have talked with Caribbean writers in exile, many of them are no longer apologising for being in exile. As a matter of fact some of them are suggesting that their exile has had a positive effect on their writing. I remember that Davies essay I quoted from earlier on your works. He ends the essay by saying something about the fact that the West Indies provides its own danger of intellectual isolation. And one person has suggested to me during my studies that perhaps you, Mr. Hearne, have had such a traumatic kind of relationship with Jamaica that exile might have been better for you. Has living in this society and being so closely concerned – I have lived here for a while and I read your articles in the *Gleaner*, and I remember a period when you actually were afraid of physical harm – has being here been so traumatic for you that it has had a negative impact?

HEARNE: I wouldn't say negative. I had written five books and three entertainments in – up to a certain period. Five serious books. I no longer was interested in doing the sort of work that culminated in *The Land of the Living*. I have a feeling that it was an instinct that brought me back for a period of the sort of involvement, sort of purely commentary writing that I did for sixteen years. I have come to the end of that now. I mean, I think that my latest work, which should come out during the next nine to twelve months, is certainly a very different book, and I have three or four more of that type to do.

DANCE: Three or four more that you have actually begun working on, or that you just…

HEARNE: Well one of them has to be begun next month; it won't wait any longer. I was just so exhausted after this one, that I couldn't, didn't have the strength to do it. So it [remaining in Jamaica] could have had… I don't know, I don't know. Certainly, I don't know whether it was realistic in these terms to put the West Indian writer into the specialist category that you would do with another society, maybe it was necessary for me to stay here. I could have stayed abroad and yet something called me back. I got involved. I think I know a little more about a lot of things now for being here, and getting involved in the way that I did. I won't know for another four or five years. I have three books to finish over the next six years. If they are as good as I think they are going to be – then, I'll know it was a good thing for me to come back. On the other hand, if I had stayed abroad – who knows, I may have been better. I neither apologise for exile nor justify return; I mean it is really a matter of what one needed emotionally. I have grown bored abroad simply because I had established the sort of reputation where most of my companions and friends were writers, painters, actors and artists, you know, the art world generally, and it is a very limited world you know – whether it's in London or New York. You tend to be just chatting shop the whole time and it's a great temptation to talk to nobody else but the sort of people you meet at publishers' cocktail parties. So, I don't know. Everybody must make up their mind on the fact of exile or not.

DANCE: And you are not dissatisfied with the decision?

HEARNE: I am not dissatisfied with the decision. Perhaps my temperament needed for a good period the sort of social and political involvement with a new society coming out that I have had to have over the last few years, over the last sixteen years. And certainly the new book I have has nothing to do with Jamaican or West Indian politics.

DANCE: Oh really?

HEARNE: No.

DANCE: Well, thank you very much.

CONVERSATION WITH

CLR JAMES

Cyril Lionel Robert James was born into a middle-class family on January 4, 1901, in
Tunapuna, Trinidad. He received a scholarship to Queen's Royal College, where he
later taught. With Alfred H Mendes, he founded and edited *Trinidad*, the magazine out
of which grew *The Beacon*. In August 1929 James wrote the novel *Minty Alley*, based
on his own observations and experiences in a boarding house in which he was living.
When he went to England in 1932 he took the novel with him; and in 1935 he
mentioned it to his publisher, who insisted upon seeing it and promptly brought it out
in 1936. In England James worked as a cricket correspondent for the *Manchester
Guardian* and the *Glasgow Herald*, and he became active in British politics. He served
as editor of *Flight*, the newspaper of the Revolutionary Socialist League, and of
International African Opinion, the publication of the International African Service
Bureau. During this period he met and became friendly with several of the young
Africans who were to play a significant role in the future liberation and political life
of African nations, including Jomo Kenyatta and Kwame Nkrumah. In 1938 James
migrated to the United States, where he involved himself in political activity on behalf
of American Blacks. In 1952 he was imprisoned on Ellis Island, and in 1953 he was
expelled from the USA. He returned to England where he remained for the next five
years, working with the Pan-Africanist movement and visiting Africa. In 1958 he went
to Trinidad and joined his friend and former student, Dr. Eric Williams, in the
People's National Movement (PNM). As a result of basic political differences with
Dr. Williams, James left Trinidad just before its independence and returned to
England in 1962.

James spent most of the 1970s living in the United States and teaching at Federal
City College in Washington, DC. He later moved to London where he died in 1989.

In addition to the novel, *Minty Alley*; the play, *Toussaint L'Ouverture* (1936); *Mariners,
Renegades and Castaways: The Study of Melville and the World We Live In* (1953), (written
while he was interned at Ellis Island); *Wilson Harris: A Philosophical Approach* (1965);
James wrote the end-word for Harris's *Tradition, the Writer, and Society;* and several short
stories and essays. James has written a host of political, historical, social and critical
works as well as sports commentaries. Among them are *Cricket and I* (the autobiography
of LN Constantine, 1933); *The Life of Captain Cipriani* (1933); *The Case for West-Indian
Self-Government* (1933); *World Revolution 1917-1936: The Rise and Fall of the Communist
International* (1937); *A History of Negro Revolt* (1938); *The Black Jacobins* (1938); *Notes on the
Dialectic* (1948); *State Capitalism and World Revolution* (1950); *Facing Reality* (1958); *Modern
Politics* (1960, reissued in paperback as *A History of Pan African Revolt*); *Party Politics in the
West Indies* (1961); *Marxism and the Intellectuals* (1962); *Beyond a Boundary* (1963); *Lenin,
Trotsky and the Vanguard Party: A Contemporary View* (1964); *Notes on Dialectics: Hegel and
Marxism* (1971); *Nkrumah and the Ghana Revolution* (1977); *Fighting Racism in World War
II* (1980); and *Walter Rodney and the Question of Power* (1982).

Collections of his work and letters include *The Future in the Present: Selected Writings*
(1971); *Spheres of Existence: Selected Writings* (1980); *CLR James's 80th Birthday Lectures*
(1984; lectures delivered in 1981 at Kingsway Princeton College in London); *At the
Rendezvous of Victory: Selected Writings* (1984); *Every Cook Can Govern: and What Is*

Happening Every Day: 1985 Conversations (1986); *CLR James: His Life and Work* (1986; ed. Paul Buhle); *Essay* [sic] *and Lectures by CLR James: A Tribute* (1989); *The CLR James Reader* (1992; ed. Anna Grimshaw); *CLR James and Revolutionary Marxism: Selected Writings 1939-1949* (1994; ed. Scott McLemee and Paul Le Blanck); *CLR James: A Political Biography* (1995; Kent Worcester), *CLR James and the 'Negro Question'* (1996; ed. Scott McLemee); *Special Delivery: The Letters of CLR James to Constance Webb, 1939-1948* (1996; ed. Anna Grimshaw) and *Letters from London* (2003); and *A Majestic Innings: Writings on Cricket* (2006). Studies of James's life and work include Paul Buhle, *CLR James: The Artist as Revolutionary* (1988); Grant Farred, *Rethinking CLR James* (1996); Tony Bogues, *Caliban's Freedom: Early Political Thought of CLR James* (1997) Farrukh Dhondy, *CLR James: A Life* (2001); Frank Rosengarten, *Urbane Revolutionary: CLR James and the Struggle for a New Society* (2007) and Dave Renton, *CLR James: Cricket's Philosopher King* (2007).

Also of interest is *A Conversation with CLR James* (1983, videocassette).

This interview took place on March 18, 1980 at James's home in San Fernando, Trinidad.

DANCE: Certainly one of the most significant periods in West Indian literature was that period in the late '20s and early '30s when, as Ken Ramchand puts it, 'in Trinidad... there was a concentration of literary and artistic talent such as had never happened anywhere in the islands before' [*The West Indian Novel and Its Background*, p.63]. Of that group that met to exchange ideas and to discuss social, political and literary matters you are now perhaps the best known. Would you tell me a little about those times and about how the group of you came together?

JAMES: We came together by accident. I was interested in literature and music, and I met a man named Mendes, Alfred Mendes. There is no discussing that period without knowing the importance that Mendes had in it. He was Portuguese. He had been to England, he had been through the world, but he was fanatically interested in literature and in music. We became friends. He naturally, [being] a Portuguese, was white and I wasn't, but that didn't prevent us becoming very intimate. We saw each other practically every day. We read books and magazines. What I read I would show him and what he had noted he would show to me. There were others around. There was a man called [H McD] Carpenter, who was a violinist and took a great interest in the analysis of the music that we bought. There was another man called Canton Comma, who came around with us. Music – he was very much interested in music and he was a very fine musician. There were one or two other people around. There was a man called [Algernon] Wharton, who was here for a while, who had made contact with a great many literary people in England. He was a lawyer. But chiefly Mendes and I were the centres of this business and we did the two first [issues of] *Trinidad*, and there was an awful row about them. But something happened that was quite important about them. I had written a story called 'La Divina Pastora' and that was published here [Trinidad] and a man called Edward J O'Brien used to publish a series of books every year, *The Best British Short Stories*, and in 1928 O'Brien published my story, 'La Divina Pastora', which had been published in one of the local magazines;

you know, we produced this and that. And he said it was one of the best short stories of 1928. I am not concerned with whether it *was* one of the best or not, but what I want you to know [is that] that gave us a recognition and people had a respect and concern for us; and then one of Mendes's stories was published the next year I think. Thus, we as men of letters and literary persons were not only working at home – and very much concerned – any people who wanted to know something about literature came to us. Anybody who came to the island, well, he was told it was James and Mendes... But that O'Brien should publish our stories in his yearly collection, that made a tremendous impact.

DANCE: I understand that 'Triumph' aroused quite a bit of controversy as well?

JAMES: Well, it aroused quite a bit of controversy and it is one of the best things I have ever written.

DANCE: Right.

JAMES: Why I am concerned about 'Triumph' and *Minty Alley* today, among other things, is I have done a lot of work in politics and literature too, but chiefly on politics, and my politics has not been confined to the Black people. It has been an international situation and I have done work on Marxism and Leninism, but I am very fond of 'Triumph' and *Minty Alley* because that shows that, while I was studying in the Caribbean all these advanced writers and went on in England to go further, the ordinary people meant a lot to me. Otherwise I couldn't have written those, so 'La Divina Pastora', 'Triumph', and *Minty Alley* represent my concern with ordinary people, quite ordinary people who were not members of any union, were not politically advanced, but there they were, and I took that to England and found that ordinary people were in trade unions and labour parties, etc., but my interest in the common people came from there. I took it with me to England and that's what those stories represent for me.

DANCE: OK. Could you tell me what were some of the issues of great controversy then? Was it simply that you had pictured in an unapologetic way this life of the yard folk? Is that why people were so upset?

JAMES: Well, no, people were so upset because we were writing in the tradition of the thirties. That is to say, literature was more and more free; people could deal with what they like. There was James Joyce had written *Ulysses*. DH Lawrence was writing freely, and people were writing freely, so we did the same in Trinidad. We wrote freely. And the life of the middle classes, to which I belonged, my father, mother and the rest of them, was very, very restrained, because my father was a young civil servant, he had a good job and they did nothing out of the way, nothing out of place. But in Shakespeare, and Aeschylus, and Dante and all the people I was reading, things were happening, and things were happening among these people, but as far as my father and my mother and the rest of them, nothing was happening: they went to work every day, my mother went to church and there wasn't much there. So that I... I saw what was happening around me. And the great passions and violence which was in all the literature, the classical literature, there it was among these people. I believe... I must have had some instinct that they mattered. I had been reading a lot of Thackeray – *Vanity Fair* – in which Thackeray was attacking the aristocracy. He wasn't attacking them on behalf of the common people, but those people up there, those who are ruling, well his usual attack was against them. So I was reading *Vanity Fair* as a boy of seven and eight, and I got the idea that, well, people had an attitude to those up there. And, well, I grew up and then it was I *saw* those people. That was more or less what I was doing and what Mendes was doing. And we got together and we were fanatically interested in literature and in music.

DANCE: Yes, yes. [interruption] OK, you were talking – I am sorry, go on.

JAMES: No, tell me what you were saying. I want to tell you something about *Minty Alley.* Now you ask me your question, but then remind me about *Minty Alley.*

DANCE: OK. We are going to talk about that very definitely. You were talking about some of the freedom of expression that you were seeing in writers around you, as you looked around the world when you started writing here, and I wanted to ask you if you were at the time familiar with the work going on in the United States among the Black Renaissance writers who were just…

JAMES: Now I regret to say the Black Renaissance writers did not appeal very much to Mendes and me, brought up in the British traditions. I believe I have always been conscious of [the fact that] I am a Black man and I know the situation of Black people in a very general way. But the British tradition did not tell us very much, and I used to read Marcus Garvey's magazine, *Negro World,* and I used to read the *Crisis* by DuBois. I read those regularly to keep in touch, but I didn't, I didn't keep *much* in touch with them. I only got in touch with them when I went to England and later when I went to the United States. I was aware of them and so on, but there was not much of that. I was more interested it so happened – my education – in French literature of the 17th century. Molière, Corneille, Racine and those were very familiar to me, and not the people in the Black Renaissance. I knew their work, I knew a poem by…

DANCE: Langston Hughes perhaps?

JAMES: Oh I knew Langston Hughes's work. I knew…

DANCE: Countee Cullen?

JAMES: Countee Cullen, I read them, but around me there wasn't much upon that. We were oriented towards the British completely and all of our education was that way.

DANCE: OK. In an interview in Texas you mentioned the fact that you went to live in a household very much like the one that is at the centre of *Minty Alley.* Is that what motivated that novel, your experiences there?

JAMES: No. No, I wouldn't say so. I went to live in a house and I took a room there and then later there were two rooms in the front of the house and I took those two. I was very comfortable. That I should get a room for myself, that was important. What happened in *Minty Alley* was going on around me, and I was very much interested in it. For the first time I had made that direct contact with people whom I had had nothing to do with. My father, the Black middle-class people – they kept away from that sort of person, you see. So I saw what was happening. It was very dramatic. The dramatic conclusion I put in. But the characters were there and most of the characters in *Minty Alley* are actual persons whom I developed. Actual people, and the dramatic episode, the most important, in which the woman went away and married the man who had been living with the woman of the house, all that happened, and I saw it, and I worked it out. Now I want to tell you something about that. It will take a little time but it's worth it. At that time I was hard at work practicing the art of fiction. I was reading all that I could get, and there was plenty to get about fiction. I was reading critiques of the art of fiction, and there were many of them published. Mendes and I were reading them. I had written a story which had been published in *The Best Short Stories*. I had written stories which had created a tremendous disturbance. It didn't trouble *me*, of that I am certain. So I sat down one day and I saw all this going on, and I said, 'Well, this is an interesting episode, interesting from what we can see, so I will write a novel about it.' And I wrote *Minty Alley*, at the rate of a chapter a day one August. Some time, about the August of '29, I wrote this thing at the rate of a chapter a day.

DANCE: That's unbelievable.

JAMES: Chapter a day. And when I was finished (I wrote it on red paper), and when I was finished, I showed it to my friend Mendes. He told me, 'That's very fine, James; I like them good.' And I took them and put them away. That was some work – I was practicing the art of fiction. So at the time I put it among my papers and the time came for me to go to England in 1932, and I took it with my papers to England. I got to know my publisher Warburg Levy fairly well, really well, and one day about 1935, August 1935, I happened to be talking to him and I mentioned a novel I wrote. He said, 'James, you have written a novel?' I said, 'Yes.' He said, 'You have no right to have put it down.' He said, 'Let me see it.' I said, 'What do you want to see it for? It is something that I wrote just to see how I could write and how I could practice writing.' He said, 'Let me see it.' So I went home and I got the papers and I gave them to him. He told me, 'I'm going to publish it,' and he gave me some money. The novel appeared. There were good reviews, in that they were not bad, but nobody was interested in the life of the West Indian people in those days in Europe. Some people said it was a very strange thing, obviously very peculiar people living a fantastic life and that was the end of that. Then time passed and about ninteen-fifty something, people began talking about *Minty Alley*, which was the first West Indian novel published in England, and John La Rose, different publisher, a good friend of, mine, a very good friend of mine, told me that he would like to publish it. I told him by all means. The novel then was republished some time about [1971], and I was astonished at the reception that it [received]… not only was the public astonished, but do you know *who* was the most astonished person…

DANCE: Not you?

JAMES: [nodding assent] Because – and this is what is really interesting and most significant, there were other people who wrote about people in the 'yard', but they wrote about people in the yard as very interesting people and people of some importance who you should know about, but in *Minty Alley* I had instinctively (I hadn't the faintest idea of what I was doing), I had made a clean distinction between an educated Black man and the uneducated Black, and every chapter in that book makes that clear. And today if people look at it, there is that problem with the Caribbean countries, the division between the educated Black and the ordinary Black person. And that is there, it is there from chapter one to the end. But what is amusing [is that] I had no such idea in my head.

DANCE: But of course you were very much aware of it.

JAMES: No, I wasn't aware of it. I was aware of it as something that wasn't done, but wasn't *aware* of it. If anybody had [asked] me what I was writing about, I wouldn't have told them *that*. I wasn't aware of *that* when I was writing that novel. I wasn't aware of it… But my eye was sharp and of course I was interested in the society and very much conscious of the difference between the educated and the uneducated, but *that* was a problem which I didn't have in my head. I want that very clear. I did not have *that* in my head and it was only when the novel was republished, some twenty years afterwards, that I read it again and began to see and people began to say, 'Yes that's it.' I think that is the most interesting…

DANCE: It is indeed.

JAMES: …thing for anybody interested in literature to do something… when something happens like that. Oh, yes.

DANCE: You mentioned the fact that the characters in the novel were very much based upon people whom you knew –

JAMES: About people who were there.

DANCE: Including yourself.

JAMES: Including myself. Now that is very important. Number one, [Laughter] I will mention; in the novel I slept with Maisie. In real life I never slept with Maisie. What happened was when I was there I was about twenty-eight. I was already in the relation with the woman I was to marry. I was a more or less mature person. What I did was to transfer myself to when I was eighteen and made the character Haynes a person not of my age, but what I was when I was eighteen, ten years before, so as to make this all very new to him. That was a literary device. So that's how people would think that I am in the novel, the 'I' in the novel was me when I had just left school… That's the work that's *Minty Alley*. And I am very glad that George Lamming tells me that when he lectures about the Caribbean now, I think he mentions three books. He says, 'I always start with *Minty Alley*,' and then he goes on to, I think it is, *In the Castle of My Skin*, his own book, and then I think he does *A House for Mr. Biswas* by Vidia Naipaul. But he starts with *Minty Alley*, and that's the basis of his approach to the Caribbean novel.

DANCE: A critic had mentioned that George Lamming is one of your most ardent disciples. Would you tell me something…

JAMES: A disciple? My goodness. He is not a disciple, in any way. He is a tremendous admirer of my work as I am of his. And I believe… but he isn't a disciple, because Lamming has done *his* work. It is not along the level of my novel, *Minty Alley*, that was entirely new. He is a great stylist, a writer of poetic metaphor and vivid illustration of what he is thinking about, a very controlled person, and I admire it a great deal, but it isn't along my *Minty Alley*. I wrote and stopped. I don't know what I would have gone on to do, but when I went to England in '32, and Europe was seething with politics and with my attitude to life and the difference between educated people and uneducated people, which is clear in that book, I joined a political group in England.

DANCE: I want to talk about that too later, but let me ask you if you ever thought about doing another novel?

JAMES: I had in mind a novel when I went to England, I had a novel in mind but I never wrote a line of it. I wrote a play called *Toussaint L'Ouverture*. I was busy working with the historical account of the Haitian revolution and being very much involved in politics and seeing there that there was a story in which Blacks had done splendid things, I thought it would be nice – not nice, but effective to produce it, because there weren't any plays that said Black people had created any distinguished events of the time. So I wrote the play. And then a friend of mine who knew some people around showed it to people and gradually it was said that the stage society would put on the play, (and they used to put on the plays by Bernard Shaw and everybody) if Paul Robeson would play the leading part. Well we went to Paul, whom I used to see, and he said, 'Let me see it.' He said, 'Yes, I'll play the part.' So that is the play. Now that was in 1936. Then came the independence of Ghana and the whole revolutionary movement, India, China, all of them. So that after twenty-odd years I thought that that idea that I was expressing should be differently expressed, and I re-wrote the play. So the play that's being shown today and it has been played in Ghana; it was played in Jamaica; it was put on by the BBC in London in their programme; and it was put on here in Trinidad the other day – extremely effective, very effective. And that is the second version. Some of the first version went into the second, but the second version meant that writing about struggle for independence in 1956 or 1960 was very different from what it was in 1936. If that was photographed I would be quite content for that to be a movie.

DANCE: Your study of the Haitian Revolution is certainly one of the most influential works of the twentieth century...

JAMES: It is still selling well, and in many universities it is used by the students, and people who are interested in the colonial question are all reading it. That book did what it was intended to do. It gave a political analysis of a struggle for colonial independence.

DANCE: But I think perhaps just as important as making the kind of analysis it did of the situation, it's been a great motivation.

JAMES: Yes. I was totally in favour as I wrote it; I was not only carried away by their struggles but I was moved to indicate that that is what people should be doing today in their own new environment... But I would like to say a new study of that revolution has appeared, and it was written by a Monsieur Fouchard, a Haitian. And I had been very emphatic that the people who made the revolution were slaves, and I thought that that was a great movement. But he has gone further. He has said the slaves helped, it is true, but the people who made the revolution were those who had run away into the forests. The Maroons. So he has written a book, and the book ought to be published. I have written an introduction to it, and I am looking forward to it. And I am very happy because after thirty years, the time has come for a new historical study... I have written the introduction voicing my satisfaction that somebody is taking it further. This to me you must always do.

DANCE: Indeed. Indeed. Let me go back to another of your studies, the one of Melville's major works, [*Mariners, Renegades and Castaways*]. But you know one thing that surprised me there: I know your emphasis was on *Moby Dick*, but you also spent quite a bit of time talking about his other works, but you didn't spend much time on *Billy Budd*, and that interested me because you were emphasising the totalitarian state and injustice and that kind of thing in the contemporary world, and *Billy Budd* seems so relevant. Do you like *Billy Budd*?

JAMES: I will tell you what happened. I was very much at home with Melville's work from the beginning, right up to *Moby Dick* and the short stories that followed. And then came a period in which he wrote around one-thousand poems and *Billy Budd*.

And when I read *Billy Budd* I was aware that Melville had added a new dimension. And to incorporate *Billy Budd* into the work that I had written, I couldn't do it.

DANCE: I see.

JAMES: But, you know something, a number of people seem to like that book. The critics who have written and told me what a remarkable book it is, innumerable, they want to reprint it.

DANCE: Oh yes. I would like you to comment on your relationship with some people who are important in history. What about Marcus Garvey? Did you know him personally?

JAMES: I met Marcus Garvey here. He came here in 1929. He had already left the United States and I had read his paper and knew about him. And I had two very great experiences with Marcus Garvey. He was here, speaking here and there at public meetings Then I came to the conclusion that I should go and speak to him in person. So I called up where he was staying and I said, 'Could I have an interview with Mr. Garvey?' I said, 'My name is James; I work with the newspaper.' He said, 'By all means: come around in the morning at nine.' So I went in the morning and there was the great man. And it has been an experience I have never forgotten. Marcus Garvey began to tell me about the Black situation in the world and in the United States… He told me nothing I had not heard before; he told me nothing I hadn't read in what he had written; he told me nothing new; but Garvey mobilised himself to talk to me as if he had discovered all this the night before, and it was making me a convert, so that we that afternoon would go out and conquer the world for Africa. And I realised then what a political leader can be more than anyone else. Then he was in England in 1934, 1935. I used to speak in the park with Padmore, and Garvey used to come in the park and speak too. And then Garvey used to say some things that were not what he had said before. So Padmore and I used to beware. We had respect for him because we knew what he had done, because before Marcus Garvey there was no Black leader in the world. All of us were built on the shoulders of what Garvey had done, so we respected him, but when he would say something that we thought was not what he ought to say, we would say, 'But that isn't what you used to say before you came to London!' So he – in England he had a very bad time.

DANCE: Could we talk a little about your relationship with Eric Williams?

JAMES: There isn't anything to say about him. I don't want to go into that. I was personally very friendly with Eric Williams when he was – I used to teach him at QRC. I was acting as a master when he was a boy. I went to London in '32. Williams won a scholarship and came there, and I saw a lot of him. He saw a lot of me from '32 to '38. I went to America in '38. Williams came to America to teach at Howard after I saw him in England in the winter. Then in '57 I was invited here. Williams used to come to me and talk to me about his plans and what he was doing, and I would introduce him to one or two people, talk to him about their needs. I was invited to come here in '57. I came and when I saw the way the people were changed, I wrote a letter, and Williams said: 'Well, if you see that and that is what we ought to do, why don't you stay and help us?' The wife said, 'OK' and I wrote to my friends in England and America and told them this is what. They said: 'By all means stay.' So I stayed. I'm going to tell you what I've seen – two things. I was here from '57 to '62 and I worked very closely with Williams. But I talked to Williams about socialism for three years. In other words

Williams was not a socialist, he never has been, he has never promised to be. I didn't
take pains to convert him to socialism. What I was concerned with: I anticipated that
the British Government would fight and oppose independence; and Williams was
determined to have independence. I thought the British Government was not
interested in Federation, but the British said, 'We are not opposed to independence.
If you want it, take it. Be quick about it.' And this is my view. When the British granted
independence to Williams – to the astonishment of everybody – I found that all the
drive that they had been showing before that faded away. So I told him, 'Look here,
we have now reached a stage where this is what we have to do; otherwise we are not
going to get anywhere.' And he said, 'We can't do it.' I told him, 'It isn't that *we* can't
do it; it's that *you* can't do it.' For the first time I told him plainly, and I said: 'If you
are not going to do that, I am leaving.' I left. Williams wouldn't dismiss me. I left here.
I left here in 1962, '63. Dr. Mahabir in a book called *In and Out of Politics* has published
a speech that he made in '65 in which he said that in '65 he had seen that the PNM
was already the servant and subordinate to the big capitalist interests in Trinidad. '65!
But I had said, but I had foreseen that that was inevitable in '63. That is why I published
that book and said I am going, because my whole life has been against those things.
So that I left. I have always made it clear that there was going to be a mess, and the mess
broke out in '70. I knew that was coming. And what I am seeing today is that another
one is on the way.

DANCE: Really?

JAMES: Oh yes. I am perfectly sure of that. But in '65 I returned, and when I reached
[Trinidad] – people don't understand this – Williams had already declared a state of
emergency for something that was going on in the southern parts. In other words, I
walked into a state of emergency where he had power to do whatever he wanted, so
he put me under house arrest. Why, nobody knows. I wasn't concerned with what was
going on. I didn't *know*. Now what was peculiar about it, George Richards was down
there and lived not far from where I was detained by a carrier. He didn't put Richards
under house arrest and he put me. But he got such a set of telegrams and letters and
protests, I mean I know one protest was: people in London got together, some of them,
and went down to the Embassy, to the Trinidad Embassy, and told the man there, 'Let
Williams know if he doesn't let James out we are going to march down Park Street and
demonstrate for everybody to know what is happening, because James has been here
for many years; the British government never put him in jail. What did *they* put him
in jail for?'

DANCE: Were you actually put in jail?

JAMES: No, I was under house arrest. So that was it. I was doing nothing. It was only
after that I was persuaded and other people told me, 'Well, let us stay and form a party.'
But I wasn't put under house arrest for anything. It was simply I happened to walk into
a state of emergency which gives him power to do whatever is necessary, and he never
gave any reason for it. But he took the chance, which didn't work. I had been writing
about him, and I had written very savagely about him. He put me away, but very
shrewd. And, by the way, what happened was he abolished the state of emergency.
Finished! Everything. So he never let me out. By abolishing the state of emergency
I became a free person.

DANCE: I would like to have you comment a little bit about your assessment of contemporary Caribbean literature. I remember in 1972 you suggested that Wilson Harris, George Lamming and Vidia Naipaul were a trio such as no other country had produced. Are there some other writers whom you would put in that august company now?

JAMES: Now, I will tell you what is happening. I would not speak any more about Harris, Naipaul and Lamming, because they are settled. At the present time, you in the United States – well, there is taking place among Black women in particular, but there are one or two Black men, but Black women, who are writing about Black people, ordinary Black people. There are Ntozake Shange, Alice Walker, and Toni Morrison in a novel called *Sula*. They are writing about Black women, all the members of the old domestic servants, who were nothing in the United States, have now been pitchforked by these highly gifted people into the very first rank of literature. The same thing is taking place in the Caribbean. Earl Lovelace and Michael Anthony are writing about the ordinary people, and I wrote about these, so did Vidia Naipaul, so did Richard Wright, but we wrote from the point of view of people who were saying: 'Well, look at them, they are OK, nothing is wrong with them, etc.' But Earl Lovelace and Michael Anthony are writing about them in the same way that Alice Walker, whom I admire immensely – *Meridian* – Alice Walker, Ntozake Shange, she's a very gifted young woman, you know… and Toni Morrison are writing about them as if to say 'These people, that's the way they are; that's the way they think; that's the way they are living. We are not criticising them or looking to see in what way they fit into the general ideas of society. We take them for what they are because what they are is what is valuable about them and valuable to the whole society.' And the same thing is going on in the Caribbean today. Earl Lovelace and Michael Anthony are writing in Trinidad about the Trinidad people, the ordinary people, in the same way that those three women are writing about all those people in the USA.

DANCE: Well, what about women writers in the Caribbean? Are there any who have impressed you at this point?

JAMES: I have not been able to – there is a woman who has written a novel – I can't…

DANCE: Merle Hodge, perhaps?

JAMES: Yes.

DANCE: *Crick Crack Monkey*. You know it?

JAMES: I have read it, but all I can say is it hasn't made much of an impact on me. I don't know about the women writers, but I want to mention one woman, a West Indian woman; she is a writer of history and a critic of politics; she is a professor at Stanford University; her name is Sylvia Wynter. When you talk about women writers in the Caribbean, I would say she would be up on top, and second to nobody.

DANCE: Really?

JAMES: Ah, that woman, that woman! And I have written that about her, in public. Sylvia Wynter. An exceptional woman. Yes, there are people whom I admire tremendously and whose work I look at; they are, of course, George Lamming; of course Wilson Harris, whom I admire beyond words; then there is a man in Africa called Wole Soyinka; and in the USA, Ntozake Shange, Alice Walker, who is beyond being super, but God she can write very profoundly, and Toni Morrison generally I like, *Sula* in particular. So that's it, that's what I think about them and the women writers. *We* haven't produced the women writers as yet. George Lamming tells me that he is waiting for the woman in the Caribbean to write a novel which will state the position of the Caribbean. Well, he is waiting for hen. I am waiting for her too.

DANCE: Mr James, your career reminds me a great deal of that of WEB DuBois, whom I know you –

JAMES: No, I am saying that, well, when you say that, he was a very big man, you know.

DANCE: Well, you aren't exactly a small man yourself. Both of you are men of many vocations: novelist, critic, historian, teacher, editor, political activist. And I think *The Souls of Black Folk* like your *Black Jacobins* is one of the most influential books of the century.

JAMES: Indeed, the book that matters most to me and that may increasingly matter is *Black Reconstruction*. That book means a lot to me, and still does. I read it all the time. I don't move without it. DuBois, very big… and you mention me in regard to DuBois! [Laughter] No… but to show you what I think of him. People don't realise what that man did. Garvey brought the movement from among people in general and brought the mass of the population. The intellectual movement was DuBois's. Those two were the ones who gave us what we have today. And DuBois did work in the United States that is superior – pardon me – that no white sociologist has surpassed what DuBois has done. I am compelled to say it that way.

DANCE: Well, one of the things that I was going to say about that is that both of you aroused a great many bitter reactions from certain people all along the way, and didn't exactly travel an easy road, but you both persevered, and the great thing about it is that I think you both have had the opportunity to experience the reactions of people who have come to appreciate your work so much. One thing that has really struck me since I have been doing this project is the great love and respect and admiration that Caribbean writers have for you, not only Caribbean writers certainly, but these are the people that I have been talking to recently.

JAMES: I have been at it a long time, you know, and I must mention, I have never wavered. At no time did I even – I know I made mistakes, but at no time did I even leave it and join the opposition. And they are very pleased with that and so am I.

DANCE: Let me end with just one question. Of the many, many contributions that you've made, as you look back, what do you prize most, what would you most like to be remembered for?

JAMES: [Long pause] I would have to be general. The contributions I have made to the Marxist movement are the things that matter most to me. And those contributions have been political, in various ways; they have been literary: the book [on] *Moby Dick* is a study of the Marxist approach to literature. All of my studies on the Black question are [Marxist] in reality. When I went to see Trotsky in '38, I said, Well the Trotskyist movement has no Black position at all. This one ought to be the position of Marxists on the Black question. So, on the whole, I like to think of myself as a Marxist who has made serious contributions to Marxism in various fields. I want to be considered one of the important Marxists. That I think is that.

DANCE: Thank you very, very much.

JAMES: No, I am glad to be able to say something that you might be able to take to some people and spread it around. I am much obliged to you.

DANCE: The pleasure is all mine. Thank you.

———————————

CONVERSATION WITH

ISMITH KHAN

Ismith Khan was born in Trinidad on March 16, 1925. After attending Queen's Royal College in Trinidad, Khan worked as a reporter for the *Trinidad Guardian*. He later came to the United States and studied at Michigan State University, later going on to earn a BA in Social Sciences from the New School for Social Research in New York and an MA in Writing at Johns Hopkins University. He worked as a research assistant at Cornell University and has taught at Johns Hopkins, the University of California at Berkeley and San Diego, and California State College. He taught in New York for the later part of his life. He died in April 2002.

Khan has published three novels: *The Jumbie Bird* (1961) and *The Obeah Man* (1964); *The Crucifixion*, unpublished at the time of the interview, was published by Peepal Tree Press in 1987. His short stories and scholarly essays have appeared in a number of journals and anthologies. A collection of his short stories, *A Day in the Country and Other Stories* was published by Peepal Tree Press in 1994. He was awarded a fellowship from the National Endowment for the Humanities in 1972.

The following interview took place at Khan's home, then in Anaheim, California, on August 14, 1981.

DANCE: I'd like to start talking about Kale Khan. How typical is he of that last generation of Indians in Trinidad who remember the old country?
KHAN: Well, I don't think that he was typical of those people. I think there were probably several people like him. But for the most part, you've got to realise that these people who came as indentured servants were people who were beaten down and if anything at all you might say he emerged as a sort of a leader, a spokesman. You see, my grandfather was not brought as an indentured servant.
DANCE: Now, let me ask you one question: Is he a portrait of your grandfather?
KHAN: Yes. Name and all. As a matter of fact a student, an English literary person who was doing some research on some of the rebellions that took place in Trinidad, went through some of the records and found his name. Now I didn't know that... Because the way I understood it was that he had made trouble and he had gotten away from the police. Now I don't think he was ever actually arrested, but somehow or another his name is on the records because they found his name...
DANCE: And this incident in the book where he's shot and all is an actual historical incident in Trinidad?
KHAN: Yeah. For just those reasons. That's exactly why.
DANCE: Are any of the other family members in the book named after [your actual family]? For example is your father Rahim?
KHAN: No. None of the other characters in the book.
DANCE: But the others are based on your father and mother, for example, and your grandmother?
KHAN: Well, actually only the grandparents are close to what they were like. It would not have been feasible to use the personalities of my mother and father because

it wouldn't have made for the dramatic possibilities. I had to create my father as a relatively weak person. He wasn't at all.

DANCE: Yes, because Kale Khan must stand out here. As I read your book I supposed that this legendary figure must have been an important part of your childhood.

KHAN: Well, I spent a lot of time with my grandfather as a little boy. He died when I was, I guess maybe about nine or ten, I'm not sure. But there is also this – I was the only grandson, you see. I have four sisters and no brothers and my father has one brother and he did not have any children. So I was the apple of the old man's eye.

DANCE: Well you know that's rather interesting. In your novels somehow you sort of do away with the girl figures, there are no sisters. So like your grandfather you kind of did away with the girls in the family [The grandfather in *The Jumbie Bird* gives away his daughter before he leaves India].

KHAN: Not because they were girls, but I didn't want to write a novel that was so sprawling… I mean the society is such a complex one. Where oh where, for example, would a writer find it… or how difficult would a writer find it to have to take in all of the racial or ethnic groups. You have to keep paring it down, at least in your first novel, and so I thought: number one, it's just going to be the East Indian community. You read that book and I think it's clear that you never realise… there is a little boy called Tommy in the book, and he's a Black kid who is Jamini's friend, but it's not made clear. There is a Black man who is a carpenter who builds some chicken coops for the old lady. But for the most part, it is really a story that deals with the East Indian community and I wanted it that way because I just couldn't…

DANCE: Yes. Yes.

KHAN: And similarly, to get back to these other characters, it would have been too much.

DANCE: Yes, but what surprises me is the attitude towards women that Kale Khan has. I suppose he is very atypical there. In the novel he gives his daughter away before he leaves India. He doesn't want his wife to have any influence on his son. And he is not too particular about his daughter-in-law having influence on Jamini.

KHAN: Well he is certainly atypical, and I think that that has largely to do with his… with himself as a very highly opinionated person. He has very strong views about a great many things, and he stands alone, his relationship to women is something which is not at all representative of East Indians. Now one of the things which might be thought about him is that he is a Pathan. And I am a Pathan… and Pathans are the people who are in the hills of Afghanistan right now fighting with the Russians, and they are an unconquered people – the British never made it into those hills. And they lead this gregarious life, and they made very good soldiers. That's why the old boy went into the military. He loved the military, as I think I mention in the book, but he hated authority. He loved women, but there was this ambivalence. In his later life, he lived by himself. My grandmother was still alive. And about the Pathans it is said you know that they love art but they, they absolutely despise artists. They love music, but they hate musicians. They love the theatre, but they hate actors and actresses and you know in my own way, I think that as I become a little bit older I begin to see some of these qualities in me. Now maybe it's just imaginary. I hate people in the theatre – not the people who write for the theatre, but actors and actresses. So, to get back to Kale

Khan I think that he would have to be thought of as an individual, and not at all representative of the East Indian community because even within the East Indian community, even in India, there are these great, regional differences of people…

DANCE: Yes, Yes. I was very impressed by the character of Binti. And I'm not so sure that you intended the kind of reaction that I had to her since Kale Khan obviously is *the* heroic figure there. But she comes off as a very heroic character. It seems to me that she would have been the one to most regret leaving India and her family, and yet there is a remarkable strength about the way she accepts the situation, about the way that she does not hate Kale Khan, whom I think she would have every reason to hate. And the way that she plans for the survival of the family and works to contribute to it seems much more meaningful than this fantasy of return that Kale Khan has. Did you envision her as such a heroic character, or is that my reading something more into it?

KHAN: No, you're quite right. I had always thought of her as a very strong, resilient person, an independent person, someone who could pick up her life although the old man had literally dumped her and taken her two sons away, and that she should then be able earn a living by herself. No, I saw her as very strong person, which is not to say that she wasn't someone whose life was saddening to me. As a child… I would go and see her and she too loved me as much as the old man did, though she knew that he would set me against her, but she was able to overcome all of that. Of course, she was always welcome in my home because my father loved her very much. But she lived alone and she made her own way in the world after her husband left her. No. I think of her as a very strong woman, indeed. I think that a great many of the women who worked in that kind of situation and who had to raise a family must have had a great deal of strength. I think that if any comparisons can be made [it is with] the Black population who survived the Middle Passage… the ones who were fit. There were lot of people who died.

DANCE: Let me ask you about the pretty constant theme of life and death in your novels. In *The Jumbie Bird* we are constantly reminded of impending death with the sound of the jumbie bird. At the end there *is* a kind of promise of life but there is this overwhelming sense of the death of everything throughout the novel. Would you like to comment on this?

KHAN: Well, I think it has to do with the East Indian community and all of the very firm and fixed traditions that they had. It had to die in a certain sense. It had to adapt if it was going to survive. I think that is true of any cultural group that migrates. Now here again, these comparisons always come up in my mind. You see, with Africans who came to the New World, we know that there were deliberate attempts to split them up so that they would not be able to communicate with each other. This was not the case with the Indians who migrated to the Caribbean. Number one, they came as families… so that there was a kind of coherence that tended to foster further the religious customs and traditions that they brought with them. They brought all of their customs with them. They brought all of their foods with them. They brought all of their seeds so they would plant and grow some of the stuff that they were accustomed to eating. Now you bring a very tightly knit system like that to such a vastly different part of the world, it's going to have to give. And it is in that sense that one laments the passing of some of these traditions because they had to be… Actually they didn't die, but they had to be modified if these people were going to be able to survive and exist in these new circumstances. But the old man, he saw he had no truck with the new world and what was going on. And that was his dream. We find parallels with somebody like Marcus Garvey, who had similar ideas. I don't know how strongly the Rastas feel about going back, but they feel their sense of identification with something that is not living where they are in Jamaica. So [it was] death in that sense, *that* dream had to die and something had to take its place and it was this adaptation; and it is for that reason that I chose to make my father out to be the kind of character who is obviously in a transitory state which makes for a very namby pamby sort of person. My sister calls me up from New York and every now and again; she says, you know, 'Why did you have to write about Pa like that?' [Laughter]

DANCE: [Laughter] She still hasn't accepted it?

KHAN: Yes, I said, 'Well, you know, it is really for fictive purposes.' But she doesn't understand that. She just keeps saying, 'Well, you know he wasn't like that!' [Laughter] But you see, that's what happens when culture travels.

DANCE: You talked about Kale Khan's dream of returning to India. But, of course, it's a hopeless dream and it leads finally to the sense that no place is home. Even Rahim has that sense that we just don't have a home. He says, 'We ain't belong to Hindustan, we ain't belong to England, we ain't belong to Trinidad' [p.54]. Is this a dilemma that the East Indian still feels in Trinidad or do we see perhaps a promise that Jamini is moving towards the sense of Trinidad as home?

KHAN: Well, I think that by the third generation, which is what he would be, one would expect a sense of belonging… Now our situation, the situation of the East Indian in the Caribbean is somewhat different from the East Indian in Africa. Now as independence comes in Africa, I think the Africans feel – and rightly so – you know, 'This is our country, what are you guys doing here?' But there is no way that anybody can say that to anybody else in the Caribbean because nobody in the Caribbean is indigenous to the area. If they want to say, 'Go home,' the only persons who can say that, you know, are the native Americans or the Amerindians. Everybody else was brought there at one point in time or another for whatever reason. But the Caribbean is very different from the African continent and other places where Indians have migrated to as well, places like, some of the islands in the Pacific, Fiji, for example. The Native Fijian can say, 'Why don't you guys go back home?' Now I don't think that anybody could say that about the East Indian in the Caribbean. It's a very different situation. We don't have a population that is indigenous to the area whom we have displaced.

DANCE: I see. Well, tell me this, have you ever had a great desire to return or even a need to return to India?

KHAN: No, I have not, and I have a certain amount of dislike for those people.

DANCE: Those people? You mean…

KHAN: People from India. I have had some very unpleasant experiences at their hands. And it is because they look down on people who have migrated like my ancestors. I think that those of them who do so do not really know the circumstances. But I worked at the Indian Embassy in New York as a messenger as a part-time student in the summer. And they would just take one look at me, you know [and say], 'What is this? He looks Indian; he sounds Indian, but he is not Indian. What kind of animal is this?' I thought many times, 'What would be a nice place… where is a good place to live where you feel a sense of belonging?' And I thought, 'Well, wouldn't it be nice to live in India?' But I never knew the language. OK. So maybe you can learn a language, but I don't think that you would ever learn the individual nuances. I don't know, maybe I'm taking this thing in too much of a highly personal way. Maybe if I were thrown into a milieu like that, I would have to find my way, and I would probably get along. But I think that part of it has to do with being a writer. It's language in that sense too. If I were a businessman who had made a lot of money, it wouldn't matter; I could get somebody to translate. But as a writer, you have to know the language that you are writing in and the milieu that you are living in intimately, and I don't think that that can ever come as a second language.

DANCE: Yes. Yes. I was at a recent conference in Haiti, the Association of Caribbean Studies and there was a paper presented there on violence in Caribbean Literature. The paper was not too well received by some West Indians who thought West Indians were being attacked, as one person said, as pathologically violent. But it seems to me that your novels reinforce the theme – the violent beating of children, you know, seems to occur in many novels and in some instances some of your characters were presented only in those kinds of situations. Would you like to talk a little bit about this picture of violence in West Indian life?

KHAN: I think that West Indian society is violent. I think that anyone who does not say so simply wishes to portray the area in a good light, and I don't know why any artist would want to do that. It seems to me that if you're going to do anything at all you're going to try to portray the society that you live in as accurately and honestly as you can. I don't like violence. I abhor violence, and it is for this reason, that I hope that people will see what I'm talking about and not feel that what I am doing is advocating violence, but that the society will see itself and try to mend its ways. It is violent, it is potentially violent. I still feel that way. I think that some of those islands are perpetually explosive for, you know, whatever political reasons… It has always been that way. It has had a history of violence.

DANCE: Yeah. OK let's talk a little bit about Carnival on which you touch in both of your novels. First of all, has Hussay sort of been worked into Carnival? Is there any relationship between that Indian celebration and Carnival in Trinidad.

KHAN: None whatsoever.

DANCE: OK. The stickman, who is an integral part of Carnival, is in both your novels – an Indian…

KHAN: Yes.

DANCE: Is there any particular reason for that? Were Indians particularly outstanding as stickmen in Carnival or…?

KHAN: Well, it comes from the Hussay, and the Hussay is not a celebration; it's a commemoration of the deaths of the two grandsons of the Prophet. This is not Hinduism; it is Muslim. And I come from a Muslim family. Stick fighting is intended to duplicate the battles that took place in the days of old. So that while you may find people who came from many of the other ethnic backgrounds become stickfighters, that is where it comes from. Now Carnival is not at all an East Indian thing…

DANCE: There is one character who appears in both of your novels as a minor character but he stands out, and that's Hop-and-Drop.

KHAN: Well, somebody told me one time that Dr. Williams felt that I was referring to him, particularly…

DANCE: To him? [Laughter]

KHAN: Yes. And that I saw – you know, there was one description of Carnival when the cripple dresses up. And his shoes are facing backward and his clothes are put on backward, and I heard – and this was by some literary critic as well, that I saw Dr. Williams as a cripple, and having him dressed up that way and walking backwards and it looked like he was walking forward; but I had nothing whatsoever of that kind in mind. It used to be typical in the old days for J'ouvert, the opening of Carnival, any old costume would do. Everybody played Mask. So, the cripple – I did not have in mind for him to be Dr. Williams. I did not have him in mind to suggest that the Caribbean was moving backwards. But, I don't know – you know, literary critics have a heyday.

DANCE: Well, you know, somehow I was inclined to read him as representative of West Indian man. There are some things that you said about him which seem to me to make him symbolic… which seem to me to make him stand out as more than an individual character – the description of his home, for example, built from odds and ends, 'discarded ends of other people's lives', you write, 'his need for true companionship; his need for understanding'; the failure of people to understand in your words again, 'the architecture of his soul'; and then the tendency to have other people look at him and see themselves in him.

KHAN: Well, I think you're quite right in that. I did intend to have him a symbolic portrait of someone who comes from the Caribbean, who has all of these bits and pieces of culture, of knowledge of other people's lives, of other people's values. He collects and stores up old newspapers about ancient things. He is a storehouse of all of these bits and pieces of knowledge, but there is no pattern to be able to make any kind of coherence out of it. I am sure, you know, all the way down to this shanty and the way it is constructed I had very much in mind to give a picture of the way I feel that people from the Caribbean, are, what they are really like, and I still believe that way.

DANCE: Is he based on one particular person whom you might have known?

KHAN: No.

DANCE: No. I don't ever remember that you tell us what his background is. Does it matter? Or is he Indian? Is he Black?

KHAN: He's a Black man. Well, when I was a very tiny tot, my father had what you would call a junk-yard, and he had a very strong Black man (his name was Peter), who would with a sledgehammer smash up engines and all the rest of it which my father exported as scrap metal to England. Peter lived on the city dump, and that's where I spent a lot of time because Peter was very fond of me, and I used to go to the dump, and there was a little man who lived there – he wasn't a cripple – but there were lots of people who lived on the city dump in these shanties and so on. All of the people who lived in the dump were Black people. There wasn't a single other nationality or ethnic person who lived in the city dump. So I remember that man. He was a small man but he was not a cripple. The cripple part was an invention.

DANCE: OK. I'd like to talk a little bit about obeah, which is central to one of your novels. Is obeah accepted by East Indians?

KHAN: Yes. There are some East Indians who… how shall I put it? You know, there's a novel by… by this well-known woman novelist… she wrote *Ship of Fools*…

Katherine Anne Porter. There is a scene there where somebody from the ship sells religious objects – [irrespective of] whether it is for Christian or Jew. And I think the point she is making is that if somebody believes that it's going to work… Similarly I have an uncle who used to be a prize fighter, and a lot of people thought that we as East Indians had our own brand of obeah. There was a lot of hocus-pocus that used to go on before my uncle went into the ring. My uncle was never knocked down.

DANCE: Really?

KHAN: And I remember as a child what used to go on before he went into the ring. Now there was a Black man who was also a fighter. You know how these fighters have a lot of other fighters around them. So he had told my parents that, you know, he would like to get some of that pzazz, and I remember my mother telling him that there were certain things that he should do and and not do like eat pork and stuff like that and drink rum. So anyway he went through this ritual on the one hand because he thought it would help, but on the other hand he continued to eat this black pudding and souse and drink his rum and so on. But of course he got beaten [Laughter] and he wondered why. I can still see this guy's face. 'I did what you told me.' My mother says, 'But did you drink rum?' And he says, 'Well, uh, uh, I had a little.'

DANCE: [Laughter] You're working now, I understand, on a novel set in New York. What stage is that now?

KHAN: Well, I wrote this novel – this is the third time that I am going over this novel. The first time around I had just given up on it. The second time around I gave up on it, and this time it looks like it might work. I never completed it those first two times around for several reasons which you wouldn't be interested in.

DANCE: I would like to…

KHAN: Well, one of the reasons is money, you know. I can't really work at my best unless I have a good deal of time, and teaching full-time is not the best situation for a writer. So that's one reason. Another reason is that when I first started to write it – today I can say this – for some strange reason I felt that I could pose as a white American who would be the protagonist of the novel. And I don't know [laughter] why I did that. And I don't know why I didn't realise that it would not work. Today I am a little bit older and a little bit wiser and a little bit more of a writer. But that was one of the reasons why the first one failed, or why I felt it disappointing. McGraw Hill was interested in it, but I could see where I was running into problems – real problems. The next attempt was a question of point of view. I wrote it from a third-person point of view. What I am doing now is writing it from a first-person point of view, and it's very much like myself. It is someone who came here as a student from an island in the Caribbean or Trinidad and his adventures and misadventures. And there again I might say after all of these years I don't know why I didn't do that in the first place.

DANCE: Now this white American character. Has he been dropped all together or is he sort of subsumed in the West Indian character?

KHAN: Well, the whole novel, the entire writing that I did was scrapped.

DANCE: So it's really a different story.

KHAN: So is the second. Completely scrapped. And of course, the times have changed. This novel is going to be set in the '60s – its a period thing. I lived in New York for thirty-two years. And I think that the '60s is a good period for some of the things that were taking place in this country, but this character is able to assimilate and to relate to and react to… So the times have changed and where the first writing would probably have been in the '50s and would have dealt with a group of artists that I knew, it is now a novel which deals with some of the political shenanigans that were going on in the Vietnam War, in the Kennedy Administration, the turned-off generation… I really don't know what it's worth.

DANCE: When you say you really don't know what it's worth, are you saying that you're not so sure how the public will receive it? Do you feel good about it?

KHAN: Well, let me put it this way. I've written some long short stories that are set here, and they have not been published. I haven't got anything that I have written set in this country that has been published.

DANCE: Really?

KHAN: It leaves me with certain questions in my mind about my having lived here all this long and how well do I really understand my environment, my world. I've lived in this country more than half my life. So if there is going to be anything at all that will be saying something about this country, it will be this novel.

DANCE: You teach a course on Caribbean literature. Who are some of the writers and what are some of the works that you include in that course?

KHAN: Well, what I try to do is to avoid the writers who are most well known like, you know, Naipaul. Most people know his work anyway. That's number one. Number two, I don't feel that I know enough about the theatre so I don't deal very much with drama. And while Eddie Brathwaite is one of the better known, if not the best poet from the area, I do use his work; and I'll tell you quite frankly, I use the work of some of my friends.

DANCE: Sam [Selvon]?

KHAN: I use Sam's work, Austin Clarke, and I also, because – you know this is the decade of the woman – I try to use Merle's work and Sylvia Wynter's so that the student will have some idea that it's not just men who write novels. And I would like them to feel that in somebody like Eddie Brathwaite, that here is the English language, here is somebody who can do that. And I will also go out of my way by using anything that is in dialect like… uh… what's her name from Jamaica?

DANCE: Louise Bennett.

KHAN: Louise Bennett's work and I have a short story that I like to use because it is written completely in dialect. I wrote it twenty years ago – nobody wanted to touch it with a ten-foot pole… I don't know, some of these people have their views about certain things. 'You don't write that way in bad English!' Well, I do write that way in bad English, thank you, and I can also write well in good English. But this is something that has to be done because I feel that it captures the total expression of the individual and I think a writer should do that.

DANCE: Is it heavier dialect than some of Sam's pieces?

KHAN: Well, this particular short story is completely in dialect because it is one character who is telling about himself and that's what the story is. There are only about five or six lines to introduce the story, and then the character starts talking like in one of the Conrad stories.

DANCE: I know you've done a lot of research too that focuses on language and identity in Caribbean literature. Would you tell me about what you see as the impact of language on identity in the literature.

KHAN: Well, it is just this use of dialect and just these differences in dialect from one island to the other which I think is a very important thing, a very colourful thing, a very meaningful thing. I think that there is an interesting relationship between our thought processes and the particular kind of languages that we use. In a certain sense, I think of myself as someone who is bilingual because I think a certain way and I feel a certain way in a certain language, and that language is the dialect language, not the language that you and I are speaking now. But if we had another West Indian here I am sure that we could carry on a conversation which would have a very different level of inflexion, but I think that the very content of the conversation would have in some way been influenced by the language that we are speaking here.

DANCE: And this could be any contemporary West Indian? The heritage *now* makes no difference in the language I take it.

KHAN: It doesn't, because you know you can meet somebody who comes from Trinidad who is Chinese or you could bring somebody in here who is Black or somebody who is East Indian or somebody who is Portuguese.

DANCE: The language would be exactly the same.

KHAN: Yeah.

DANCE: Well, now, most dialects change quite a bit; so having been away this long, when you go back to Trinidad has the language changed enough so that some of the nuances and expressions and so forth…?

KHAN: There are words and there are expressions, but there is something about the language which, I think, for the greater part of it… the substance, has to do with the rhythmic pattern of the language and the enunciation of certain words. But certainly there are expressions, there are words which have cropped up which are new. The last time I was there, it was after an absence of about seven years, so there were some words that people were using, and I had to ask them, 'What does that word mean; what does that term mean?' Because there again it's a very inventive kind of thing.

DANCE: Would you talk a little about what you see as the important aspects of contemporary Caribbean literature. What is happening in the field? What are the problems?

KHAN: Well, I think that the problems have not changed too much, the major problems. One of them is the lack of publishing houses; the second is an audience. What kind of audience is there going to be for the literature that comes from the Caribbean besides the people in the Caribbean and possibly some people from some parts of the so-called Third World? That's a real problem and I think that those two questions can be looked at when you look at a writer like VS Naipaul. I don't know that he writes for the people in the Caribbean anymore. I don't know that any writer has to be told what he should write about, but I think that there is a great loss because people will say, 'Oh, well, here is one of the world's finest novelists', (which he is), but I don't know what that does to revivify the milieu from which he comes, and I would like to be able to feel that that is what I do, that I wish to do; and the fact that I have been living abroad is just one of those historical happenstances. It would have been impossible for me to have become a writer if I had stayed there. The same thing is true of a number of writers who went abroad and some of them continue to live abroad; some of them returned and I think that any number of them will tell you that while they have thought of returning, they found a rather hostile community. But apart from the community as an audience, I think that for myself I really needed a community of writers and artists when I wished to become a writer, and it was most helpful to me. I think that at the point in time when I wished to be a writer, there wasn't that kind of ambience in the Caribbean; there wasn't a group of not only writers but fellow artists, and I have the feeling that that was very necessary for me. And I found it in New York by way of the school that I went to which was called The New School for Social Research. There were a couple of people at that school who started the writing workshops there; there was an older man by the name of Gorham Munson. He was a friend of Hemingway and Gertrude Stein, and some of those people, and then he and two others, Charles Glicksberg and Don Wolfe, both of whom were full professors at Brooklyn College, carried on this writing workshop, which I was a part of. And I also had friends who were in some of the other arts. I had a pretty good picture of what was going on in the theatre, I had a pretty good picture of what has going on on 57th Street in painting and sculpture, because some of my friends were also in those fields. And while I came from the kind of background that I did and was trying to do something with that, it was nonetheless very important to me to be in the company of these people and exchange ideas with them and have some sort of picture of where is literature headed; where is painting headed; where is sculpture headed? How are all of these arts related to one another? And I don't think that it would have been possible to find an ambience like that in the Caribbean. Oh, I'll tell you a little story that I didn't mention early on. When I was really struggling so hard to write my first novel, Sam had already had I don't know how many novels done, and so my mother, my dear old sweet mother, said to me – in a letter she said to me, 'If you want to write a book all that badly, why don't you get Sam to write it for you?' I told Sam this story. I don't know if he remembers. [Laughter]

DANCE: What about Trinidad today? Do you think that the environment is different for a writer? There are a lot of active writers there, Lovelace and Anthony. Do you think it would be a different kind of situation for you?

KHAN: Well I think that it must be. I think that it must be. But, I don't know just how that works because I know that it happens quite frequently that writers don't, when they get to a certain point in their development, don't fraternise too much. So I don't know if some of these writers really create that kind of ambience that would be helpful and encouraging to younger writers, but it is certainly true that there are more people there today who are accomplished, who have arrived, than used to be the case when I was growing up, but as I said, I don't know. I know that Earl [Lovelace] lives way to hell and gone behind God's back in some place called Matura. When we were there, you know, I never made it out to where he lives, but I have the feeling that he maybe enjoys being away from places where people can just come and knock on your door. Yet, they're there, and they have chosen to be there. I don't know about Michael Anthony, whether he's going to do another stint of teaching abroad or what, but some of the artists have chosen to return and live there, you know, permanently. I myself am – it's a thought that goes through my mind all of the time. Now, who knows? You know. Maybe this tape that replays in my mind constantly will become a reality one of these days and maybe I will – go back.

DANCE: I read somewhere that you frequently make trips to the Caribbean to...

KHAN: I go back as often as I can.

DANCE: Un-huhn. And you find it helpful to you as a writer to return?

KHAN: It is. It is. Because as I said, I still write about the Caribbean, and you have
to know what's going on. That's the other side of the coin of these writers who live
abroad, because there is no question in my mind that, OK, so you have to be way over
here, but if you are way over here, you know, maybe you will learn a lot of things, but
in the meantime, you know, there are certain things that are going on down there that
you would want to know about if you are going to keep writing about it. Some of us
apparently have good memories. Some of us have retained our ear for the language.

DANCE: Is there anything else that we should [discuss]? Any other interests that
you want to talk about, any other goals that you have as a writer?

KHAN: Well, one of the things that has always turned me off is political things, and
I don't mean by that that someone who is an artist should not have political views, but
I would prefer to feel that the kinds of characters and the kinds of situations that
writers are dealing with, as they have in the past, have still to do with some of the
elemental questions of life, and existence, and that to me a novel – and I think I can
name one, you know – like *The Prime Minister*, which is Austin's book, is a direction
that I don't find interesting, you know, as a reader. Now this is not to say that that book
may or may not be important. Then of course, there is the total question of the
Caribbean which has more recently more and more to do with politics and political
things – Cuba, Grenada, the United States and some of its commitments to the area.
I don't know how that will influence writers – certainly some writers will feel, you
know, that they want to get into that. But, I don't think that's a good way to go. I think
if a writer has political views (and I think he should express them), there are lots of
places for that; you can write an article, a non-fiction thing and express your views,
whatever they happen to be, and as I say I'm not questioning anyone's particular
politics. What I'm questioning is the temptation that some writers have succumbed
to, to use political kinds of things as themes in their work. I don't think that's the place
for it. I have views if somebody were to ask me. The last time I was down in the
Caribbean, I wrote a few technical papers, non-fiction things, I don't do that all of the
time because it's a waste of time for me. I do it if I'm asked to go somewhere and
somebody asks me, 'What do you think?' Now I get into a lot of trouble – I will grant
you that. Now that is something that you could get up there and argue with people
about, but if I write a piece of fiction, there's no argument about that. If anybody wants
to argue, you know, they can argue with *it*, they don't argue with *me*. You know,
somebody comes up to me, and says, 'What do you mean by writing about women the
way you have in *The Obeah Man*? Look at the way this woman is treated! And children
– look at how children get beat up' and all the rest of it. I say, you know, 'That is the
way the society is.' I don't argue with that at all. You take my word for it, or you don't
take my word for it. I'm not advocating any of that. What I'm trying to do is to hold
a mirror up to that society and that culture so that they will see. That is not an opinion
that I'm expressing as I would if I were to write something of a technical, non-fiction
nature. To continue on this line – it's a very violent society. That very name, Hop-
and-Drop, and that very inventiveness which we have for language. You just go off
the beaten track for one moment and we will find a name for you – we will pick up
on it like that [snap of the fingers], and I tell you it's going to be a name that is going
to try to straighten you out. You call somebody Hop-and-Drop, my God! You know.

What does that mean? That is the kind of inventiveness that my society has with language. That is the kind of manner in which my society will immediately try to bring you into line, and they're very sharp people that way – they don't miss a trick... I've got another novel that nobody wanted to publish. It's called *The Crucifixion*, and it's in some ways quite similar to *The Obeah Man*. It's about a man who thinks that he has had a call and he wants to become one of these wayside preachers – it's complete – it got some pretty nice comments from some people, but there were some people who felt that it was too close to the Christ story. And it is.

DANCE: And it was intended that way, I assume?

KHAN: Yes, but I didn't go through the Bible and choose all of those situations. It happens to be just that way. We live in the kind of society where, if an individual as a young man wants to find some kind of meaning to his life, some kind of direction, something to do, there's nothing to do, there's nothing to do. You might say this poor devil thinks that he has heard the voice of God one day, and God told him that what he has to do is to go out and save the people in Port of Spain because they are sinners. The novel is finished, it's sitting there, I don't know what will ever happen to it. I don't push these things too hard, but that was one of the things that was said, and I get pissed off real fast, and I don't bother to trouble publishers and editors. I suppose that's one of my failings. I don't know. Maybe one of these days when I am dead and gone, somebody will find some of these things tucked away back there. That is the kind of story that I've written. People ask me about *The Obeah Man*, you know. It's a purely symbolic novel – I don't know the first goddamn thing about obeah – just as *The Crucifixion* is a symbolic novel. Both of those books have largely to do with a society or a culture where a young person growing up finds himself in a situation where he is looking for some sort of meaning in life, if not, you know, some sort of job.

DANCE: Yes. I don't want to keep dwelling on Hop-and-Drop, but he seems to me one of the most fascinating characters I've ever met and yet not really know that much about... we still don't know where he comes from. There are all these legends about him. You often raise questions in these scenes about what he's really thinking – we usually see what happens to him, but we really don't get into him in the way that we do with some of your more fully-developed characters, which is not a criticism – it's simply to say that he seems to have so much more story than you've told yet.

KHAN: Well, he's a good vehicle... and to get back to what I think I said earlier on, I think that he's a good vehicle because he is so representative of the Caribbean – we are all of us always coming up with some sort of voyage. Eddie Brathwaite has told me about his journey to Africa. Vidia Naipaul has been to India, his brother [Shiva], I understand, has been to India, I don't know how many times. Now what are these people doing in all these places they have gone to? They didn't just go to make a fortune, I think, but they are still looking for themselves, or looking for some ancestry. Well, for some of us, it has become a reality, but I think that it is something that is very elemental to all of us, a special significance to people who are so far removed.

DANCE: Well, thank you very much.

CONVERSATION WITH

GEORGE LAMMING

GEORGE LAMMING

George Lamming was born in Barbados in 1927, the only child of a demanding and stalwart mother, who inspired his now famous phrase, 'my mother who fathered me'. Lamming won a scholarship to the prestigious Combermere High School, where he played cricket, but where he was not very happy. However, one of his teachers there was Frank Collymore, one of the founders of *Bim*, who encouraged him and made available to him his extensive library. Collymore's influence is acknowledged in the dedication to *In the Castle of My Skin*: 'To my mother and Frank Collymore whose love and help deserved a better book.' After finishing Combermere, the eighteen year old Lamming went to teach in Trinidad. There he began writing and published some poems in *Bim*. In 1950 he went to England, travelling on the same ship as Sam Selvon. Lamming has worked extensively in broadcasting and has held a number of positions at various colleges and universities. From 1967-1968 he was writer in residence at the University of the West Indies. Since then he has taught at numerous colleges in Denmark, Tanzania, Australia, Kenya and the United States. He continues to be a Visiting Professor of Africana Studies and Literary Arts at Brown University.

In addition to the highly acclaimed *In the Castle of My Skin* (1953), Lamming's novels are: *The Emigrants* (1954); *Of Age and Innocence* (1958); *Season of Adventure* (1960); *Water With Berries* (1971) and *Natives of My Person* (1972). Some of his uncollected short stories can be found in *West Indian Stories* (ed. A. Salkey, 1960) and in *Stories from the Caribbean* (ed. Salkey, 1965). *Natives of My Person* was published in Cuba as *Partes de mi ser* (1988). Other works include his seminal collection of essays, *The Pleasures of Exile* (1960); *George Lamming in Suriname* (1980; interviews); *Conversations: Essays, Addresses and Interviews, 1953-1990* (1992; ed. Richard Drayton and Andaiye); and *Coming, Coming Home: Conversations II: Western Education and the Caribbean Intellectual* (2000). He also edited the anthology *Cannon Shot and Glass Beads* (1974).

Lamming has received several awards: the Somerset Award for Literature in 1958 for *In the Castle of My Skin*; a Guggenheim award in 1955-56; a Canada Council Fellowship in 1962; a Writers' Award from the Association of Commonwealth Literature in 1976 ; a Felix Varela Award from the Consejo de Estado de la Republica de Cuba; a Langston Hughes Festival Award; and he was recently honoured with an Honorary Doctorate from the University of the West Indies.

Critical readings of his works include an essay in *The Islands in Between*, ed. by Louis James (1968); *The Novels of George Lamming* by Sandra Pouchet Paquet (1982); *Critical Perspectives on George Lamming* by Antony Boxhill (1986); *Caliban's Curse: George Lamming and the Revisioning of History* by Supriya Nair (1996); *The Luxury of Nationalist Despair: George Lamming's Fiction as Decolonizing Project* by A.J. Simoes da Silva (2000); Curdella Forbes, *From Nation to Diaspora: Samuel Selvon and George Lamming and the Cultural Performance of Gender* (2005) and ed. Bill Schwarz, *The Locations of George Lamming* (2007).

Though much of his adult life has been spent in London, Lamming has spent much time during the last twenty-five years in the United States and the Caribbean. He has a son and daughter, both grown, who live in Trinidad, where his mother also now resides.

The following interview was conducted on September 30, 1979, in Philadelphia at the home of the poet Sonia Sanchez. George Lamming was the only interviewee who requested that before the interview I submit to him a copy of questions to be asked. Having submitted questions I, at least initially, felt obliged to limit the conversation to these questions, and this did slightly inhibit the spontaneity of the interview. Inevitably, however, the conversation moved beyond the prepared questions.

————————————

DANCE: What is a West Indian writer? Would you help me with that? How would you define…?

LAMMING: Well… I would say that the term 'West Indian writer' could apply to anyone whose work was primarily concerned with the West Indian reality and in whose work, to put it another way, what one would call a West Indian reality was the central focus or the central preoccupation; and that may therefore include people whose home has remained completely in the West Indies. It might, in a sense, almost include people who may not even have been born in the West Indies, but for whom the West Indies was the major shaping influence of their imagination. It would not include people who, for example, had found in a West Indian island the occasion for the setting of a book. For example, there is no way in which you could regard, say, Graham Greene's *Our Man In Havana* as a West Indian novel. That is because the Caribbean reality is not central to Greene's preoccupation. So that's the definition I would use. Once the region, its history and its predicament were central to the body of the work, then I would say that that constituted an aspect of literature of the Caribbean.

DANCE: This definition seems a little bit broader than one that I found in *The Pleasures of Exile*. There you speak of the 'instinct and root impulse which returns the better West Indian writers back to the soil. For the soil is a large part of what the West Indian novel has brought back to reading; lumps of earth: unrefined, perhaps, but good, warm, fertile earth' [p.46]. In that essay you sort of omitted Hearne because he doesn't deal with the earth and with the peasant sensibility, I think.

LAMMING: You know that's a good point to raise, because, in a way I'm not omitting Hearne. That's a good point.

DANCE: But where are you not omitting Hearne – in which of the definitions?

LAMMING: Hearne is essentially a West Indian writer, and what I'm saying here is that, as I recall that chapter, there may be certain West Indian writers who may have chosen to relate to the Caribbean reality in ways that I did not think – and this is a purely subjective judgement – did not think sufficiently authentic, OK? of that reality. That doesn't mean that they're not West Indian writers. And that passage on Hearne in particular was really a criticism of Hearne, who I believe was capable of, and whom I thought should extend his range of exploration a little more…

DANCE: Beyond that sort of upper class?

LAMMING: Yes, but he's certainly a Caribbean writer. He's nothing else but a West Indian writer… I have a slightly different view of Hearne since *The Pleasures of Exile*. I would – while not leaving that criticism – I think it's incomplete, and I have more recently come to think of Hearne as representing a kind of relevance that I did not state in that criticism.

DANCE: Relevance to West Indian literature in particular?

LAMMING: And to the total West Indian reality. That is what I was speaking about – that I thought the strongest books were informed by that peasant sensibility. What I would say today is that while that remains true, the area of investigation of Hearne's books is very important – that is that Hearne is dealing with a Jamaican – inverted commas – middle-class and that he is looking at that class sympathetically; and I think that's a very important thing, because the role and future of that class raises very serious questions for the destiny of the Caribbean.

DANCE: OK. Well, I want to get back to the idea of the significance of the land and place in terms of the West Indian writer's imagination. And in this statement you lament: 'I have lost my place, or my place has deserted me… the West Indian writer abroad… hungers for nourishment from a soil which he… could not at present endure… yet there is always an acre of ground in the New World which keeps growing echoes in my head. I can only hope that these echoes do not die before my work comes to an end' [p.50]. Do you have a sense that you are, because of your distance from home, losing those echoes?

LAMMING: No. I think it is a very good indication of how a period may have an effect on emphases. The way I organise statements, they contain paradoxes, that I'm saying something which while it is true, the relevance of the truth varies from time to time, so that – that comes from *The Pleasures of Exile*, which was published in 1960 – I think it's perhaps true to say that the echoes of the Caribbean reality are louder in my head today than they probably were in 1960.

DANCE: Oh, really?

LAMMING: Yes. And I think that there is a reason for that. That book is also coming out of a certain kind of pain about the – I mean it's quite clear that there has been a total betrayal of the creating of a regional solidarity, the whole of the Federation thing is not doing well, and so on, and it's a period in which people like me who are completely regional in their perspectives of the Caribbean, were taking blows, to see something that they thought their life's work was about, not taking place; but there have been, you know, later developments that have helped correct that attitude, so that if I were writing *The Pleasures of Exile* today, I don't think that basically some of the things I said there would have changed, but I think that there would be different emphases.

DANCE: So that leaving does not have that terrible detrimental effect on writers that I think you have suggested it might have? Eddie Brathwaite, for example, said something about the difficulty of writers in exile for whom so much has changed and who don't really know the land anymore. Is this no longer a real problem for the expatriate writers?

LAMMING: The problem varies according to who is talking. I think the thing that one has to bear in mind is that writers are very individual, and they relate in a very individual way to what may be the same common experience. I think there is a certain kind of writer for whom the separation is less of a deprivation than it is for another writer, though all writers would of course prefer that they were within the arena from which they were drawing materials…

DANCE: But you don't feel as strongly about this as you did when you told students at the University of the West Indies that they must not leave?

LAMMING: Oh, I feel very strongly about that. What I wanted to say about that question is that it's a question which I don't care to discuss in that way. That I believe that the subject of the writer in exile should be dropped, completely. I don't think it's any longer relevant. And I'm saying this as one who perhaps initiated the discussion… I don't think that it should be on the agenda now in a serious way. What is on the agenda in a serious way is how does the Caribbean society organise itself and politically relate to its cultural life in such a way that there would not be a repetition of that movement – that is the issue – not that past movement or what is happening to them. I don't think anybody in the Caribbean now should lose any time about what's happening to the writers who migrated or to writers who are in exile. The only thing they have to do is to look at what books they are writing and so on…

DANCE: So you are suggesting that there is a need to correct the situation that causes writers to go into exile?

LAMMING: Oh, absolutely. That is the only issue to be discussed. I mean how do you make the ambience – how do the writers themselves make the ambience workable?

DANCE: May I assume from that that you are suggesting that if the situations were different you might return to live in Barbados?

LAMMING: Oh, yes, oh, yes.

DANCE: But it is mainly a political situation which prevents that at this point?

LAMMING: Basically it's a political situation, but then political is used in a very wide sort of way. If… it's a very big if, a nonsensical kind of if in a way… but if I were Cuban, I would not be living out of Cuba.

DANCE: It's that kind of revolution…

LAMMING: It's that kind of situation in which the cultural life is an organic part of the whole and in which the cultural worker is seen and organised as an organic part of the working life of the people.

DANCE: Might that not also take away some of your freedom as a writer? Is there any problem…

LAMMING: Well, that's another kind of struggle. But problems of freedom are ongoing, and they arise in all kinds of society, and there is that problem of freedom in the neocolonial society in Jamaica or Barbados or Trinidad. I mean the problem appears. And writers left because they were not free to be writers. They weren't ordered not to be writers, but a situation existed which said this had no meaning, you know, in society, so you weren't really free to function any more than, you know, than roses are free to bloom in the Sahara. If a situation is so organised that your particular activity may have no meaning, that is a serious deprivation of freedom to exercise that activity, so I think the problem of freedom is not peculiar to socialist societies. I think that it is an ongoing problem in all types of society.

DANCE: OK. Let me ask you about another subject, and that is the subject of Africa. You have travelled in Africa and you know many writers from the Americas make that voyage to Africa a very symbolic kind of thing, a quest for roots and so forth. Did you go to Africa in that sort of romantic vein, or was it just a trip?

LAMMING: Oh, no, I think it was a serious… I mean… you say romantic. Yes, it probably was romantic, but I would use romantic in a very serious sense. There are different ways in which you can use romantic. I tell you how that came about. It came about because of increasing interest in the political struggle, the anti-colonial struggle, which was really spearheaded from West Africa. And then I had arrived in England, and a lot of my earliest and first personal contacts were with Africans either from Nigeria or Ghana, and therefore I was not simply dealing with Africa as an abstraction. I was dealing with Africa via the guy who lived in the same room as me, and with whom I talked every evening, and I used to go then, I think, every Sunday or every other Sunday to a place called the West African Students' Union, where they used to gather there for all sorts of discussion. So it was not only the other romantic thing; but it was the actual concrete experience of talking to and with people, many of whom became my friends – that concrete experience in African reality. But, as I say, I would think that at that stage my linkage was political. That is that the more we talked, the more I realised that there was a very common experience in relation to that whole imperialist and colonial empires. That I think was the trigger point for me. And then I had the choice – I got an award – and one of the conditions of the award was that you were not to use the money in England, you had to travel. I used it to go to what had then become Ghana.

DANCE: This discussion of your early relationships with Africans in Europe, which I assume was the first time that you probably had any type of real contact, seems reasonably positive, and yet I see suggested often in your written accounts of contacts of Black people from the Americas with Africans in Europe a kind of negative thing. As a matter of fact, in one book you even wrote that they weren't supposed to like each other [*The Emigrants*, p. 165] which sort of suggests the inability of Blacks from the Diaspora to relate to Blacks from Africa when they first met in Europe.

LAMMING: Well, I think one has to be careful about that, because I mean that's made up of a lot of different people, but I think that... there would have been tensions. The people who became close and very friendly were the people who were aware of those tensions and could talk about them, and where they came from, and what they were about, and what we had to do about them... We realised, for example, that if you came out of that Caribbean situation, you did encounter the African, you did see the African person there in front of you through that filter... of that colonial education, and so on, that you had been given about the dark continent. I think there are some scenes in *The Emigrants* which are very authentic. You had West Indian women who had great difficulty or felt they had great difficulty in dancing with an African man whose tribal marks, as they called them, were over-pronounced; you see that as a scratched up face which in some way had to do with savagery.

DANCE: Yes. Let me ask you about what I see as a general theme in a lot of your novels and in a lot of other novels by West Indians, and that is the sense of death in Europe. For the West Indian going to Europe, you know, they go there to make a living, but they can't live in Europe. In *The Emigrants*, for example, they all come to rather sad ends. Some lose their minds and there's a pervading sense of death. But particularly in *Water With Berries*. You know, the characters are described in terms of death... one plays a corpse all the time, you know, Derek.

LAMMING: Yes.

DANCE: And you call the city a mausoleum; the houses rise like vaults; the steps echo the silence of the grave; the theatre rises like a tomb. Are you suggesting that West Indians cannot live in Europe?

LAMMING: Well, I think that the images of a tomb and so on are images that have to do with the death of empire. Not of a death of the West Indian so much, but the death of his original connection with the British Empire. That's the, I think, meaning of the Old Dowager in *Water With Berries*. The Old Dowager does represent that last, fading, but very potent voice of empire. OK. It's an empire that is in decline, but its psychological force is still very operative on all who come within its orbit.

DANCE: So that's why Teeton can't leave her?

LAMMING: That's why he has to kill her. And that is a symbolic murder that then has not only to do with Teeton, and not only with West Indians in England. It has to do with *all* the post-colonial world that was connected with her. Gentlemen's agreements about transfer of power cannot touch the psychological weight of the historic influence.

DANCE: That's very interesting. Let me ask you then. It is very interesting that Roger cannot believe that his European wife Nicole is pregnant with his baby. [*Water With Berries*] Does that mean that the West Indian cannot bring his life into this old empire, and so she must die before she can give birth?

LAMMING: Of course that was very special to him… Roger, as I recall, his special thing was that he was afflicted with notions of a purity – of a special kind of purity, and…

DANCE: Racial as much as anything else?

LAMMING: Yes. Racial, yes, but racial-cultural, and couldn't commit himself to the idea of that sort of miscegenation without the feeling that some portion of him would be diminished. I don't think that Teeton, whom we do not see in that kind of relationship with women, might have been so strong on that. Teeton's was a much more starkly political confrontation and a political-psychological confrontation with the Old Dowager.

DANCE: I see. OK. In an interview, which I think was the one at Texas, you said that New York was replacing London as a literary centre for West Indians. That was in 1970. Do you see that trend continuing?

LAMMING: What I meant there was that the movement of the West Indian writers to Europe was part of a certain historical development, which was gradually coming to an end. OK. Just as politically all decisions about change involved the journey of politicians to Europe whether they went from Martinique to Paris or from Jamaica and Trinidad to London and all kinds of constitutional things and so on. As part of that same movement, the Caribbean writers saw, say London, as a cultural metropole that would even bring them to the attention of the Caribbean people, which is precisely what happened. I don't think that you would have heard of any of the novelists, certainly when you heard about them, had it not been for that movement. That's one of the curious paradoxes of that cultural history, but with increasing developments, developments of authenticity in the area, the territory would gradually begin to see itself more as part of the Americas. OK. And that politically as well as culturally (because this doesn't only apply to writers) the movement, so far as there has to be a movement, would increase towards the United States. I mean Caribbean leaders don't go to England. There's no reason to go to England unless there's a Common-wealth Conference or something like that, but Washington is crucial… the network of power manipulation, aid, business, how you settle what you're going to do with the powers that be, is American… in the sense not only of the United States – but an affair of the Americas.

DANCE: Another move I would suppose is also towards Cuba?

LAMMING: Yes, the move to the Americas has a further extension, logically… And the extension logically, it seems to me, is that I think that Havana will become a major cultural centre for the Caribbean intelligentsia, even more major… than say New York. And then what has happened really is that the thing is coming back full circle from the dependence relations to Europe, to coming back to the Americas where you belong, and then back inside the Caribbean region, if you see Cuba, as I do, as a Caribbean country.

DANCE: Is there any chance of Jamaica becoming a centre…?

LAMMING: Well, Cuba is the more advanced, but what I'm saying is that the way that the wheel turns is that the Caribbean will become its major cultural centre.

DANCE: Let me ask you some questions about your family now. I'm not so sure – are we safe in reading *In the Castle of My Skin* as pretty straight autobiography…?

LAMMING: No, not really.

DANCE: No? Is the mother there very much like your mother in terms of encouraging education and…

LAMMING: Yes, the mother figure is… but it's a composite of fiction and… yes, I draw from the actualities of my situation…

DANCE: Was your mother an educated woman?

LAMMING: No, literate, but not what you would call educated…

DANCE: Well, any mother would of course be pleased with her son's success, but I would suppose with your mother it's sort of reinforcing what she planned for you all along? Is that?

LAMMING: Well, yes, I suppose a part of her is.

DANCE: You are an only child?

LAMMING: Yes, yes. She has a double way of dealing with me, I think. I mean a part of me is that writer, of which, yes, she is very pleased, but there's still a part of me that's still silly and…

DANCE: Well, you know, I would imagine that if I may just guess, which is a dangerous thing to do, that a lady like your mother might have some misgivings about your wanting to become a writer rather than say a teacher.

LAMMING: Well, it wouldn't have made… at that time, no, no sense at all to her. None at all. It only makes sense later with books and with, you know, critical judgements and things… But I don't think that the actual occupation of professional writer… why, I mean, she still thinks it's a very weird profession… But I've found her one of the best critics of *In the Castle of My Skin*, and she raises some questions, some very, very real questions. She was very disturbed by – my mother is a very fundamentalist kind of Christian, who actually lives that life – and she enjoyed that book, and she knows, she can tell you who everybody is, and that sort of thing… What happened to A and what happened to B and what happened to D and so on. She objected very much to language and treatment of language, you know, things that she calls bad language and that sort of thing. And she doesn't think that's necessary at all, that there must be some other way of doing things. And the other thing – she reads some parts of that book in which there appears to be disrespect – some of the boys are speaking with disrespect of God, and that she is very firm on. That she will describe as ignorance, in the Pauline sense of being a fooled fool, not necessarily an ignorant person, but a person who is not aware of his or her ignorance... And she is disgusted by that. Like she thinks that no matter how good a writer you may be, or people say you may be, you did not give yourself your gift, you see, and therefore if you are honest to it, you really have to see yourself as a vessel through which some things must flow, a chosen vessel, as we would say... I think she is perceptive. She doesn't like to see me in the company of political people, particularly people who are in office, people who are at the ministries, and so on. She is convinced they're up to no good... and that they're seeing me for some reason that has nothing to do with me. She may have a point.

DANCE: Yes. May I ask you about your father?

LAMMING: Not very much, because I hardly knew him. I've been trying to search my memory in more recent times. He never grew up with us and I didn't know him in the house at all.

DANCE: Did you ever meet him later?

LAMMING: Oh, I met him. Not later, I met him earlier. I remember him coming on occasions some Sunday mornings to take me out and that sort of thing, maybe twice a year or something like that. And then somewhat later when I was in my teens and started to go around to have a drink, and so on, I'd run into him at the same bar, and he was always very proud and would do a big thing about introducing his son... but all fathers who've never carried the responsibility of their children tend to do that, if their children are about to make something of themselves. But I don't really know him.

DANCE: Is he still living?

LAMMING: Oh, no. He died. He died, as I recall, he died shortly after I left to go to Trinidad, because I remember, vaguely remember, a letter from my mother saying he had died.

DANCE: Most of the boys in the village pictured in *In the Castle of My Skin* seem to grow up in homes without fathers. Was that a realistic kind of picture of the Barbados village in which you grew up? They talk about it themselves in a very humorous passage at one point.

LAMMING: Yes. There were different levels of that. Many without any experience of paternal responsibility – that's very different from without fathers. I mean the fathers were there or around or in and out, and so on, but I mean fathers in the sense of being responsible for them.

DANCE: Yes, I remember one of the boys said something about the fact that a father who doesn't live at home can't beat you or can't discipline you or something to suggest that he thereby lost his right to function as father.

LAMMING: Yes.

DANCE: Do you think this kind of experience early in your life where your mother was, you said, your father too, and the boys talk about father like that... do you think that has anything to do with the fact that for the most part, as I read your novels, men have a certain kind of weakness in terms of their ability to form a strong relationship with women?

LAMMING: I don't know, because that problem of the man/woman relationship and so on exists also within the more solid structures, I mean, even within the Caribbean. I mean if you went from that level to what you might call the middle-class family, and so on, I think that… I think that, perhaps before I was aware of it, or before it was being stated in that way, probably some part of me was aware of the fundamental failure in that man/woman relationship. I wasn't articulating it then in the way that it is articulated in *Natives of my Person*. I mean by the time they get there, and the organisation of that book in terms of the officers and their wives – that is very highly conscious, and I'm saying things there that I would not have been in a position to say when I was writing…

DANCE: So you are there articulating a view that has been developing: that women 'are a future [men] must learn' [*Natives of My Person*, p.351].

LAMMING: Oh, yes. It's a view on which I think the whole feminist movement is based. And *Natives of My Person* is doing that very consciously. It's not quite so conscious in *In the Castle of My Skin*. It's simply reportage in a way.

DANCE: Let me get you to specify a little more distinctly exactly what you're saying there so I won't misread it: the men are not able to accept the strengths and moral values of the women, right? They cannot see…

LAMMING: In *Natives*, yes. And the problem that they can't resolve, hence the scuttle of the enterprise really – they can't resolve the basic conflict between power and love – that their entire destinies are linked to the realisation and the exercise of power, and in the process of achieving that, they live almost a total negation of the experience of loving the women who are in their lives… And they will then be in deep trouble when women suggest that there has to be some other basis for that connection, which is done in the Lady of the House. While they are waiting, what they are saying there is that they're waiting, but when the men arrive – because they're sure they will arrive – it will be different, it will have to be.

DANCE: Would it be oversimplifying things to say that that ideal society that the men envision there in that book can be realised only when they learn from the women how to love. Is that oversimplifying it?

LAMMING: No, I think that the society that they wanted to shape, yes, is a society which I think would have to be made with women, yes, the dominant and formative influence in that society. It certainly couldn't be made on the basis that produced them and produced their earlier relationships.

DANCE: It's rather interesting that, in these books, the women are sort of the moral norm, they set the mode of morality, they're very good beings, they will do anything for their men, and so forth, and yet they're so shallow. It seems that you want to make them positive and yet in one sense they seem very negative because…

LAMMING: Yes, I saw that comment of yours. I don't think they're shallow. I don't think shallow is the word. I think that they are women who have accommodated themselves to certain kinds of roles, but in those roles they function with great intelligence, as in the case of the Lady of the House. They are trapped by this thing they call love, and of course they are in many ways, in that particular era, very dependent on their men.

DANCE: Yes, accepting that era, certainly I realise that has something to do with it, but you know a woman like the Lady of the House who can do all of these things in terms of manipulating leaders, getting the ship for the Commandant, and so forth. I mean she's a very strong person in one sense; it's kind of hard for me to accept that a woman with that possibility, with that kind of strength, can walk around filling her days for years, with collecting leaves, counting the days until a man returns – I mean that's one thing. That's what I'm talking about when I say there's a kind of shallowness…

LAMMING: Well, I think that was just an image, really, of her devotion, in the sense of her capacity for loving, that she wouldn't see the separation as an adversity and so on, that the love that she had couldn't cope with it. I think that is done really to heighten the disproportion in the involvement because, though he can't do without her, when he is out on the expeditions and so on, she's not really on his mind.

DANCE: That's because he's a more complex person.

LAMMING: But that is general; that is true of the Prime Minister or the head of a business corporation or what have you. There's an area in him which can't function if she leaves. OK. But the arena in which he has chosen to realise himself is one in which he doesn't think about her because it's not an arena that is made by her and it's not an arena in which her real decisions operate.

DANCE: That's perfectly understandable, and I suppose the main thing we must see with her is her influence on him, but somehow it seems to me that she would be complex enough that she would find something else…

LAMMING: But what alternatives would she have? I mean, out of revenge, she gets married and so on to a man whom she says is a husband. There's a very important distinction between a husband and a man, and she gets married to a husband. Well, in that world and very much in all worlds – but the world I was thinking about was the Caribbean or that post-colonial world – women have been trapped in a world that has been created by men, and whose organisation is male, and while they are functioning within it, there isn't really an alternative, because the alternative isn't this man rather than that, but because the male then represents a sort of class which is dominant in their lives, the only alternative would be a disruption in that arrangement. And I think at the end of *Natives*, what is left there is the suggestion that that disruption is in the making. I think the book ends with her saying something about 'We…'

DANCE: 'We are the future that they must learn.' Is that why their ship is the *Penalty*?

LAMMING: Yes. And they weren't going to make it back. In a way I don't think that a man of that social formation will be able to meet the demands of a woman who has decided that the way has to be altered…

DANCE: I want to ask you about the title *Natives Of My Person*. Now I read the explanation that you gave to George Kent about the post card from the African with his children on it saying, 'These are all the natives of my person.' I can't quite see how that relates to the novel where the characters seem sort of alien to *you*. You say they are the natives of your person.

LAMMING: Yes. I mean they are alien if you want to put them in a historical sense. In another sense what *native* means there is that they are the creations, they are the children of this particular imagination as it has been shaped by the history that includes me and those people, like the Commandant.

DANCE: I see, and there's a little irony I suppose in that…

LAMMING: Yes, I suppose you could say, yes, in the sense that I, the creator of them, was also created by their enterprises, yes…

DANCE: I want to ask you about the idea of combining artistry with politics. At one point I think I remember reading something you said that that can go too far, that a writer may forget, he may sacrifice his art if he does not work in the area in which he's qualified to contribute, which made me think that a writer can become too political.

LAMMING: Yeah, I remember that very vaguely. I don't think he can become too political. What can happen in our situation is that the political context may not be established in which he can make the best possible use of his gifts for political ends. You see we have been living in a situation in which that divorce has seemed natural, I mean I think that divorce is unnatural, and if you have a political situation which would carry the socialist context, that divorce would not be on the agenda at all. I mean the writer would be just a cultural worker, another branch, OK? of work within that kind of society. We don't yet have that kind of society…

[During a break we talked about two questions which I had submitted to Lamming and which he preferred to write responses to after he had an opportunity to look over passages in his books. Then he started to speak rather specifically about one of the questions, and so he permitted me to turn on the tape.]

DANCE: [written question] I have a problem with your first-person narrator, who seems sometimes to simply disappear. In the scene on the beach in *In the Castle of My Skin*, the boys do all the talking and the narrator hardly seems to be there. In many discussions on the boat in *The Emigrants*, the narrator hardly seems to be there, so much so that he can tell us that he didn't see Queenie after they got on the boat, but yet I assume he is narrating the scene when she appears at the dance.

LAMMING: I have been trying to work out, more consciously now, a device where there is an observer/participant, and in such a way that the 'I' slides into the 'we'. Now this is very central to a lot of the fiction in the Caribbean in which the 'I' of the writer is hardly inseparable from the 'we', even when the 'I' is speaking only of the 'I'. The opening of *In the Castle Of My Skin* is the 'I' of the 'I', but that 'I' is in a sense not only the 'I' of the 'I', but the 'I' of any of the others. That 'I/we' arrangement I want to keep; and it will work differently in different books. *The Castle* is a good example of where this silence is functioning, and I think perhaps it is more successful there than in *The Emigrants*. You asked where is 'he'. He's very much there. Right? But if you remember, if you look at that again, when that chapter opens, as I remember that, his relationship to the boys is very troubled and alienated; as a matter of fact, they don't want him there.

DANCE: So they could easily ignore him,

LAMMING: OK. And he's only there, I think, by virtue of the fact that they're also partly accepting his difference. I mean they resent it and then accept it. There is a passage in which one of them says how they had overheard the mother telling him what she would do if she saw him in their company.

DANCE: Yes.

LAMMING: That's very heavy. That's very heavy. So what is happening is that while he is with them, he's really on the periphery of the world and he doesn't really feel the right to speak in that world: and I think if you look at how that section opens, you will see that his silence is functional in terms of being with them but not being of them. And then if the echoes of that remain, by the time you're reading, then the almost straight statement about the high school when he's saying what will happen to A, B and C, then the silence of things becomes more real. There he's saying what the school has now unapologetically done to them, and in a way, because the book works that way, that ripple, echo, ripple, echo, and by the time he and Trumper meet on the eve of departure, I think the silence of it should become more real.

DANCE: OK. I want to ask you something about your relationship with American writers… first of all, Richard Wright, to whom you dedicated *Natives*. Did you know him well?

LAMMING: No. I didn't know him well. I got to know him, because as you know, he did the introduction to the American edition of *In the Castle*… it turned out that the man, called Ed Aswald, who was going to be my editor at McGraw-Hill, had been Wright's editor. Aswald had a very big thing about *In the Castle of My Skin*. He wanted to use all the ploys and so on for the promotion of it. And I think Aswald sent the book to Wright with a request that if he felt it was worth it, would he do an introduction. So the American edition of *In the Castle of My Skin* came out with a long introduction by Wright… Very interesting introduction. Very interesting. I hadn't known Wright.

DANCE: Do you think he fully appreciated the book?

LAMMING: Oh, yes. Well he makes emphases that are of his own kind. But it was very interesting to see how he read it, and it fitted very much into things going on in his head, and I think quite correctly here he saw the movement of the Trumpers of this world and so on as not too different from the movement of Bigger from the South to the North, the throwing up of a peasant, agricultural man into this new industrial world. What happened is that about a year after that I was going to Paris for the first time, and on the strength of that I sent him a cable – I'd never been to Paris – to say I was coming, and Aswald had kindly introduced me to him by letter. And he was, you know, he was wonderful… He got me rooms, and I spent a month in Paris. And that was the limit of my knowing him. I saw him almost every day…

DANCE: You mentioned somewhere that you were surprised to find that you had copied many passages from *Black Boy*…

LAMMING: Oh, earlier, yes. That was before I ever wrote anything.

DANCE: So, there was an admiration I assume…

LAMMING: Oh, very much. I was moved by that. I think I still have it – that exercise book, with sections of when he returns and sees the father, and the section where he sees the father on the eve of the departure.

DANCE: You have commented on Baldwin's work…

LAMMING: My only comments on Baldwin were in *The Pleasures of Exile*, in which I was making a critical observation of what I thought was in Baldwin an incorrect view of Europe. Baldwin has a passage in *The Fire Next Time*, I think it is, in which he speaks about when he was in Europe looking at peasants and so on that he was not, in the way they were, related to the cathedrals and… the Eiffel Tower and all of that, but when he looked back he had nothing to claim, and there is that reference to bush… the fact that if he looked at his own history the way they were looking at theirs, he had no Eiffel Tower, and what I was trying to say is that two things were wrong about that – he was part of the notion that the only meaningful history was the history of Eiffel Towers, and there was no history of an African civilisation because it had no Eiffel Towers. OK. I don't think he would make that mistake again. But that was the comment I made. And, point two: it was also, it was also an American distortion of the European reality – that the only people who see the continuity in European civilisation are Americans, because the European working class men don't have that relation to any Eiffel Tower either. The Eiffel Tower is a monument of a dominant ruling class and he doesn't have that kind of relation to all that that tower means either...

CONVERSATION WITH

EARL LOVELACE

Earl W Lovelace was born in Toco, Trinidad, on July 13, 1935, and grew up in Tobago. His early training was in agriculture, and for two years he worked as a forest ranger. He then turned to writing, and after the publication of his first novel he came to America and studied at Howard University and Johns Hopkins University. He returned to Trinidad, where he lectures at the University of the West Indies. He was in residence at the Writer's Program at the University of Iowa in the 1980s, and has now been appointed to the Board of Governers at Trinidad and Tobago University. He lives in Trinidad.

Lovelace has published five novels: *While Gods Are Falling* (1965); *The Schoolmaster* (1968); *The Dragon Can't Dance* (1979); *The Wine of Astonishment* (1982) and *Salt* (1996); as well as a collection of short stories, *A Brief Conversion and Other Stories* (1988). He has also written several dramas, some of which are published in *Jestina's Calypso and Other Plays* (1984) and many plays performed in Trinidad. A few poems and short stories have appeared in anthologies and journals. *Growing in the Dark*, a collection of essays by Lovelace, was published in 2003 by Lexicon Press. In 2004, he wrote the 'Introduction' to Stefan Falke's *Moko Jumbies: the Dancing Spirits of Trinidad*.

The first extensive study of his work is *Caribbean Literature After Independence: The Case of Earl Lovelace* (ed. Bill Schwarz, 2008)

Lovelace has been the recipient of the British Petroleum Independence Literary Award (1964) and a Guggenheim Fellowship (1980). In 1997, the Commonwealth Writers Prize for best book was awarded for his novel, *Salt*.

At the time of the interview, Lovelace was living in Matura, Trinidad, with his first wife and three children; he has since remarried. The following interview was conducted in Port of Spain, on March 11, 1980.

––––––––––––––

DANCE: In an interview [*Kas-Kas*, 1972] CLR James has contrasted the education of himself and Lamming and Naipaul, which was in the literary tradition of Western civilisation, with the experience of you and Anthony. He rather humorously recounts a conversation with you. He says: 'I [James] said, "Have you read so and so?" He said, "No, but I intended to." "Have you read so and so?" He said, "Well, I started but I didn't finish, but I am going to."' Then he goes on to say seriously that while you are not literary in the traditional sense, you are native and national in a sense that the previous generation is not. Have you read this interview?

LOVELACE: No, I didn't read the interview as such, you know – but I do know that he has made some comments like that. I don't want to contradict CLR – I understand the spirit in which it is said – the thing is though, that I think what CLR wants to emphasise there is that there were writers who are not only educated in, let's say, in the Western tradition, but who were imbued with the ideas of, almost the superiority and the over-prevailingness of the Western tradition. I would say that I am aware of that tradition. I have read, I think, all the writers, yeah, or many of them at least and perhaps my attitude to them is that, 'OK they have written that.' I mean they are seeing things from one kind of 'eye' and from one world view, as it were, and I am seeing something different. I think basically this is what he wants to convey, that they have not impressed me perhaps in the same way that they have impressed Lamming and Naipaul and James himself.

DANCE: Is it simply a matter of not being influenced by these writers or do you see yourself as consciously rejecting the Western tradition and looking for something that you see as more pertinent to your concerns here?

LOVELACE: Well actually I don't think it is so much rejecting them, because I think there have been people who I respect; but it is really more looking to see what I have to say, what we have to say, as it were. One thing I should say is that when I look at the movement of Caribbean writing (let me say Caribbean for the time being), I see one stage at which we had to prove to the Western world that we can write like them. Right? I think that that work, in a kind of way, was done by people coming before me, let us say, like James, Lamming, and so on. Right? I don't think I have to prove that I can write like them. I am not interested in writing like them. Of course the literary standards that one gets, I wouldn't say involved in, you know, but that one accepts, right, and one deals with. One has an idea of what standards one wants for oneself. I am not suggesting that we are dealing with any slipshodidness, or just being native for the sake of being native in that kind of way.

DANCE: Were there any writers who led you to this? Any Caribbean writers who impressed you with doing some of the kinds of things that you consider yourself…

LOVELACE: Well, I would say at various points, you know, and not necessarily in a chronological order, but I would think that Selvon, for example, who deals with the vernacular of the native speech and a lot of the underlying pathos, and writes in Caribbean English, if you want to call it that, is one person who I feel I have looked at with great interest. Then there is Césaire, who while I can't say that he influenced me at an early point in my career or writing, learning to write or whatever, I am certain that he has had an influence in helping to solidify some things that one might have felt, that there was another way of viewing things. Right? So those are the principal writers, you know, those are all I can think of.

DANCE: What about James's influence on you?

LOVELACE: Right. As you mention James now, James – yes, I think he has had a great influence in the sense that he was perhaps the first Caribbean intellectual that I came in contact with, not necessarily personally at the beginning, but in terms of his writings. I do know that he has had some influence in terms of clarifying a lot of things, of presenting, of proposing a lot of ideas. If one reads James carefully, one would see that he has dealt with many, many things, you know.

DANCE: Yes. Did you ever consult him when you were writing, ask him to read manuscripts, seek his advice?

LOVELACE: When I was finished, more or less finished… like I remember, I didn't know him personally when I was writing *While Gods Are Falling*, which was my first novel. But when I was finished with *The Schoolmaster*, I let him see it, and generally it has been that kind of way. When I am finished with a book, I say, 'Well, look,' you know, and he would comment, or what…

DANCE: Have his comments resulted in any changes, modifications?

LOVELACE: You see he is not that kind of – to me at least – that kind of person. I think he watches you grow or develop according to how you want to develop, and he would make a comment that would not necessarily be emphasised, but if you listen carefully you will find probably what he wanted to tell you, you know. I remember in *The Schoolmaster*, he said to me, 'Why did the schoolmaster have to die?' or 'Why did you kill the schoolmaster?' or something like that. And I thought about that, I didn't change it. I thought about it and then I understood what I think he was saying, and it seemed to me that what he was saying is that the schoolmaster is alive. I mean that kind of person still exists in the society and to have killed him off is probably kind of romantic, you know… I think that in a certain respect James [in his comments in the previously quoted interview] is correct. I think I would say that I am largely a self-educated person and it would be giving the kind of wrong impression, I think, if I emphasised degrees. When I went to Howard I thought I was going to study, you know, which is something I had always wanted to do. And when I got there – what it did for me is to make me see people studying, be at university, understand what that was, understand some terms that people used, the way they studied, and so on. And after a while I felt as if I didn't want to pursue that, you know, that academic kind of career – right? So I left. Going to Johns Hopkins was – when I left there, incidentally, I came back and I worked in the newspaper, I continued writing, and then I went to Federal City College and taught in a programme there. And after that, after gaining a lot of experience and understanding some things about the world as it were, and then I went to people. Friends of mine said it would be useful to have a degree and there was this writing degree offered at Hopkins, and indeed it was a friend of mine who filled out the forms and everything, took me up there, he took me personally. And I decided to go (kind of halfway, you know), and before the course started the person who was teaching the programme got a Fulbright Fellowship, I think, and they asked me to teach the programme. So from the point of view of emphasis really… I don't think it is true to say that organised education in that kind of way has influenced me that much.

DANCE: All right. While you were in America, were you introduced to the works of any writers that impressed you or influenced you?

LOVELACE: Well, right here [Trinidad] I had read – I suppose that I always have to talk about it because I think the most important influence perhaps in my own *life* actually – not only in writing – is reading. From a small boy I read a great deal, you know, and I had read not only novels and so on, from the time I was quite small, about, let us say, three, four, five, six.

DANCE: Were you reading novels then?

LOVELACE: No, but from about six, seven, I would say, I was reading novels. Actually, at a certain time I used to think that I had read more between the ages of let us say, six and twelve, than afterwards, you know. And what am I saying now about this reading? Oh, that I had read all about the Black Americans, Frederick Douglass… Harriet Tubman, all that stuff I read as a child in the library in Tobago, right, where I grew up. And later on I read, not as a child now, but as a man, I had read the Black writers, you know, like…

DANCE: Wright, Hughes…?

LOVELACE: Wright, Baldwin, not Hughes, but Baldwin and those writers. I had also read Hemingway. In fact I had read a number of the American writers, and I had read the American writers principally because I found the English writers boring (that's the truth, you know). They didn't have as much action for me as the American writers. I like action a lot and… so I was led to the American writers for that reason… Oh, I have read Faulkner, who I find a tremendous writer, who to me is one of the greatest writers, you know.

DANCE: What about the group of more militant writers during the '60s like Don L Lee and LeRoi Jones and that group?

LOVELACE: Well, I read them as well. Don L Lee, LeRoi Jones – I don't know. On the one hand, there is a certain affinity and understanding of Don L Lee and LeRoi Jones – Black people struggling against a system that is probably more oppressive than, let us say, it has been in the Caribbean in a certain milieu. Because of the differences that I think you will understand – and I myself was involved in the Black Power movement – it was a part of me, you know, that whole move to establish your own identity, power, and so on – I found the writing a little straight-line, by that I mean concerned with one dimension, I think, simple, one dimension at a time, not sufficiently complex and capturing the subtleties and contradictions of human beings, you know. Well, that is the way I respond to them.

DANCE: OK. I noticed in your work that race does not seem to be as significant as it is in much West Indian literature, particularly that by writers who have gone to Europe and America and have developed, I think, a more… more of a sense of racial identity; your characters seem to me to be looking for manhood, rather than identity as Black men specifically in racial terms. Bee in 'Every Step Is a Station' [in *New Writing in the Caribbean* ed. AJ Seymour, 1972] declares that he seeks freedom to express himself in his own way: 'A man is what he is.' Walter in *While Gods Are Falling* seems constantly seeking for a way to feel and assert his manhood. Benn, in *The Schoolmaster*, struggles to keep his sense of manhood. Is this your theme, your major theme?

LOVELACE: Well I think that perhaps 'personhood' might be a better word, and one is looking at it from the point of view of – well, you know, we grow up in a male chauvinist society, so I don't want to get the slant on 'manhood' as separate from 'personhood'.

DANCE: But it's always the male, and it's always what we associate with 'manhood'.

LOVELACE: But I am not so sure you know. I am not sure it is always what you associate with 'manhood'… What do you associate with 'manhood'? Maybe I could try to throw some light on that in terms of some of the characters. Or do you want to say what you are thinking?

DANCE: But with Walter Castle, for example, that matter of manhood has to do with things that we associate with being a male, including providing for his family in a certain kind of way; and with Benn in *The Schoolmaster* it's a matter of showing another man what a man he is, you know. For example, I don't think with a woman that situation with the horse would ever have been so significant as it was to him. So there seems to be what we call 'typically' male kinds of drives.

LOVELACE: OK. Well, I would want to leave out Walter Castle from that a little bit, for the reason that, the first book was, I would say, a young book, very groping, and so on. Right? OK. Then I suppose what I should be trying to do here is to define or to look at what I am calling personhood, you know. Right? I think we are talking about personhood, and I've been talking, as it were, about manhood. Right? I think that what we're talking about is a man in a community, man's view of his integrity, and this is defined, not by him alone, but by the community in which he lives. Right? So manhood would appear to be rather stereotyped, but behind it what I am talking about is the integrity of the individual, and one begins to decide what that integrity is in terms of one's own growth, that later you begin to add dimensions to it, that you haven't had before, or to de-emphasise certain things that you had emphasised before.

Right? So I don't think it is placed in terms of the chauvinist man as opposed to woman in that kind of way. It is really dealing with the integrity of the individual.

DANCE: OK. I don't want to press…

LOVELACE: Yes, press me.

DANCE: I don't want to press the issue too much, this is slightly different but it certainly gets down to the matter of sex roles. And this is the question that comes to my mind as I have read your novels. You create some striking and fascinating female characters, but you seem to resist dealing with them in the way that you deal with the male characters. And this is particularly apparent in *The Dragon Can't Dance*, where your procedure is to introduce a character and then give us a detailed background, so, you know, you take us back sometimes to a grandfather or a father, an early life. You do that with Aldrick, and then we meet Fisheye, and you do that; you do that with Pariag, you do that with Philo, and when you've finished with these male characters one has a satisfying feeling, you know, that even when they are introduced you begin to expect that you will learn all that there is to learn about their background, and you give a very close historical and psychological view. But when you come to Miss Cleothilda and Miss Olive and Sylvia, all of whom are interesting characters, you view them largely from the outside and you don't put them in this larger perspective, so that the whole thing seems to be given from a completely male perspective, and there are times when it really disturbed me, when I really wanted to know, for example, what Miss Cleothilda was feeling in that closing scene with Philo. I know that there were some very strong feelings that couldn't come through in the conversation which you would in a similar situation, I think, give us with your male characters.

LOVELACE: Right, right. I think I have to agree with you, you know. Right. And I think that I suppose responsible for that is one's own development, I would say. I hadn't looked at it like that before, but as you – immediately you began to talk I see that you are right.

DANCE: But now in this latest novel, *The Wine of Astonishment*?

LOVELACE: Well, this latest novel… well, it is before *The Dragon Can't Dance* actually. It is seen from a woman's point of view, and I think it is probably – she is the mother, but again I still have the same role in which you were querying, you know, in a kind of sense. But I agree with you that I am not viewing the women as fully as persons as they might be viewed. Now I wonder why? You have any opinions?

DANCE: *You* must tell me that. [Laughter]

LOVELACE: I have – having done it, I think that it has been largely unconscious. Let us take *The Dragon*, which is the latest book and which probably I would want to feel represents, certainly in the things I have written, one of the more recent developments. Let me see. The characters we have are Aldrick, who is dealing with the world from a man's point of view, yes, the male. Now let me look at the women characters. Cleothilda. Yes, yes. I think that I haven't understood the woman's question or the woman's struggle for personhood as fully as I might have, although I feel that I understand a good bit, you know. I think that people have to see themselves in terms of relations. What is called Women's Liberation is leading one to what I call the individual family, and a lot of the demands are made on the basis of what men have achieved and what men are doing, and so on, as if that is so tremendously important – which it might be. I don't know. But we have had the nuclear family where the tribal or let us say the larger elements of the family like the grandmothers and grandfathers and so on have been left out; and now it seems to me we only have the husband and wife and a couple of children. Now it seems to me that we are moving towards the individual family, and one of the reasons why I see us moving in that direction is because people are not talking about people in relation to each other any more, but talking about individuals set off by themselves. Now – so I tend, I believe, to see women, right, in terms still of a family structure and therefore in one kind of way, one might say, dominated by the male.

DANCE: The family seems to be a major concern in your first two novels, and it seems also that you are suggesting the destructive impact of the city on the family, and there it is family, the extended family. Would you like to comment on that a little bit?

LOVELACE: Maybe you could tell me where in the book…

DANCE: OK. In *While Gods Are Falling*, for example, when you focus on this yard or ghetto area, the whole thing seems to be that all the families are falling apart, and again you go back in the background and when we see the history we see a rather strong family unit in most cases, people have a kind of unity. And with Walter we just see the family falling to pieces, you know, relationships even with sisters, brothers; and then what you do is have Walter bring the whole community together as a kind of family. And the same thing seems to me to be true in *The Schoolmaster*. You have in that rural community very strong families when you introduce them. I mean they are loving, they have values, they have standards that they live by and that hold them together, and then the city seems to encroach. The schoolmaster comes in, the shopkeeper comes in, from the city we assume, and they absolutely destroy these families…

LOVELACE: When I am harking back for the idyllic past… I don't know if it is something I am focusing on very deliberately, and I don't necessarily want to make out a case for its appearance in the book. I think that somehow it seems to be a consequence of what is called 'progress', of moving to the city. Right? I suppose I see the move to the city as having to leave things behind, as it were, and moving on alone, and in that kind of way I think it is a movement that we recognise existing in societies at large. What we are going to do about it is quite another question; I don't know that I have tackled that.

DANCE: Well, you certainly did in *While Gods Are Falling*. Walter brings everybody together and they start functioning as one big family unit.

LOVELACE: I feel that book was in a kind of way, kind of romantic, you know, and also quite young.

DANCE: So that's not really a practical answer to the dilemma.

LOVELACE: No, I think… well let me see. I think it is a possibility, you know, of having communal living and so on, but I wouldn't like it answered exactly in that way. I don't know that we have one answer to the questions that face us in life. We have a number of possibilities, right? Which brings to another question, you know, of the uniformity and diversity, which is one of the questions I feel that as Black people we have to deal with, and this is what I was talking about: the work of people caught up in a political kind of struggle, wanting to find answers for that struggle immediately, and I don't know that life – I mean the older I get – that life provides these clear-cut answers, nor do we want to emphasise one uniform answer, you know. I certainly do not want to. I think in a kind of way if I have any difficulty with the Western world it is that it has emphasised one kind of answer, and has not had, let's say, a number of possibilities going.

DANCE: You mention Black. The people in *The Schoolmaster* in that community aren't Black, are they? They are Indian? What are they? Spanish?

LOVELACE: Well, the people *are* Black. They are mixed with Carib – let me tell you a little bit. The Amerindians, Caribs and Arawaks, used to inhabit these islands, and when the Spaniards came here, they killed off a great number of them; they had battles and what not and so on. And so one would see in the history books that these people have disappeared. Well, they have not really disappeared. I think some people took to the hills and they have been intermingling with Black people and so on, and they pass under the name 'Spanish', meaning those people generally who were under the dominion of the Spanish, when Spain ruled the island, that was up to, I think, 1789… Oh, and that leads me, because when I was talking earlier on about reading as a small boy, really what I was saying is that at that point I was in search of my identity, you know. Because I remember… I am also partly Amerindian – vaguely. [Laughter] And because of my features, you know, people used to say, 'You are Spanish.' Now that is why I understand the thing about the Spanish. I taught Spanish so I looked at the Spanish side of my ancestry, and I read some things by the Spanish writers and so on to find out this thing. And of course I investigated the African, you know. And that is what led me at a very early age to understand a lot of things which people much later on began to deal with.

DANCE: OK. You begin *The Dragon Can't Dance* with an anecdote which is evidently legendary in Trinidad. I've seen references to it in Selvon and Naipaul. Could you tell me a little about Taffy?

[In *The Dragon Can't Dance*, Taffy goes up on Calvary Hill, puts himself on a cross, and says to his followers: 'Crucify me! Let me die for my people. Stone me with stones as you stone Jesus, I will love you still.' Lovelace continues, 'And when they start to stone him in truth he get vex and start to cuss: "Get me down!… Let every sinnerman bear his own blasted burden; who is I to die for people who ain't have sense enough to know that they can't pelt a man with big stones when so much little pebbles lying on the ground"' (p.9).]

LOVELACE: Well, actually Taffy is another fellow. The man who is celebrated more is a fellow by the name of Brackley, who was supposed to be a Baptist preacher and who went on a hill one day and said to his followers, 'Well, I have to be crucified. Crucify me.' But Taffy, the man I have, was a fellow I heard of. I don't know that I ever saw him, although he lived around the time that I was growing up. He had a church and, you know, just from going to school I heard people talking about Taffy, and the story was very closely – they had said the same thing about Brackley, but I had heard about Taffy; so I dealt with Taffy, and I was very interested to know afterwards, having written it in a kind of innocence, that Taffy was a man who indeed had a very respected church; he was one of the early Baptist preachers, if you want to call it that, who had a certain respect even in times when the Baptists were persecuted, which is actually what *The Wine of Astonishment* deals with.

DANCE: This is twentieth century, late twentieth century?

LOVELACE: Yes, that happened from 1919. They passed a law outlawing the Spiritual Baptists of Trinidad. They outlawed the beating of drums, African drums. There was a lot of outlawing of African customs and so on in colonial times here. And the struggle of these people, the Baptists, to maintain their integrity and to continue and to eventually exist today – so in a lot of fiction therefore there has been a kind of ridicule, you know, and I don't know what kind of overtones we get from the Taffy thing.

DANCE: It was hilarious as you recount it. Are the tales usually told that way or is there some admiration for him?

LOVELACE: Well, in the case of Brackley, I know he was a figure of – a 'legendary' figure in the sense of his exploits with women and so on, you know, a whole lot of stuff there. Taffy is probably much more restrained and I understand he used to wear a white suit and a poke hat, which suggests a kind of European dress for the tropics, so that tells you a little bit about him, but he was also quite a respected figure with a church up on, I think, Duke Street.

DANCE: You give an extremely sympathetic view of Pariag, the lonely Indian desiring to be accepted by the Blacks in the yard. What motivated your interest in this type of character? Are Indians seeking acceptance in the Black community in the way that this man so strongly seeks it?

LOVELACE: I think that one has to say yes and no. Yes, there is a problem in the society, that because when 'slavery' was abolished (you see I don't even like to use the word 'slavery'; I prefer to use the word 'enslavement', which suggests people fighting against that condition and seeking to liberate themselves), but when that institution was abolished in 1834 here in the West Indies, the colonial people who were in charge had to look elsewhere for labour in the new colonies like Trinidad and Guyana principally, because Black people being liberated from enslavement were not so keen to go on the estates and so on. And what they introduced were the East Indians, indentured immigrants. Also it was a plan to prevent – to keep the society split up really, having a homogeneous population to deal with, and the Indians were accepted on a different kind of base in Trinidad, you know. His religion was accepted and so on; the difference was accentuated then between the Indian and the African. It was not totally a colonial – I mean, what has resulted is not only because of the colonial, but certainly they set the stage for that kind of thing. But the end of it is, because of the place they lived and so on, is that Indians and Africans developed apart, and the Creole society, which is not really African – I mean you see when we talk about the Africans accepting them in that society, it is not that the society is African in its full sense – that society is a creation of the Africans, the Europeans and so on; it's a society where Africa has a great deal of input, but the dominant figures and the dominant codes are European. I mean the official codes. Right? And in that kind of situation the Indian has, in order to be accepted, has to give up his culture and give up certain other things at a certain point. When we have Black Power now, where Africans were seeking their own identity, you found that power began to exist in the situation. It's something that has its own complexity, eh? But basically I think it is true to say that the Indian has not been easily accepted in the Creole society unless he gave up something of his culture. Right? And I think this is what you see presented there.

DANCE: Yes, what what surprised me was his eagerness to give it up and to find acceptance…

LOVELACE: No, he wasn't… I don't think he wanted to give it up; he wanted to get in with his integrity intact, with his culture intact, he didn't want to – for example, there is another boy in the book, another fellow who is an Indian [Balliram] who had become creolised, right, and who had given up that Indianness in a kind of way.

DANCE: Well, you know what made me say that was that after you have them live in the yard for a long while, he returns home, and it seems that he had almost completely broken those ties. I am misreading that?

LOVELACE: Well, I would say he has broken – you see people have to venture out of the bosom of race, tribe, family, and so on into the world. You see this is my thesis. Right?

That people are moving to become the universe, and therefore to embrace everything in the way, everything that is in the world. Right? And so he had to be leaving, he couldn't remain in that room, in that bosom of the family and so on; he had to move out, but he wanted to move out with his integrity, so what really you saw there wasn't so much rejecting the family and all it stood for, but not being restricted by being limited to the family, but moving out beyond it, and it is the difficulty to move beyond that that presented the dilemma to him.

DANCE: Your novel centres around Carnival. No Carnival seems to be quite like Trinidad's Carnival. And I wanted to talk a little bit about that. Is it very much the same Carnival that you knew growing up in Trinidad now?

LOVELACE: It has changed a lot I think, but it is also, this year's carnival, for example, involved a lot of the things I have been talking about. For carnival you have, principally, three elements, the music which would be the steel bands and string bands – what we call string bands; the calypsonian, an element of the music, the calypso and the masqueraders. Now we have had two elements of masqueraders, one is what they call 'Pretty Mask', mask being short for masquerade. Pretty Mask, principally on Tuesday, and what we call 'Old Mask' on Monday morning at J'ouvert, which means 'day open' – it's a French form of patois. So there are all these elements and one has seen lots of changes in all of them, like the Pretty Mask, which is in a way the central attraction for the eye… Of course we have the calypso tents and you have the steel bands beating and these have been developing in their own ways… I mean you can say a lot about them, each one of them, but I'm trying to give you a picture of it in a nutshell. All right, and then we have had – one element I left out that functions somewhere between and within Old Mask and Pretty Mask, I think, is what we call traditional Carnival characters, like the Moko Jumbie, which is derived from an African god actually, an African masker, Mask, if you can call it that, and stick-fighters and a whole lot of stuff. Right? I don't know that it has changed in some respects; it has changed in the sense that the violence that we were talking about in the steel band is gone now… The Pretty Mask is there, but it seemed to me this year, in particular, that people went back to a lot of traditional mask. And it was very interesting to me because I have been a great watcher of this Carnival to see, to find out why we going back at this point. And there are a number of reasons that occur to me. One is that people seem to be seeking some kind of rootage: some point at which to move off. I mean people have replayed all the kinds of mask, you know, by that I mean everything historical, a lot of historical things, you know, the glory of Greece, the fall of Babylon, English, French, Ethiopia, Africa, all sorts of things we've played, you know, or performed, and people have come back now to the traditional mask as if needing, as I say, a footage for another movement forward, and I have a whole lot of ideas concerning this which would take a little time to explain.

DANCE: I would like you to, if you don't mind.

LOVELACE: All right, let me see. I have to try to separate them. One of the other elements I see functioning, no not one element – *two* – addresses to our existence. One is what I call the imitative and the native; this gets back again to the earlier question when you asked about my difference from Walcott and Lamming and so on. Increasingly I think that we have been largely imitative, because everything was external, you know, we never looked inside; we were always looking outside, and I think increasingly we are coming to a consciousness of being a people (to use the word *native*; I don't even want to use the word *nation* in the same sense because of certain kinds of connotations of the word), but certainly, as people with a culture and possibilities of our own, while we perform being everybody else, it is as if we have exhausted being everybody else and it has led us back to ourselves, in a certain kind of way. And I see this – maybe I am imposing this view on Carnival – but I think I see signs of that in the Carnival and corroborated elsewhere, I think, because it doesn't seem to me that a great deal that is energising and providing vitality is coming from the rest of the world. At this point there seems to me at least to be a lull in the world outside. You know no large movement that is captivating people's imagination – disco – so that I think that hopefully what we are seeking is another look at ourselves. It's not a repetition of the old ideas, but it is looking at the old ideas now; and moving off from them. Right?

DANCE: OK. Now Aldrick obviously is unable to express this, but yet he feels a sense of his playing the dragon as a tie with his past, with his father, with his uncle, and then it takes him back even to Africa. I am not so sure how aware you suggest he is of that, but you certainly suggest that. But then again you keep emphasising the acting, that it's all play-acting and indeed I think you used the word *acting* when you were talking about it there. So are we to see it as a kind of symbolic link that's just about completely lost so that people can only play it?

LOVELACE: No, invariably I use the word *playing* for acting in two senses: one, there is when I say: 'Play Mask', you see. I don't know if you understood exactly what I meant. I meant act out a character so I was trying to explain *that* to you on one level, right. When we talk about masquerade we talk about playing mask. Another term we use, 'Playing Mask' which means to say you dress up in a costume and you dance on the street; that is what is called 'Playing Mask'.

DANCE: But it's not the kind of negative connotation that I am suggesting…

LOVELACE: Play-acting, no. Although there is that connotation too which we can deal with. Right?

DANCE: Yes. Because I sort of thought you emphasised that that's what it was when they go through this rebellious thing [the attack on the police] when they play the…

LOVELACE: Right, right, right.

DANCE: You know, and in other words it kind of takes the meaning out of the thing.

LOVELACE: Hummn hummn. Hummn hummn.

DANCE: There's one line I have written down here which seems to suggest they are fooling themselves. You say – this is Aldrick thinking as he prepares to play the dragon for the last time – that this is 'the last symbol of rebellion and threat to comfort Port of Spain' [p.103]. Is Carnival a hoax to allow the people to fool themselves?

LOVELACE: Right. right, right. Now Carnival has functioned in many ways, eh, and from many perspectives. Now I thought it was very useful to make the connection with Africa because that exists, you see. [But] in a lot of the books I have read – almost all – there is not a mention of Africa; and yet the people who are playing mask are Africans who have come from masker societies, and the Moko Jumbie, for example, because that's big on stilts and so on. What used to be pagan Carnival is almost taken fully and whole from African tradition. I did a little thinking and imagining, you know, to make some of the connections, but I think that, and I asked also around, you know, from people who played mask, who played particularly things like dragons and bats and certain things, and they had this sense of it being that sacred kind of thing, you know. Now, so there is that connection on the one level, but nobody is saying anything about it, nobody noticing it except the individuals playing those kinds of things. Right? Now, on the other level you have a sense of threat; it seems to me that there are a number of ways in which people have confronted their day-to-day existence, you know, or their powerlessness. And interesting, in 1970 I went to Guyana, and I saw what is called the Flounce dance in what is called a masquerade band. Now because of different influences, like Guyana is more English or, I think, Dutch and British than – here is more French, Spanish, and Greek, and American, so they say these different terms and they also have different experiences too. Right? But they call that the masquerade band; it's nothing like Trinidad Carnival. There is a small band, there is a fellow with a flute and a man dancing in a costumed uniform with a little head-piece, and this fellow dances and everybody apparently throws a coin on the ground and he dances, swoops down in a very beautiful gesture, takes up the coin very quickly and rises in a gesture almost to confront the person who has thrown the coin, so that he appears taller and more beautiful than the person who has given the coin. Right? Now this to me represents one response to powerlessness; he had to stoop to pick up the coin. but yet he confronted the person with his own beauty. Right? That seems to me to be one way.

DANCE: But Aldrick can't do that.

LOVELACE: No, not only can't, does not do that because the tradition *here* is to confront in a different kind of way. The confrontation here is to pretend to be terrible, you know. You have a particular example, in fact, that I have emphasised in *The Dragon*, which comes from something that we know here as 'Jab Malassie', which was originally molasses devil or black devil, in which people paint themselves and the fellow has on little short pants and a little tail, and he used to have cow horns on his head; little boy behind him beating up a drum with two sticks, and on his fingers he would have long fingernails of tin, right, and he would be very black and greasy. He would paint himself. And he would come up to people and threaten them, and they would give him the money, you know. So there are two different postures to powerlessness, and one posture is that of threat. There was certainly possibly the potential for the actualisation of that threat, but somehow we got caught or trapped in the centre without ever organising the threats to take power.

DANCE: And so that 'revolution', if you call it that in quotation marks, is actually a parallel to what happens at Carnival.

LOVELACE: In that kind – a lot of things happen, but in that particular frame.

DANCE: The whole novel seems to me to be suggesting the fact that this is all coming to an end and Aldrick certainly suggests that this is the last Carnival in which he will play dragon.

LOVELACE: Yes, the last *performance* of that kind. Right. Has it come to an end? Do you know?

DANCE: Well, I know actually it hasn't come to an end, but I am wondering if you are suggesting that the *meaning* has been lost, if *it* has come to an end: or maybe I should ask you in what way has it come to an end?… Let me ask you this way. Why can't the dragons dance any more?

LOVELACE: In that same flounce dance that I saw in Guyana in 1970, I went back there in 1972 and I was looking for this dance because I was very impressed with it, you know, and I wanted to see it again. And when I went there I saw the band and the dancers and so on, and I was waiting for the fellow to do this pretty dance, but somebody handed him the coin *in his hand*. The relationships had changed in the society so there was no need for him to go down and pick up the coin anymore. Right? I suppose that when relationships change that there is not the need to make that same gesture anymore. I think that, now in terms of why the dragon can't dance, I think that – I mean the book probably expressed better, you know, than I could now, why the dragon couldn't dance, why he couldn't perform, you know, you couldn't carry on that one-dimensional almost rebellion all the time. And I suppose a question that man has to face, I mean even beyond Carnival, is, 'Can one continue to rebel all the time in a certain dimension?' What about life? And what is life, you know. These are very difficult questions; I don't know that I answer them at all.

DANCE: But, you know, you raise the question of whether meaningful rebellion is possible, don't you? All of this is *dramatic* rebellion.

LOVELACE: Oh, I think that that rebellion too is real, you know. I think that even the rebellion of threat is real, but one rebels always in relation perhaps, I say perhaps, to one's power, to one's potential. At a certain point you might have to make a sort of little gesture because you can't do better. I am suggesting now that you can do more than that and politics says you can play more than a mask. You can do better than that, you know. It is not that that is absolutely inauthentic or has inauthenticated your existence. Right? You've been doing that because that's the only way you saw out, but now that you can do better you have to do better; we always have to do better, you know; we can't just keep within the habit of a gesture, you know, that we have grown accustomed to without going beyond it. And I suppose that is probably what I am saying about rebellion. You can't just rebel in the practiced way; you have to do more.

DANCE: Is it significant that Philo's successful calypsos are those that don't really express him? I mean when he was singing the calypsos that really expressed himself you know, he wasn't successful, and then when he began writing lyrics that were almost antithetical to his personality, everybody became excited about them. Does society simply refuse to recognise the realities and reward the fantasy?

LOVELACE: That is increasingly a serious question I think. But of course if that person that you're presenting is a threat to their ease, it seems society is going to try to discourage that person from existing, and encourage what they are more comfortable with. I suppose that is the problem of a number of people who function in the world, you know, in a society where they don't have the power, and where the audience, as it were, or the people they relate to, want to be comfortable; they don't want to be bothered, so they accept what makes them laugh or what they can be comfortable with.

DANCE: And they are very comfortable with the image of the Black male as sex symbol?

LOVELACE: They are very comfortable with that image I would say.

DANCE: Were you satirising anyone in particular in the professor of English who explicates Philo's calypsos?

LOVELACE: [Laughter] I don't want to say anything. But I think that people have written about calypso in that kind of way, you know, and make great points about it. I think that there is some validity in what they saying too, you know, but it is almost for another audience, you know.

DANCE: OK. Would you like to talk about any other aspects of your work that we haven't touched upon that are very important to you?

LOVELACE: I think that, well, I think I should ask you some questions now maybe.

DANCE: Oh, no. This is my interview!

LOVELACE: All right.

DANCE: But go on.

LOVELACE: No, I was thinking that while the man/woman situation which you raised earlier, I think you raised it in relation to the absence of wholeness, of the women, right. I thought that there was also some element of love, you know, on a man-woman basis involved in the book, the relations between the men and women. Do you see that as a significant dimension of the book?

DANCE: Yes, I think I see some (if what you mean is fulfilling relationships) some promising relationships.

LOVELACE: Yes, an attempt at grappling with relationships, both in terms of Pariag and in terms of Fisheye – even when he left the woman and so on and was searching for her again and what not. Even within the framework of Aldrick's relationship with Sylvia.

DANCE: But all having some disturbing features.

LOVELACE: Well tell me. Male domination? What is it?

DANCE: [Laughter] Well simply that of male recognition. With Pariag, for example, you bring him to a scene of recognition that I think is great, but it is extremely disturbing to think that that woman has lived with him all of these years, and you know he has been motivated simply by selfish things as finding himself a place in the community and that sort of thing, and not being lonely, and all of a sudden he looks around and here is this woman who could perhaps help keep him from being lonely, and for the first time he thinks about saying, 'Would you like to go to a movie?' You know?

LOVELACE: OK. Good.

DANCE: The same thing with Aldrick. I mean he is absolutely afraid of the relationship. You know there's a very promising possibility there, and you leave the suggestion that something might occur here in terms of fulfilling this relationship, but throughout the work he is absolutely afraid of relating to a woman in a male, a man-woman way.

LOVELACE: Well, I am not so sure. Right. Now let us deal firstly with the Pariag thing. And you said something there in which I was interested: that Pariag is selfishly pursuing – I don't want to make too big a case about the 'selfishly', but is pursuing as it were for himself –

DANCE: And it's not because he doesn't *want* to think about her; I don't think he even realises that she is there to be thought about.

LOVELACE: All right. Good. All right, OK. Now there are certain concerns – in the Pariag instance. I mean I understand what you're talking about – the recognition of the woman eventually, or as being driven to the recognition, and *eventually* I think there is more in the recognition in the final chapter where they come together when he says, 'We have to live', which suggests our living is the beginning of our dealing with the world. But you see I think it is not any particular malice; it is not motivated by malice.

DANCE: Right. I definitely agree with you there; it's a blindness… I agree with you completely there that there is no malice, even the schoolmaster, who *is* a villain, wants to correct the relationship, but he cannot even imagine what this girl whom he has raped and impregnated is going through. I mean he thinks that he will say, 'I will marry you', and she will be happy, you know, which is not to consider her humanity at all, you know…

CONVERSATION WITH

TONY McNEILL

ANTHONY McNEILL

Anthony (Tony) McNeill was born in Kingston, Jamaica, on December 17, 1941, the son of a Minister of Government. After completing his early education at Excelsior School and St. George's College in Jamaica, he went to the United States and studied at Nassau Community College and Johns Hopkins University where he received an MA in 1971 in the Writing Seminars. He completed an MA in English at the University of Massachusetts (Amherst) in 1976.

McNeill, who has worked as a civil servant, a journalist, a script-writer, and a teacher, was Assistant Director (Publications) at the Institute of Jamaica from 1975 to 1981.

He is the author of four volumes of poetry: *Hello Ungod* (1971); *Reel from the Lift Movie* (1972, revised ed. 1975); and *Credences at the Altar of Cloud* (1979). A further volume of poetry was announced as *Choruses in the Summer of Clear* but has not been published. With Neville Dawes he coedited the anthology, *The Caribbean Poem* (1976). He is one of the poets represented in Mervyn Morris's *Seven Jamaica Poets: An Anthology of Recent Poetry* (1971). His poems 'Black Space' and 'Ode to Brother Joe' are on Caedmon's record, *Poets of the West Indies*. Peepal Tree Press published *Chinese Lanterns from the Blue Child* his final collection posthumously in 1998.

The style of McNeill's poetry ranges from the familiar and traditional to the highly innovative and experimental; one might even occasionally label bizarre the blurred type, the unusual layout, the unconventional punctuation, and the consciously retained typographical errors of *Credences*. Despite the controversy that will undoubtedly follow as more critics turn to intensively study the work of this complex and extraordinary writer (McNeill's good friend Dennis Scott labels *Credences* 'annoying, confusing and beautiful', 'Lightning Words' [*The Sunday Gleaner,* January 1980]), there is no doubt that Tony McNeill accurately and appropriately defined himself when he wrote, 'a poet is someone who lights/ words' [*Credences*, p.93].

McNeill was awarded first prize in the Jamaica Festival Literary Competition (Poetry) in 1966 and 1971, and the Silver Musgrave Medal for poetry in 1972. He won the Jamaican National Book Award in 1995 for *Chinese Lanterns from the Blue Child*.

He died of a heart attack during surgery on January 1, 1996.

The following interview was conducted in McNeill's office at the Institute of Jamaica in Kingston on March 2, 1980. I had met him at a dinner party a few days before, and had felt that he was so shy and reticent that the interview might be difficult. In our meeting McNeill was gracious, and though obviously reserved and sensitive, there was nothing uncommunicative about him. He was certainly not garrulous, but he responded honestly and eloquently to all my questions. I went away from the interview knowing that Dennis Scott was quite accurate when he described him as 'one of the warmest and most honest human beings I have met' [Introduction to *Reel*, p.3].

DANCE: I notice that you dedicate *Reel* to 'my grandmother, who taught me the language.' You weren't raised by your grandmother were you?

McNEILL: No, I wasn't, but she had a number of schools when I was growing up, you know, before high school. I think there were at least two of them that I can remember that she was headmistress of: one of them was in her own house, so that when I say headmistress, I use the term loosely, because really it was just a question of her setting up a school in her own house. And then I think she took over a church school or something; but she taught me English you know, and I think she is the best English teacher I ever had.

DANCE: What do you mean by she taught you English? This may seem like a stupid question, but does it have anything to do with the kind of poetry you write? Does it have anything to do with the rhythms of the language or do you simply mean subject-verb agreement?

McNEILL: Well, as you probably know, Jamaica is a two language country: there is the Jamaican Creole and then there is English. Right? Now, I hate to bring class into it, but my class background was such that my parents invariably spoke English, you know. It is true I heard Creole from helpers and from people who worked on the property, because my father had a farm at one time. But I guess the models, which would tend to be the parents, were speaking English most of the time, so that I guess for the most part I think (and I think at least one other West Indian poet has said the same or a similar thing) in English. I mean I don't know whether people really verbalise too much when they are thinking, but if I do verbalise it tends to be in English; so I have the feeling that English is the more intimate language. I mean I am not really concerned with the fact that it was the slave masters' language. I have assumed it as my own.

DANCE: That was the language that your grandmother taught you as well?

McNEILL: Yes, yes.

DANCE: OK. Why then weren't your parents the model for language?

McNEILL: Well, as I did mention, I was saying that the parents would tend to be the models, you know, even though there were helpers and there were people who worked on my father's farm; but I would like to point out at the same time that even though the parents were the models, the grandmother was an even more direct transmitter because she was actually teaching me the mechanics of the language, which I think is like learning to swim. I mean, if you start off with the wrong stroke, it is very hard to correct it, but if you are given the best ground rules possible, then, you know, you can always function within the machinery of the language; and when the machinery runs out, when for instance, a comma or a semi-colon or a dash no longer suffices for the kind of stuff you want, well you move away from the tradition into things like spacing, wide-spacing, massed colons, the use of the virgule and other things which you might find especially in *Credences*.

DANCE: OK. Are you apologetic about your upper-class background?

McNEILL: No, I am not you know. There was a time when I had a strong indentification with, you know, the proletariat or the urban lower class or whatever you want to call it. All the words for class always seem to be so ugly, including bourgeoisie, you know. But there was even a time when I thought about becoming a Rastafarian, as I have said in other interviews, but just about the time when the desire was quite strong to possibly go over to Rastafarianism, I was offered a fellowship at Johns Hopkins University so…

DANCE: Put you right in the heart of the bourgeoisie.

McNEILL: Yes.

DANCE: And so being away from Jamaica has redirected some of your goals?

McNEILL: Yes, and also latterly the amazing amount of writing I have done since '76. You know, I wrote a great deal, about twenty manuscripts or something, between, I think, June '76 and, I think, February 1977, and then again between January '78 and September 1978.

DANCE: These aren't full length manuscripts?

McNEILL: Yes.

DANCE: Really? How many of them do you plan to publish?

McNEILL: Well, you see there is a problem with them. One problem is that many of them use the same poems, you see.

DANCE: Do they become part of a narrative? Is that why they appear and reappear?

McNEILL: No, it's just that I have some favourites and I tend to put them in all the manuscripts, but I think that even with those included it would roughly come out to about twenty when you are through.

DANCE: At what point in your interest in Rastafarianism was 'Ode to Brother Joe' written? Was that after you became disillusioned?

McNEILL: No, that was before, you know, but there is a certain sense in the poem of, you know, disillusionment or, I don't know if the word is disillusionment as much as scepticism.

DANCE: May I assume that the return to Africa never appealed to you, because you seem to satirise that in that poem?

McNEILL: Well, no, I would say that I am not really interested in returning to Africa. I see myself very much as a man of the Western World.

DANCE: And even at that time, if I remember the poem correctly, you were very sarcastic about the belief in Selassie?

McNEILL: Yes.

DANCE: So that never was part of your attraction to Rastafarianism?

McNEILL: No, no.

DANCE: Do you think had you stayed in Jamaica though that you might indeed have become a Rastafarian?

McNEILL: Well, I doubt it, you know, and I don't think so, because, that would be something that would take me so many years of deliberations to really arrive at that. By the time I would have thought of becoming a Rastafarian so many people with similar backgrounds to mine had in fact become Rastafarians that it would seem to be an unoriginal choice.

DANCE: Was it simply then a kind of fashionable rebellion for young men of your class?

McNEILL: Well, it has become so over the past few years, and it is, like how people became hippies in America or in England, well you become Rastafarians out here.

DANCE: OK. A rather personal question that your poetry motivates. Has your father discouraged your writing poetry? There is a rather negative image of your father in your poetry.

McNEILL: Well, I would say that I picked up a kind of, you know, patronising attitude possibly, or the question as to why I was sort of wasting my time, you know, writing these things. But after I achieved a certain amount of success, then it became a, you know, a different thing.

DANCE: One question that comes to mind as one reads your poetry, quite obviously, is influences, and I think one reason it comes to mind is that you mention so many other poets in your poetry. Who do you see as the most important influences on your work?

McNEILL: Well, actually, there are two things I'd like to say by way of a preamble. First of all, I was very careful in *Reel* to make sure that no influences were apparent; and I am almost sure that, you know, *Reel* is quite monolithic in that sense, quite, you know, my own book. But *Credences* is a different thing. I had undergone a tremendous change of style, if you want to call it that, although I prefer to use the word form. The forms had changed, and there were poems which are – in part anyway – could have been written by other poets; and the poets that have the chief influence were I would say, WS Merwin – and I am thinking of his latter works, the work since *The Moving Target*, the unpunctuated poetry that he has written since about half way through the book *The Moving Target*. So WS Merwin was a very strong influence, and he also influenced me in the sense that he has poems which are divided by rules or lines, and I think in his case, apart from, you know, one that I can remember which is a suite of songs, for the most part I think Merwin regards these poems separated by rules or lines as one poem. Even though the music of each section is different among them, I think he sees it as one poem; at any rate it has only one title. In my case I see the poems separated by these rules or lines as separate poems. Some of them hinge very close, sometimes even structurally they hinge on each other, but for the most part I regard them as separate poems.

DANCE: Others?

McNEILL: Well, Whitman. You know there is the poem that goes in part, 'turn I am dizzy/ the world turns/ out of the cradle/endlessly rocking' [*Credences*, p.48], so that of course is directly from 'Out of the Cradle Endlessly Rocking', from a Whitman thing, so that is actually more than just an influence, it is an actual borrowing.

DANCE: Was 'The God-maggot' [*Reel*, p.25] influenced by Emily Dickinson?

McNEILL: I didn't think of Emily Dickinson at all.

DANCE: Did you know her poem 'I heard a fly buzz – when I died'?

McNEILL: Most likely, because I did read her at some point.

DANCE: Do you like her poetry?

McNEILL: Yeah, I like her poetry.

DANCE: What about the contemporary militant American writers? You mentioned Sonia Sanchez.

McNEILL: Yeah. Well I like her work, you know, and in fact as far as form goes I learned a lot from the Afro-American poets who began writing, say, seriously in the '60s. I learned a lot from them, but I think that they in turn also learned a lot from EE Cummings, so I am not quite sure who it is I learned from primarily, Cummings or the Afro-American poets.

DANCE: Who did you come to first? Did you know Cummings when you were reading the Afro-American poets?

McNEILL: I knew him before. I read him before.

DANCE: OK. You don't mention some of your friends here in Jamaica who obviously share with you their impressions of your poetry. I am thinking particularly of Dennis Scott and Mervyn Morris. Have their comments had any kind of influence on your development?

McNEILL: Yes, a very strong influence because several years ago, you know, we used to exchange poems and exchange criticisms of these poems, and I learned a whole lot from Mervyn and Dennis in particular.

DANCE: Tell me what effect their comments have on your work. Do they lead you to revise sometimes?

McNEILL: Well at a certain point of my life you know – you see, *Reel from 'The Life-Movie'* is very much of a product of discussions that Mervyn and Dennis and I had in terms of poetry, and poetry form and all that; and one of the big things of course was economy, you know, the under-usage or I would say the fact that adjectives were not used very much in *Reel*. But *Credences* – was a braver book; it took more risks, you know; it is not the sort of book that seems intended to elicit approval from Mervyn and Dennis: I know they are not happy with some of the poems in the book.

DANCE: OK. Could you just give me a few bits of information about some allusions you make in your poetry. Is Olive your wife?

McNEILL: Yes.

DANCE: Who is Jennifer?

McNEILL: She is my sister, one of my sisters. There is another sister called Carol, who appears as 'C' in the poem that starts, 'boy dem coud fight/ dem pickney' [*Credences*, p.17].

DANCE: In your poetry, you quite often define poetry: at one point you write, 'everything you say is a poem/ everything you write/ everything you do/ even deceit is lovely because the…' I can't read my own writing…

McNEILL: '…the tongue fell on the word/ once/ and it woke' [*Credences*, p.89].

DANCE: Yes, yes. That's a pretty warped definition of poetry.

McNEILL: Well, at that time I was open to more forms, you know. I am not as eclectic as I was then. And in fact I would like to correct something I said earlier. You asked me if all these manuscripts were poetry. Well, there are two of them, one called *Arrows & Orchids* and one called *Angels and Willows*, which may be either prose or prose-poetry, although if you remember the discussion that we had at Mervyn's, both Mervyn and Dennis feel that *Angels* is made up of poems, as against prose poems. So I leave a question sign beside two of those manuscripts. There are also other manuscripts I have written which are made up entirely of – or contain – what I consider prose poems.

DANCE: Why do you consider them prose rather than poetry, since that's a part of everything you say and everything you write and everything you do, which at one point would be poetry.

McNEILL: Yeah. Well I have moved away from that position. In fact I have moved away from several of the poems in *Credences*. I will never write some of those poems again in that mode, you know. Just never.

DANCE: Let me go back. You have poets who know each other's work so well, one insists it's poetry and you suggest it's prose. What are you doing there that's so different from what you have done before that makes you consider that prose? Are you telling a story? Is it narrative? Are you developing characters?

McNEILL: Well, actually, no. [McNeill later informed me that he has since written several manuscripts of prose poems in which both narrative and characters are developed. He terms these works 'novellas-in-verse' (letter to Dance, September 6, 1981).] I would say if there is any character at all it's the language; it's the peculiar slant that the language takes; you could say language is character. But really, for the most part, these are brief iconic or aphoristic things which I see as a form of prose.

DANCE: I would think that what you are saying describes *Credences* too.

McNEILL: As a form of prose?

DANCE: Well, I think that the brief, aphoristic statements and so forth you certainly have there.

McNEILL: Well, maybe those were the forerunners of the stuff I am writing now and in fact at the very end of *Credences* there are selections from *Arrows & Orchids*, because *Credences* uses material from about nineteen of the manuscripts. I feel it necessary to add that there are others that I've since discovered to be (with the help of a brilliant assessment of my work by Mark Douglas) prose poems in the book.

DANCE: OK. Those last poems if I remember – this may sound crazy – but they go all the way across the line whereas most of your earlier poems don't. Does that have anything to do with its becoming prose?

McNEILL: Well, I think that in some of the poems, especially the ones that move at higher speed, the influences there were not only the Afro-American poets and EE Cummings... especially the Afro-American poets. I would say in the case of some of the poems I am thinking of one of which starts, 'howlin de local' [*Credences*, p. 80], and there is one which ends, 'de resurrection be/ comin/de resurrection be/ comin/ know' [*Credences*, p.122] – well those poems were to a large extent influenced not only by the Afro-American poets, but by Afro-American musicians because I feel more of a nexus with music than I do with poetry. And in fact, I don't know which one, which of the two entities is more important to me, music or poetry, because when I am at home I saturate myself with music. And I find that music can become a method of breaking through into other forms. In other words, when I went to America first I liked what people used to call 'jazz', but which I call jz. because I don't like the word 'jazz'.

DANCE: What do you call it?

McNEILL: J – z. with a full stop beside it – jz. Because jazz seems to be a word that is suspect now, you know. But anyway, my experience of jz. mainly focused on the bop era, you know, Charlie Parker, Miles Davis and the 'Cool School', Brubeck, etc. But when I went to America in '70 I discovered the later Coltrane. I had heard him before and I couldn't come to terms with him, but once I discovered him emotionally. once I reacted to him and admired him and loved him for his music, he opened a whole, you know, just a whole world of music to me. I mean people that I didn't like before, like Stevie Wonder, suddenly became very accessible. But to get into these people I have to go through Trane first, and I am sure I learned a lot from him in terms of incoherence, or seeming incoherence, when the music becomes very staccato on the surface, but it's not really that way. But I think that that has a lot to do with some of the poems in *Credences* which I term the intermediate poems and which end with a usually luminous boldfaced line; well, that's what I get in Trane. After these periods of discordancy, or discordance, or whatever, you have the lyric gift which survives from the Miles Davis era coming out, and the whole thing just becomes beautiful.

DANCE: I remember seeing somewhere, I don't know whether it was a poem or what, that you one time intended to be a musician.

McNEILL: Yes, that was in the 'Notes on Contributors' of *Credences*.

DANCE: Was that said jokingly or had you seriously...

McNEILL: Well, it was half-serious, I mean, you know, I don't think that at any stage of the game I really thought I had the talent to be a jz. pianist, but I do play the piano a little bit.

DANCE: You deliberately retain typographical errors in *Credences*, I am told. Why?

McNEILL: Well, I don't call them typographical errors; I call them mutants. You see what was happening to me was that I was writing very quickly. In fact there was one weekend when I wrote four full-length manuscripts, you know, between let's say, some time on Friday...

DANCE: Not from the beginning! The poems were developed over a period of one weekend? Four manuscripts of poems!

McNEILL: Yeah, yeah. I mean some of them use the same poems, but I guess you would get about four sixty-page manuscripts from that, you know, even though they were about eighty pages or longer; but I mean one was in fact fairly short, about forty pages or something. But in typing at that high speed and with working with a defective typewriter, you often had mutations coming in. But at that time I was, you know, as Dennis Scott said in a review, in a kind of trance-like attitude towards poetry, and I believed that language-in-music, as I call it, could not lie, so that once something was in music it had to tell the truth. But I no longer believe that, but I still believe that most poetry is not really written in music, it is written in a kind of half-music so that if you read it very quickly, you know, it comes across as music; it plays a beautiful illusion. But for the most part it doesn't really sing and that's one of the reasons I like the Afro-American poets and Cummings, because their work sings.

DANCE: Another question that arises immediately from reading your poetry is your reaction to critics. There is a frequent concern with critics in your poetry: 'May scholars not read these poems' [*Credences*, p.31]; one time you write: 'de critic will sey dem line crude' [*Credences*, p.37]; and also: 'he sang in-/ viting the bullets of critics' [*Credences*, p.102]. You write, it appears, expecting to be attacked?

McNEILL: Well, some part of me must have because as I say I was in a kind of trancelike state for a lot of that period. In fact, the night of the breakthrough, you know, I had written a poem called 'Choric unGod' and I figured that like the years between '72 and '76 what was going to happen was that 'Choric unGod' was going to be the only poem I'd keep for the year because in '72, '73, '74 and '75, I kept one poem for the year. All the rest that I wrote were discarded and I considered them drafts.

DANCE: Permanently destroyed?

McNEILL: No, no, I keep them, but I mean I don't consider them as poems. But after 'Choric unGod' something very strange happened to me one night, you know, it was like automatic writing. I wrote about fifty pages of poetry, and it may be the best poetry I have ever written... and it was just coming out on the typewriter like that.

DANCE: I have never talked to a poet who created this way. That doesn't mean anything, but it is just coming as a surprise to me. Frequently you mention a problem with alcohol. Were you ever an alcoholic?

McNEILL: Well, I had problems with alcohol, you know, I used to drink too much.
DANCE: Does that have anything to do with this period when you did not write poetry… even though some writers insist that they write better under the influence.
McNEILL: Yeah. Well, I think that was true of me too.
DANCE: That you did or did not write better?
McNEILL: Did write better. I was able to concentrate for long periods of time.
DANCE: OK. You know this constant concern with critics… seems to me unusual in a poet who is as personal as you are. Because sometimes the poems are so personal that obviously nobody else can understand. I mean there is one poem that says simply 'jennifer' [*Credences*, p.16], which suggests that at that point you don't care whether anybody else understands it or not.
McNEILL: Well, I do care, you know, and I think that 'jennifer' is a small song, and usually what I have found with a lot of the poems is that tunes come out of them for me, you know. Like I am reading and then all of a sudden a tune will come, and that tune will remain, and whenever I read the poem I'll honour the music. So whenever I say 'jennifer' I don't just say 'jennifer,' I say [singing], 'jenn-i-fer-r'. Well, that's the way the poem communicates itself to me; that is the music that comes out of it.
DANCE: In a letter to Dennis Scott you write, 'I don't think I could write if my first concern weren't for the aesthetic…' And yet I don't think that anybody could get much blacker than 'The Lady Accepts the Needle Again'. 'It's shitting on the white woman. It's savage. It's dread black' [*Reel*, p.2]. I want to ask you two things about that. One, was that motivated because you were accused of not being racially conscious, something like that?
McNEILL: Well, no, but you know in *Reel*, like in the earlier poetry, a lot of the earlier poetry, I was very concerned with, you know, certain trends which were in the air, certain types of speech, you know. The Jamaican urban Creole really fascinated me, so I integrated some of it into some of the poems; and there was also a Black consciousness thing in some of the others because that was a trend. But, really, 'The Lady Accepts the Needle Again', as I went on to say in another part of the letter, or in a later letter to Dennis, I said that it concludes with compassion, which it does, because I see this female figure as being renewed by the sexual experience with the Black man. So that the poem is circular, it never stops. It gets to the end, it starts over again, she is ravished, she is renewed, she is ravished, she is renewed.
DANCE: Is the racial element important with the renewal there – that it is a white woman and a Black man?
McNEILL: Yes, it's important, it's part of the, kind of, well, it's Black consciousness but it's also – you see the Black consciousness comes out in the fact that the poem, if you go by the dedication, 'for Dennis & all the brothers' is a kind of warning… to stay away from white women, you know, I guess so.
DANCE: There are a lot of poems that might be called paeans to the Black woman, but there's one poem that suggests you feel guilty about being sexually attracted to a white woman.
McNEILL: Oh, you mean the one about 'haven't I lusted/ for white/ pussy and pass/ ing above me/ beauty   the bell' [*Credences*, p.2]?
DANCE: Yes. Is that a reflection of a sense of guilt you had?
McNEILL: Well that poem was written that night, I believe, when I wrote the fifty

pages, so there was very little conscious intellection going on; it was automatic, so…
DANCE: But one can analyse himself and even though it wasn't conscious, obviously it's coming from the subconscious, which is meaningful; so if you think about
it now could you respond?
McNEILL: Well, I haven't had that many relationships with white women, so I don't
know if there have been enough of them to set up any sort of guilt within me, and I
think it's counterbalanced by the paeans, as you said, to the dark wife.
DANCE: Well it's more than counterbalanced. I want to ask you about something
that I see as a kind of thematic progression in your works. Your earlier works seem to
me, and I say this very reluctantly, because I haven't given them the kind of study I
would like to, but they seem to me to be obsessed with death and dying and killing –
they're very morbid – suicide in particular, very morbid. And then at one point in
Credences you write, 'I am going to live, the morning is coming up… I am going to live'
[p.66]. I am not so sure, but I think I see a progression towards a more philosophical
view of life?
McNEILL: Well, I think that what happened is that when somebody gives up
something like alcohol, you know, he tends to feel happier, he or she. And, you know,
it's true that I have not been entirely without alcohol since, say, '75, but I have had less
problems with it because I rarely drink, I hardly ever do drink, and when I do it's
usually not more then two drinks, three at the most. So that, you see, that morbid fear
of death and all that is something that vanished for a couple of years anyway, you
know; so that at some point I believed that people would live for ever, you know. That
was when I was in that kind of trancelike stage. I really believed that, because it seemed
to me that the whole mechanism of the human body was oceanic, you know the breath
coming in and out, eternal like the sea.
DANCE: Did you indeed feel suicidal during those early years, yourself?
McNEILL: Well, the thing is that I may have felt suicidal, but I didn't tend to write
at that time because when I write I tend to be happy no matter what the subject matter
is.
DANCE: Let me ask you a question that I don't quite know how to phrase, but of
course *Credences* brings me to it. And that is about the matter of religion. Would you
say that you are a religious person? Would you say you are seeking for a religious
meaning in life? Or are you simply satirising religion?
McNEILL: Well, I grew up a Catholic and I was a very religious one, but there were
a number of theological questions that I couldn't come to terms with in the Catholic
religion, and then for a time Rastafarianism appealed to me; and then after that I got
to the point where Earth, you know, became the deity for me, and I addressed my
prayers to leaves, trees, the earth itself and various other phenomena, natural
phenomena. Well that lasted quite some time you know, but then I think I have gone
back to God now, you know.
DANCE: And who is that God?
McNEILL: Well, I suppose the traditional…
DANCE: You mean Christianity? Jehovah?
McNEILL: Yes. This time, I think.
DANCE: OK. And Ungod?
McNEILL: Well, Ungod was a compromise figure, Ungod was a prayer, you know,

represented a kind of prayer to absence, you know; in other words, it is like inventing a god since the one who was already there seemed, you know, inadequate.

DANCE: So when you gave him the name Ungod it suggests that your invention was absolutely, what? Incomplete? Void?

McNEILL: You mean like it is a prayer to a void?

DANCE: Well, Ungod. You can't really believe can you... I am just asking you.

McNEILL: You mean in Ungod? Well, I suppose Ungod is the reverse face of God or the reverse figure hinging on Lucifer.

DANCE: Are there any other things about your poetry that you would like to talk about that we haven't covered that are very important to you in terms of what you are attempting?

McNEILL: Well, I would like to come back to the whole business of language-in-music and say that, you know, if something is written in music it starts off with two advantages. The first is that only certain words can fit if you are writing in pure music which cuts down the options. So even though I no longer believe that language-in-music has to be the truth, it would seem to me that it would tend to be closer to the truth than something which is not written in real music, because the options are cut down. And the second thing is that when something is in music it has a kind of charm and beauty that is not really true of things that are not written in music... I see that poetry – it's not really an original idea because Jean-Paul Sartre for one has talked about that – but I see a close affinity between poetry and music and such, and architecture. I don't think Sartre mentioned architecture but I mention it too. So to me a poem is something that has all of these properties.

DANCE: And a question about audience. In a letter to Dennis [Scott] you said, 'We and all the other purists who claim to be writing only for art's sake... [are] writing... with an (elite) audience of our peers/fellow-practioners somewhere at the back of our minds' [Reel, p.1]. So are you addressing yourself to an elite audience?

McNEILL: Well at that time I was, but in Credences... I mean I am surprised that Credences hasn't sold better because I think that there are poems in it which anybody could enjoy, quite simple.

DANCE: But there's a great deal in it that's extremely complicated.

McNEILL: Well, I don't see it as that at all... I see it as quite an accessible book... In Linstead, when I was living in Linstead – that's in the country – I had some Rastafarian friends who are not as educated in the formal sense as some other people who will have problems with the book. But if I can believe what they said, they liked the book and I mean they pointed out some things that they liked, you know. That gave me a tremendous feeling because I really want this book to be read by everybody, and I think it can be.

DANCE: All right. Thank you very much.

McNEILL: You are welcome.

CONVERSATION WITH

PAMELA MORDECAI AND VELMA POLLARD

Pamela Mordecai was born in Jamaica is 1942 and educated at the University of the West Indies at Mona. She worked for fifteen years as TV anchorwoman/commentator for JIS/API. She also was hostess on a magazine-type programme focusing on the arts. She taught on the faculty of the University of the West Indies in Trinidad and served from 1974-1988 as Publications Officer at the School of Education, University of the West Indies at Mona, Kingston. She is founder and director of the Sandberry Press.

She has co-edited several anthologies: Mordecai and Mervyn Morris, *Jamaica Woman: An Anthology of Fifteen Jamaican Women Poets* (1980); Mordecai and Betty Wilson, *Her True-True Name* (1989); Mordecai, *Don't Ever Wake a Snake: Poems and Stories for Children* (1991); Mordecai and Grace Walker, *Sunsong Tide Rising* (1994); and Mordecai, *From Our Yard: Jamaican Poetry Since Independence: The First Twenty-Five Years* (1994).

Mordecai has also co-edited several pedagogical works and more recently, she has written four books for children: *Sunsong: Tide Rising* (1994) with Grace Walker Gordon; *Ezra's Goldfish and other storypoems*; *The Costume Parade* (2000) and *Rohan Goes to Big School* (2000).

Her poems as well as her pedagogical and critical articles have appeared in various journals and anthologies; whilst she has published three volumes of poetry: *Journey Poem* (1989); *De Man: A Performance Poem* (1995); and *Certifiable* (2001). Mordecai's poetry is widely anthologized, such as in *The Oxford Book of Caribbean Verse* (2005; eds. Brown and McWatt) and *Poetry International 7/8* (2003; ed. Fred Moramarco). She has also published a book of short stories, *Pink icing and other stories* (2007).

She won the Jamaican National Book Award for children's literature in 1994.

Ms. Mordecai's husband, Martin Mordecai, is also a poet. They have two sons and a daughter, and live in Toronto.

———————————

Velma Earle Pollard was born in Jamaica on March 26, 1937, and educated at Excelsior High School in Kingston and the University College of the West Indies at Mona. She received an MA degree in Education, Administration and Curriculum from McGill University in Montreal in 1968; an MA in the Teaching of English from Teachers' College, Columbia University in 1974; and a PhD in Language Education from the University of the West Indies, Jamaica, in 1987. Ms. Pollard has taught English and occasionally Spanish and Latin at Kingston College in Jamaica; St. George's College, Trinidad; McDonald High School, Montreal; Knox College, Jamaica, where she was Head of the Department; Hunter College, CUNY; and the University of Guyana. She has been on the faculty of the School of Education at the University of the West Indies, Mona, since 1975, where she was Senior Lecturer, Dean of the Faculty of Education, and Head of the Department of Educational Studies. She has recently retired.

Ms. Pollard's collections of poems include *Crown Point and Other Poems* (1988); *Shame Trees Don't Grow Here: but Poincianas Bloom* (1992); *The Greatest Philosophers I*

Know Can't Read or Write (2006); and *Leaving Traces* (2008). She is also the author of two collections of short stories, *Considering Woman* (1989); and *Karl and Other Stories* (1994); the novella *Karl*, originally published separately in 1992); and a novel, *Homestretch* (1994).

She has edited a number of anthologies: *Nine West Indian Poets: An Anthology for the CXC* (1980); *Over Our Way: Caribbean Short Stories with Introduction and Notes* (1980; co-edited with Jean D'Costa); and *Anansesem: A Collection of Caribbean Folk Tales, Legends and Poems for Juniors* (1985). Among her pedagogical works are *A Handbook for Teachers of English at Elementary Schools in Guyana* (1975); *Caribbean Poems and Stories for Children* (1976); *An Introduction to Caribbean Poetry and Some Caribbean Short Stories* (1976); and *From (Jamaican) Creole to Standard (Jamaican) English: A Handbook for Teachers* (1990). Other works include *Dread Talk: The Language of Rastafari* (1994) and with G. Covi, C. Sassi and J. Anim Addo, *Caribbean Scottish Relations: Colonial and Contemporary Inscriptions in History, Language and Literature* (2007).

Ms. Pollard received a Fulbright Hays Senior Research Fellowship in 1986, and she won the Casa de las Americas Literary Prize for *Karl* in 1992.

Her work is cited in Carole Boyce Davies' *Black Women, Writing and Identity: Migrations of the Subject* (1994), but similarly to Pamela Mordecai's writing, scholarly research on Pollard is yet to be formed.

Ms. Pollard lives in Kingston. She has three children.

The following interview was conducted in Pamela Moredecai's office at the University of the West Indies in Kingston on March 12, 1980.

DANCE: I was delighted to discover this anthology, *Jamaica Woman*; I would like to ask you what made you decide to do this collection, because I understand it was your idea.

MORDECAI: Yes, it was. I was writing myself, I was in touch with other people like Velma who were writing also, and I think accidentally, almost, it turned out that the people that I was talking to who were writing, were mostly women. There is one young man who also works in the building, who was writing, but most of the people it turned out who were writing and who had not had a chance really to have their work represented anywhere were in fact women. And as it started out, my interest was not primarily in Jamaican women; I was interested in the Caribbean because I have only just come back from two and a half years in Trinidad, and so I thought, hell, it would be nice to get a collection together of Caribbean women poets. I went to Guyana, and did a bit of searching around in Trinidad, but interestingly enough many of the Trinidadian women poets, it seemed, were publishing out of Canada. They were not at home. I was not in Guyana long, and I only turned up one person whose work I saw, and I heard of another person, so it seemed that most of the people who were writing were in Jamaica.

DANCE: What about that one person? You decided not to include her?

MORDECAI: Well, for various reasons, right. Because so many women were here, and so few seemed to be elsewhere that I thought it might as well turn into a collection of…

DANCE: So almost accidentally it became Jamaica, and almost accidentally it became women since you thought about including men?

MORDECAI: No, I would say the woman thing was very early you know and so, decisively. There were so many women who were writing and whose work had not really had the kind of exposure…

POLLARD: Can I say something here to the point about women whether they are in Jamaica or Trinidad. And I say that if Pam did not know the Jamaican women so well she probably would not have picked up a number of us. Certainly me, I am sure. In other words if I were living in Guyana and anybody came there looking for poets, they wouldn't have picked me up because I don't show. So that in a way I think it is less that there are no women poets there than that she knows more Jamaican people, and so she would be aware of what they are doing. So perhaps the significant thing is that she is a Jamaican and therefore knows more people in Jamaica.

MORDECAI: I take that point, I take that point.

DANCE: It is very interesting that every one of these women is unpublished in a full volume work. [Subsequently Christine Craig, Lorna Goodison, Pam Mordecai, Velma Pollard and Olive Senior have published collections.] Everybody has published in a journal or something like that. And I want to know if the fact that they are women has anything to do with the fact that they have not had the kind of exposure that I suppose a lot of male writers of similar talents would have had.

MORDECAI: Well I think that would be [true]. I am no feminist by any manner of means, but I certainly think that this has something to do with it. Judging only from myself it has had to do with the fact that – I am – well, not any more, but up to about three or four years ago, I would say, I was fairly tentative about my own work, about letting anybody see it, about putting it in journals and so on, about simply small things, letting people know in fact that I was writing and here is what I was writing. Now I think that this has something to do with the fact that you are a woman and a sort of [acceptance of the] historical thing where most of the people who are doing it are men, anyway. You are not quite sure of how the response is, you don't necessarily know some of these people very well, and so on and so forth. In fact I would go as far as saying that even when you do know – I mean Dennis Scott, for instance, is somebody that I have known for a long time, and yet I wasn't bold enough to show him my work. Right? So I would say the whole woman thing has definitely something to do with it.

POLLARD: Well I see it as a woman thing in a way, but let me just expand on that a little bit more. For me, I am sure it is that maybe because I am a woman, I have seen myself as a mother, as a wife, as a person who earns, and a writer, really, only as something I do for myself. So I think it is less because of my female sex than because of my sex roles. The roles that have become important have been getting the children out of the way and all the rest of it, so in the same way that writing has had to just take a little pigeon hole out of my real life in terms of time: *after* the children have been put to sleep, or *after* the children are gone to school, and *after* you've done the groceries, *after* everything else, then you get a little moment – certainly poetry is something you write and you enjoy it and so, but you don't see yourself as a poet.

MORDECAI: That is exactly what I'm saying.

POLLARD: But I am saying that it is less because of just [being] female as such, than because there are all these other things that you have to do. And I am not saying that a man does not have a career and all the rest of it, but after the career what else does he have? Everything else he has can be put somehow onto the wife and mother in a kind of way. He may help you with the groceries, but finally it is your responsibility. He may help with the laundry, but finally if the sheets are not clean and ready, it's your responsibility. So I think that there is a way in which our whole lives are set up to put this kind of thing last. Now if I were not also a working woman, then I may have been a mother first and a poet next, but because I am also a working woman there is the job next.

DANCE: We are more or less talking about poetry today. Do you work in any other genres?

MORDECAI: Yes. I won't speak about the plays: I have written a couple in my life. But I have, for a long time, been working on two novels, one of which is about two-thirds of the way through, I think. It is a novella rather than a novel, a sort of political thing. The other one is a sort of humorous folk kind of thing. I write for children as well, poetry for kids. I am very pleased about those, and Mrs. Pollard is a very enthusiastic fan of my children's poems.

POLLARD: Have been all the time.

MORDECAI: Yes. Again, I would say in terms of getting stuff out, a major concern of mine (and Velma is going to have something to say about this too) is getting the children's stuff out, because this is the West Indies and we don't have enough indigenous material for children out. But I must say that the metropolitan publishers do not have any kind of interest there, you know. OUP publishes children's stuff for the illustrations and so on and so forth; so really to get that kind of stuff out is to decide to publish it yourself.

DANCE: Have you published any of that yourself?

MORDECAI: No, but I think that I am about to do that. A bit of it has got out in anthologies here and anthologies there but nothing compared to the amount of it that there is. Right? And so I think I am going to do something bold about that fairly soon.

POLLARD: And I hope that when she does something bold that she will do the illustrations herself because I have said over and over again that Pam does not remember that she draws! [Laughter] Though now I notice she has very boldly exhibited as one of twenty-three women in an exhibition going at the Bolivar now. Her illustrations for those children's poems are going to be models. I have said all the time, 'You know what you should do: do your children's poems and do the illustrations; it's going to be great.' Now whether the metropolitan countries will like it or not, I don't know, but I know that I like her children's poems and I like the fact that she can illustrate them very well, you know.

DANCE: Very interesting. Let me ask you how you happened to approach Mervyn Morris to co-edit the book with you. Did you think you needed an established figure, which might also be male?

MORDECAI: No, the maleness – I was thinking about exactly *this* this morning. Right? The maleness is a function of the historical thing we have been talking about. Right? Mervyn has been very helpful to me personally. Edward Brathwaite was the first person who helped by looking at my stuff many years ago – I won't tell you how many, a long time ago – and being very positive about it. And then I was away for intermittent periods. Tony McNeill was supportive, but Mervyn and I work extremely well together, and he has a very, to me, very useful talent, and he is the only person I know who does have it – which is that he will take a pencil and he will just apply it to what you are doing in ways that are astounding sometimes. It is as though he has an intuitive understanding of the poem from inside of it; and it is your poem from inside of it. So you take him something and he will not merely say, 'Oh this is good, I like it.' He will say, 'Why don't you do this here?' And he will do little things with his pencil and it will turn out really to work very well.

DANCE: Do you mean he will write a comment or make a suggestion for an actual change?

MORDECAI: He will actually doctor, yes, he will doctor the stuff right. I mean everybody might not find this a useful thing, but I found it very helpful. So in fact he had been helping me with my own work and I suppose the tentativeness and the, I don't know, I guess it has something to do with timidity and cowardice. Right? Though I am not really – and I don't strike people as a timid, cowardly person, inside you know is this tremulous creature; and I think that's why I went to him. I'll tell you an interesting thing though, for the women. In the beginning he said, 'Oh, I'll help you with this thing, you know, but you don't have to put my name on it.' The standard thing. Right? You see it just started up as an idea in my head and then it just sort of got bigger and bigger because there were more people who were writing (many of whom Mervyn knew of and was in touch with) and the work was very fine I thought, and eventually I think when he saw that something was going to come out of it, and I went and hustled up somebody who said I'll publish it, which is always very useful… So I was delivering a publisher and the thing was carrying itself.

POLLARD: But I asked Pam that same question. In fact, before I asked her I wrote a few lines called 'Woman Poet, or Mervyn, with Your Permission', and then I told her. I really wanted to find out whether it was that she didn't think she could do it alone, as a woman, because I knew how long she had had the idea and I didn't see why she shouldn't just get whatever there was going for it, and then she explained this away to me. And as she said, the business about encouragement, I think that I should say that when I was in Guyana I wrote something that I though sounded, well, sort of 'goodish', [laughter] and I sent it to my sister [novelist, Erna Brodber], because we used to send stuff, not necessarily serious stuff – all kinds of things, references – anything. We would keep in touch and keep the theme there. And she showed it to Eddie Brathwaite apparently, and he thought it was – well, he probably used a lot of superlatives which she relayed to me. That is on the prose level, a story thing. The particular piece of work has never gone out because it is part of a novel, which seems never to be about to finish anywhere inside my head [Laughter] but the point is, that just that part he thought was very fine. And then the business of somebody who can look at your work and fix it. There is a line in one of my poems, 'After Cages' in that collection there [*Jamaica Woman*] 'newly old'. I remember I had it attached to another line and Eddie just took his pencil and said, 'What about here?' And now it looks so right I can hardly remember when 'newly old' was not standing there significantly. So it does help if somebody can just look. And I think that after a while one picks up the skill oneself. You can then look at your own stuff and see where to fix the line, you know.

DANCE: I know what fine poets Eddie and Mervyn both are, and personally I like them a great deal, but it is very interesting that as we are talking (and what I think we are seeing is influences and what have you) you are referring only to males. Are there any women writers who have assisted or encouraged you?

POLLARD: But there really are not many female models. I mean people like Una Marson and so, for some reason they are not the generation just before us; they are older. There are women poets and story-tellers if you think of say even Louise Bennett, she is not really the generation just before me; she is not five years older than I. I think that what happens is that, well, Mervyn is exactly my age except for a month; Eddie is seven years older. So I think it is that they are accessible, because they are so close to your own time. I think we have missed out a whole set of women poets, whether they didn't write or they didn't publish…

MORDECAI: I think a whole new sensibility thing has happened though between them and this lot. Right? For me, I must say that I know Louise Bennett's work very well. I can't see influences in the thing where, if you looked at what I write and looked to see her thing – I don't know about her as an influence in that way, but certainly in terms of the voices I hear in my head. And I write orally; a poem is completely written in my head and I carry most of my work in my memory, whole poems, right, other people's work too. I relate to work in this kind of way. The oral tradition for me is alive and well and that is how I work. And Louise's voice is loud and clear in my mind. Right? I am very intimate with her work, so if that counts for anything, that's a plus. I think too, in a weird kind of way – and this is a very weird lady – Sylvia Plath. Right? The weirdness of her sensibility: I relate to that. But as far as West Indian women and the generation that Velma is talking about, I think that the sensibility and the definition of West Indian woman has grown so between that point and us.

DANCE: What is the age range of the writers in this book?

MORDECAI: Twenty to forty-five. I think it's about something like that.

DANCE: You seem to minimise the significance to the work of the fact that the writers *are* women, I think, in the preface. Am I correct in saying that?

MORDECAI: I don't know if it's really minimised. There is strong feeling, right, on the part of some of the women in here about the fact that they are not women poets; they are poets. And they write, and they write good work that they are sufficiently confident about, that they will expose publicly in this kind of way; I don't think they would quarrel about your saying that their sensibility is influenced by their feminine-ness, right, but I think that certainly a couple of people that I can think of are very anxious not to be put in a box which is a woman-box.

DANCE: I can understand that, but even so let me ask you if there are some concerns that are significant here that are pretty clearly concerns of women, or perhaps I might rephrase the question and ask you the degree to which the usual concerns of Caribbean poetry are found here.

MORDECAI: I think that many of the usual concerns are found here and found here in ways that they are not (let me be careful about this) [found in the men's work]. I am particularly impressed by the fact that, for instance Heather Royes in a poem like 'Theophilus Jones Walks Naked Down King Street', works in a kind of way that is absolutely unsentimental. Right? I think somebody like Tony McNeill is parading his angst in a kind of way that Heather is not. She describes a Rasta Man walking down King Street on the way to committing suicide. And in fact the normal sort of complaints about women's work – it's sentimental, it's wet, it's soppy. Right? I think the men write sentimentally, and wetly, and soppily, in a way that many of the poems in here do not fill. They absolutely do not fill. Christine Craig's work, similarly, is remarkably distant and yet utterly concerned, and utterly sensitive; and what is being dealt with are issues like poverty, alienation, isolation, the whole business of the West Indian psyche getting itself together, the struggle, the struggle to be alive and so on. There is some of this in Lorna Goodison's 'The Road of the Dread'. I see a connection here with how Velma and Lorna and other people in here use the language, because the kind of language you are using is intimately tied to what you are talking about. And I think the fact that the women have been bold with the language, in a kind of way that the men have not been, is part of this sort of thing.

POLLARD: I think I will go along with what Pam says. I do think that the period sensibility is different, and I think that one of the reasons that we will not be soppy about the man walking down the street to commit suicide is that we can only think of practical ways in which we can help him, if help him at all. I mean the comments, I mean people will look at him and they will say, 'Well, boy, another naked man!' or what have you. But I think that the woman is going to try to figure out, 'Now what can be done about that guy?' whereas the man is going to sound soppily sentimental. So I think that there is a way in which I am conscious that perhaps we are too practical in the way that they are too sentimental; but I think however that the things that men expect us to get soppy and sentimental about are love things. And a lot of these poems are not about love things. I think they believe that if we were writing about love we would be slobbering over.

DANCE: But you do write about love.

POLLARD: But not as much as one would expect from a book of poetry written by women. People traditionally think, don't you think, that women sing songs about love and so, and that's what they expected. That has not been. I am perhaps the most guilty and I don't think it's love I am talking about.

DANCE: Oh? But you use the word 'guilty'?

POLLARD: There are these two or three poems there which I consider anti-love. They are not love, they are the other side of it; they are what happens if it isn't. Right? But when I say I am the most guilty, if I have six poems and three of them are what happens when love is not, then it means that I am thinking about it more than some of the others who will have maybe one representing that whole thing, and three about problems in the society, you know.

MORDECAI: I think that Dorothea [Edmondson] had some anti-love poems in there. I have lots of anti-love poems in there; I have a nasty poem for my husband that says, 'if you won't let me be myself just let me go do my thing somewhere else.' By an accident of selection I have several anti-love poems. A large portion of my work is anti-love poetry.

POLLARD: But maybe we should not call it anti-love; I think it is, in this sense, woman trying to get out of what I see as a sort of cage, because no matter how you think about it, when you think about female identification in terms of a man/woman thing you are in a cage.

DANCE: I think that if there is just one image that runs through [*Jamaica Woman*] it is the idea of being trapped. I see it so often there.

POLLARD: It is. I have a whole thing called 'Cages', and this poem which says 'After Cages' is about what woman can see once she has got…

MORDECAI: …out of her cage. I am looking at something by Alma Mock Yen that says 'I am wallowing/ in my store/ unsure/ that tomorrow/ can afford me/ I am sinking/ in my bed/ back to the fountain-head', and so on. I take that point; it is all through the work.

DANCE: Well, let me follow that up a little bit. You decided not to use the word anti-love, but I…

MORDECAI: We don't have another word to back it up.

DANCE: Is there a kind of disillusionment with love among the women poets?

POLLARD: I don't think it is with love, you know. I think it is the disillusionment with what has been carved out for you if you love. I don't think it *has* to be and I think it will change, but certainly in our society, *if* you love, you become a wife. If you are a wife your concerns take on a pecking order which I described in the business of – you are a wife, you are a mother, then you are a career woman and… Now it is only after you have organised that kind of thing and set up a new hierarchy to please yourself that you can even write. So I think that it is significant that we are writing about it as if it were anti-love now that we are out of our cages in a sense, because if we were not out we could hardly look to see what those cages were. I think the fact that we can write about it must mean that we are not as much into it, although even if you are into it and you are aware that it is a cage, so I think it is the limitations that loving tends to place [upon] some people rather than loving itself that we are worried about.

MORDECAI: Yes, I think that's true, if I can go on a little… I am very lucky because my main relationship is very satisfying, and he has… well, I got out of my cage early. I have a continuing problem though with relating to men, right, in work kind of ways, in affection kind of ways and so on. I am constantly encountering a fairly meagre kind of concept in their minds for what a woman person is; they have a concept of woman and it is an extremely limited concept. So I am always fighting battles, right, very up-close battles. I think I fight them well too. But I am always fighting them and they definitely have to do with the fact that a woman is a person and the broad thing, you know, that definition of person that obtains for a man ought to obtain for a woman. I am fighting my son who is thirteen years old on exactly this point right now. And you know I think it's kind of dread.

DANCE: Let me ask you – because I think we are sort of talking about images that males have of women or at least the little slot they'd like to place you in – what do you think about the images of women that appear generally in Caribbean literature which are by and large images created by male writers?

POLLARD: Well, I think that the image of Caribbean woman in Caribbean litera-ture is the same limiting image of the woman. I will say this, and I say it because I meant to write it down, that the only Caribbean poet or Caribbean literary person who I think has seen any wider role for woman is Edward Brathwaite, and that is because I think that he has given to women some very significant roles in his poetry at least. There is somebody called Francina [in *The Arrivants*] who is a little half-crazy woman, in a way; she picks up a turtle which suggests all that is home, all that is for real as opposed to factories and concrete things that are going to go up, and going to usurp whatever we have that is still good. And when they remove this nice place where the turtle was and they are going to put up some horrible structure, the person who buys the turtle is a little half-crazy lady, or so regarded, called Francina. Now I don't know if this is the way Mr. Brathwaite wanted it to go, but for me what it says is that it is the woman who really saves whatever there is worth saving. He has other women, but I think of her most because in real life she would be such a minor person. Then he has a group of female philosophers, I call them, in a shop, in another poem called 'The Dust' [*The Arrivants*] about which I have written. And all these female philosophers are saying some very, very important things for the Caribbean psyche; well eventually he gets to *Mother Poem*, which is the whole thing about mother in all her phases. I think that every time he touches woman she is very significant and I would sing loud for Francina.

MORDECAI: I would agree with all of that. I would see turtle too in the oldness of turtle, the preservation of the tradition back to…

POLLARD: Yes, and the sheltering, you know, that cover that it has, that covers everything. As I said, I keep saying that poets write down things and I am sure they don't even know how much they are saying sometimes. I don't know whether it was conscious, but that is what I think it does, whether he know it or not.

MORDECAI: I want to say that I have read something of Garth St. Omer's recently that has struck me, because I think that it is the first honest, decent attempt I think that a West Indian male sensibility has made to analyse in a rigorous kind of way the whole business of how a man deals with a woman. He has really been very rigorous in *Nor Any Country*. Now I hope to write something on that soon. I know his other work is quite different, right, because there is the same existentialist thing in a lot of the rest of it, but I think *Nor Any Country* is an important move forward, because he explores in the minds of a number of men how the men regard the women, and the absolute callousness of that regard is exposed in an almost medical kind of way, right, and I think that that's important: I am about to write, in fact I am writing now, a paper called 'The West Indian Male Sensibility in Search of Itself'; it's going to deal with some of the novels, because I think in fact male criticism has suffered from not having women deal with the work. And again we are back into the trap of woman critic. OK. But I think that women must bring to response something that has to do with the fact that they are women. And that perhaps has been missing. We create the history, we keep the societies going; they say the societies are matriarchal. Velma has spoken about Francina preserving what there is worth preserving, and so maybe you know we should have woken up long ago and started to talk about this sort of thing the men were writing and pass some kind of helpful judgement on that.

DANCE: I may have missed something myself but one thing that struck me as I looked over this volume of poetry, was, with the exception of Miss Tomlinson's poetry, an almost complete lack of humour. Is that observation correct or…

POLLARD: You're right. When there is humour it's like Goodison's 'Ocho Rios' when it is not humour that you are supposed to laugh at. Because it is very concerned humour. Having attempted to laugh, you can't laugh because it's not a joke. So there is the humorous streak, the possibility of humour, but I think the material is not humorous.

DANCE: Does that occur very often, even the possibility of humour there?

MORDECAI: I think it is here, you know, and in particular Goodison comes to mind: her 'For R&R in the Rain'

POLLARD: Yes, this is what I am saying, but you cannot laugh.

DANCE: Nor can we with your spider and the fly can we? ['Fly']

POLLARD: Yes, but it is not outright humour, because it is putting humour into a serious thing.

MORDECAI: I think that some of Olive's stuff too, well, perhaps not much that is represented here, but there is a little quality to 'Madam at Traffic Lights' [*Jamaica Woman*] which, you know, I think, you could relate to too. But perhaps overall – ah, Bridget Jones too, some of her stuff is funny in the kind of way we are talking about.

POLLARD: OK. Well I was about to say that her stuff comes closest to being funny, but hers are very short, cryptic almost, and I suppose inherent in that kind of poem is a funny streak. I think all hers are in that general way.

MORDECAI: Sandy McIntosh too is in that kind of style: the short, the cryptic, the funny thing: 'night people/we're not bright/ in the morning/ (yawning)' ['Darn!'] you know; you could see it as having that kind of wry voice, if you want, rather than straight.

POLLARD: But it is still not straight humour. You're right. And even Cyrene Tomlinson, hers, it's humour in a kind of way, but, I thought you were going to say, when you mentioned her that all of the others are mostly in English while hers is in dialect.

MORDECAI: It's the Creole I suppose that signals the laughter.

POLLARD: And in a way that is normal, because what has happened so far, here we get historical again. The poetry that we have had in dialect so far has tended to be laughter-raising; the plays that we have had that use dialect are mostly Bim and Bam stuff so that the business of treating dialect seriously is going to be very new. In poetry I think we are only accustomed to it for laughs, in a lot of ways.

DANCE: OK. Let me go back to the idea of some of the themes that I see in a great deal of West Indian literature and ask you if they are indeed significant here, and perhaps if not, why not. One of them is the quest for identity; you know, throughout at least contemporary West Indian literature, the men are trying to determine who they are; they are travelling to determine who they are. Here you might say that [the concern is] the sense of identity as a woman, but people aren't looking for it; they are just asking to be allowed to express it. They aren't lost, in other words, wondering who they are. Would you…

POLLARD: Well, I don't know how it is going to be documented, but I have a feeling that it perhaps is because the men have been looking outward, here and beyond. I think you only begin to search for your identity when you compare yourself in some kind of way with another world. As long as we are here and we recognise it, this is where we are. Then you don't have to speak to the identity problem, but I think the first thing is that for a very long time our education was outside of here. So that the people who went away were always into the identity search. I think it has carried over, even to a lot of the people who did not go, because when you are writing, if you are writing for some big publication it is going to go beyond here. And then there is a way in which you start questioning. Also if you are reared on literature, the literature that we have is a literature that does not include us. So long as you are dealing in the world of books, in the early twentieth century, say, you will never see yourself. And I suppose you start to question, 'Well where am I?' In a sense, I think that the women are lucky for two reasons. The men have done the whole of that – of the fighting about who they are, and so, if they find out who they are, then if they are the Black men then we are the Black women and we don't really have to fight about it again! [Laughter] But our concerns again are more practical. I remember, I think it is – which is this wife and husband popular in the comics? – Andy Capp and his wife I think. And she was saying that, you know, he looked after the large things, like I suppose, World War whichever and so, while she only dealt with the small things. He looked after the big concerns, and he was very proud of it, but the big concerns were all the things that really are not the day to day things. I think that it could be (I don't know if I am right) two things: one the business of books and education and going away and dealing with the world and us being just Caribbean people and then the business of woman, where you tend to look after the close things, the man down the street, the problems around and *then* now yourself. So I think that this whole definition, to wit, we are more anxious to define ourselves as people as Pam pointed out. The struggle, to be a person at all, to get out of our cage, even if it is a pleasant cage, or to function as if you are out of it, has already been so difficult that I don't think we have started sitting and thinking of ourselves.

MORDECAI: I mean there is something very ironic about – because on the one hand, you look at the sociological writing on the West Indies. The societies are matriarchal, and this is true. All right. So that in the close-up sense, in the sense of who the woman is when she is making the tribe and growing up the tribe and when she is a grandmother going through the whole set of processes again. And you can hardly be dealing with that and don't know who you are. You must know who you are, right?

POLLARD: It can't be defined for you.

MORDECAI: Good. But then on the other hand there is this thing where you start to expand your concerns a little more and there is the man with his cage, right. Sometimes I think he is just 'fraid of what will happen to di whole a dem, if we get out of di cage. This whole business of who you are in the sense of being alienated from the West Indian place is something of which I have no experience, and I don't think the women who write have any experience of that. I think that we identify very closely with our people and with this place and we don't in any way feel alienated or isolated or reduced by the fact that we are Black people in the West Indies of now.

POLLARD: All right, but you can't feel reduced being Black in the West Indies of now, but what I am wondering, however, is whether the same women if they went into another society whether they wouldn't have other concerns? And I think they would, in fact. In fact I was just one week in America in a conference that was national so that people from all over the States were there – but here again I suddenly became very depressed in a way with the fact that, 'Here I am again', because I have been in the States before, right in the middle of the late '60s I was there (what now, '68 to '72). And there was I again, suddenly a Black person, which I hadn't been for a long time. [Laughter] I had been a person. And I came and I said it to my sister and she said, 'Yes, you know, I had thought that *I* had gotten myself together totally. But you only need to sit on a plane in America once to realise that you can't get the Black world together by being together yourself.' So you are right back, so I have a feeling that this

Caribbean which we insist is confused in many ways, is also a very safe little harbour in which to be. The men, because of their outward look, I think anyway, have had to go through a lot of stuff.

MORDECAI: Yes. I think you are right about that.

POLLARD: But we are not – we will not necessarily have to go through it. I think the society does not ask us to do that. It really asks us to bring up the children, to keep things going, and even if we go abroad with our men, frequently we are not called upon to think or deal, just to work and do whatever, because while we are there it's because of the big stuff that *they* are doing. Now we will start going out doing big stuff ourselves, presumably they [women] will perhaps think about it.

DANCE: When you were talking about what happens to the West Indian woman who may go abroad with her husband, I was thinking about the theme of the exiles, lost away from home and so forth. That does not become as significant for the woman either because she simply keeps the same role in a different location:

POLLARD: Right and there are problems. She has to work and sometimes she has to face the music out there. But I think she sees it in a way as a means to an end. She is just there; she will just deal with that for the time being until *he* is finished and she gets back home. She doesn't really think about, well, 'How would I accommodate my psyche to this sort of thing?' because it isn't her thing and she is there with her husband – she is not there, she is really there with her husband.

DANCE: And coming home likewise, to continue the usual theme, wouldn't be the traumatic thing that it is for the male?

POLLARD: No, because the male will have gone and he will have found a whole lot of new things in a way, and having started to deal with these crises, I am afraid he continues…

MORDECAI: Yes, she is likely in either situation (I am thinking of St. Omer again), whether she is at home or in foreign to be faced with the same kind of thing.

POLLARD: Yes, I am thinking of him too.

MORDECAI: Yes, because for instance, you know, the thing of the Black man dealing with the white lady and what the white lady is, you know, in his consciousness and that whole thing. I mean she is as likely in a way to buck that up at home, you know, in a-kind of way, as she is to buck it up there. Right? And so, you know, here or there, when it intervenes it's the same syndrome that has…

POLLARD: No, *there* it is a bit more terrible, more poignant in a way, because there you bet she is working hard to keep things going and she doesn't have her mother to cry on, she doesn't have her friends to tell how bad this man is, she doesn't have all the social supports that she needs.

MORDECAI: That's true.

POLLARD: And here too, there is a way in which here, at a pinch she can go and tear up the white lady, if she is really serious. [Laughter]

MORDECAI: Oh, but that Patsy – I love. Oh-h-h! [Character in St. Omer's *J–*, *Black Bam & The Masqueraders*].

POLLARD: Here she can tear her up.

MORDECAI: Absolutely decimate the white lady.

DANCE: Here?

MORDECAI: No, man, he mek her do it there, and I think it is the *nicest* thing in that book. [Laughter]

POLLARD: I didn't know it could be done *there* because those societies have a tendency to have all kinds of little rules – you really just don't think of tearing up somebody.

MORDECAI: Man it was really nice! I want to say how that went. Right at the end of *J–, Black Bam & The Masqueraders*, right.

POLLARD: I don't remember that.

MORDECAI: You must see the picture, it's lovely. Where the wife sits waiting for the husband to come and the sister arrive with a big stick and just reduce the lady!

DANCE: Let me ask you this, that triangle, the Black male, the white woman and the Black woman, is frequently treated by male Caribbean writers. I think I saw an allusion to it in that book [*Jamaica Women*] and only one. That's not too important a theme then among the women writers?

POLLARD: No, because you see here again, I think the 'other' woman is a theme, but not the woman as white, necessarily. But I don't think anybody has written about it, because I do believe that the other woman is just one other of the limiting things that happen to you. I think you will find that it falls in place as one thing.

MORDECAI: But a whole lot of other things.

POLLARD: Right. He talks down to you, he doesn't realise that you have a mind even half as big as his, he thinks you can settle for half a relationship – it's part of a whole lot of things, I don't think that we single that out.

DANCE: I think in 'Roots-Man' [Dorothea Edmondson, *Jamaica Woman*, p.22] there is some…

MORDECAI: 'The Roots-Man', who is, you know, striking all the poses, right? 'In town/ they say he's/ charismatic:/ Comrades, who is robbing you?/ Who who who?/ And you, black woman woman,/ [This is the guy saying, you know] 'black woman [must] stand behind your man;/ … Black in his rebel roost/ he's strangely subdued/ A red-haired woman rules the roost.'

POLLARD: But let me say this – that she is writing there out of a white experience. I think that that is from a set of poems that was not written on this piece of earth. She lived for a long time out of a white experience. She was living in a white country when that poem was written. So it is to the point and I think she is addressing herself to the sixties American business.

MORDECAI: I think it could be easily in one place as the other, right? The complaint is that the guy prefers the wife. Talks Black, but his main alliance is the white wife.

POLLARD: Yes, yes. White, it needn't be a traveller here at all. And now that is something that I think that many Black women who have lived abroad have become very very aware of, that this whole rhetoric that the Black man gives you is really – maybe it is in his heart, but sometimes it isn't as obvious as one would expect. I mean for a man whose heart is so Black, you keep wondering how his wife is so white. And then you have all these men who say. 'The only black things in my house are me and my car.' You have all these quotes supposedly from Black men. Now I hear them from Black, cynical women. I don't know whether they make them up. So we have had that, though I tell you I think that we had a lot more of that in the '50s when the men were going abroad to study. To a man they were coming back… I think you got your degree, you came back, you got your big job and you had your wife. You have a house on the hill; a big car, a big job, a white wife. I think they went together. And you will see a lot I think in the literature too – it's not about white, certainly about brown, and about the whole business of milking your coffee, and marrying up and the lot, you know; we have had the whole of that, though I think that by the '70s, well… Now I must say that I took this thing to a West Indian man, this point, and he argued that what he was not sure about is whether the women wouldn't do the same if women were the askers. In other words, he is saying that men ask, women wait to be asked; he does not know whether if women were in the asking position whether Black women would not take white men. I told him I don't know the answer, I really don't. [At this point Pollard had to leave for class.]

DANCE: The female writers seem to be a little more traditional in terms of form and style. There is not a great deal of experimentation in these poems, I think. Would you like to comment?

MORDECAI: Well, I would agree and disagree. I think that, somebody like Lorna Goodison comes to mind because I do think that she is doing absolutely new things in exactly the area that we are talking about. I think she is exploring the range of language, at an interesting point, because it isn't deep Creole, it certainly isn't the standard language. She is exploring its rhythms in a new way; she isn't working in any of the metrical modes at all. The line length is long and it moves with the rhythms, with the speech rhythms, right? Lorna comes to mind. Velma also comes to mind, but I don't think it shows in the poetry that is here; Olive Senior in her prose work, a lot of which I would call prose poetry… the organisation is tight and close and so on. It's the same kind of thing that Lorna is doing. For most of the other people I think that what you are saying is true, that the traditional types of constraints are there. I – well I won't talk about my own stuff except to say that there is a problem with mine because I do write in my head and the stuff when it gets down on the page has a way of not looking quite right.

DANCE: And just one last question. Your 'Protest Poem' offers an extremely dramatic ending to this book. Was it placed at the end for that reason?

MORDECAI: Well, as it turned out we decided that there were so many kinds of exigencies that were going to manifest themselves if we had started dealing with the work in terms of say, themes and so on, that the best way would probably be to do it alphabetically. Happily, Jennifer Brown has that beautiful poem 'Africa and the Caribbean', which I think is a lovely way of starting this kind of anthology, and I went at the end as editor, right? And I am afraid that I am very attached to 'Protest Poem' because I think it deals with something that for me is very important. I have a strong political sense, awareness, interest. In fact I think I would like to actively enter politics at some point in my life and I think this poem does that. I would also like to say that where it has been read it has worked on I think practically every occasion: and one or two of the gentlemen who looked at it in the beginning said, 'Ahhh, I am not sure, you know I am not sure this works at all.' So it represents a kind of triumph of my own confident judgement.

CONVERSATION WITH

MERVYN MORRIS

Mervyn F. Morris was born in Kingston, Jamaica, on February 21, 1937. He finished Munro College in Jamaica and then went on to complete a BA at the University College of the West Indies (1957); a BA at St. Edmund Hall, Oxford, 1961; and an MA at Oxford (1965). He has taught at Munro College and has held various positions at the University of the West Indies, Mona Campus, where he is currently Professor Emeritus of Creative Writing and West Indian Literature. He has also served as visiting professor at the University of Kent in Canterbury, England, and the University of Miami in Coral Gables, Florida. In 1992 he was the United Kingdom Arts Council International Writer in Residence. He serves as the general editor of Longman Caribbean Critical Studies of Caribbean writers, the theatre critic for *The Daily Gleaner*, a weekly columnist on public affairs for *The Jamaican Daily News*, and occasionally as a broadcaster on the BBC, JBC and RJR.

Morris is the author of five volumes of poetry: *The Pond* (1973); *On Holy Week* (1976); *Shadowboxing* (1979); *Examination Centre* (1992); and *I Been There Sort Of: New and Selected Poems* (2006). In addition, his poems have appeared in newspapers and journals in Jamaica, Barbados, Trinidad, England, Canada and the United States, and have been included in over twenty anthologies. He has edited several anthologies: *Seven Jamaican Poets* (1971); *Jamaica Woman* (1980; coedited with Pamela Mordecai); *Focus 1983: An Anthology* (1983); *Voiceprint: An Anthology of Oral and Related Poetry from the Caribbean* (1989); and *The Faber Book of Contemporary Caribbean Short Stories* (1990). Also of interest are his monograph, *Is English We Speaking: West Indian Literature* (1993); *Progressions: West Indian Literature in the 1970s* (1990); proceedings of the Second Conference on West Indian Literature, held at UWI, Mona, (co-edited with Edward Baugh); and *Caribbean Theatre* (1986). He has also written *Is English We Speaking* (1999) and *Making West Indian Literature* (2004).

In addition he is the general editor of Louis James, *Jean Rhys* (1978); Jean D'Costa, *Roger Mais: 'The Hills Were Joyful Together' and 'Brother Man'* (1978); Claude McKay, *My Green Hills of Jamaica and Five Jamaican Short Stories* (1979); Pat Persaud, *Childhood Whispers* (1981); Louise Bennett's *Selected Poems* (1982); Michael Smith, *It a Come* (1987); Jean Binta Breeze, *Riddym Ravings and Other Poems* (1988); Louise Bennett, *Aunty Roachy Seh* (1993); and posthumously edited Dennis Scott's volume of poetry *After-Image* (to be published by Peepal Tree Press in 2008). Morris was also the editor of *The Faber Book of Contemporary Caribbean Short Stories* (1991). With Carolyn Allen he edited *Writing Life: Reflections by West Indian Writers* (2007).

He has written introductions to Dennis Scott's *Uncle Time* (1973); VS Reid's *New Day* (1973); Claude McKay's *My Green Hills of Jamaica and Five Jamaican Stories* (1979); Louise Bennett's *Anancy and Miss Lou* (1979); VS Reid's *The Leopard* (1980); Paul Issa's *Mutabaruka: The First Poems (1970-1979)* (1980); Trevor Rhone's, *Old Story Time and Other Plays* (1981); Louise Bennett's *Selected Poems* (1982); Samuel Selvon's *Moses Ascending* (1984); Namba Roy's *Black Albino* (1986); Trevor Rhone's *School's Out and Two Can Play* (1986) and *Smile Orange and Old Story Time* (1987); and Abdur-Rahman Slade Hopkinson's *Snowscape with Signature* (1993).

Morris was a Rhodes Scholar from 1958-1961. In 1976 the Institute of Jamaica awarded him a Silver Musgrave Medal for Poetry, and in 1978 he won a UNESCO study grant.

At the time of the interview, Morris was living in Mona, Kingston.

Our interview took place at Morris's home on November 17, 1978, before I envisioned this collection.

DANCE: Tell me about your family? Was it sort of middle-class or…

MORRIS: Yes, I think definitely that's how it can be described. My mother was head-teacher at an elementary school, ultimately; and my father was an accountant at the Island Medical Office, so that we're not really 'working class'. I sound as though I am apologising for not being working class. But that's the way it happened… I am not sure exactly where they are from. They are both from the country – which parishes I no longer remember.

DANCE: Were your folks interested in the old folk tales, that kind of thing? Did you grow up hearing any of them?

MORRIS: Not directly through my folks, because one of the things which I think is very important in my personal background is that my father in relation to things like culture and the dialect was relaxed and comfortable; whereas I think, on the whole, my mother was not. I can still remember that we used to tell and listen to Anancy stories at the neighbours', you know – sitting on the step and so on. And I remember we used to enjoy when they first started to come out, Anancy stories in print, when the Pioneer Press started to put them out. That's not when they first started to come out, but I mean I had never heard of Jekyll [Walter Jekyll, *Jamaican Song and Story*, 1907, new edition 1966] when I was a child, but we all knew of and admired, at least all the children knew of and admired Louise Bennett and my father certainly admired Louise Bennett's stuff. But one of the, I think, peculiar things about my personal family background, especially in relation to literature, is that we were a family that read things aloud from time to time, and it was a family in which we would read Louise Bennett's poems in the *Gleaner* – aloud – and enjoy them, with my mother looking faintly disapproving. And we would also read aloud passages from PG Wodehouse; so that there, in terms of growing up, I was never taught to be uncomfortable with the very English any more than I was taught to be uncomfortable with the folk thing.

DANCE: Your interest in poetry then stems perhaps from the family sessions and the oral reading of poems…?

MORRIS: I guess it must have in a way, in that an interest in literature certainly – and what I think I have been stressing – an interest in a wide range of literature, certainly in terms of cultural origin, was being developed, but I don't think we read aloud very much serious poetry. I don't recall this. I mean obviously one learnt things at school and we would recite them, and we did recite them…

DANCE: Let me interrupt you one minute to ask you – you don't consider Louise Bennett's poetry serious poetry?

MORRIS: I consider it *very* serious poetry, but at that time we read it for the pleasure it gave us and we would not have called it 'serious', and in fact, of course, years later, you know, when I was writing on Louise, at first it seemed important to make precisely that point – you know, the thing I wrote was called 'On Reading Louise Bennett, (comma) Seriously' [*Jamaica Journal*, 1, Dec. 1967]. Right? In which you know I was trying to argue the case for her as a serious worker. But what we knew is that we liked it, and we didn't ask too many questions about whether it was serious or not. We knew it was good. Now, what's also interesting, I think, is that we knew that PG Wodehouse was good, as I told you, and we enjoyed that. But my father, who had quite a sense of humour, also read aloud the newspaper poets who we all knew were bad… poets who were obviously inept in terms of basic skills, so that you would stop before the rhyme and we would all try to supply it, so that there was a kind of critical sense developing in those early days, because we certainly knew what gave us pleasure and what we wished to deride because we felt it so incompetent.

DANCE: I'd like to ask you now about your process of writing. Are your poems the result of some great inspiration momentarily or are they the results of hard labour over a long period of time?

MORRIS: They vary a lot, Daryl. Now that is a question I have been many, many times asked. You know, anytime you give a sort of creative talk you get asked that. And the truth though is that the most of the poems are a result of a lot of work, and now and again it has happened that a poem has come comparatively easily, but when the poem *has* come easily, certainly in later years – the point is one keeps writing and keeps practicing and you know one writes bad drafts which are never shown to anyone, but that is a kind of practice – so that when you receive what you call a gift, it's a gift that comes to somebody who has been practicing, and who has been trained to receive the gift, so that if a poem comes quickly and seems adequately formed and shaped, it doesn't mean that writing poems is easy, you know. But by and large I rework poems a great deal.

DANCE: What writers or teachers do you consider as having been most influential in your development as a poet?

MORRIS: No, no names that come immediately to mind… I think as you could guess from some of what I was saying about the family background, I have always been interested in wit and humour, and in fact as a writer of verse, from my schooldays, long before I ever thought of writing anything I thought was a serious poem, I was interested in doggerel and in writing doggerel and satirical verse… Also in the Sixth Form at Munro, we did a very unusual special paper on the age of Johnson, getting away from all the mushy romantics, and I think that probably had an important influence on my whole background, because it meant that a certain kind of rationalist verse, not without emotion of course, but something very much the way the prose flowed, was among the formative academic influences. I did like reading Johnson and Gray, whom we happened to study at that time.

DANCE: All your formal education I suppose was mostly British poets?

MORRIS: Yes, almost entirely.

DANCE: At the time you were at school there was not much emphasis on poets from the West Indies, I suppose?

MORRIS: No, and in fact the only one with whom I was really intimate was Louise Bennett. At that time I don't think I knew anything about Claude McKay. A bit later perhaps I did, and I, by the way, am not a fan of his verse at all. I am a great fan of Claude McKay, but I do not think that his poetry is very good. I think it's very important, you know, very important historically, and some of his prose is marvellous in my view, but if you set him… with someone like Countee Cullen, for example, there seems in Countee Cullen to be an integrity of – an integration between voice and vision, which I find isn't there in McKay. McKay keeps sounding to me as though it's someone else's voice – you know, the whole prison of the sonnets, it sounds as though there is some other voice there. He never frees himself of it for me.

DANCE: Let me ask you about your reaction to some other American poets.

MORRIS: I tended to read the 1960s poets when they were fashionable. I haven't read them all hard; I mean one of the ones whom I have read a lot of and liked a lot is Don Lee. I like some Sonia Sanchez. I personally think Nikki Giovanni is overrated. I like Baraka, you know, some of it, but I feel like I should be reading the whole of Baraka. I feel very close to – I like the sort of classicism that I sense in Gwendolen Brooks, you know a kind of tightness, which is much closer to the kind of English poetry thing I was brought up on than most of the others, for me, anyway. Somebody I am very, very keen on, this is one book that really grabbed me, and I don't see anybody talking about her as very important, Mari Evans – I think she is a tremendous poet. Now you asked me a question which I didn't answer, so let me go back a bit and answer a little of it. What poets did I like?… We were introduced to the Metaphysicals at the University, and of course I loved Donne and Herbert. I happen to prefer Herbert to Donne, which I think is unusual. Now I suppose the first individual poet whom I was attracted to, was RS Thomas, a Welsh poet. I don't think I can trace any influence of RS Thomas in my work… I picked up this thing called *Poetry For Supper*, I think it was, and was astonished that the thing gave me quite a lot on first reading of a few poems and it seemed hard-edged and it really caught me… But people like Dylan Thomas I have never really wanted to read personally; you know I have sometimes had to teach and analyse and look at his individual poems. but the whole thing of a kind of noisy rhetoric – that's very horribly against my temperament – and certainly against the particular background I have been telling you about, which is the rationalist poetry.

DANCE: Let me ask you about *Seven Jamaican Poets*. In the introduction you wrote that 'This little book could serve as an introduction to recent Jamaican verse,' and yet as I read it and other collections of Caribbean literature, I sense that perhaps, at least in terms of tone, these poets may not be considered as representative as some others?

MORRIS: I think that's a very fair comment. There was a problem with that book in a way… In the introduction I tried to make it apparent really that one was not trying to say, 'These are *the* seven poets' or that this is the full range of their work, but our intentions were fairly widely misunderstood and I think obviously misjudged in a sense, because all that happened with the making of that collection was that Bolivar asked me to put it together. What the poets wanted in most cases was simply to publish some poems which they were not ashamed of and which they had not published. There was no attempt either by the poets or the editor to represent their actual range as poets. Simply the attempt was to put together a number of poems, none of which in the view of the editor, or the writers was a bad poem. So that, if I had to do that again, I would certainly protect myself much more carefully by in fact trying to make it representative, because many of us, for example this is certainly true of Dennis Scott, Tony McNeill and myself, had dialect poems, and poems which were angry and so on which we could easily have put in, but we were simply putting out some new poems and, you know, had no idea it would be received the way it was. And one or two reviewers, I remember Andrew Salkey, for example, spreading the notion really that this was an attempt to cull the best of these poets, and there never was any such intention.

DANCE: Let me ask you about the theme of the quest for an identity which became very important, in the '60s, particularly in Black American literature and in Caribbean literature it seems to me. In some of your poems you seem to treat that theme a bit sarcastically – 'To A West Indian Definer', 'Journey into the Interior', and so forth. Would you care to react to this?

MORRIS: Love to react to that. I don't like 'To A West Indian Definer' as a poem – all right? And in fact when James Livingston wanted to reprint it for *Caribbean Rhythms* I tried to persuade him to put in something else instead, but as a statement about my position, it remains entirely what I would subscribe to. I do not think that identity can be put into a capsule. Everybody, each person, has an identity, and it is also at the same time true that each person is searching for an identity. I think that the way in which the question about identity tended to be framed at the time when it was most popular, was strictly in terms of a precise relationship, the degree of one's relationship to Europe and to Africa; and a lot of that really is inadequate, a lot of the way in which it may be framed is inadequate, because each person is a person and we define ourselves in terms of interpersonal relationships – what's going on inside one's head and so on. And in the way that people who want to talk, especially in an academic way, about the search for identity, tend to talk, you know, that is about our relationship to Africa, to the folk, relation to Europe and the Great Tradition and so on, the human person tends to get lost, actually, because the neatness of the academic categorising doesn't allow for the untidiness of the human being.

DANCE: This looking to Africa in terms of the quest for identity in the poetry, many writers of the '60s and '70s have been doing that in quite a romantic way, and I noted in one of your poems, 'A West Indian to an African', you write, 'I like you, brother/ But tell these bloody men/ We're different. Our closest bond's in history books.'

MORRIS: Where did you find that actually?

DANCE: Let me see. Where did I find it?

MORRIS: Because I have never published that.

DANCE: I think someone was quoting you; it may have been James [*The Islands in Between*, p.7].

MORRIS: It doesn't matter, it doesn't matter. Anyway that's a bad poem which I have never published.

DANCE: But it's yours?

MORRIS: Yes, I wrote those lines… What to say about that? I mean, I think that that is a simplistic poem, … you know they are obviously a response – I have developed certainly beyond that. There are important senses in which I recognise that we are different from Africans, but there are important senses in which I recognise real continuities. I think a crucial thing, something that you will find very helpful for defining a position which I think, I hope, I have moved beyond, would be my essay called 'Feeling, Affection, Respect' in *Disappointed Guests*, an essay written soon after I was a student in England, and there are some attitudes to Africa and Africans which

I have certainly moved beyond, but I think that I was setting out what my attitudes at this time were, very accurately. You know, my actual response at that time was I found Africans very strange, and found it much – well, you know, I found I understood the social interchange of the English having been taught by the English – I felt very much more comfortable with it than with a very African African, and you know, that's shorthand, of course, it's very crudely put. But there were one or two Africans whom I did like, but they were precisely the ones who seemed to me to be easily mistaken for West Indians; they were so comfortable with Englishmen. I think, though, one has moved beyond that. I mean one of the things that the late '60s has done actually in terms of my own development, I think, the influence, though I keep resisting him in various ways, the influence of Edward Brathwaite, is very, very strong in terms of you know, increasing my understanding of the continuities between the Caribbean and Africa, though I have never visited Africa. There are some people who still question the academic validity of what he is saying, but increasingly I find myself accepting that there are continuities which are observable, you know – food patterns, particular patterns of dress, etc. etc. etc.

DANCE: One great irony in reading the little that I have read about Caribbean literature, is that most of the critics tend to see you as outside the contemporary trends, in a sense, in Caribbean literature, and they speak of your 'formal classicism' and talk about your consciousness of 'the elegance of the Great Tradition' [Salkey, *Breaklight*, p.XVI], and Gerald Moore insists that you remain 'faithful to the iambic pentameter and to a general stanzaic regularity' [*Critics on Caribbean Literature*, p. 132]. The irony it seems to me is that these same critics who say that, usually quote you to illustrate trends in Caribbean literature. Would you like to comment on that?

MORRIS: No. I wouldn't know what to say, because – I really wouldn't know what to say. You see there are particular poems that I have written which really are very convenient for illustrating particular historical moments. It's not necessarily got anything to do with whether the poem is any good or not, I mean, though I think I am in no way ashamed of or embarrassed by 'To an Expatriate Friend', which is one of the ones that they keep quoting. Now one reason why I think it is reasonable, sensible for them to keep using that poem is that it really does focus lucidly, you know, which a lot of very good poetry doesn't – it focuses lucidly so that people who are reading it for the first time can perhaps grasp quickly what, whoever is quoting, is talking about. It focuses that tension which really was a very, very important part of the whole cultural mood of the late '60s, you know.

DANCE: Was it worth losing that expatriate friend for the revolution?

MORRIS: In a sense that's not what the poem is about, and I didn't lose that friend, you know, the particular person on whom it is modelled, though there are lies in the poem as there usually are in most of my poems. The particular person is someone with whom I keep in touch even now, and this particular friend happens to be very far away. I mean, the friend isn't lost in a sense, and also the revolution didn't come in a sense. No, what I think that poem is about, Daryl, what I'm sure that poem is about – is a particular moment when there is a shift in values, a moment, a pressure moment. And what has not always been noticed by people reading the poem, is that I am not only talking about the way in which the white man is beginning to feel rejected. When I say, 'new powers re-enslaved us all', I mean *all*, and when I say to the person 'it hurt to see you slowly going white', it's not only that the white friend is getting more and more white, feeling attacked and so on, but that the 'I', both the letter 'I' and the e-y-e of the poem, is getting blacker, and I *have* got blacker.

DANCE: Well, let me ask you about the poem 'The House Slave'. Was that written before or after?

MORRIS: Written very much in the same period; there's a whole series of poems written in the same period.

DANCE: Is that autobiographical?

MORRIS: No, not at all, not at all. It is autobiographical in this sense, and I will be more candid than perhaps I should be about the origin of the poem, because it is not really important to the poem as an artefact. I quite like that poem still, because, you see, it's a poem that comes from where important poems come from; you know it is not fully in control, actually. You know it is something happening underneath. It really arose out of the tendency of people to throw the term 'house-slave' around, so that originally it was an attempt to deal with that; but what it becomes (and I am getting further from it as I talk now), what it seems to me to become really is a reading of a historical moment which is true and a moment in history which relates to the present, so that 'they'll burn this building,/ fire these books, this art,' you see part of what was happening at that time; you were getting a lot of sheer nonsense talk (which isn't talked now and that is one of the ways in which we all grow up, I think) about the need to reject the British tradition. Right? And there was a time when people were saying 'Burn Shakespeare' and so on, so that in fact the House-Slave, in so far as he is an image of a contemporary artist, if you like, or a contemporary 'person of culture', somebody who is appreciating books and art – right? – the House-Slave is threatened. But the House-Slave also inherits. You know, 'these are my books now', 'my pallid masters fled'. So it is a sort of very tense moment, insofar as it relates to the present, but I mean I don't think I would consider that in any simple sense autobiographical, and certainly, I would want, I mean that last line is the line that seems to me to make the poem and it is a very, very complex line or meant to be. I mean, 'the terror of the dark', hasn't necessarily got much to do with colour, but you know, the colour is there in it, the terror of the dark is the dark forces, the forces that destroy, as well as the forces that might energise.

DANCE: But the terror of the dark has nothing to do with those new aspects, let us say of one's heritage, and I say 'new' in the sense that they haven't been a part of this House-Slave's background? That's a part of it too?

MORRIS: That's there, that's there, but I think that it would be an inadequate and unfair reading of the poem to let that line freeze at colour, you know? Because, and in fact, you know, it relates to a whole lot of other forces, the whole thing of getting people, you know, 'stumbling down his own aesophagus'.

DANCE: Yes. You know the suggestion in the '60s particularly, that whiteness was death, coldness, that kind of thing and that Blackness was vibrancy and light and so forth. You say my 'pallid masters' here have fled. Are you suggesting the same thing?

MORRIS: Yes… no. The pallid masters are both the pale-skinned masters and the masters who, because they are terrified, have got paler, but also they are pallid in the sense that you mean of not having the richness, the particular kind of richness that darkness offers, but a different kind.

DANCE: I want to ask you now some things about your image of the poet, and I was led to this question by some poems of yours, particularly 'The Stripper' which seems to me a rather pessimistic view of the poet: the poet 'pursues mirrors', the stripper's writhing is 'an image of his line'; and having set up the image of the stripper as a sort of metaphor for the poet, then I guess the poet wears 'performing pieces', and makes a fuss of 'skimpy little veils'. He never displays his parts…

MORRIS: But the thing is, is it pessimistic? No, I think it's – is it? The whole idea is that it's the basic thing – where is it from now? *As You Like It*? 'The truest poetry is the most feigning.' OK. Poets seem to tell the truth but they are liars; we tell lies perhaps sometimes to reveal another kind of truth and so on, but there is a sense in which we are like strip-teasers in that we seem to reveal, but we don't reveal. I mean the ultimate revelation, you know, I suppose is just on the edge of suicide.

DANCE: Oh, but you do strive for that, don't you?

MORRIS: For what?

DANCE: The ultimate revelation, the final truth.

MORRIS: We keep saying this but sometimes I wonder how true it is.

DANCE: But if you know you are strip-teasers, then it is a pessimistic view of the poet, isn't it? If you don't know it, I can see that it wouldn't be so pessimistic, but if you know you are veiling things and you have on 'performing pieces'…

MORRIS: Yes, because you see the 'performing pieces' matters a great deal, because you see this thing about revelation and truth and all that, all the poets – we always say we are interested in this, but at the same time we are aware of the element of play in writing poetry, you know. There is a sense in which it isn't serious at all, you know – the two things have to be driven together. I don't know whether pessimistic is something that I would want to say about that particular vision – it's just that you tell the truth and you don't tell the truth; you tell the truth but you do it by an illusion; you tell a lie in order to get at the truth. You know, the paradoxes are always there.

DANCE: Let me ask you about the image of the poet in 'Prologue by the Maker' in *On Holy Week*, and I realise the slightly joking tones throughout that poem, but on the other hand, you do call yourself the Maker, so I guess there you are the divine Creator!

MORRIS: No, only in an ironic sense, because you know poets were of course called Makers; there is a book about Chaucer called *Chaucer the Maker*, so I mean there is a sense in which any creator sees something presumably of an image of the divine creation, but insofar as that is true it is manipulated very ironically in that preface, which is, you know, in a fairly careful way sort of making cracks.

DANCE: Why do you make the two who were crucified with Christ speak in Jamaican dialect?

MORRIS: I don't know. It came that way, and I am not absolutely happy with it, actually; no, I am happy with the poems, but not happy with the fact that these are the only two that are obviously in dialect. You know I wish I had done more. Whenever I happen to read this aloud, the whole sequence, it becomes apparent that many of the other voices are related to dialect, including Jesus actually.

DANCE: Have you written anything using, shall I say, the Rasta dialect, is that the appropriate description?

MORRIS: Rasta language. Yes. I have. 'Give T'anks' [*Shadowboxing*, p.30] is a very, very short poem which is a kind of love poem and that is completely Rasta language really.

DANCE: Do you feel you have been influenced by the Rastafarian movement in any way aside from what you have already said?

MORRIS: Oh yes, it's hard to measure, but I'm sure I have been influenced by the Rastafarian movement. You know everybody has been influenced by the Rastafarian movement who lives in Jamaica, and certainly they are a very, very important influence in the arts, in that artists write about them, use them as particular symbols, and so on. They are important because, for me, one of the things that – I can't trace it in the verse – but many Rastafarians – is it many or some Rastafarians? – seem to me to have a kind of spiritual quality which communicates through faces and eyes and which I find very, very moving.

DANCE: Would I be wrong to say that there still seems to be a great deal of negative reaction to Rastafarians, particularly among the more educated Jamaicans?

MORRIS: No, I think you have come – that's perhaps true – but I am inclined to think that you have come at a time when the picture is changing and changing rapidly because Rastafarianism has been used as a cloak increasingly for elements that are not primarily religious, or Rastafarian at all, and the backlash is beginning. Also Rastafarianism has been increasingly treated with official respect, and some of the intelligentsia are beginning to rebel. Rebel because they feel that at its centre, intellectually, Rastafarianism is not defensible. A book which I admire, and which a number of my friends despise, is the Joseph Owens book called *Dread*. I like it because it gives me a feel of talking to Rastafarians; it's very much a book based on tape recordings, and sort of arranged to make the kind of theological point that he's after. But the author sort of withdraws, you know, from the book so that you hear lots of Rastafarian voices throughout; you get the feeling of immersion. But some people dislike it greatly because they feel that it is intellectually indefensible. He argues, for example, that Rastafarianism is not racist and he argues this, partly on the basis of his own experience as a white man from Boston, who found that it was not all that difficult to get accepted by the Rastafarians; but some commentators feel that it is very silly of him, because Rastafarians like other Jamaicans often have a special kind of attitude to, to – like social workers and priests, and he is in a special kind of category and that he doesn't really know what it would be like to be, say, an ordinary white tourist wandering into a Rastafarian camp and so on. But, no, I think Rastafarianism is important in the arts; I mean everybody is influenced by it.

———————

CONVERSATION WITH

ORLANDO PATTERSON

Horace Orlando Patterson was born in Westmoreland, Jamaica, on June 5, 1940. He grew up in Clarendon in the little town of Maypen. After completing primary school there, he moved to Kingston to attend Kingston College. He went on to earn a BSc in Economics from the University of the West Indies at Mona in 1962, and a PhD at the London School of Economics in 1965. After teaching sociology at the London School of Economics for two years he returned to the University of the West Indies as a lecturer in Sociology in 1967. In 1970 he left Jamaica to take a position as Visiting Associate Professor at Harvard where he is now John Cowles Professor of Sociology. Patterson was also, for eight years, Special Advisor for Social Policy and Development to Prime Minister Michael Manley of Jamaica. He wrote a guest column for several weeks with the *New York Times*.

Orlando Patterson is the author of three novels: *The Children of Sisyphus* (1964); *An Absence of Ruins* (1967); and *Die the Long Day* (1972). His short stories and reviews have appeared in a variety of journals, and two of his short stories have been anthologised. His first two novels will be republished by Peepal Tree in 2009. His academic works include *The Sociology of Slavery* (1967); *Black in White America: Historical Perspectives* (1975); *Ethnic Chauvinism* (1977); *Slavery and Social Death: A Comparative Study* (1982); *Freedom in the Making of Western Culture* (1991); *The Ordeal of Integration: Progress and Resentment in America's "Racial" Crisis* (1997); and *Rituals of Blood: Consequences of Slavery in Two American Centuries* (1999). Numerous essays have appeared in a variety of journals and books.

Orlando Patterson received the First Prize for Fiction for *The Children of Sisyphus* at the Dakar Festival of Negro Arts in 1966. He also won the National Book Award for Non-Fiction in 1991 for his *Freedom and the Making of Western Culture*. He holds honorary degrees from several universities, including the University of Chicago, U.C.L.A and La Trobe University in Australia. He was awarded the Order of Distinction by the Government of Jamaica in 1999.

The following interview was conducted in Dr. Patterson's office at Harvard University on December 10, 1979.

———————————

DANCE: Quite clearly certain Western writers such as Camus and some other existentialists have influenced your work, and Bridget Jones has done a study of that [*Savacou*, XI XII, 27-38]. I'm interested in some other possible influences. Are you conscious of other writers who have influenced you?
PATTERSON: Well, the whole tradition of existentialist writers and many others who weren't considered existentialists when they were writing themselves (but they've been seen as sources of existentialist thought) were influential – in particular, Dostoevsky, whose novels were very important in my development, at least in the writing of fiction. I read and I was influenced a lot by the short stories of several writers, particularly De Maupassant; when I was quite young I read him. But, apart from those influences – Camus, Dostoevsky, and De Maupassant – I read other

writers, but I wouldn't sort of single out any of them as being sort of particularly strong influences.

DANCE: OK. As I read your picture of yard life in Jamaica, I thought about CLR James and Roger Mais. Had you read their works when you wrote *Children of Sisyphus*?

PATTERSON: No, I had read CLR James's academic works.

DANCE: But not *Minty Alley*.

PATTERSON: But not *Minty Alley*. No. I don't think there was a copy of *Minty Alley* around. It was already out of print when I was a student. And it was much later that I sort of went out of my way to get it. And Roger Mais – I'd read his works, but I wouldn't say they influenced me greatly – a bit, but not, not very much. I mean they were people who had gone before and they gave younger writers encouragement by having written. But, say, actually, now that you mention it, Roger Mais, more than any other West Indian novelist would have been the person I would say was the most influential, but, on the whole, as far as selecting my themes and working, there really were very few models to go on – in writing *Sisyphus*. Most of the other novelists had worked on other themes.

DANCE: OK. I want to ask you about a review which I'm sure you don't respond too favourably to, and that's John Hearne's review of *Die the Long Day* in the *Caribbean Quarterly* [XVIII, 78-81]. He suggests that parts of the book are so good that they should be required reading for any history student, and he acclaims your knowledge of history and sociology but he attacks the novel and he attacks it with so much vengeance that I wonder if there's some personal attack there?

PATTERSON: I've known John for a long time, and we have radically different views of literature. On the whole, I simply neglect what John has to say. In fact this is my first time even hearing about that review.

DANCE: Oh, really?

PATTERSON: I don't usually read what John has to write, because I find a lot of his stuff very pretentious and very forced and sort of – he has a very cultivated kind of sensibility which is very artificial. But more important than anything else we sort of differ radically in what we think literature is all about. He has a rather – well, a very special purist view of literature. Actually I wouldn't mind that very much if he actually wrote literature that way, but I find most of his novels basically boring and sometimes overwritten, but lacking basically in depth, more than anything else. We just fundamentally see things quite differently. We meet, we talk – I mean we don't particular like each other. He belongs to another generation, another style and comes from a class of Jamaicans who are sort of obsessively involved with the need to identify with certain values and certain traditions…

DANCE: OK. There was one thing that he said in the essay (and I'm not going to prolong it beyond this), a sarcastic reference to metaphors concocted in Harvard. I wondered if that suggested also some sort of attitude towards your leaving the University of the West Indies to come to Harvard? Did you leave to come to Harvard?

PATTERSON: Well that's typical of John, you see, who loves to invent clever phrases. The truth of the matter is that *Die The Long Day* was written, the first draft, before I came to Harvard, but it sounded like a nice thing to say, and John cannot resist saying something nice even though it may be completely ridiculous. I brought with me to Harvard the first draft and simply revised it here. But it was written while I was teaching at the University of the West Indies.

DANCE: Are there some people who think that you have deserted your...

PATTERSON: Well, that's the craziest view of how people should live their lives. On that basis no one should leave their village, or their hometown, or anywhere else. Well, this would be true of all West Indian writers. Almost all of them who live outside, including many whom in other respects are greatly admired by the same people: Lamming lives outside; CLR James, who is the great grandfather of West Indian literature and is greatly admired by all the people who would dare to say that I've deserted them, has lived all of his life outside of the Caribbean. So I don't take that seriously either. And besides, I've been in very close touch with the Caribbean, much more so than a lot of people at the University, since I spend four months each year advising the Government of Jamaica on urban problems... I mean I've never lost touch with the group I wrote about in my first novel. I mean a half of my research work is devoted to working on the slums of Kingston, and not only working, researching the problem, but developing programmes for ameliorating the conditions in the low-income areas of Kingstown, Spanish Town and Montego Bay. That's a lot more than what a lot of people are doing at the University of the West Indies. Again, I don't take that seriously.

DANCE: OK. A lot of criticism of your work stems from the fact that some people see you as more of a sociologist than a novelist. Now if you think it's possible to make the distinction, would you tell me whether you see yourself as more of a sociologist than a novelist, or is it a distinction that cannot be made?

PATTERSON: Well, it's not a meaningful distinction, I see myself as both. Again it's a sort of stereotyped kind of response. If you're sociologist, people assume that you're going to be using your sociology – using your novels as a medium for expressing sociological ideas. As you know that's not the case in the United States. Again it goes back to a certain purist tradition in the British tradition of writing, one which is rather modern by the way. It's not even true of the Victorian novelists. It's certainly not true of French novelists. It's really silly to assume that there is necessarily any conflict. I'm both, and I've never had any problem in keeping the two separate.

DANCE: All right. There's a very naturalistic view of life in *Children of Sisyphus*: one critic even calls you the Caribbean Zola. In the novel Solomon suggests that the horribly destitute and hellish life these people are fated to live and too weak to escape is indeed the plight of all mankind. Do you see that work as treating, in terms of the philosophy of the book, not just the situation of those people there in the area...?

PATTERSON: Why, yes. In the novel I did attempt to see the Dungle and the struggle for dignity, and escape and meaning as a symbol of the human condition generally. I was very much in my existentialist phase then. So, yeah, there was that attempt, and Brother Solomon was the main symbolic means for expressing this idea. I try to make it not very intrusive. I mean, lots of people read the novel without recognising that.

DANCE: But you did feel then that in a sense we are all children of Sisyphus?

PATTERSON: Oh, yeah, sure, and I mean, you know, the philosophical background of the novel was Albert Camus's *Myth of Sisyphus*. Several of the problems posed there – basically the fundamental problem of why is it that although one may recognise life as meaningless one still continues to live and want to live; the important element of hope as critical – struggle and hope – as critical factors in answering the absurdity of wanting to continue to do something that you consider meaningless. It was the sort of philosophical foundation of the novel and it was understandable at the time that these people were hoping for something which, standing outside, one could see that it would not be achievable, but from their perspective it made all the difference.

DANCE: OK. I want to ask you some more about that idea of hope in a minute, but let me go back to something you said earlier. You began by saying that you were really into existentialism *then*. Does that suggest that your view has…?

PATTERSON: Well, somewhat, somewhat. I mean, you know, one moves on and I am – it's helped to form my own intellectual development. At that stage I was very much into it and very much, overwhelmingly influenced by it. Since then I've not so much abandoned it but integrated it, moved on, I hope, to other, more mature views of the world.

DANCE: What does 'more mature' suggest? Less pessimistic?

PATTERSON: Yes, less pessimistic, but also a recognition of a greater complexity of the world, not only in sociological terms, but even in moral terms, that the phenomenon of absurdity may be an over simplified view of conceiving of the world. Sartre's basic precept, coming out of his own despair, that you should commit yourself, again simplifies a great deal, and one must ask, commit yourself to what? And how? There are times in which you may not want to commit yourself. And also, not everything is absurd, and I think in general, I've come to recognise the possibility of moral absolutes.

DANCE: Let me go back to the matter of hope, which you were talking about just a few moments ago, that some of these people can only hope, even though given the world of the novel which you've created, we know that their hope is destined not to be realised, but there are some people there who don't even hope, who have resigned themselves to the fate that they know is going to come, and I'm wondering, within this world, how we are to respond. Is it better to be like the Rastas and have this foolish dream of tomorrow, or is it better to be like Rachel and realise that everybody is going to end up back there in the Dungle?

PATTERSON: No, I wasn't passing judgement on any of them. They were both quite bleak actually, they were both equally bleak, but in different ways. One can be wholly realistic, and there are advantages to realism, you know – trying to get out of it – Dinah and Rachel – but the disadvantage, of course, is that one has nothing to hold on to. Realism allows for the possibility of a more genuine escape, but it also means that failure is going to be that much harder to bear. Having hope, whether it is religious hope or hope that you create in one way or the other, offers you support, and in the long run it might even be a means of escape in a *real* way. In a sense religion has always done that, in the sense that in the process of trying to attain an unreachable, unrealisable goal, you may, nonetheless, find ways of escaping other kinds of problems.

DANCE: Yes. OK. Let me ask you about the violence in the novel. I know of course that there is this violent element in human beings, and I know that it's accentuated among those living in the kinds of conditions in which your characters in the Dungle live. But I still find it difficult to relate to the extreme violence of these people. They are like, as you describe them one time, 'a wolf pack at war'. Are you exaggerating this for any particular reason – just to show us how the society has completely destroyed their humanity.

PATTERSON: No, no, it's a very violent society. It's very violent. In fact the violence has gotten worse.

DANCE: But I mean they don't just fight. They bite off ears; they bite off breasts.

PATTERSON: Well people bite off – people always bite when they fight in Jamaica, and you do get – I mean, pick up the newspaper any day, people are always biting each other, if they're not cutting each other up – usually they're chopping each other, you know, most people go around with machetes in the urban area, but if they don't have weapons, they bite. Yes, it's very violent, no doubt about that.

DANCE: And you don't think it's exaggerated?

PATTERSON: For a society that size, it has one of the highest crime rates in the world. No, it's not exaggerated. In fact, I mean, the violence – there are kinds of violence there which I didn't include. I mean, what I wrote was quite tame. Read some of the stuff which you get even in the newspapers – in the evening tabloid, the *Star*. Oh, it's the most bizarre kind of – I mean, I didn't include a lot of more bizarre crimes and violence which I knew existed because I think people would think I was exaggerating, but biting people's ears off and so on is quite common.

DANCE: OK. Were you exaggerating the poverty of the people – in the scene, for example when Dinah had never seen an egg. I found that hard to believe that a person who had been a whore in a city…

PATTERSON: Well, she was a city girl you see. I mean no one who's grown up in rural Jamaica would not have seen an egg. I guess she should have seen an egg, but I mean, it's quite possible that she had never had one. Sure, I mean, I've known all about that. An egg is always an expensive thing when you realise that people are living, at the time when the novel was set, around the '50s, on a few shillings a week. An egg was always an expensive item. Yes, it's quite possible that she had never had one before.

DANCE: All right. Let me turn now to the Rastas. As I was reading the novel, sometimes you seem to satirise their ignorance and gullibility; and at other times they're treated pretty sympathetically. What is your personal view of the Rastafarian movement?

PATTERSON: Ahhh… I understand their condition. I can see the forces which create it, but I myself am not a religious person, so I'm not going to be sympathetic in the sense of identifying with them. I think in the long run one can't confront reality that way, although in the short run one can easily see how it is that they came to do that. You see, human beings create out of nothing, and even if you disagree with what they create, you can admire the process whereby they assert dignity and give meaning to their lives, even though the way in which *they* give meaning to their lives, one may not oneself want to participate in. It's a mistake which people make all the time. One can understand the mechanisms of nationalism and why it is and admire the people's courage without embodying all of it or necessarily oneself accepting the content of what it is they develop.

DANCE: OK. Had you studied the Rastas?

PATTERSON: I'd spent a lot of time among them while I was a student, gathering material for the novel, meaningful enough but not for writing anything. No, I've never studied them sociologically. I did write a paper, but it came out of the work I did collecting material for the novel.

DANCE: And the study of the Rastafarians was a study that you started with this novel in mind?

PATTERSON: Yes, it's more a matter of collecting material. Yes, as I said, I did an article once several years ago, but not a full-scale, sociological study.

DANCE: Are the Rastafarians a very sexist movement? I know there are female Rastas, but they don't seem to be very visible. And I was noting Cyrus's relationship with Dinah here. It starts with his rape of her; then he uses his religion to rationalise his prostitution of her; then he uses his religion to rationalise also his design to beat her, kill her, for leaving him.

PATTERSON: Yes, it's a very sexist movement. Like many nationalist movements – somewhat like the same thing you get in Black American – the early phases…

DANCE: The Muslim movement, perhaps…

PATTERSON: Not only the Muslim movement, but you know, the problem that Stokely Carmichael had with the woman in the Black movement – I mean a lot of men assert their own sort of male pride – a lot of pride is usually male pride and it involves putting women in their place, especially in the context in which women were traditionally breadwinners and, if anything, had more to be independent about, even though it was not much, but more than men; so there's a compensatory, conservative view that males demand, to be made at the expense of women; you get that in a lot of nationalist movements. Once men start getting protective about woman and start talking about 'our women', that's always the first bad sign. Yes it is; it is sexist.

DANCE: Is the Dungle down by the harbour?

PATTERSON: It was originally. It's no longer there. It was located near to what is now a housing scheme called Tivoli Gardens… The Dungle was wiped out completely. It was bulldozed, the whole area, and part of it is now a housing scheme, part of it has developed for industrial purposes.

DANCE: So that the people who live in that area – I suppose their lives are – at least their homes and what have you – are a little bit improved.

PATTERSON: On no, not necessarily at all, because one of the evils of housing schemes is that you tear down all the houses, but the people who get them aren't necessarily the people who've been displaced. In fact, very rarely are the people who receive new units the people who are displaced. Usually the people who were displaced can't afford the down payment or instalment, even though it may be very small; and even when they can afford it there's usually lot of political patronage in who gets it, so usually they're outsiders who come in. So, all these people – they moved to form other slums.

DANCE: What does Dungle mean?

PATTERSON: It's sort of a mixture of different words. Sort of dung hill, and jungle. Jamaicans do a lot of that sort of combining. It suggests both. It's quite graphical – mainly dung hill.

DANCE: You do not name the religious sect that the Shepherd leads. Is that a Pocomania sect?

PATTERSON: Well, there are scores of these little sects. And some of them are Pocomania, some of them are Revivalists, some of them are all sorts of little one thing or the other, and they sort of phase off one into the other; some of them are fundamentalist. This one was more what you'd call Revivalist – on the border of

Pocomania. Pocomania has more African elements in it; this would be more Christian than African – the cult I had in mind. Actually, it was a cult I knew quite well.

DANCE: Is the flogging of Dinah a part of the religious ceremony or just the personal sadistic drives of the Shepherd?

PATTERSON: You see, a lot of these Shepherds, as in America, have become very sexually involved with their church sisters, and the idea of – well it's almost, it's partly medieval – but it's also found in other cultures, of exorcising spirits by flogging. Well, this particular Shepherd, it's sort of a mixture of this kind of exorcism which is blended in his mind – well, exorcism always has a sexual component anyway, the business of flogging and witchcraft and so on is very closely tied up with it. It's just being explicit in this particular case.

DANCE: I want to ask you about a quotation. You say in an article, 'Blacks in the Americas', that Black Americans have a greater sense of racial and cultural pride than West Indians. Now I know that such a generalisation is probably defensible because I've heard other West Indians make similar observations. But that seems particularly ironical to me since most of the main periods of Black awareness in the States have had West Indians in key positions – Marcus Garvey, Stokely Carmichael, Malcolm X, whose mother was from the West Indies. Was it that these people needed the United States experience to develop that racial awareness?

PATTERSON: What I said – I think what I said was a greater sense of racial consciousness, maybe pride. What I was getting at in that work was that in the modern period in particular, perhaps because they are a minority group living in a white society, you have to become more racially conscious, and the need to assert racial pride is going to be greater in this society. In the Caribbean, Blacks are considered the majority of the population and the whole issue of race is not as great, you know, and you don't grow up with the overwhelming presence of whites around you. In the village, in the town in which I grew up, I mean, there were only about two or three whites and we hardly ever saw them; they were just not within one's… I mean you had no sense that you were living in a white society. You didn't. And all of the authority figures were Black. All the teachers were Black. All the public officials were Black. All the policemen were Black. Of course in Kingston, you see it was a colonial power, the governor was white. But that was all very distant from one's life growing up. In terms of your real experiences you had no sense of being a minority; you had no sense of being in a white society. Where it differed was that the culture was very white. They were the very dominant culture, although you also had the Creole culture. Later when you went to school, however, you had to confront the predominent white culture, but this was seen as British rather than as white and the sense of racial oppression was not great. And so later on the need to compensate and assert racial pride was not a real – but of course, when you grow up in that kind of society and then come to America, it strikes you much more than if you'd grown up all your life in it…

DANCE: The Rastafarians are pretty much a racially conscious group though.

PATTERSON: That's right, the Rastas are unusual in having developed a sense of racial identity. As an urban group, they are much more aware of the white control of the economy. Well, once the need to deny the British cultural influence became evident, it would take the form of racial nationalism, as happened in the case, not only of the Rastas, but also people who go to the University and begin to reflect on the colonial situation…

DANCE: Then you begin to have that developing awareness?

PATTERSON: Right, but it's very much an intellectual awareness, and to some extent the same is true for the Rastas too, because, you know, it isn't a case of them growing up with white cops and so on. It's cultural imperialism they're objecting to, and they themselves are not hostile to whites. In fact, in actual face-to-face contact, one of the ironies is that many whites go down there and sort of mix freely with the Rastas, much more than whites could in a Black nationalist group here, because, strictly speaking, what the Rastas are objecting to is the cultural imperialism, which they identify with whites, you see, so there's a difference.

DANCE: I see. OK. Now, here's a statement I want to ask you about. This is from *Ethnic Chauvinism*. You're writing about Black anti-Semitism, and you say, 'In their demand for community control, Blacks increasingly turned on the white merchants in their neighbourhoods, who, in most cases, happened to be Jewish. Ironically, the Black demand for control of local business, so-called Black capitalism, was encouraged by none other than Richard Nixon in a stroke of pure malevolent political genius, for it killed several birds with one stone. It won some support from black spokesmen who were foolish enough to believe in such economic idiocy.' Now by 'economic idiocy' do you mean Black control of their communities or Black antagonism towards Jews.

PATTERSON: No, no, I was referring to the whole Black capitalism movement.

DANCE: Why do you call it economic idiocy?

PATTERSON: Well, the way it was set up then, was essentially a ghettoised view that by having a few Blacks owning, you know, a few supermarkets and dry goods stores in the ghetto, that could in any way solve the Black economic problem. Of course, it was a completely ridiculous idea. I mean, even if Blacks were to own all the stores in Black neighbour-hoods, it would have little effect on Black employment – they mainly employ Blacks anyway, and the vast majority of Blacks earn their income outside the ghetto in the large concerns. And the whole strategy was one that claimed that Blacks would own their own local stores and shops and so on. I mean, that would be good for the few Black entrepreneurs who owned them, but it wouldn't have much effect on the Black economic condition. Furthermore, the important thing is that none of this referred to Black control of any of the major firms or Blacks in the board room of any of the major companies, which is what determines the fate of all groups in America.

DANCE: All right. You explain in *Ethnic Chauvinism* that you understand the extremes of the Black Power movement of the '60s, and yet I think I detect a great deal of sarcasm, as when you write, 'It seems to be typical of all human groups that psychological compensation can only be achieved by overcompensation. To cure the deep racial hurt and self-contempt it was not enough simply to "prove" by means of Black solidarity that Blacks were people like everyone else... Sanity and self-respect demanded the celebration of things black, and solidarity demanded the homogenisation and loyalty of all. Thus Blacks had to believe first that all Blacks are beautiful, Black culture and "soul" had to be declared superior; and all Blacks, no matter what the objective differences, had to become alike, or else be condemned as "Toms".' There's no question about the fact that that kind of overcompensation was there. But I want to know if you personally were attacked by members of the Black nationalist movement for your views as a 'Tom'.

PATTERSON: Occasionally I got a lot of threatening letters, but since I'm not a political figure, I never really got into any physical scrapes, but I'm sure there were lots of people – intellectuals – who were hostile to the position I took. The position I took comes from a rather Marxian perspective, which was sceptical of, or fully recognised the limits of, chauvinism. I wasn't criticising it from a conservative perspective, so a lot of the people who may have disagreed with me nonetheless recognised the intellectual context in which I was being critical of extreme chauvinism, and that muted their criticism somewhat. I would say that people are changing anyway, I mean, you know, the tide seems to be moving very much in the direction of the position which I've taken.

DANCE: Would you like to elaborate on it?

PATTERSON: Black intellectuals and leaders are recognising the limits of just pure chauvinism – simply being proud and having a lot of culture, and having people recognise your heritage and your roots – in fact people are only too willing to do that. You know, that's free. It's not going to have any effect on whether you have any real control over the system which really ultimately determines your life. I mean realistic demands for being in the board room or controlling important assets in the society

DANCE: OK. You make an interesting argument about the way ethnicity has hurt Blacks economically, and how the American establishment has found it easy to give us what we wanted: and I want to ask you about another statement you made within that context. You wrote, 'It was ridiculously easy for the establishment to respond by changing the colour of a few faces in the ads for the Pepsi generation, by introducing a few network shows in which the traditional role of Blacks as clowns and maids was updated (with the added boon that these new 'soul' shows have been extremely profitable), by publishing a spate of third-rate books on the greatness of the African tradition, by the glorification of Black roots, and, most cruel of all, by introducing into the curriculum of the nation's colleges that strange package of organised self-delusion which goes by the name of Afro-American Studies.' Have you had many reactions to that last part in particular?

PATTERSON: Yes, yes, a lot of people were upset, but far fewer than I thought would have been, because by the time I wrote that there was a general dissatisfaction with the way Afro-American studies had gone, not only among white college administrators but among Blacks – Black students and so on. Maybe I should point out that actually I'm not against Afro-American studies; in fact I take it very seriously as a serious discipline, academic discipline. [But] it became a political whipping boy in the curriculum of all the colleges. College administrators very cynically responded by simply making it a way of keeping Black students quiet. No one was really committed to it; it became a place where people could jive and so on, and what should have been one of the most serious areas of study and one of the most legitimate intellectually, it just became a joke as far as I…

DANCE: Your objection here is not to the concept then of Afro-American studies?

PATTERSON: Oh, no! My objection is to what it became. An organised self-delusion. I mean people were sitting down, you know, jiving and going on unrealistically about culture…

DANCE: Can we talk a little bit about your present work. Are you writing now?

PATTERSON: Yes, I'm just finishing up the first three-volume work on slavery – the first volume.

DANCE: Slavery in?

PATTERSON: Comparative – all through the world – ancient Greece and Rome, the Orient, in Africa, and in the New World.

DANCE: What about creative work?

PATTERSON: Creative work? I've got three works which are in the penultimate draft by now, but I've just not been able to complete them because I've been totally immersed in writing and getting this book out for the past several years. I have a novel called *Harvard Square*, which is the first novel I've written set in America. There's another novel which was written earlier than that which was in a rough form, which I in a sense revised last summer, set in Jamaica, again set among the working class; and I have a volume of stories. All of these have been written. They just need to be revised.

DANCE: Have any of the stories in the volume been published in journals?

PATTERSON: Yeah, the stories have been, several have been published, yes: in journals, and in anthologies, one edited by Andrew Salkey, [*Stories From The Caribbean*] in fact. A long one was published in *Jamaica Journal* [I, 1968] and so on.

DANCE: I see. Have you any observations you might want to share with me about what you see as either outstanding or unfortunate trends in contemporary Caribbean literature?

PATTERSON: Well, the first major phase, modern phase; seems to be coming to an end or has come to an end; and it was overwhelmingly informed by the tradition of Negritude and of the nationalist movement – Negritude in the case of the French Caribbean (Césaire and so on) and also by the nationalist movements in a lot of Lamming's novels, and the whole need to express and explore a West Indian identity. A lot of those kinds of questions were the questions we used to talk about – what is a West Indian? In asking the question, what is a West Indian novel, you're really asking what is the West Indian identity invariably. And that first phase has peculiar elements which were found in most of the writers who lived abroad and so on. I think a new phase is perhaps beginning as more and more writers will be writing locally and are going to be published locally because the interest in the West Indian novel has dried up virtually abroad, while at the same time there is a sufficiently large readership, just about, for local publishers, to make a living on that. So I see a second phase in which a lot of the new writers are going to come from the urban, working class groups, and it's going to have a strong realist element. In a sense, I mean, *Sisyphus*, while it was involved with the early phase in time, was, I think, more a model of what – certainly to judge from what I've been reading, it's going to be more of a nationalist element...

DANCE: More of a nationalist...

PATTERSON: Yeah. We-l-l, yes, in a sense, partly an imitation of America, so that earlier form of the movement was more an assertion of cultural independence, an exploration of identity; the racial element was not very strong. Let me say, I think the racial business is partly influenced by the Rastafarian movement and partly in other areas. But I think this itself is going to be very short-lived. The move toward realism is also going to be concerned with the movement away from the exploration of a sort of general identity towards, on the one hand, I think, more of a kind of exploration of personal identity and on the other hand, more a kind of realism in exploring the crisis of modernisation and poverty.

DANCE: That exploration of the personal identity almost always, in the earlier works that you talked about, took the searcher to Europe and then to Africa...

PATTERSON: Right, right.

DANCE: But that trip's not going to be necessary in these novels?

PATTERSON: That's right. No, I don't think so, I don't think so.

DANCE: That's very interesting. So your novel might in a sense be seen as one of the early works in this tradition. What about Vic Reid?

PATTERSON: Well, Vic Reid was very much in the nationalist tradition – the earlier thing I mentioned; and was very much influenced by the independence movement – bourgeois nationalism. Vic is the classic bourgeois nationalist novelist. I think that sort of thing we won't get much of any more, because people have seen independence and realise that it really doesn't bring a great deal and they're exploring the realities of class and the realities of personhood. So it will be, on the one hand, more a class type novel and a lot of working-class people will come – already the urban class, urbanites, are writing a lot of poetry – it reminds me very much of the sort of thing Black Americans were writing in the '60s, the sort of things I heard in Chicago – we're getting a lot of that now. I think there's a racial element, but it's very realistic, it's more a class phenomenon.

DANCE: OK. Are there any novels that come to your mind that are suggestive of this new trend? Or is it mostly poetry so far?

PATTERSON: Not really. because they move away from novels. I mean novels are more expensive to publish, and, as I said, the foreign publishers are not publishing very much. Local publishers find it very easy to publish poetry, so I don't know of any…

DANCE: Dramas, perhaps?

PATTERSON: Drama. That's right. I mean that's where more – in fact, I think another important development is the shift away from the novel as the main medium of expression. There's an enormous amount of plays being turned out in Jamaica. At one point in Kingston when I was there last summer there were something like six different plays going on in Kingston to packed houses.

DANCE: Yes, yes, that's very interesting. Who are your favourite writers among the Caribbean writers who are publishing now? Which ones do you consider the most significant?

PATTERSON: I like Walcott's poetry very much. I have mixed feelings about Naipaul. I think he is a very good novelist, and I like his earlier works enormously. I think he's grown far too bitter and I think his own alienation (and I have nothing against alienation and exile – it can be very creative), but I think he runs the risk of alienating himself from his subject. What a lot of American and European admirers don't realise is that Naipaul's peculiar sense of irony is not something he invented, but something he simply took straight out of the Trinidad working class and refashioned. He didn't invent it, that particular kind of irony, and he's alienated himself from it. He can continue writing, but if he doesn't want to end up as a kind of Iris Murdoch, in which what you write is very witty and technically superb, but lacks a certain kind of substance simply because one piece is not real life – it would be sad if that should happen to Naipaul. You see you can be ironical and can even reject your society, but there are creative ways of rejecting and destructive ways of rejecting, and I think perhaps in his later works he may – although of course he can always change again. I enjoy his stuff very much. The other West Indian writers – I find Lamming tedious, actually, too precious, too arty, his style much too poetic. The language becomes obtrusive. I don't like his work very much. Hearne is shallow – writes well, but really quite shallow; his characters are shallow and the substance, the content of his work, is shallow, and partly because the writer himself is perhaps quite shallow. I shouldn't say Hearne is shallow – I mean he's a very complex person: but I think basically he rather early lost his creative faculties, partly due to all sorts of problems which he has never been able to resolve. So whereas Naipaul has been running the risk of alienating himself from his material by being physically removed from it; John is one of the few writers living there, but he's also alienated himself because his own personal relation-ship with the society is so traumatic that in a sense exile would have been much better for him. I think he would have written far more if he were in exile... it's like a masochistic relationship he has, living there; he can never come to terms with the society or with himself.

DANCE: I see. Well thank you very much. It really has been pleasant talking with you.

———————————

CONVERSATION WITH

VIC REID

Victor Stafford Reid, born on May 1, 1913, in Kingston, Jamaica, was a graduate of Jamaica High School. He worked as a farm overseer, journalist, editor, and advertising executive. He also held a number of Government positions, the most recent being that of Chairman of the Jamaica National Trust Commission and Trustee of the Historic Foundation Research Centre in Kingston. Vic Reid travelled widely. As a young man he journeyed to Britain in quest of work in publishing, but soon found his 'passion for Jamaica was too strong for the pallid English area summer'. Thus he remained in England but a few weeks. Only after he had written his novel set in Africa (*The Leopard*) did he visit that continent for the first time – on a government mission, exploring in East Africa and West Africa the possibilities of the repatriation of Jamaicans at the behest of the Rastafarians. He frequently travelled in the United States and lived in Manhattan during the year he received a Guggenheim. He also spent a couple of years in Canada. Most of his life, however, Vic Reid remained in Jamaica. Of his travels he says that he was 'always heading back home, and recharging my batteries and going out again with some zest and gusto'.

He is the author of one of the best known of all Jamaican novels, *New Day*, a work widely regarded as a landmark in Jamaican literature. In addition to that novel, which was published in 1949, Reid has written *The Leopard* (1958) and *The Jamaicans* (1979). He has also done four works specifically for children: *Sixty Five* (1969); *The Young Warriors* (1967); *Peter of Mount Ephraim* (1971) and *Nanny-Town* (1983). His biography of NW Manley, *The Horses of the Morning*, was published in 1985.

Reid won several honours, including the Musgrave Medal, two Canada Council Fellowships, a Guggenheim Fellowship, and the Mexican Escritores Award. The title of Officer of the Order of Jamaica was conferred on him in 1980, and he received the Norman Manley Award for Excellence in 1981.

Sadly, Victor Stafford Reid died in Jamaica on August 25, 1987.

DANCE: It is generally conceded that your novel *New Day* is a landmark in Jamaican literature. Gerald Moore writes, 'It was with *New Day* that a new generation of West Indian writers really began the task of breaking free from the colonial cocoon and flying with wings of their own in a distinctly tropical sky' [*The Chosen Tongue*, p.6]. Peter Abrahams says that *New Day* 'marked the beginning of the emergence of a whole new school of Jamaican and West Indian novelists' [AL Hendricks and Cedric Lindo, *The Independence Anthology of Jamaican Literature*]. And I find that most of the writers I talk to respond to *New Day* with this kind of enthusiasm. Did you have any idea that you were initiating such a new day in West Indian literature?

REID: At the risk of being humble, Yes. [Laughter] Well, I knew. The point is that before, this dialect had been used in verses, had been used in prose, but almost as pure dialect, which confined it to a very small audience. I very consciously determined to place it in a text which would make it available to all peoples, but at the same time keep the atmosphere and the rhythm and the similes and so forth together.

DANCE: Were you concerned about how that would be received?

REID: No, because it was done deliberately. I mean, I'm a professional and I knew how to get it across so that people would get the feeling of the language at the same time that they would understand it.

DANCE: Who were some of the other people that you mentioned who were writing in dialect? Claude McKay?

REID: Well, yes, Claude McKay. There are several short story writers – no novelists. The short story writers very frequently wrote in dialect.

DANCE: Did you know Eric Waldrond's works when you wrote *New Day*?

REID: No, I'm afraid not. I did know then my contemporaries who are dead, people like Ulric Simmons, who was my colleague in the newspaper. He wrote one or two short stories. Ogilvie did several. [WG Ogilvie, author of *Cactus Village* and *The Ghost Bank*] I have an idea that Roger Mais did some dialogue in dialect.

DANCE: Was this before *New Day*?

REID: I'm not sure. I really can't remember, you know. But I know that at that time nobody had done any novels. A few people had done some dialogue in dialect. Nobody had used dialect in the body of the story, within the narration. This wasn't done.

DANCE: It's very interesting to me to note as I read your latest novel [*The Jamaicans*] that you use no dialect, not even in the conversation.

REID: Yes, isn't this odd.

DANCE: Well, I wanted to know why.

REID: Ah… I suppose because at bottom one speaks English, one writes English at bottom, and one unconsciously preserves one's dialectical conversation for driving home points in conversation because dialect is remarkably good for driving home the points – the images are superb. But there is no reason why. As a matter of fact I'm engaged in a novel now. I'm almost finished. Knock on wood for that. And the dialogue is dialect, today's dialect – Rastafarianisms and so on, and the body of the book is done in a dialect English, but very faint. I suppose you'd probably think in terms of some of those Southern American writers who would write what they call a dialect, but it would be thoroughly properly spelt, you couldn't mistake what the word was, but in the use of the word, the formation of the sentences, the range of the syntax and so on would tell you that this is an American dialect, you know.

DANCE: Yes, yes.

REID: Well, this is the way this is being done. I have a feeling that we can't begin talking to ourselves unless we write in this use of dialect. I believe that if you're writing that you should endeavour to get to your widest audience possible, especially in a place like Jamaica which is just, if you like, emerging, and which requires that people know about us, and all this helps in uplifting the kitty, so I really think one must be a little careful about this 'purity of dialect'. What the hell is that anyway? Dialect is…

DANCE: It has to be communicated.

REID: Of course. Dialect, unlike [standard] language changes so fast, you know.

DANCE: And I think one of the most striking things about it, at least for me as I was introduced to it in *New Day*, is the rhythm rather than the pronunciation.

REID: This, I think, is where the power of dialect comes.

DANCE: Could you tell me something about what motivated you to write *New Day*.

REID: Above all, 'twas the need… in my mind to tell the Jamaicans who they are, to remind the Jamaicans who they are, where they came from, to show them that the then-self government we were aiming for, the then-change in the constitution that we were getting, was not entirely a gift. The fact is that historically we had paid for it, and we had been paying for over three hundred years, four hundred years counting Spanish times, and therefore they should accept it with pride and work at it with the knowledge that it is theirs as a right.

DANCE: Is John Campbell's family based on any historical person?

REID: No, John Campbell's family is not based on any historical persons, but I will tell you that many of the members of the family are really based on members of my own family. For instance, my grandfather was John Campbell and Cairo, the girl in the book, is named for and quite resembles my own Aunt Carol.

DANCE: Your latest novel is as far as I know, your first novel with a contemporary setting. Is that correct?

REID: Yes, as far as Jamaica is concerned.

DANCE: Oh, *The Leopard*, yes, yes.

REID: But all my short stories, almost every one, are contemporaries.

DANCE: Have you done a collection of short stories or would they be found in journals here and there I suppose and anthologies.

REID: All over the place.

DANCE: Do you plan to bring them together in a collection?

REID: If I can, but that takes a man-sized job.

DANCE: OK. Let me ask you if you will comment on some of the other writers who, following your lead, have done work in dialect. I'm particularly thinking about Samuel Selvon.

REID: I think… Well, remember this, that what I'm talking about is non-Jamaican. Dialect in other islands is different. Sam Selvon is a superb professional, top-class writer and a man of soul and insight, and consequently what Sam does with the dialect is easily understood. I think his job is beautifully done.

DANCE: Let me go back to your family background. One of the things that impressed me, as a person very much interested in folklore, was the use of folklore in *New Day*. It's almost an anthology of folk beliefs and practices and so forth. Can you tell me a little something about your background, particularly in terms of folk influences.

REID: Yes, well I was born in Kingston, which would make me non-existent as far as folklore is concerned except for one good factor – that my mother was a country girl who had come to Kingston and a woman of almost total recall, and she's still alive. And some weekends (she's over by the sea at Yallahs) we sometimes go over for weekends and she regales me with stories.

DANCE: Really? Even today?

REID: Even today she is good. As a matter of fact I tape her regularly. And she would tell me those stories. Of course I was a person of… I suppose I was more than normally curious about things, and I listened to… Well, in those days, even in Kingston, Anancy stories were part of the growing up, and all these stories lodge in my mind. I suppose other story-tellers helped, you know. So a lot of these things came out without even knowing that they were there when I began writing. Even today, today it comes out beautifully.

DANCE: Let me ask you about the oral history tales. Many of your works are historical romances. Would you object to that description?

REID: Yes. But go ahead. [Laughter] I suppose so.

DANCE: And I wondered to what degree they might have been based on oral history tales of those characters who were passed down, and to what extent they are based upon your research?

REID: Uh, you are talking about *New Day*?

DANCE: And *The Jamaicans* and *Peter of Mount Ephraim*.

REID: I see. You see I go through the countryside, even today, and for years I have lived up in the mountains. We keep a flat in town but I really like living up in the mountains. As I go through the countryside today, I never turn on the radio in my car. You know why? I am listening to the countryside… and everywhere I stop I can hear people's voices. And, you must understand that I don't want to sound like a bloody jingle-jingle person, but I have a thorough unbelievable love for this land. I hear those things and I hear people talking and I pick them up and I must keep them because I just think that the whole rhythm of the country is part of me, and the rhythm of the talk is part of me, and the rhythm of the stories is part of me, and wherever I go I pick them up. So it is a little difficult for me to pin-point any particular one. Just… I can only say… that this is from all over the country, all from inside the people and it comes naturally I suppose.

DANCE: Now when I was here, I heard some folk tales (I was here specifically to study the folklore) of Three Finger Jack, people like that, but never – do people still tell tales, for example, of Juan de Bolas?

REID: No. You see this is my role in life at the moment. I'm trying to let people know what their background is. The oral history of, say Juan de Bolas would have been lost because of severance, amputations, and so on; and remember that the people who were with Juan de Bolas would have been eventually scattered and were assimilated. It is really sickening to know that so few people know anything of Juan de Bolas, of anybody. I sometimes go on the radio, call to a place and talk about Juan de Bolas. And they look at you as if you are crazy – you're talking about some Cuban or Spaniard… Bogle of course is quite different and even there during the first fifty or sixty years after Bogle's execution you would not find anybody willing to say, 'I'm a relation or I'm a descendant of Bogle.'

DANCE: Oh, really?

REID: It was cut off completely. And after *New Day* came out, then there were people who were willing to say, 'Hey! Bogle was one of my ancestors.' This is how it was in countries like these. You were cut off, either from fear or from… separation… cut off from your history.

DANCE: Did you do much research in the preparation for the writing of this novel?

REID: Yes, I read a great deal of history. You see Jamaican history was never written. What was written were some works done by English telling the English side of the Jamaican history. And consequently, I went outside of the published books – there is a great reference library – a great West Indian reference library at the Institute of Jamaica (I'm a member of the board there) and it is perhaps the finest in this hemisphere. And I used to read old council minutes written in script, you know, in long hand. And you could pick between the lines, see how frequently the events were distorted to show the conqueror's point of view – the Englishman's point of view. I am not blaming him at all. This is very natural, but somebody has to show another point of view, and in the absence of written language, I suppose the stories that come down out of the folk tales, and some of the old history also, I got probably second-hand and my own imagination, and the hindsight that would come from being alive after the events and seeing the results – these thresh out the incidents and give me my stories.

DANCE: The historical figures in your works like Bogle and Daddy Sharpe are usually presented through the eyes of a child, who, bright though he may be, lacks the maturity to give us a mature vision of them. Why?

REID: Bogle and Daddy Sharpe are presented through the eyes of a child because, frankly, I think that it is the children to whom we ought to go with our Jamaican history. We old ones are on our way out, but the kids growing up ought to know something about themselves and ought to develop a pride in themselves. And so, subconsciously I suppose in some cases, but in the ease of *Peter of Mount Ephraim* and in the case of *The Young Warriors* and in the case of *Sixty Five*, these were written deliberately towards the children. Even *New Day* had this bias, as you mentioned.

DANCE: Yes. What you're doing here in these historical novels is very interesting to me because it is quite different – the impact – from what one gets in reading most of West Indian literature which is very (like most contemporary literature) very disillusioning – it deals with weak people, with lost people – and your characters have a certain kind of moral and physical strength. And you seem to be celebrating the strength of man, rather than the… weakness of man.

REID: Because it's the truth. You take this island which I know intimately, and as historians will tell you, there was hardly a year – there was no year passed in which they didn't have some sort of revolt. You take after emancipation in 1838 when all these Black women and Black men went up to the mountains – left the bloody estate and decided not to work on the estate. They knew where they were going: they were going up to the mountains (and the mountains are not particularly good soil) to plant those limestone hills, eking out an existence while at the same time sending their kids to school. Now those are heroes. Sending their kids to school barefooted! One little bloody school – they go there. They go to primary school for five or six years, they come out in what we used to call Sixth form. I think you call it about the thirteenth grade or something like that. And those same kids would descend into the city and become important people. They hadn't gone beyond the primary stage, but because they had good primary schools – I must say this – and because of the drive that their parents had. So these people are conquerors – not this bloody weakling thing about people backing up. But you know in America, this was the same sort of feeling about… you know, the 'Uncle Tom' situation. And what happened when those kids exploded in the '50s. I was up in America in the early '50s…

DANCE: Oh, were you?

REID: …and they fought as…I was ashamed to walk, to go through some of these Southern towns. I went through in fear because of the fear that I might explode and get killed. Because I was angry as hell when I saw what was happening to all the Africans. I rode on the train and I almost had a nervous breakdown because I was dying to blast somebody! OK? [Laughter] Now look when those kids – and it wasn't because

American Blacks were weaklings, because the whole construction was against them at that time. Once the time came and they exploded...

DANCE: They saw their strength.

REID: ...stood out like a volcano!

DANCE: Will your new novel, which has a more contemporary setting, have similar kinds of characters, not based on real people, perhaps, but...

REID: Well, all characters I suppose are based on real people. These are the characters who are not necessarily heroic in the accepted term but people who know where they're going, quite hard and cynical to what's going on around them, especially outside of the country, and above all determined to use their folk intellect, and their folk understanding, and their own historical precedence to find a place for them in this world. This is what the Rastafarians are doing in a sense. Laugh at it as much as people might, it is bloody significant.

DANCE: I've been surprised to find how much respect the Rastafarians have, at least from the literary world in Jamaica and in the West Indies.

REID: Those who go to America, so very few of them could be real Rastas! They are people who take up their attitudes and the dress and the language.

DANCE: So what we get is a kind of bastardisation of it?

REID: That's right.

DANCE: Do you have any kind of relationship with the Rastafarian movement? Have you ever been involved in it?

REID: Oh, I've been deeply involved in it. I was a co-leader of the Government mission to Africa back in 1963, '64, when the back to Africa movement exploded among the Rastafarians and we took about four Rastas over to Africa touring to see what the position was about returning to Africa and so on. And I have been... I have been an admirer and – admire is the wrong word, I have understood them and they have my respect as much as, equal to the respect I give, quote, 'Christians', unquote, perhaps more.

DANCE: That whole effort to return to Africa just fell through, didn't it? I understand a few actually went back but...

REID: Yes, if you will. It has fallen actively. But I think it is much healthier now in that *spiritually* people are returning to Africa. And the idea of transplanting yourself physically to Africa was quite impossible because we didn't speak the language, we were there as foreigners – as Americans have found out – we were there as foreigners. But the idea of having that spiritual feeling and understanding that you came from somewhere, that this country was great at one time, still is great in its own way, and the feeling of being a people with a past – this was what was bugging us all along, you see. So many people thought that our history began in 1655 with the coming of the British or some foolishness like that. Are we never going to let them know where they came from and who our people were? Alex Haley all over again.

DANCE: Let me go back a minute to your time in the United States. How long were you there?

REID: Well the first times I only spent two weeks, three weeks. I had a Guggenheim once and I spent the better part of a year there, this is the '60s.

DANCE: I think LeRoi Jones was in that area at that time; did you know him?

REID: I met LeRoi; Langston Hughes was my friend before I went to America, and so I spent a good deal of time with him. I was at that concert at Carnegie Hall when Harry Belafonte sang Langston's love poem and I met quite a number of fellows there.

DANCE: Did Langston Hughes have any influence on you as a writer? Because he was very much doing for America what you are doing for Jamaica.

REID: I don't know. I think we came together [gesture] just like that. I don't think it was a question of influence as much as to recognise that here was a guy who was talking my language and a person of enormous charm, enormous understanding, and a great companion; and I really liked Langston… it was good to be with him. He knew Harlem like the palm of his hand. And he would take me to all *sorts* of places… [laughter]

DANCE: There are many prominent writers here in Kingston and in Jamaica generally. Is there much interaction between you?

REID: Well, one meets writers, but I don't have any special friend among the writers in Jamaica. We all meet now and again, and we'll have a drink or so. I suppose Jan Carew, who lives in America – he's a Guyanese – would be my closest acquaintance among present-day writers, but they're good fellows – Brathwaite, Morris, Scott – yes I like them.

DANCE: Let me move on to *The Leopard*. Could you tell me something about what motivated you to do that novel.

REID: Darling, sweetheart – sheer anger! I was angry because the Western press (UP, AP) and the writers were treating the Mau-Mau as if they weren't human beings, as if they were sheer animals. Now that is pure… I won't use my French. [Laughter]

DANCE: Feel free.

REID: Because people are people. And I knew from our experiences out here in the 1865 outburst in Morant Bay, I knew what the Western soldiers were capable of, what the white soldiers were capable of, and I knew that this couldn't be so, so I decided to write a book about it since there wasn't any, quote, 'getting into the newspapers'. Well, the main thing, of course, is to find out what the hell did I know about Africa. I had been there before. But of course, I am sure Africa is underneath this skin, it's inside my pores, and the time we lived up in Gordon Town in a beautiful old house on the banks of a river, a sort of rainforest and I said, 'But look, this is Africa?' So as far as the physical descriptions were concerned – because we weren't there, I used these. And also I steeped myself in African folklore. For about a year I read everything I could lay my hands on, I read about the tribal customs and everything and then I, I became Africa. I really became Africa and I wrote this book straight out.

DANCE: But you were very careful not to, I started to say not to romanticise the Africans, even though I think there is *some* romanticising of them, but for the most part you seem to suggest there that it's not so much that the Europeans are so good, it's just that *everybody* is pretty bad.

REID: Everybody's pretty bad and everybody's pretty good. You see, all I wanted to make a point of is that these are human beings. That's all, not that they are any bloody angels!

DANCE: But they all almost become animals in your book, including the white man.

REID: Right. Well this is a way of saying [laughter], 'Look, stop that… we are all alike, you know?' – I saw a weakness in attempting to make these fellows noble

savages, and I had no intention of doing this. All I wanted to say is, 'Stop regarding
these as animals, because if *you're* an animal you won't regard others as animals.' You
see, if you know that you're made of glass, you won't notice any other guy's really
made of glass. You'll accept it; it's just another glass. Now, the whites who are writing
these stories regard themselves as being fine, Christian, human gentlemen and other
people as being animals. OK so, you become… you understand that you are all as
much animal as the others. Consequently, whenever a white man was killed I said he
was made beautiful.

DANCE: Was that a phrase that you got from them?

REID: No, no.

DANCE: You made that up.

REID: Yes, this was contrived. I was making a point.

DANCE: Yes. Quite clearly. Let me ask you to comment on this: the leopard seems
most times to symbolise the white settler, even though I think sometimes he requires
a broader interpretation. Would you comment a little bit on what you intended.

REID: I think the leopard – we could regard him in the latter phrase: 'a broader
interpretation'. The leopard was… largely Africa. He was a kind of mother, which is
probably a felicitous phrase, but it meant that you are all, white or Black, you belong
to me. This is the country… this is the country that supports you, whether you are
born here or not. This is what is there and if you don't learn to live with me then I will
destroy you. Now, I don't know if you got this impression. Sometimes I wonder if
people think the book ended rightly or wrongly because the idea is not that Nebu died,
the idea is that the leopard died. OK? And then the further idea is that the white man
died because he didn't understand the country, he didn't know it, he didn't respect
it, if you like.

DANCE: All right, let me pursue the idea of why Nebu died. Let me pursue it in an
indirect way by going back and asking another question and hoping you'll help me be
sure that I work up to this because I think it's related. The central part of the novel is
the relationship that Nebu has with the white woman [Msabu Gibson, wife of his
master] and the child that's born of that union. I want to ask you why this happened
to come in, since I don't think it's immediately representative of what was happening
in the uprising that you were concerned about, so it must symbolise some broader
issues in terms of racial relationships there. And what I'm getting at is the issue of the
Black man and the white woman which seems to come out there, because he
compares at one point his reactions to these two women.

REID: Why did Nebu have this relationship with the white woman? Of course it had
a symbolism, and the symbolism was directed at the weakness in certain white urban
cities in Africa, in that they would almost corrupt the Blacks, almost. It also had to have
this grey child who was neither black or white. To get that child you have to have this
relationship because the child also represents this certain situation that is… that is…
very much West Indian as you perhaps know, very much American also, and to a lesser
extent African. It also was a professional ploy to gain what you needed, a conflict, and
it produced the conflict that you needed. So, you have to think of it in terms as being
a professional piece of construction, and also for its symbolism. Let me ask you first
of all: does the presence of the white woman affect your reading of Nebu?

DANCE: Well, the white woman becomes pretty symbolic in a great deal of West

Indian literature it seems to me – Nebu feels that he has wronged the white man in this way, and of course other than this, he would have no reason for feeling guilty about his relationship with whites. But it's the white woman that makes him feel this sense of guilt. So I'm wondering if symbolically this suggests first of all an attraction that weakens him, and it's this that makes him an easy prey for the white man. For example, I think you suggest that quite clearly he could have destroyed this white man without any injury to himself but it is that moment of pause which stems from his guilt feeling…

REID: But doesn't this do what I mentioned before? Doesn't this lift Nebu a bit out of the animal even more than everybody else because he has this feeling of guilt? It wasn't a question of she being white, it was… the white situation was used because you had to formulate this conflict. But the fact that he took over a man's woman, this was what made it morally important for him to pay, and then on top of all that to have this child.

DANCE: But isn't it important that she's white? You write at one time, 'he would have fought lions with his hands for the white woman.'

REID: Well, this is… it's a woman… Men will fight lions for you people! I think that I thoroughly justified his position as a male and also as a human being by the juxtaposition of the Black and the white woman. When he sang those songs and poems to the Black girl, I think they're perhaps the most beautiful part of the book, I don't know if you remember…

DANCE: Yes, I do, I do.

REID: This at once said what man is all about. Being with a white woman was a… was a natural… natural feeling for the poor Black in the urban community to attain to what they think, what they think is a success. OK. But in doing that, he confronts the dilemma arising out of the moral condition as a human being in that he took another man's woman. But his repayment also included his memories of this Black girl who, to him, was more important than anybody else in his life. There is a line there when the white woman's power and situation in society was hitting hard at him and then in a sudden defiant retort he pointed out that the African girl is the daughter of a prince.

DANCE: Yes, you… you on at least two occasions in your works have impressed me with the image of the Black woman that you've given. It may be romanticised rather than real. I'm not sure, but it's impressive to me, particularly in a body of literature where I don't think women always are pictured in such a positive light. And I'm thinking of *The Jamaicans*, in the picture of Ked.

REID: Oh, that I did… well, you see… remember I am twenty years older – *The Jamaicans* is twenty years older than *The Leopard* and at that point I think I could write with much more authority on the Black woman because this is what I want to bring out, you know, that you are devils, but you are the greatest, most wonderful people in the world! [Laughter] Just to stop you from getting too swell-headed. But, I really think – I shouldn't tape this – it really doesn't matter… I really think that the girl Kedela in the book is one of the most moving characters – to myself – that I have written about. I think she was just marvellous!

DANCE: Why would you be hesitant to tape that?

REID: I don't know. I might sound bloody sentimental [Laughter]. But, you see, so many people don't seem to pick this up, what that girl meant, that girl means to the whole construction of the book, that the Black daughter must be written about. You know what I have found difficult, what I know that so many Black men writers find difficult: you see, we have grown up on the blue-eyed literature which tells us that… they talk about blond hair and long tresses and blue eyes and thin lips and so on, and of course that destroys your image of the beauty of our people. And then, now that for some God-given reason the Black women of the world realise that their own beauty… just a few years ago as you know… some realised that their own beauty was there to be sure, and it has changed the entire concept of males. I don't know if you realise this…

DANCE: Well, I do, but I think the process may be a little different. I think the male concept may be necessary to help the woman reinforce her own self concept.

REID: Of course, well you see, once she almost stumbled on that, it meant that the male would have to begin seeing her. Once she almost stumbled on that, on the fact of her own peculiar beauty to her people, rather than trying to get it out of a jar. You know, I remember the first time I saw girls with the low cut hair was one day when I was in another Nigerian village, and I went to one of those puberty rites. I wasn't supposed to be there but an African woman (she was tall, about fifty, sixty), anyway, she said, 'OK. I want you to see this.' And she took me to this place and I saw these girls and they all had the low cut hair. I think they were the most marvellous… I just stood there agape, just looking on saying, 'Is this how it really is!' Here were these beautiful creatures in their own setting, proud of themselves because they were… terribly proud of themselves… and being perfect. And then I knew back home there were the girls hasting to the hairdressers to get their hair straightened and so… [Laughter]

DANCE: …because they thought you wanted it that way. [Laughter]

REID: That's what I know now… I know that now. I didn't know that before.

DANCE: You are working on a biography of Manley, I understand?

REID: Yes, that has been finished. I don't know when it's going to come out. It has been a long hard work, but it's finished now.

DANCE: What were some of the difficulties?

REID: The man is dead. You see, when Manley asked me to do his biography, I said of course I would. But I had the expectation that Manley would be alive for years and I saw visions of us – he has that lovely place up in the mountains there, lovely place, and he liked to go up there on weekends – and I saw visions of us sitting there working on this book.

DANCE: Was he able to work with you on it at all?

REID: Not really. We had a couple of talks… we made some notes. Maybe about a tape of notes… something like that. You see he became ill and the death was quite sudden, so it meant going back and picking up things. Luckily, I knew him very well so his character was clear to me.

DANCE: And I suppose all of his papers were available to you.

REID: Oh, yes, what there was, but there were certain House minutes and so on I couldn't get at easily. In any case I wasn't writing… I wasn't about to talk about when Manley passed a law to put shingles on roofs. I wasn't thinking of that. I was thinking of just a book about Manley, the man who was a great guy, a formidable person! And this was what I set out to do. Well, of course you have to bring in his politics and his law. As a matter of fact, I think that in law, Manley is much more interesting than in politics. Because as you know he was a great lawyer and a man of really brilliant mind.

DANCE: Who is publishing the book?

REID: I don't know yet. I don't know whether it will ever get publication in America. I hope, I expect it will get publication in Britain. What I would like is to get publication here in Jamaica. You see I have been trying for years to get books published in Jamaica. We have just begun now.

DANCE: Yes. Are you pleased with the way you are progressing in that direction? I noticed quite a few coming out of the Institute of Jamaica.

REID: Yes. I had hoped to get it done faster, but we have begun. You know on *The Jamaicans*, for instance – I had my own printery once, you know, I've given that up now. I was in printing at one time.

DANCE: Oh, I didn't know that.

REID: Yes, so I know that end of the business, I did all the sending it through the press – it wasn't my press, it was somebody else's press – but I oversaw all the preliminaries, chose the paper myself and everything because I liked this, and the only trouble of it was it is difficult to get proper covers and so on out here and what you want you don't get, you know!

DANCE: What about the circulation after publication?

REID: That has been quite good, but what we are trying to do now is to get more Jamaican books in schools. This is a disgrace, it's a scandal that so many English books and even American books are in our primary school system – in our entire school system. It's a real scandal – almost a little Black Sambo situation, but I hope that will change.

DANCE: Tell me about your experience with foreign publishers. I'm sure that's what's led to this concern about finding means of publishing within your own country.

REID: Yes. The experience is that foreign publishers naturally are looking for money. The odd case is when they think in terms of literature. Maybe all do, but probably they say, 'Let's think of literature once and then think money a hundred times.' OK. And you find that, well, if you know a work is good and that you know it is right for your country and so on… but because it wouldn't probably sell a hell of a lot in America or England that they wouldn't touch it, you know. On the other hand I think I have always thought well of a man like Alfred Knopf who saw *New Day*, an excerpt in an English magazine, I think it was *Life and Letters*, a literary magazine (Britain), and Knopf himself at once wrote me and asked me if this book was finished and if I would show it to them, and I don't suppose you could have hoped to make a hell of a lot of money out of that, but the fact is that he saw that here is something that is new, and from there on he just grabbed hold of the book. Very few publishers would do that, you see. Now what I am expecting, what I am hoping is that – you see we have books in the school system [that] can pay the author and also help the whole country and I want to get as many good books – I don't want any second-rate stuff – good books in the Jamaican school system which talk about the Jamaican children – you know books like *The Young Warriors* – I've written about three books to be used in schools.

DANCE: Yes.

REID: *The Young Warriors* – you go to the country and you go to schools and then the teacher says, 'Children this is Mr. Reid. Mr. Vic Reid who wrote *The Young Warriors.*' And their faces say, 'Aaahh!' And then they pelt you with questions because some of them see themselves in the book.

DANCE: Right.

REID: They don't see some little Red Riding Hood. And this is all, this is all I want! I mean everybody needs money, but believe me, the money is secondary to see that they are getting what I never got. I had to divorce myself completely from Robin Hood and Sexton Blake and Buffalo Bill and all that stuff.

DANCE: Would you like to make some general comments about what you see as the state of Caribbean literature these days, perhaps, to comment on some of your contemporaries?

REID: I don't think so. To me it is a wait and see period. You see my generation of writers are giving way, should be giving way – not are – *should* be giving way, giving way in this sense – not to stop writing (don't misunderstand me) but to have more young writers coming out. Now this I don't see happening in Jamaica. I don't see enough of them. Now for instance the National Trust has a residential centre at Port Henderson. These are some restored eighteenth-century houses, small cottages, self-contained, and because I know how difficult it is for the Jamaican artist and writer to find peace, quiet and absence of anything else but his profession to work on, we have this place, these six cottages available to any writer who only has to present us with a sample of what he is doing, particularly a man or a woman who is working on a novel – a sample of what they are doing and for us to assess if they are serious writers and they can go there. And this I hope I will see the young writers taking up. There aren't enough of them even thinking about this now. I suppose they are probably impatient with the whole situation. I can't blame them. I was impatient as a young person also, but I wish that they could really just set themselves up for six months or a year of serious work and see what happens, because they have it in them, I know that. It's just that they aren't working at it. So we have the Port Henderson complex named for Carl Parboosingh, who was a painter. He died a few years ago – a brilliant Jamaican painter.

DANCE: Is this representative of the kinds of involvements that you have in your position with the National Trust?

REID: Absolutely. I am completely and thoroughly involved in… I research the history and then I go about the country trying to find the various sites where these things occurred. You see the history books treated us very scantily, and very frequently quite ungraciously. And what we have to be doing now is to realise the heroes, to bring them up, to realise the other side of the story in the same way that we realised the other side of the story in the Paul Bogle case, in the same way that we have realised the story in Tacky's case (Tacky was one of the great warriors in an important raid); Nanny (who is a national hero), so are realising these other sides of these coins and this is what I am doing wholly and solely, plus my writing.

DANCE: Well, you're certainly doing that in your writing too. Thank you very much for this interview.

CONVERSATION WITH

DENNIS SCOTT

DENNIS SCOTT

Dennis Scott was born in Jamaica on December 16, 1939, into a middle-class family. Typically he attended, as he put it, an 'establishment school'. Then he studied at the University of the West Indies, Mona. He left to teach for two years in Trinidad, after which he returned to Mona and completed his BA. In 1970-71 he received a Schubert Playwriting Fellowship at the University of Georgia. During 1972-73 he studied in England under a Commonwealth Scholarship in Drama-in-Education. Scott, who has worked in the Extra-Mural Department at the University of the West Indies and has served as Assistant Editor of the *Caribbean Quarterly*, was at the time of our interview Director of the School of Drama at the Cultural Training Centre in Kingston, and also a member of the National Dance Theatre Company of Jamaica. He later served as consultant to the Playwrights-in-Residence Program at the Julliard Theatre Center and as Chairman of the Directing Department at the Yale School of Drama. He played the part of the father-in-law, Lester, on the popular Cosby Show.

Scott is the author of *Journey and Ceremonies, Poems: 1960-69* (which was privately published in 1969); *Uncle Time* (1973); *Dread Walk: Poems 1970-78* (1982); and *Strategies* (1990). His final volume of poetry, *After-Image*, is forthcoming with Peepal Tree Press (2008). His poetry has appeared in a number of journals and anthologies. He has written several plays which have been produced in Jamaica and Trinidad. These include: *Terminus, An Echo in the Bone, Dog* – a verse adaptation of the Middle English poem, *Sir Gawain and the Green Knight, The Crime of Annabel Campbell*, and *Live and Direct from Babylon. The Fantasy of Sir Gawain and the Green Knight* was published in 1979. His poetry features in *The Heinemann Book of Caribbean Poetry* (1992).

Scott was an extremely versatile individual who has won recognition for his activities in a variety of areas – all of which he saw as related to teaching, the vocation he chose when he was a young child. As a poet, dramatist, dancer, actor, director, radio broadcaster, teacher and literary critic, Scott enjoyed a great deal of success and recognition. *Uncle Time* was an International Poetry Forum selection and earned him the 1974 Commonwealth Poetry Prize. His dramas *Chariots of Wrath* and *The Passionate Cabbage* won Jamaica Festival awards in 1966 and 1969, respectively, and in 1972 he was the recipient of the Best Director Award. In 1983 he received the Prime Minister's Award for Contributions to Art and Education.

The following interview took place in Jamaica on Tuesday March 11, 1980. Dennis Scott died in 1991.

DANCE: Tell me something about your education. Through university here in Kingston, right?

SCOTT: I went to an establishment school at the time when it was just about to begin becoming non-establishment. I was on a scholarship. From boredom I went from there to the University of the West Indies. Far too young because I was very precocious.

DANCE: How old were you?

SCOTT: Seventeen. Late sixteen. And I spent four years there very happily having adolescent angst and failing one of my courses which invalidated my degree. [Laughter] I went to Trinidad for two years… taught in Trinidad. Came back home. Taught – wasn't appetising – for a year. Took a year off and lived on friends and family and wrote that first full-length play which was a very well-made play *à la scribe.* It was quite bad. It was done here in my absence. Went back into teaching. Ended up at the university doing a part-time job in the Extra-Mural Department, editing the *Caribbean Quarterly*, and while I was there John Hearne said to me, 'Well, Dennis, why don't you just finish your degree?' So I did, very well, and had a great time. And then got married towards the end of that year I finished here. And we packed off on a playwriting fellowship to Georgia for a year; came back home for a year; went off on a Commonwealth scholarship in Drama-in-Education in England for a year. Came back here.

DANCE: How long have you been writing poetry?

SCOTT: Probably since I was eleven or twelve.

DANCE: Really, do you have any of the earlier pieces?

SCOTT: I think I must have. A while back I got in the habit of keeping everything, you know, which one doesn't do at first… So I probably have it somewhere, but I hope I don't find it.

DANCE: I know you are a close friend of Mervyn Morris. Has he been an influence on your development as a poet?

SCOTT: Yes, he has. He criticises, that is, looks at closely the work that I show him, very usefully. You know, he has a good, tough, critical mind, and we trust each other enough for honesty to be nothing but useful. So that helps a great deal.

DANCE: Do you always accept his criticism: that is, if he suggested a revision would you necessarily revise?

SCOTT: Not necessarily.

DANCE: But do you often?

SCOTT: I think I probably have more times than I haven't. Really, what – he certainly has taught to me – what I use him for is to reassure me that my own instincts about the crap that I am writing at the moment are right, or that my own feeling on it is right, is correct, you know.

DANCE: Have you published more than one volume?

SCOTT: No, I have one and a half manuscripts ready at the moment. The second one is called *Dreadwalk*, to be published by New Beacon.

DANCE: I read that you had written a novel too?

SCOTT: No, I started one but it was very self-indulgent, and I gave it up wisely after about three chapters. I am a playwright really. When I am not doing poetry, you know, I am a playwright.

DANCE: In his introduction to *Uncle Time*, Mervyn Morris suggests that your poetry is usually addressed to an audience, and he quotes the opening and closing lines of the first poem, 'The poet is speaking… Clap a little' [p.xvii]. Edna Manley disagrees and her letter to you comments, 'I do not think that you write really to an audience, rather that you have something in common with George Campbell, who had to an intense degree the gift of engaging in discussions with himself' [*ibid.* p.xiv]. Are you carrying on a dialogue with yourself, or are you writing for an audience? Who is correct there?

SCOTT: I think it varies. I think they are both right to some extent at some time. And this has changed. The balance has remained constant I think for me. Sometimes I do one; sometimes the other.

DANCE: What audience do you have in mind when you write for an audience?

SCOTT: It depends. It depends on what the poem is trying to say, I think. Sometimes it is to an audience which is very like myself: mongrel, mulatto, multicultural, those –

DANCE: West Indian?

SCOTT: West Indian, yes, with certain built-in tendencies to bias of one sort or another. Sometimes it's to people very much like myself who have exactly the opposite set of prejudices for precisely the same reasons, that they are multicultural, pluralistic. I started a suite last year which is now eight poems long called 'Letters to My Son', which I find a very useful device at the moment for crystallising my perceptions about whatever it is I am seeking or think I am. I am focusing the statements, addressing the statements to someone who at the moment is only seven, isn't capable of dealing with the statements – I have an idealised *him* in mind, which is an interesting, as I say, device, because it then forced me to address a person whom I like, and therefore the tone can be as intimate and as vulnerable as it can be in conversation with people that one likes.

DANCE: All right. Mervyn Morris again in that same introduction projected the responses of varied audiences to your work. He warned that some of your poems 'will be faulted by a narrow West Indianism for seeming to bear no distinctive marks of [your] Jamaican origins'; and others 'because of their local language and reference' may be 'imperfectly received by readers unarmed with a knowledge of our Jamaican context'. Do issues like this concern you when you are writing?

SCOTT: Not when I am writing; before sometimes, afterwards occasionally.

DANCE: Well, if before, then you certainly write with that in mind?

SCOTT: Right. What I try and do is avoid letting the truth – hopefully – of the work be unduly influenced by any designs I may have on an audience.

DANCE: But you are concerned that a reader outside the culture would perhaps understand your work?

SCOTT: I don't think I really am.

DANCE: Are you writing then for a West Indian audience?

SCOTT: I am writing for *me*, I am writing for my perception, I am writing to be as true to what I think and feel as I can be.

DANCE: In a line from 'Let Black Hands', you note, 'Song must swell/ from native throats, but tell of all men's state,' which suggests that you are striving for a kind of universality – I hate that word – but…

SCOTT: Yeah, me, too. No, it suggested, I think… I'd like to clarify that. It's not a kind of multinational thrust in it at all; it's rather… my perception of myself is that… it is a perception I think all people should have, which is that you are the only one of you there is. And there is a subsumed universality – I happen to be human; I function as human beings always function, and therefore, if I am true to that, that capacity and that potential, then there will be something that is relevant to everybody else who is human, who may come across this work.

DANCE: Let me ask you about the poem 'Infidelities'. If you remember… that built up to what was to me a very unexpected ending. [We] were led to believe as you viewed the scene that it was a rather romantic one in which two boys were battling for the narrator's sister and they seemed very pleased to stop their battle to sample the flaked flour-cakes she brings them. We assume they are affected by her 'water-cool voice', they seem to be excited by her smile, and then all of a sudden the poem concludes: 'my sister is safe; when boys, at night/ in these islands, dream, their dreams are white' [*Uncle Time*, p.4]. Am I more shocked by that than I should have been?

SCOTT: No you are supposed to be shocked by it. I think that poem is no longer, I hope, as relevant as it once was. That is, our appetites for Europeans as friends and lovers simply because they are Europeans has diminished considerably.

DANCE: Really?

SCOTT: Well, I would like to think so. [Laughter]

DANCE: Did the Black movement have something to do with it, do you think?

SCOTT: I think it did have quite a lot to do with it, and the fact that as we went economically further and further out on our own, or were pushed out on our own by a combination of circumstances, we have had to look inwards more and more as a people, each island and the whole Caribbean.

DANCE: 'Out on our own' doesn't mean geographically at all, moving from Europe, to America to Canada, it means simply…

SCOTT: No, no. It means an ideological construct that you try and work your life around.

DANCE: Were the poems 'Exile' and 'Homecoming' written after you had spent some time away from Jamaica?

SCOTT: Yes, I think they were, but they probably dated back to after I had been to Trinidad. I lived there for two years in the '60s. It was a very interesting period for me because I had been around the Caribbean a couple of times before that, but I hadn't spent much time in any one place, and, if anything, I think the experience intensified my awareness of being a Caribbean man and also made it very clear that I was very much rooted, not only in the Caribbean, but in Jamaica specifically, because the differences between the two places are quite large.

DANCE: Your sense of the exile in that poem ['Homecoming'] seems to be a person who can never fully return. Was that a temporary state or permanent in your case?

SCOTT: Well, no – this is very much after the event this critical judgement – but I think the poem is probably more about psychological exile than about geographical exile.

DANCE: Yes, I know but does one psychologically overcome –

SCOTT: Oh yes, I think it is harder to come back psychologically than it is to come back physically. Always, yes. Once you leave psychologically you are in trouble I think.

DANCE: In this poem, the lines I had in mind – well, let me start here: 'the old affections hang loosely./ Suddenly, mouth is dumb; eyes/ hurt; surprised, it is we/ who have changed/ glad, now,/ to have practised loving before that departure/ To travel/ is to return/ to strangers' [*ibid.* p5]. That's not…? That's only temporary?

SCOTT: Hmmn. Hmmn. I take your point and all I can do is say that 'Exile' is about leaving home and needing to come home, and 'Homecoming' is about having come home…

DANCE: But not completely?

SCOTT: ...remembering that you were away.

DANCE: OK. In the same poem, 'Homecoming', you talk about the journey and you used terms that suggest the journey was some kind of impractical fantasy, an 'El Dorado voyage', 'wanting a rainbow', and speaking of the appeal of other places you write, 'The sirens sing' [*ibid.* p.6]. Do you think for yourself and for most islanders, the journey away from home is really that kind of unreal, somewhat foolish, probably doomed quest for something?

SCOTT: I think it is a very real kind of quest and I think we have to do it, apparently we have to do it, in order to learn that it was finally unnecessary, you know. It is like that thing, burning your fingers or something; you do it and then you learn that your fingers get burnt.

DANCE: OK. Mervyn [Morris] talks a little bit too about your ambiguous use of words in the introduction. I suppose you mean for me to accept *Uncle Time* as a combination of things?

SCOTT: No. I am told that it is to be accepted as such, but it wasn't intended that way.

DANCE: OK. Well then my question is... Well I have problems determining who Uncle Time is; if he is Time I can't understand why he moves so suddenly – except in the first stanza. And if he's Death, I'm not so sure why we should weep as we do, and if he's Anancy, then I would think the results wouldn't be quite so grave.

SCOTT: Hmmn. I should have written you a short story.

DANCE: [Laughter] Well, it's such an interesting thing: I must know who he is, I mean I should. Who is he to you?

SCOTT: Well, isn't he old? Isn't he old? He is a little old man who is very quick, who is also the Anancy, god-figure, the web-weaver, the blesser of homes and houses. But he's also Death. Why are you insisting that he is an image?

DANCE: So that he is a combination of things?

SCOTT: Oh, he is all of them, he is all of them, yes. I think one of the things about my poetry that intrigues me is the fact that it's very, as Mervyn I think has pointed out, very influenced by my interest in the theatre and specifically in more traditional forms of theatre. For me, a poem is something which happens in an image or a series of images; it is like taking a snapshot or a series, a collage of shots, for me, which demonstrate, because of what is happening in the photograph and feeling content, the background story, the scenario, the moral and intellectual judgements being made by the poet, so that I was very interested to hear your actual comment a while ago, which suggested that images tend not to work with each other, not to form sometimes, in my work, a fully integrated picture. Maybe I heard that wrong?

DANCE: I attributed the problem to myself rather than to your poetry.

SCOTT: No. I think that's unfair. I think it is my problem, it is not the reader. What the reader is being offered deliberately is a shot or a group of shots which the reader is asked to fill in, the interstices between... I have used the word *cool* before about it, and really I want to create like a short picture, a short drawing, a sketch, and then say, 'Well, you have got to fill in the rest, you have to do some of the work. If I want to do all of the work I'll write a novel, I'll write prose which does fill in very many of the spaces.' Which makes it a very teasing and a very... my approach tends not as a result,

I think, to move terribly strongly; it excites and, if you are willing to let that excitement carry you into deeper feeling areas, I think it works. If you are not, it tends not to work… I remember being hurt years ago (and of course concealed it very effectively) by critical statements that one or two people made about my work not being very full of emotion, to the effect that it did not move the reader. And I think I was very wrong. The judgement was unfair, but my response was also wrong, because I don't want to move first with the gut. I think I want to make – both in the theatre and on the page or with the voice in poetry – I think I want people to be affected by something they can't forget: an image that holds them, that they are forced to deal with at gut level, subsequently, or simultaneously. I suppose poets are always trying to write myth, invented or reinvented, and that's where those icons are.

DANCE: Do the images in your work just suddenly occur to you or do you work on them and work on them and polish them until finally you get just what you want? You know some of them would be impossible for the… I mean I could never, for example, imagine some of those very striking images that you have in your poetry. How do they come?

SCOTT: I think they come as I said partly because – I'm really serious – I am a science fiction fan, an addict. Science fiction tends, science fantasy, speculative fiction, tends to move – I have heard it described as a genre in which the field of discourse is far wider than in normal, the traditional fiction, because… the possibility of creating interactions, of new relationships between imagined people, places, objects and technologies is so much vaster. And I think this is a very freeing kind of activity for me, the sense of pleasure in playing with unfamiliar relationships. It's, I suppose, lateral thinking in a funny kind of way, in pictures.

DANCE: The moment you started that observation, I started trying to think of any science fiction works that I had read coming out of the Caribbean. I can't think of any…

SCOTT: No, there aren't any. I once started to write science fiction stories and they were all very bad because it is difficult to find new concepts, you know; there is one that holds me for instance. It came out in the '60s, I think, it must have been. The image of slow glass. It's glass that – forget about the technology – but what it does is to retain the light striking it long after the event which the light blocks out has passed. So that you get pictures which are of the past, you know, and this haunted me partly because I am so desperately intrigued with the concept of time, of mortality, of things passing.

DANCE: Could you comment on that opening poem [in *Uncle Time*], 'Black Mass', it's simply that I don't have the feeling that I have completely understood it.

SCOTT: 'Black Mass', I think, may have been an important poem for me because of using a very specific form, the form of the Catholic Mass and trying to use it in such a way that finally what the poem, I think, says is also what the Mass says – the hope of Resurrection. I think craftwise it was a very important piece of work for me. Whether or not it really works as a poem, just as a poem, I'm really not sure any longer. And I think this is what I miss in a lot of poetry that I read – a sense of form as being the controlling element. It's not enough for me to be intense and clear and evocative and create images and so on. I think the shape of the thing of course has to help communicate what you are saying.

DANCE: Where do you start? Do you start with form? I am beginning to sense that perhaps you do. You know where you're going to begin. You know where you're going to end, and then the rest comes later.

SCOTT: Sometimes – sometimes that's true. But always in the reworking I'm interested in seeing exactly what is the shape that I've made. And this again is a spin-off from the theatre where form is so terribly obviously important.

DANCE: Would you say that that is a weakness of a lot of contemporary poetry, the lack of form?

SCOTT: I think it is. Yes. The control is always there in the energy, but not in the shape.

DANCE: Can we talk a little bit about the critical reception to your work. Have you been pleased?

SCOTT: It hasn't been enough. And it is partly my fault and partly the fault of the times we live in and partly the fault of the critics themselves. It's my fault in that I tend not to want to push for recognition. I think it's a corollary to my intense absorption with getting the work right for me. And that sounds dreadfully vain, and that's cool. It's partly the fault of the times we live in because like Morris's – but with an added problem – and Tony's [McNeill's], I think my work is concerned with keeping up a line of sanity in the middle of a whole lot of pressures – social and political – that are trying to push you into either being Black or being one of the haves or whatever it is. And that will never work, you know. It's partly the fault of the critics for – well, I'm not sure if I should blame them. The work is not easily accessible sometimes – literally you can't get at it. And it's partly because it was published by the University of Pittsburgh and it's hard to get the books down here and they're expensive, and so on and so on. I think that my work has been improving over the last four years – certainly since *Uncle Time*. My new work is much clearer and I think much warmer in many ways.

DANCE: Can you tell me about the new collection?

SCOTT: *Dreadwalk*.

DANCE: And tell me why that title.

SCOTT: Dread is one of the many words for one of the many kinds of Rastas. And it's one word – Dreadwalk. And again the concept of journeys and travelling from A to B and growing and learning as you go along, because my own development, and I think that of many West Indian writers, has been a process of moving from a position of privilege and travelling further out into the community.

DANCE: OK. So you're really travelling inside yourself or travelling back so to speak. It is not a matter of what we would generally say, up and out, but in.

SCOTT: Yes.

DANCE: Where are you moving in your new work?

SCOTT: I think there are two areas that are still very clear; one is an entirely personal and domestic sector, inquiring into the nature of my existence and my person, and the other is a reaching out towards establishing relationships and the rules for relationships between myself and the communities of which I am part – the society, the groups, the ideologies that I come in contact with. Maybe a third of the poems are in fact in a third area, in which these two interests are both equally involved, in which my relationship (I think this is accurate for everyone) within my own small home circle is influenced and modified by my relationships outside, where I have to cope with the society and the community. I think the language of those two or three areas of inquiry is becoming clearer and is making more energetic use of the Creole forms of communication and is reducing itself to a much more conversational, casual statement, a very shocking image.

DANCE: Do you think the increased use of the Creole, the perhaps more political aspect of the poetry, will make it (I hate to use the word) more popular – will mean that critics will pay more attention to it?

SCOTT: Yes to both those questions

DANCE: The use of the term *dread*, of course, raises the question of your association with the Rastafarian movement and its impact on you. Would you talk a little bit about that.

SCOTT: I think it's the most vital and healthy – at its finest – vital and healthy movement that the Caribbean has seen in that it explicitly rejects very many of the values which are associated, necessarily, with materialism, with imperialist attitudes and activities, with the metropolitan values and centredness of metropolitan values. It appeals, it cries out (Rasta does) for a return to a sense of self, a sense of individual identity and worth. It cries out for a return to simple living within the economies created by our situation as a set of very poor Third World countries.

DANCE: You seem to be dealing with the Rasta philosophy, economic and so forth, but not the religious aspect of it.

SCOTT: That's right. I think it's no less absurd in many of its tenets than any other religious body of beliefs and no more so. What is regrettable for me about Rasta is that it is so easily (and maybe not any more than any other religious belief or political concept), it's so easily used for selfish and unhealthy ends by individuals and by groups.

DANCE: You mean just the excuse for smoking grass or something like that?

SCOTT: It's an excuse for attitudes of hate and hostility and violence which I think tend to work very often against the value of the body of beliefs that we very loosely term Rasta. It is also a symptom quite as much as it is a phenomenon; it's a symptom of disaffection, of a need for something other than the faiths and dogma that we've been fed for so long. It has also created an enormously energetic language.

DANCE: That's exactly what I was about to ask you – if you thought the language had had a great impact on your work, and I suppose just the mere fact that you've chosen the title that you have begins to suggest that.

SCOTT: I don't use Rasta, Dread-talk 'I' talk, often, you know, in the work. When I do it is very often to set up polarities of attitude and of social behaviour within the poem, out of which some kind of meaning can then develop. Now I have been experimenting deliberately with Creole, not an awful lot quantitatively, but in quality I've put quite a lot of hard work into it. I have been trying to keep the voice very clear and conversational. When I began writing I was very – Derek Walcott once told me, more than half seriously, that I have too much blood and flesh in the poems, I needed more muscle, more tendon.

DANCE: And you think – you are striving for that?

SCOTT: I think I have moved away from the blood. It's cool now.

DANCE: Has Derek Walcott been an influence on you in other ways?

SCOTT: Not really, I am not sure why except perhaps that his stature very early on was so impressive that I may well have decided that I wasn't going to simply try and be another Walcott.

DANCE: As I was looking through your new collection of poetry I noticed the poem that you wrote when you were in Cuba. You were in Cuba to...?

SCOTT: For judging the Casa de Las Americas – the first year that the prize was offered to an English work.

DANCE: Well, tell me something about the impact of that trip on you, I know it motivated that poem.

SCOTT: Hmmn. At the first level I found myself ambivalent, as always, towards the politics of the situation. I think that what they have achieved has been quite incredible, and I am very satisfied for them. And I remind myself that it took them twenty years; and what the first nine years or ten years of that experience must have been like after the Revolution I would prefer not to have to live through. The fact that they have now created a society, with whatever help people may mention, like from Russia perhaps, in which people can live as I think I saw them living is marvellous. I wish it weren't necessary to go through certain stage in order to arrive at certain stages. And this perhaps makes me very much not a revolutionary. I'm not sure whether it makes me a reactionary.

DANCE: Let me be sure I understand what you are saying. Have they arrived at what you see as perhaps, if not an ideal stage, at least an advanced stage over most of the islands.

SCOTT: It seemed to me that more people there seem to be happier more of the time, or at least to be contented far more of the time, than anywhere else I have seen. Whether you define happiness in those terms, is I suppose another question altogether. But at least the children are fed...

DANCE: OK. So the impact on the masses of the people is quite clear. Let me ask you about your impression of the cultural life since what you were there for is very much related to that. Were you impressed with the way the Government encourages...

SCOTT: Very much so. The State as a centre of all activity is a marvellous system, if the State is well liked, thoughtful, has created with the help of the people systems which it operates.

DANCE: And you did not see the kinds of restrictions that sometimes inhibit creative writers in communist countries?

SCOTT: I didn't see them. I'm fairly sure that they exist. It's a question of choice and balance once again for me. Some freedoms aren't worth having because of the prices one has to pay for them. I return, I think always, to a dynamic of morality in which one has to make choices constantly and programme yourself, I think you shouldn't programme yourself to one thing or the other – that's a system – and use labels and finally all you have left is a label that you have to live in. Maybe what I am saying very very badly is that I like the dynamic that is happening in the West Indies in which we are constantly being forced to choose day after day between courses of actions with implications of different kinds. That I think is a way of surviving and of maintaining some kind of sanity day by day, which may well be preferable.

DANCE: To what is happening in Cuba?

SCOTT: To going one way or the other way. I don't want to be American, I don't
want to be Cuban. I don't want to be Russian. It's very uncomfortable…
DANCE: But you want Jamaica to be something else?'
SCOTT: I want us to be whatever it is we have the potential to be and we can discover
that, I think, patiently and sometimes violently, and very unhappily in some cases. It's
not an easy choice. It's far less easy than opting for one or the other.
DANCE: Last night we were talking about the project that I am working on, and you
were looking for perhaps some unifying trends that I see among Caribbean writers,
and you suggested that one unifying trend may be the matter of tone which you
defined as possibly 'a malicious tolerance or tolerant malice'. Would you talk about
that a little bit. What did you have in mind?
SCOTT: I'll talk about it only if you permit me not to be as serious as you want me
to be about it. I definitely think that that tone is a very strong element in our use of
language. That tone, it seems to me, is very strongly a product of being artists in the
society which traditionally has, or had lost its faith in artists and attempted to replace
that faith with other things which were less useful than artists are. So that one is
constantly being aware that one's own judgements as an artist are, even from the very
moment of speaking, questionable, questioned by the public. We have to constantly
assert in various ways, sometimes in very complex ways, the fact that we do know what
we are talking about, that our experience of life in the Caribbean, of life generally
perhaps, is very acute and a very self-aware kind of thing. There is, of course, also the
fact that because – if I am right – we see the place and its problems and its richnesses
so clearly, then our resentment against the stupidities with which the societies here
have been imbued is very sharp, but needs to be adjusted in order not to distance the
reader, in order to tune the reader in sympathetically.
DANCE: Is there a kind of condescending then to your reader?
SCOTT: No, there is an accommodation; we do not speak a foreign language to
people. If you know the reader understands you, you try and find at least a Creole that
you can share. And I think the process of forging language in the West Indies has very
often been a process of creating out of necessity the language in which you can
communicate fairly clearly and people can receive you very clearly. It is not conde-
scension. If you want to communicate, you try to communicate as best you can.
DANCE: Do you see any other distinctive characteristics of West Indian literature
or of West Indian writers?
SCOTT: Oh, all the good old themes, you know, the journey, the exile, the quest,
the high concentration of human beings in a small living space, whether you treat that
as the 'yard' or as a town or as a village, or as the whole Caribbean, the political
disappointment.
DANCE: Do you think among the younger group of writers that these themes are
as important? For example, I don't think I see them so much in Tony McNeill and
Michael Anthony and Earl Lovelaee. I am not so sure I see them that much in you. Are
these old themes that are getting to be outdated?
SCOTT: Good question. I don't know. You may be right. Hmmn.
DANCE: Who would you consider the most important poets writing in the Carib-
bean now?
SCOTT: Walcott. Brathwaite. Morris. Important in the sense of what they have to

offer than their acceptance by an audience. It's a nice question… I have never had to answer it before. One of the – Lorna Goodison, I think, Pam Mordecai, two Jamaicans here. I am out of touch with letters in the Caribbean.

DANCE: Drama has really had a big upsurge in the Caribbean in the last ten years. Why do you think that is? Does it appeal more readily to the folk?

SCOTT: Hmmn. I think some of it is because the cinema fare had got worse and worse, and people have turned to the live theatre, and as the social-political tensions have increased, public gatherings which the have-nots frequent have a sense of danger and urgency, so that, again, the people who prefer not to feel threatened, because they have a little more than the have-nots, have tended to move towards a different kind of entertainment.

DANCE: These are the middle-class people…

SCOTT: The middle class is always the one that worries, you know, the middle class has always been rising. Also, of course, with the recent nationalism and political consciousness, there is a tremendously high degree of politicisation taking place across the Caribbean. The art which speaks, if not in political terms, at least with political prejudices that can be demonstrably entertaining, has become more and more popular.

DANCE: But those of you who are involved in drama have made a real attempt, haven't you, to involve the folk in things like the yard theatre – is that what it was called, the experiment here? And the emphasis on folk tradition in the theatre and Caribbean plays as opposed to more European plays, that kind of thing.

SCOTT: That's true too.

DANCE: Has that developed another kind of audience other than this middle-class audience?

SCOTT: Oh yes, there always is a very wide circle in Jamaica, but the popularity, the size of the audience in itself is, I think, a result of those factors, and oh yes, it spirals up nicely. You know the more theatre there is, the more of the middle-class audience there is, the more theatre there can be; the more theatre there can be, the more you can play with types of theatre before you extend your range of product. The more involved the private sector is beginning to become, the more money that there is to plough into productions. The more the educational system starts accepting theatre and the fact that the culture is what you live in from birth and not something that you learn in the school, then the more readily people accept the vitality and validity of the arts in general, and the more prepared they are to form audiences.

DANCE: I have enjoyed this talk with you. Thank you, very much.

———————————

CONVERSATION WITH

SAMUEL SELVON

Samuel Selvon was born in San Fernando, Trinidad, in 1923, to descendants of Indian immigrants. His maternal grandfather was Scottish. After receiving the Senior Cambridge Certificate at Naparima College in Trinidad in 1938, Selvon served as a wireless operator in the Royal Naval Reserve from 1940-1945, and then worked on the *Trinidad Guardian* from 1945-1950. In 1950 he emigrated to England, where he established himself as a freelance writer. Selvon was visiting lecturer at the University of California, Dundee University (Scotland) and the University of Victoria (Canada). At the time of our interview he was writer-in-residence at the University of Calgary. A spellbinding reader of his own works, he was a popular guest artist at colleges and universities around the world.

Selvon is the author of numerous well-received novels, including *A Brighter Sun* (1952); *An Island Is A World* (1955); *The Lonely Londoners* (1956); *Turn Again Tiger* (1958); *I Hear Thunder* (1963); *The Housing Lark* (1965); *The Plains of Caroni* (1970); *Those Who Eat The Cascadura* (1972); *Moses Ascending* (1975) and *Moses Migrating* (1983). His collections of plays, *Eldorado West One* (1988) and *Highway in the Sun and Other Plays* (1991) were published by Peepal Tree Press. He wrote three books for schools, *Carnival in Trinidad* (1964); *A Cruise in The Caribbean* (1966) and *A Drink of Water* (1968). In addition to the short stories collected in *Ways of Sunlight* (1957) and *Foreday Morning: Selected Prose 1946-1986* (1989) his short stories have appeared in numerous anthologies and journals and have been broadcast by the BBC in London and CBC in Toronto. His novels and short stories have been variously translated and have appeared in German, Danish, French, Tamil and Japanese editions. He has written numerous radio and television dramas, mainly for the BBC. He co-scripted *Pressure*, a London film which appeared in 1975.

Selvon's work has been recognised through the awarding of numerous fellowships and honours, including two Guggenheim Fellowships (1955 and 1968); the MacDowell Colony for Writers and Artists Fellowship (1955); The Society of Authors (London) Travelling Scholarship (1959); The Trinidad Government Refamiliarisation Scholarship (1962-63); The Arts Council of Great Britain Writing Assistant Grants (1967-68); The Trinidad Government Humming Bird Award for Literature (1969); The Dundee University Fellowship in Creative Writing (1975-77) and Doctor of Letters at the University of the West Indies in 1985.

Selvon's writing has been scholarly discussed, particularly following a revaluation of his work where its aesthetic innovations with the form of the novel and the use of dialect in narrative voice have been given proper consideration. These include Sushelia Nasta's *Critical Perspectives on Sam Selvon* (1988); Clement H. Wyke, *Sam Selvon's Dialectal Style and Fictional Strategy* (1991); *Tiger's triumph: celebrating Sam Selvon* (eds. Nasta and Anna Rutherford; 1995); Mark Looker, *History, Community and Language in the Fiction of Sam Selvon* (1996); Roydon Salick, *The Novels of Samuel Selvon: A Critical Study* (2001); ed. Martin Zehnder, *Something Rich and Strange: Selected Essay on Samuel Selvon* (Peepal Tree, 2003) and Curdella Forbes, *From Nation to Diaspora: Samuel Selvon and George Lamming and the Cultural Performance of Gender* (2005).

At the time of our interview Selvon was living in Calgary, Alberta. He is the father of four children, one by his first wife, and three by his second wife.

The following interview took place in Richmond, Virginia, on February 20, 1980. I had the opportunity to spend two days with the novelist before the interview, as he was participating in the Virginia Consortium for International Studies Program. Selvon did not really enjoy talking about his writings, nor about literature in general. He greatly preferred simply to read from his works and to allow them to speak for themselves.

Selvon had a pleasing, friendly personality. His soft spoken, easy-going, sincere manner is captivating. The only time he showed any strong emotional response and raised his voice during our interview was when he commented on the divisiveness recently developing in Trinidad with Negro anti-Indianism.

Samuel Selvon died in Trinidad on April 16, 1994.

DANCE: I know you are not one to trace family roots, but just briefly tell me about your family background. Your folks from…
SELVON: My father was East Indian and my mother, my mother was half-Scottish; her father was a Scotsman, and her mother was an East Indian; and as I told you the other day, I am not quite sure what that makes me, what percentage of the Scottish blood I have got, but those are things that don't really interest me. I'm not bothered very much about ancestry and about going back and tracing things like that.
DANCE: OK. Were both your parents born in Trinidad?
SELVON: I hope so. I think so. As I think about that part of my life, I really remember growing up as a child, that they never really held me down to any particular cultural line as such. My mother, strangely enough, she grew up with her father, who as I say was Scottish – I think he had a coconut plantation in the south of the island, and she grew up there in an Indian village and she spoke Hindi fluently. And I don't think my father, who was East Indian, I don't think I remember him speaking any Hindi at all. She tried to urge me very much to learn it at school, because during those days they did teach Hindi at school, as a sort of extra class, and she used to say, 'Boy, why don't you learn to speak Hindi!' and so on. Even at that early age I was growing up in that sort of cosmopolitan, mixed atmosphere, even from childhood days where things like – you know – I had no interest in learning to speak any – I would rather go and see some American film at the cinema [laughter] than go to school.
DANCE: I see. Did your family situation, growing up in Trinidad, approach any of the situations that you recount in your novels? Was it close say to Tiger's situation, or to Adrian's or…
SELVON: Not really. I've been asked this question before – I haven't really written that kind of novel; it is something I have notes on, that I want to make – I think in a way that I am freakish in the sense that the things that I write about I haven't really experienced, like when *A Brighter Sun* was published, everyone though that, well, there must be a great deal of biographical material in this book, and strictly speaking, there is absolutely none at all, you know. The story of my private life and my parents and my childhood and how I grew up is something that is entirely different from

anything that I have written yet… I think to get an idea of how I was thinking during those earlier years, the best thing might be to refer to *An Island Is A World*, where I tried to express certain lines of thought that I had at that time.

DANCE: Let me ask you a little bit about your education. I have noticed that most West Indian writers have extensive formal education, university education, which is kind of different from Black American writers, many of whom have had very little, or no university education at all… You seem to be the exception; you have not had university education, have you?

SELVON: No. I never went to university. I finished high school with what was called Senior Cambridge Certificate, and then I had to get out and go to work.

DANCE: When you say you 'had to', was it because of family financial…

SELVON: Yes, you know, I didn't come from rich parentage. I think my parents did have some money, but this was – I guess I must have been a baby.

DANCE: You mean that money was lost?

SELVON: I guess it was spent or dissipated or whatever, but I never had much. When I started to grow up, by the time I was about eight years old, whatever money they had had started to disappear, so that by the time I could really appreciate the fact that they did have some, I learnt in turn there was none left, you know, and I had to go out to work.

DANCE: Was this a great disappointment to you, or…

SELVON: No. No. No. At that age, you know, I didn't think about things like money, you know.

DANCE: Well what about things like university? Was that a goal for you or something that you did not consider as a possibility?

SELVON: No. I think I started to – my thoughts began to become formative during my college days, and perhaps if I had had the opportunity there, I might have gone on to university, but it just happened that I couldn't at the time, and I just accepted it. I didn't want to get out and go abroad and study to be a professional lawyer or doctor or whatever.

DANCE: What about writer? When did you decide that you were going to be a writer?

SELVON: I don't know, I don't think I have ever made that decision, and I am not quite sure if I have decided yet, you know. That is a very strange thing. Let me tell you what I wanted to do, what I have always wanted to do. I wanted to be a composer. I wanted to write music.

DANCE: Really?

SELVON: Yeah. Now I wanted to write music and then I wanted to be a philosopher.

DANCE: Are you combining those with your writing?

SELVON: Well, I'm trying in a way to combine the philosophy with it, but the music is a bit more difficult. I actually started to write – I used to sit down at a piano and try to write out tunes and things like that, and its something that still lingers at the back of my mind. I mean I never consciously made the decision to be a writer. It kind of worked out because about the best subject I was good at at school was writing essays, and I think it just sort of evolved on me. During the war – I spent five years in the Navy – and lived a great deal by myself – when I say by myself I mean in the sense I was away from the friends I had grown up with, I was away from family, I was out at sea, on ships.

DANCE: Were you married then?

SELVON: No. No. And I started to become very thoughtful and wondered some-thing, something, almost something like say Tiger of *A Brighter Sun*, you know, well, what the hell is life all about? What directions am I going to take and so on. And during that time I guess I did a fair amount of reading. I have given up reading for many years now, but I am sure that during those earlier years, that I recall reading about anything I could put my hands on.

DANCE: Do you remember any authors who stand out from that early reading?

SELVON: Not particularly. Here is a strange thing – because I think that what you are daring…

DANCE: Influences – that terrible word!

SELVON: …to ask here is: am I being influenced by any writer? OK. No matter how you couch it I know what you mean. Now I would say yes, but listen to the – anomaly or whatever. I was influenced by an English writer, Richard Jefferies [1848-1887], who wrote a great deal about the English countryside. He was a naturalist; he used to write about flowers and plants, and living in little villages, and the peasant life or small farming life of England, and the birds and the seasons and things like that. And that had a very strong influence on me in those earlier days, because when I first started to write I transposed that feeling and love that this writer seemed to me to have for nature, I transposed that into Trinidad and saw myself in a way as a kind of local Richard Jefferies, who was going to try to get all of the physical aspects of the island and the beauty, the natural beauty of the island; I was going to be the one who would write that sort of thing. And if you look at my earlier – the little articles I used to have published in the local newspapers and so on when I started writing, you would see that this tendency to be always talking about the seasons and the rain falling, and all the beautiful flowers we've got in Trinidad, stuff like that.

DANCE: What about Caribbean literature at that time, which I know was a bit limited, but did you read, before you began writing, men like CLR James? *Minty Alley*, for example?

SELVON: No. No. One thing I started with and one thing which I think I still kept with me, is that I don't see why *I* have to read other Caribbean writers to write anything. I just want whatever comes out of me, belongs to me, and it is how *I* think and I don't want to read other Caribbean writers to find what *they* have to say. I know they have certain things to say and they say it well and they do it *their* way, and that's cool. I want to do *my* thing – just how *I* see it, and what *I* want to say.

DANCE: But at this period we were talking about, you weren't reading, thinking about writing were you? You were just reading for enjoyment, and what I am asking is if during this period any of the reading you did was Caribbean literature, or was it mostly English?

SELVON: No, no, I, I, mark you, mark you, I did have – you see I'm going to be contradicting myself continuously during this interview and I will tell you why. I used to sub-edit a magazine for the local paper, *The Trinidad Guardian*, called the *Guardian Weekly*; it was a weekly little magazine that we published along with the newspaper, and we used to publish some poetry and prose writing, and I used to edit those stories that were submitted from different people and so on. So there you are, you know, in one way I am kind of denying any kind of wholly literary influences or what have you, and at the same time I know consciously that I was involved to some extent. In fact, you know, I published some of the earlier writers like Eric Roach and Alfred Mendes and some names I can't remember. And well, there you are, even some of my own short stories that I started to write then and compose poems…

DANCE: Were your first works published in *The Guardian*?

SELVON: My earlier work, yes, and broadcast by the BBC in London.

DANCE: OK. When did you move to England?

SELVON: I moved to England in 1950.

DANCE: OK. I know that you have already told me that you were not closely associated with CAM [Caribbean Artists Movement], but can you tell me anything about that association of Caribbean writers in London?

SELVON: I don't know very much about it. I know that it was founded by Eddie Brathwaite, Andrew Salkey, John La Rose, and some other people perhaps. CAM is something that is much later in my career; I mean I don't know if you want to skip years and come up to CAM, but CAM, well, you know, CAM I heard about it after I had written four or five novels. I read of it; I heard that they had formed this group.

DANCE: But you were not at all a member of the group?

SELVON: No. I was not a member. Well, I was never an active participant in anything – I don't like getting together with writers and talking about writing. If I get together with writers I would rather talk about women and drink and that sort of thing… I am very suspicious of these kinds of things, you know, where they try to group people together, and get very serious about this whole business, and you know, I don't like these organisations. In a way, it sets up inhibitions in my mind; I don't like to be associated with things like that.

DANCE: You have lived abroad more than half of your life, certainly since you have been a writer, an established writer. Has that had any effect on your work?

SELVON: Well, yes, of course it did; it had a great deal to do with it. I mean I look back on my life and figure that, well, what would have happened to me if I had stayed in Trinidad. I don't know; I was working for a newspaper as I said, and things were pretty good. I was even stupid enough to feel that, 'Ah, well this must be success, you've had some stories broadcast by the BBC in London, and you've had some stories published, and so on here and there, little poems. Boy, you know this is great!' and so on. And apart from that there was, there was the social life; I was earning a fair wage, and I kind of saw myself settling down and figuring, 'Man, this is it', and so on. I just felt that I was too young for that to happen, that I ought to get on, out of Trinidad. Because I felt kind of cramped in the island, I wanted to come abroad before making any further decisions about what direction my life would take. So that I didn't really leave Trinidad with the sense of I was going abroad to be a writer. I left Trinidad for more personal reasons in trying to discover myself and what direction my life would take. So I went to England like an ordinary immigrant, you know; it was on a ship and I think I told you George Lamming was on that same ship too. I had known George a little before that, and I was surprised to see him on the ship. I don't think he knew I was leaving on the same ship either; we just met on board.

DANCE: Very interesting. As one reads your fiction, and the works of other Trinidadian writers, one notes all kinds of relationships between Indians and Blacks. Now the first Black Trinidadians that I met shared with me childhood anecdotes which suggested extreme racial antagonisms. And I have read that Naipaul said that the race problem in Trinidad is not Black versus white but Negro versus Indian. And you allude without comment in some of your works, to prejudices of Indians against Blacks. And yet you have a relationship like Adrian's and Mark's, where you have a Black and Indian who are very close friends. Could you tell me a little bit about the relationship between Blacks and Indians in Trinidad: would a relationship like Adrian's and Mark's be the exception rather than the rule?

SELVON: Well, it might be the exception to some writers who want to write about racial issues. While I was growing up in Trinidad, I had friends with Blacks, and I had friends with Indians, and I grew up in that sort of atmosphere, and in fact, you know, this isn't like saying, 'Some of my best friends are Black,' you know, or 'Some of my best friends are white,' you know, the usual cliché talk. But I grew up in that kind of atmosphere and this is, say, the late '20s and throughout the '30s. I think that during those years the racial situation between the Indians and the Blacks was much less hostile and much more inclined to be on a give-and-take basis than how it developed after the War, and through certain developments in the island, political, and things like that, and then came, say, from the '50s, then the situation became more and more antagonistic for certain reasons. But the kind of atmosphere I grew up in – I know that it's changed, you know – but the people I grew up with during that time, when I go back to Trinidad, even today, and I see them, they remember what it was like in the same way that I do. They are just as friendly to me as we were during the earlier years. So, of course, what is happening generally in the island is something else.

DANCE: And it has gotten worse rather than better?

SELVON: Yes, and you know, this is a great, great, a bitter disappointment to me, you know. I feel that it is something that I regret very much.

DANCE: It was very interesting to me as I read your works to note that you deal as comfortably with Black characters as you do with Indians.

SELVON: Yes, well there you are, this is exactly what I mean. As I say, growing up in that sort of atmosphere I identified as much with Blacks as with Indians; in fact, strictly speaking, if you talk about the creolising process, you're not Indian, you're not Black, you're not even white; you assimilate all these cultures and you turn out to be a different man who is the Caribbean man. And what I think still remains the idealism that the whole chain of islands is aiming for is to form one sort of Caribbean unified nation, and this is what I write about. I want my work to be – don't only want to write about Indians – want to write about everything.

DANCE: OK. I note the frequent portrait, not just in your work, but in much of West Indian literature, of the Black West Indian who is obsessed with the white woman: Carew's *Green Winter*, Dathorne's *The Scholar Man*, Williams's *Other Leopards*, some works by Salkey and Austin Clarke, in varying degrees of course. It seems that this obsession motivated usually by the conflicting passionate sexual attraction and the vehement racial bitterness overcomes some of your Indian characters as well, like Tiger, who is a man of great dignity and who, seemingly, intentionally allows himself to be degraded by a callous white woman, whose attraction practically destroys his life; and with Adrian you have the same kind of situation. Would you comment on this?

SELVON: Hmmm. Well, maybe it's more than racial, I mean it could go right back to, back to the whole concept of being colonised, of the feeling that white, of white supremacy, of looking up towards the white man as if it is something that, as if it is a goal, a goal to be attained. I think – didn't I mention this in *A Brighter Sun*? – I think that when Urmilla was looking into the house or something, and she says they wish they could – that everybody could be like white people or something like that. Something that's there, that's to be attained, this high high level of life and society that we are indoctrinated to feel that this is where we should aim for, we should try to imitate our masters… There probably are a lot of reasons, I mean I haven't gone into all the psychological implications of it, but this is where it stems from, I would think. I could see this happening to Tiger; I mean I could see this happening to any Black guy. I like white women myself you know, in that sense, that I would like to, I mean I would like to have sex with them. I sometimes – I haven't really probed into this, maybe it is a feeling of – I tell you what I think it is. OK. Fine. In my second novel, *An Island Is A World*, and this is a complete, almost a chapter that was cut out by the English publisher, where I had… it was either Rufus or his friend, I can't remember who – there was a white English girl who came down to the islands to meet him. I think they were both interested in painting and things like that. And he had sexual intercourse with her and actually during the process of it he was shedding all this feeling of white supremacy, you know, saying, 'I'll fuck it all out of you, you white bitch!' You know what I mean… almost as if now he's trying to shed all that feeling that this race is supreme. And that is a very vital part of the book, but I got into a lot of trouble with the publishers about it. Apparently they didn't like it. Anyway it's water below the bridge.

DANCE: Well, let me ask you – I don't want to belabour the point, but in *Turn Again Tiger* everything works up to this moment when he suddenly attacks this white woman; he has been desiring this and evidently she has been desiring it too and all of a sudden there is this kind of animalistic act, and after this life begins to resume a kind of normal course. Now are you suggesting that that is some kind of symbolic attack there on white supremacy which helps him to come to terms with himself and with his life?

SELVON: Yes, I would say so. I would say that maybe this is what I did do in *Turn Again Tiger*. That same incident that I referred to in *An Island Is A World*, I used that same motivation there, because once Tiger had done this, it was like a purge, he got rid of the whole thing out of his system. I think he actually dives into the river and washes it all away.

DANCE: OK. Your treatment of the conflicts between young Indians and their parents who insist on the old ways, is sometimes very humorously painted and sometimes very poignantly done. I assume that this was not really a problem that you faced growing up, even though your mother for example wanted you to learn your native tongue. She didn't force upon you…

SELVON: Exactly. That is what I am saying about my whole background now, my whole childhood, is that I grew up completely differently and there were no fetters at all from my parents; and it's something that I remember with a great deal of gratitude. If I had to go to an Indian ceremony like a wedding or feast or anything like that, my attitude towards that would be the same as a Black who would be going, because my parents never insisted that I should grow up like an Indian and learn, you know, learn all the ways and customs and mannerisms and religions and all that sort of thing. I would go to the ceremony and I would sit down and eat roti and things like that, but *that* was it. I mean there wasn't any cultural attachment that I felt about it.

DANCE: In one of your stories – 'When Greek Meets Greek' – you introduce one character whose name is, what is it? Ramkilawansingh.

SELVON: Ram…

DANCE: And you wrote, 'After this, we calling this man Ram,' and you introduce another character with another long name [Chandrilaboodoo] and you say, 'after this, we calling this man Chan.' This rather flippant dispensing with the complexities of Indian culture and facilely accepting…

SELVON: Well, it isn't entirely flippant; it's my attitude towards it. You know I had figured this, that this is the whole thing and the ideal of being the Caribbean man, and in that sense, I feel strongly disappointed in certain Blacks too – now, who are militating for, you know, African roots and Blackness as opposed to any other racial group. In that sense, I think that if we start to become isolated as racists in the Caribbean then the whole dream of the Caribbean man is going to be shattered again.

DANCE: OK. Is *your* name exactly as it was given to you?

SELVON: Yes. Yes. I don't know where the name Selvon comes from. It doesn't sound Indian at all. I used to think it was French. I heard some story that my father grew up as a child in Martinique, which is a French island, as you know. I don't know, maybe the plantation overseers might have given him the name Selvon. I don't know. But I tell you this though. Later on, not so long ago, I found out from someone who lives in the south of India, when he mentioned my name and I gave him this story, that I didn't know where it comes from, he says, 'Oh, there are people in certain parts of south India who have that name – Selvon,' so I figured that well, that's good for me to know anyway. Not that it's important to me.

DANCE: One of the most striking things about your work, and one that I am sure you are most often asked about, is your use of dialect, not only in the dialogue but frequently also in narration. Would you tell me a little bit about how and when you decided to use this technique?

SELVON: Well, the decision came when I wanted to do that novel, *The Lonely Londoners*, which dealt, as you know with the whole Black scene in London as I saw it through the eyes of a man from the Caribbean. And I couldn't write it unless I used the Caribbean idiom. I tried to write it in standard English and it just would not work, and suddenly it dawned on me that perhaps if I did both, both the dialogue and the narrative in this way of speaking, but at the same time being conscious that I was – that it would have to be understandable to predominantly, at that time, a white audience, that I would have to modify it slightly. Therefore, starting from that book onwards – because if you look at my earlier works, you will see that where I use dialect that I spell it phonetically – [in *The Lonely Londoners*] I avoided for one thing the phonetic spelling, I just used the straight word, because the kind of dialect as it is spoken in Trinidad is really a jumbling up of – it's a grammatical jumbling up, rather than very much of the words that come from other languages like African tribal languages, or even Spanish and French and so; although there is a bit of it but not such a great deal as say the Jamaican dialect which is something else, you know. I don't know very much about that; I don't understand it myself many times. However, to get back, I thought that this way of speaking, perhaps if I tried to express the feelings of these people from the Caribbean through this medium that it might work better. And, thus I started to write a novel and it worked, and it worked, and suddenly you know it was like sailing along, it seemed, it fitted so naturally that the novel just sailed along, no difficulty at all. It seemed as if what I was trying to write about, the Blacks in Britain, and using that language form just melded into one another and just pushed the whole thing straight along, and I don't think it would have worked at all if I had tried to do it in standard English.

DANCE: Is that success attributable to the fact that you find the dialect the best way to tell these people's stories, or is it attributable to the fact that you write more comfortably in the dialect?

SELVON: Well, I think it is a combination of both. I write more comfortably in that language form – I don't like to use the word dialect very much – I have heard it so many times. In writing in that language form about the Caribbean experience or at least the Black Caribbean experience, that it is suitable and it is best. Now, even in *The Lonely Londoners* there are passages where I revert back to standard English for the lyrical quality, English, where I feel not so much as a contrast but because the dialect wouldn't work (here I go using the word dialect. OK, well, to hell with it!), wouldn't work in that particular section. This is what I am going to continue to do in my work because I don't think that I'm ever going to forsake the Caribbean image; I am not ever going to write a book about my experiences with the English people in England unless I do it in this language form as a Caribbean man. Or in any book for that matter. I am always going to be writing as a Caribbean man.

DANCE: OK. Now we have been talking about this language form and a dialect, as if, you know, it's all the very same pattern, but Gordon Rohlehr has noted the distinctions you make between the form spoken say, by the East Indian who has not been creolised, and the language say of a Tiger, who has grown up in the West Indies and has been fully creolised [in *Critics on Caribbean Literature*, pp.153-161]. And I was also looking to see if there were any distinctions between the Black speakers and the Indian speakers which I imagine would be the case in the Trinidad you grew up in. How many different dialects, if I may use that word, are you using, or how many different forms of this creolised language are you using?

SELVON: I am using the Trinidad form of the dialect, the Trinidad form as it developed during Tiger's generation and not Tiger's father's. Tiger's father was from the older generation and they still used to talk like the old Indians, would say, 'Give-am', or 'Have-am this' and so on, which I did use in *A Brighter Sun*, but if I ever have to come back to write about characters of that older generation, certainly I would not have them talking like Tiger.

DANCE: OK. Let me move to another subject. In the novel *I Hear Thunder* we see two relatively strong men attempting to resist the total nihilism that accompanies middle-class, modern life in Trinidad. Both of them in varied ways try to hold on to moral values and cultural manifestations of a simpler life that is both more moral and more fulfilling. But in the end we know that though they can continue to manifest outward signs – they can speak the dialect, they can go to Carnival and so forth – they are hopelessly lost. Must this happen or is it simply that there is some weakness in these two men that makes it happen; could they live there, in other words, and hold on to those values they want? [Pause] You know what I am talking about?

SELVON: Yeah, I know exactly what you are talking about. I think it's very difficult. Because of the social patterns that exist in Trinidad community life – that's the way I see it, that's the kind of society I grew up in. I didn't grow up like Tiger in the carat hut – not that I am spurning that in any way – I am just explaining how I grew up in that kind of Adrian and Foster society and those are things I saw happening, and those are the things that I see happening even now when I go back to Trinidad; it still exists.

DANCE: When you were talking about why you left, you sounded very much like Adrian to me.

SELVON: This is exactly it, you know, that's part of it too, that's part of the reason why I left.

DANCE: As I think about the situation of Mark, I wonder if it is supposed to be as tragic a situation as it impresses me as being. You know, here's a man who would like to love his mother and who would like to keep his friends, who would like to remain the kind of Black Trinidadian who really loved Trinidad, who loved Carnival, who loved flying kites, and who finds himself forced to move into the white country club set that he obviously doesn't really like.

SELVON: I think that this is true. I think that this still obtains. I do not know, myself – and know some – any Black-White marital relationship that does not have to face all these pressures throughout the Caribbean. I would go so far as to say that, not only in Trinidad, throughout the Caribbean, those relationships become shattered and destroyed, many times. I am not saying, mark you, that there might not be one or two who survive all that, but certainly I would say it is extremely difficult, and for that reason you would find that such individuals tend to come back out of the islands and live abroad, or don't make the mistake of going back down to the Caribbean at all.

DANCE: You know I can certainly see how the wife is the motivational factor in his joining the country club and all that, but I didn't tend to blame her for all this. As a matter of fact even though in one sense she emphasises the distance from the mother, I didn't have the impression that she would intentionally alienate him. As a matter of fact I think she would find it interesting to become a part of that life. I thought it was something in Mark's character and his experience and so forth that made it difficult for him to ever be the Mark he once was…

SELVON: Oh yes, I was much more interested in Mark and his reaction than Joyce. I mean, you know, she was just a kind of figurehead to motivate and to show certain facets of both Adrian's and Mark's relationship. These are the people I am interested in. I am not interested in Joyce. I mean she has got her problems, I am sure she has, but I don't know much about the white psychology to put myself in her place and I am not going to attempt to do that. I mean I think I am intelligent enough to perhaps attempt it and do a passable job. I don't only like a passable job – I really want to get down to grips, and if I had tried to get into her too much I think, you know, I would have gotten into trouble in the same way as I might have got into trouble with Doreen in *Turn Again Tiger*. I mean I put her down superficially as a kind of promiscuous woman, you know, who would like to have an affair sort of thing; but I mean, I am not saying that this is my image of the white woman in the Caribbean. There must be quite fine ones; and the *best*, to tell you the truth, the *best* white people I know in the Caribbean are those who are as creolised as I am, and to me those are the ones with whom I get along best.

DANCE: You know that's very interesting. It makes me think about your portrait of the white woman. And I wonder if you realise, at least in the novels I have read, how extremely negative it is. You know, they are just there really waiting to be attacked by some darker man and relishing being ravished by them, I mean the moment there is the opportunity they literally throw their legs in the air!

SELVON: Well, I can see what you mean, but as I have just explained, I use them merely as figureheads. I am more interested in the other characters, in the Black man who has intercourse with her and his motivations and things like that rather than see it out of the eyes of the white woman.

DANCE: No white female critic has ever reacted to this?

SELVON: No. No. Not that I know of. Again, I say that I know that there are white people, white families who are completely ignored in all this talk about the Caribbean, who have been living there for a number of generations and have got children who have grown up and who are to a large extent just as creolised and un-racial as my characters are in the sense of identifying strictly with one race – they just grew up.

DANCE: Is Randolph in *I Hear Thunder* supposed to be representative of some whites of the time that you grew up – callous, greedy, epicurean, you know; he would not consider himself a racist and yet he has no respect for anyone?

SELVON: Yeah, he is a type too. He is a type that exists and he would perhaps typify a certain section of this same white Caribbean society that I am talking about.

DANCE: Now you were talking about the process that you envision in the Caribbean of all races coming together as one, which is a very positive thing. In this particular novel I was disturbed that all races were moving towards Randolph, that Adrian and Mark were moving towards becoming one with Randolph, a kind of whitening process that in this case is extremely negative.

SELVON: Yes. Well, there you are. I mean I know in many ways that *I Hear Thunder* is a depressing novel towards that idealism that I talk about. Still, it is, I think, a truthful image that I try to project as I saw it at the time. But let's put it this way, that it's an ideal that I am striving for myself in my own life, and it's an ideal that I would like to see among my own peoples of the Caribbean, and it is, if I have a theme, if I have an axe to grind, it is this – that I would *always, always* show why this thing *isn't* working and try to show positive elements towards why it *should* work.

DANCE: We tend to refer so often to Caribbean literature, to West Indian literature, as if all of you writers from whatever island or of whatever racial background, are all in one bag, and I would like to know if you see some distinctions in Trinidadian literature, shall we say, which makes it distinctive from Jamaican or other West Indian literature; should we consider it – the area – as one?

SELVON: I don't think it is possible to consider the area as one purely because, as I say, the object of a unified nation still hasn't been attained and it would be – well let me put it this way – I think if I were born in Jamaica and grew up in Jamaica I might have been a different kind of writer entirely. I feel that in Trinidad the society is much more mixed than it is in any of the other islands.

DANCE: If somebody calls you a West Indian writer, do you correct him and say, 'No, I am a Trinidadian writer'?

SELVON: No. No. I don't. Because that again is my ideal you know. I like the word Caribbean and I like it to be used throughout the whole area. I don't really like the word West Indian. I think that it is a misnomer. I mean what do I call myself: an 'East Indian Trinidadian West Indian'? Jesus!

DANCE: I know you don't like to comment on other writers, but what about Naipaul? What is your reaction to, assessment of him?

SELVON: I have no reaction. I admire his *work* greatly. I think he has reached a certain level in world literature which he probably rightly deserves. And that's as it is, and his politics, his beliefs, his directions are his own; and I think every man, *every* man is entitled to those decisions. I mean I neither approve nor disapprove. I just grant him the right to be what he is and what he thinks about and what he writes about. That's good enough for me. I hope that everyone would think of me and my work in the same way, whatever direction it takes.

DANCE: One final question. Are there some aspects of your work that you'd like to talk about that I should have asked you about today? I've covered everything?

SELVON: I think so. I don't like these taped interviews really, because I would rather sit down and write out my thoughts. This is why I am a writer, I guess. I don't think that everything comes out of me in a very fluent and spontaneous manner in the way I would like it to, but I don't think I have said anything that I would want to go back and erase out the tape – To hell with it! This was meant to be a conversation, and as long as it's taken with that understanding, I feel pretty good about it.

———————————

CONVERSATION WITH

MICHAEL THELWELL

Michael Miles Thelwell, now known as Ekwueme Michael Thelwell, was born into a well-known Jamaican family on July 25, 1939. His father, the late Morris Thelwell, was a member of the House of Representatives during the 1940s and his brother, Richard Thelwell, served as Permanent Secretary in the Ministry of Mining and Natural Resources during the Manley administration. After finishing Jamaica College, Michael Thelwell attended Howard University, where he received a BA degree in English Literature in 1964, and the University of Massachusetts, Amherst, where he received an MFA in 1969.

A prominent activist in the Civil Rights movement, Thelwell served as Director of the Washington Office of the Student Nonviolent Co-ordinating Committee (SNCC) from 1963-6, and as Director of the Washington Office of the Mississippi Freedom Democratic Party from 1964-65. He was Chairman of the WEB DuBois Department of Afro-American Studies at the University of Massachusetts, Amherst, from 1969 to 1975, and is currently Associate Professor of Literature in that department. He serves on the editorial boards of *Okike*, *The Black Scholar*, and the *Massachusetts Review*.

Thelwell's first novel, *The Harder They Come*, (Grove Press, 1980) is based upon Perry Henzell's and Trevor Rhone's movie of the same title, the first feature film made in Jamaica. Thelwell's essays and short stories have appeared in numerous journals and anthologies. His essays have also been collected in *Duties, Pleasures and Conflicts: Essays in Struggle* (1987). His most recent work is his assistance in the writing of the political autobiography of the late Kwame Ture (Stokely Carmichael): *Ready for Revolution: The Life and Struggles of Stokely Carmichael* (2003).

Also of interest are the American Audio Prose Library cassettes, *Michael Thelwell Reads* The Harder They Come *(excerpts)* (1981); and *Michael Thelwell Interview with Kay Bonetti* (1981). Thelwell has received several grants and awards for his work. Two of his short stories received honourable mention in the *Story Magazine* Short Story Contests in 1963 and 1964, and his 'The Organizer' received the first prize in that contest in 1967. He received the National Foundation in the Arts and Humanities award for the essay, 'Notes from the Delta' in 1968. He was a Fellow of the Society for the Humanities at Cornell University in 1969, and he was the recipient of the 1969-70 Literary Award from the Rockefeller Foundation.

I interviewed Thelwell in Amherst on December 9, 1979.

———————

DANCE: When we first met and I talked with you about this project you suggested to me that there were certain writers whom I planned to include who weren't really West Indian writers or who should not be included. Let me ask you how you define 'West Indian writer'. What is a West Indian writer? Who is a West Indian writer?
THELWELL: Well obviously a West Indian writer is a writer who uses as his material the people, the experience, the languages and the culture of the West Indies – I mean, somebody who is involved with the culture of West Indian people and is involved in

their process of shaping a modern or contemporary literature out of the resources that that cultural experience represents – that's what a West Indian writer is. And I think for the record that one ought to say that I don't recall suggesting to you that certain writers shouldn't have been included, or weren't West Indian writers.

DANCE: [Laughter] You suggested VS Naipaul should not have been included.

THELWELL: Well, I mean since you're raising the name of Naipaul, Naipaul is *not* a West Indian writer, and I suspect that he would be the first one to affirm this. It's very clear, even though he does use the Third World, whether it be Africa, India or the Caribbean, as a setting for a lot of his books, he's really concerned with making a kind of Western literary statement; in addition to which, he has a great hostility, contempt even, evidenced by the judgements and comments he has made, for the peoples and cultures of Africa, for the people and cultures of India, for the people and cultures of the West Indies, so that while he may *write* about these areas, I don't think that really makes him in literary terms, in terms of his literary concerns and preoccupations, a Caribbean writer or a West Indian writer, any more than Conrad, as a consequence of having written *The Heart of Darkness*, could be considered an African writer.

DANCE: Tell me a something about your family. I gather from what you told me that they were reasonably well-to-do. Upper-class? Middle-class?

THELWELL: Well actually they were quite poor. My father died when we were very young, and after that time the only income we had was what my mother earned from working in an office, so that we were in point of fact quite poor in terms of what Mr. Nixon called his cash flow, but the fact is because it was a class based society – I mean we had a certain position in what I suppose one might term the Jamaican middle class – and we had a certain amount of credit and by scrimping along, we lived in genteel poverty.

DANCE: Let me ask you about folk influences in your early development. The folklore is a very important part of your novel. Where, when were you introduced to the folklore? In your family or elsewhere?

THELWELL: I mean it used to be that any Jamaican kid was introduced to the folklore everywhere. I mean the traditional kind of things that when you are a kid people would, you know, put you to bed, tell you Anancy stories and riddles, that kind of stuff – especially the people from the masses, the African element of Jamaican society, would tend to carry that stuff with you. I mean it would be a vital and living part of the experiences of people in the country. Also my family's background was from the country, and I used to spend vacations there, and in the country [among] the peasants the folklore is a kind of, a medium of communication and entertainment and exchange. And that's when I really learned a lot about duppy stories and Anancy stories, and riddles and that kind of stuff. My interest in it, and I was always interested in it as it took place around me in Kingston; that is to say again – if you're aware of the class divisions – the class into which I was born didn't have much to do with Pocomania churches or barnyards or the folk expression, the religious expression, the culture of the masses of the people. I found that fascinating and used to hang around those neighbourhoods, those poor neighbourhoods where these things took place, just to observe them, [including] the Rastas. I had a lot of friends among what the Jamaican middle class would refer to as the poorer class. I moved in that society – I can't pretend that I was a part of it because I always was a little middle-class young man visiting, but I had friends there and learned about it that way.

DANCE: I noticed as I looked over your resume that you directed the Washington Office of the Student Nonviolent Co-ordinating Committee and the Mississippi Freedom Democratic Party from 1963-5. How did you become so involved in the Civil Rights Movement here?

THELWELL: I came to this country in 1959. In 1959, if you recall, the student aspect of the Civil Rights Movement was about to erupt. That is to say prior to that time there had been [the] church-based, largely from the Montgomery bus boycott; but students started in 1959 coincidentally to take a very active social role, going into the streets. The non-violent direct action aspect of the movement became very pronounced. And so the first year I was at Howard, Howard being situated in Washington, students on campus started talking about having a demonstration or getting involved in the wave of demonstrations that were sweeping the South. And at that time Washington was still largely segregated and if Washington wasn't completely segregated, certainly Virginia and Maryland just outside the District were. It was impossible to be a Black student in Washington without experiencing certain levels of overt discrimination, which I had not been accustomed to in the Caribbean; and so when the movement started, I had one very simple question: how can I allow my friends and peers to go down town and demonstrate and not accompany them? Of course, the difficulty was that the Immigration wasn't likely to – there is a certain danger involved in doing that if you're a foreign student because you might then be deported, and it required a certain amount of thought on my part. In point of fact I remember the first demonstration which I had helped to organise: I had thought that discretion should prevent me from accompanying the people, and I stood watching the students getting on the buses to go downtown and I realised – I said, you know, 'Fuck it, there's no way that I'm going on to campus while this was happening,' and having made that decision I became involved in the Movement.

DANCE: You speak of it as if it's something one feels an obligation to do, and yet as I read the reactions of some West Indians to this Movement, it was something that some of them viewed with some suspicion, sarcasm, even contempt sometimes. Did you find most of the West Indian students at Howard as involved as you were?

THELWELL: No, but I didn't find suspicion, sarcasm or contempt either. I would suspect that if you found that attitude towards the Movement from West Indians, they'd be: (a) West Indians who didn't live in this country or (b) West Indians who were operating out of a very basic ignorance. I mean it is absolutely inconceivable to me that any borderline rational person could view that Movement as other than what it was, which is an enormous expression of the will and determination of Black people in this country to... at least to be treated equally. I started to say to be free, but that might be overstating it, but at least to remove the overt signs of racial discrimination from the body of society. No, the West Indian student at Howard did not become deeply involved in the Movement for precisely the reason that they were vulnerable to deportation, but I know none of them that were not sympathetic, I know none of them that were not very, very supportive, and I know none of them that didn't frequently express regret and make excuses for not being able to involve themselves more fully and overtly.

DANCE: Would you like to talk a little bit about your activities in the South, actually out in the field, during the Civil Rights demonstrations?

THELWELL: No, I don't want to talk about that, but I will say that the experience was one of the more significant experiences of my life – on a number of levels. I think this was the experience of everybody from the North who went South. There's a point at which, for Afro-Americans anyway, the South is the home country, and what I was surprised to find, when I first went South, to Georgia and to Mississippi, was how remarkably much it reminded me of the Caribbean. That surprised me, because I had grown up in a Jamaican situation thinking of Jamaica as a country which might have had a class problem, but essentially having the same Jamaican middle-class smugness about its sophistication and progressiveness in racial matters. That is to say, there was no overt racial segregation and discrimination, at least not segregation and discrimination which was legitimised in the legal system which was established by law. And going to Mississippi and looking at the plantation society, which had not evolved beyond that, and seeing a plantation society in which the racial attitudes which were prevalent during slavery had simple been taken and established in the code of law which governs the society was, first of all, an enormous kind of shock; and second of all, it enabled me to see certain things about Jamaican society, which at that time (and I'm talking about the '50s) were not quite so obvious, and in point of fact, regardless of whether there are overt signs of discrimination in a society, it is a victim of its history, a history very similar to the American South, a victim of its history. And what Caribbean people tend to term simply a class problem is basically a race problem which derives from patterns of relationships which evolved between the races during slavery and which still impose a kind of inertia on the class structure of the society and still impose that impression, still give form and content to social relationships. And so that to say that this is simply a function of class and to ignore the historical origins of it and its basis in history, and its basis in racial history, is to obscure the situation. So to say briefly what I've said at great length and not very well, the experiences in the South led me to a much clearer view and perception of the realities of the society which produced me, the Jamaican society; and the next thing that was significant – I think I have probably written as much about the American South as I have about Jamaica (since this is the first book on Jamaica that I've done), but the other thing I perceived was that there were certain elements which were absolutely common to Black Americans in Mississippi in the South and to Black Jamaicans, which could not be explained in terms of their history or in terms of the culture in which they were produced; and these things, by the way, are not true so much of middle-class American Blacks in the North or of middle-class Jamaicans regardless of what race. I'm talking about the Black people, and Black people who still live in the proletariat, but particularly the rural proletariat, the peasants.

DANCE: What are some of those similarities?

THELWELL: It's very difficult to talk about. But there is a style for example, a relationship to language, even though the dialects are quite different, a sense of social relationships, a body of religious imagery, which, when you analyse it, represents a view of the world. It's very subtle and yet very real because what it amounts to is a world view and a cultural tradition both in language and in song and ritual, a cultural tradition which clearly, while they may not even resemble each other superficially, in a very profound way essentially are the same; and that, I concluded, had to originate in African culture. And so I started studying traditional African culture and discovered that perception was accurate.

DANCE: OK. Let's talk a little bit about your forthcoming novel. Tell me something about what motivated you to write this book.

THELWELL: Well, there was a period, a time in which I hadn't written anything significant. I'd done a few movie scripts and stuff like that – *only* on assignment – when I needed some money and somebody asked me to do it, and I wasn't particularly interested in writing anything serious, and I'll tell you why. You see I don't regard myself as a *writer* the way a lot of writers I know do, and that is people who get very upset if they go through a week without having written something. And they define themselves: 'What I do is I am a writer. Therefore everyday I must write, everyday I must produce and I've got to publish a certain amount.' I think that is a misguided attitude, and it led, you know, to the chopping down of a lot of trees to publish a lot of crap which should not have been published in the first place. Writing is something that is very important to me and I enjoy doing it very much, but I regard it as something which is more purposeful than simply a means of self expression. I mean, I'm very opposed to a kind of bourgeois notion, bourgeois literary notion, that writing is some form of therapy for the people who do it. As far as I'm concerned writing by Black writers has to be historically and culturally very purposeful and very pointed. I mean there are certain historical roles and functions that the Black writer has at this time in the existence of Black people which is largely to reclaim and define our culture for ourselves in the way the white folks have been defining and elaborating their own cultures for a long time. And when I write fiction, obviously that is my responsibility. All my fiction has political themes, and all my fiction attempts in certain ways, with perhaps not as much success as I'd like, to use the cultural resources, the cultural traditions, the linguistic traditions, the very rich linguistic traditions of Black people, and to selectively mine these resources, which [are] the legacy of the Black writer, and weld them into, you know, literary forms, into modern literary forms – short stories or novels. I think that is an activist function for the writer, and a political one. And I see myself as a political activist who writes. Consequently I don't need to be writing all the time. And I also don't publish anything for purposes of building a reputation and a career. And there was a period of time in this country, not that I'd been very actively trying, when the kinds of stories that I would want to write, the kind of issues that I would want to deal with, the way I wanted to handle Black people and the culture weren't of great interest to white publishers.

DANCE: Do you have many stories that you've written and not published?

THELWELL: No, because I don't believe in writing stuff – that's what I'm saying, you know, I'm not going to sit down and write stuff because I *have* to write it and I'm *driven* to write. Usually when I write something I know where I can publish it; except some apprentice pieces I wrote in college, which I didn't get published, I don't have anything that I've written that wasn't published. I mean writing is a lot of work, to be writing stuff on speculation.

DANCE: You don't mean that you necessarily have a publisher *before* you write a story? If you find a theme that you're interested in developing you wait to write it until you find a publisher? You don't mean that, do you?

THELWELL: Yeah, I pretty much mean that. I mean, I pretty much have a good idea
– not necessarily a contract – but a good idea what I'm going to do with a story before
I sit down to write –

DANCE: Can we begin more specifically with the novel and how you came to write
that?

THELWELL: OK. Well, and I'm getting to that, actually, although it may not sound
like it. So that for a period of time since I didn't think that the white publishers were
interested in the kind of stuff I was interested in, I found it better not to write anything,
anything serious; and I also had been very actively involved in a project, that is
building the WEB DuBois Department of Afro-American Studies at the University
of Massachusetts, and that took a lot of my time and that accounted for five of the years
in which I didn't write; and my perception of what the white publishing industry
wanted accounted for another three or four years in which I didn't write; and I think
this is important because Black writers who think they always have to be publishing
consciously or unconsciously start to edit and structure their works around the
fashions of the white industry – the fashions and the assumptions of the white
industry and you can end up then writing works about the Black experience which
lack integrity and which lack authenticity because ultimately they're shaped and
structured around values and attitudes which don't come out of that experience. They
become distortions, and the same thing is true when writers become too enamoured
of the literary establishment – the Western literary establishment. So, having said all
of that, and I think this is a subject that I'll probably get back to in the course of this
interview – when Grove Press approached me and said that they thought the film *The
Harder They Come* had in it the basis for a very good book about Third World
experience, I agreed with them and expressed my interest in doing it, and my interest
was particularly this: ever since the government in Jamaica changed, I had started to
take much more of an interest. There was much more of a political interest on the part
of young people in Jamaica and it seemed to me that the whole intellectual atmosphere, despite what people are saying, had opened up a great deal. The realities of
Jamaican society and culture were being discussed in a much more accurate, a much
more meaningful and productive kind of way, and I wanted to make a contribution
to that. What I didn't think was that any white publisher in this country would be
interested in the kind of book that could do that, so that when Grove Press came up
with this idea it struck me that here was precisely the vehicle I was looking for. I
respected the movie and I thought the movie was perhaps more political than the
makers had intended it to be – more politically accurate than the makers had intended
it to be, and so I thought that since here was a publisher interested in this project it
would give me a chance to write a novel about the peasants and the workers in Jamaica,
about their culture, about their view of the world – and I'm not sure that Grove Press
expected exactly what they finally ended up with – so I was very anxious to do it and
that was how I came to write the book.

DANCE: Have they objected to any of what they've ended up with?

THELWELL: No, I think they respect it. I think they respect it. We had a lot of
arguments about how much Jamaican dialect the work could support and how
accessible it had to be to the general reader. When they say to the general reader what
they basically mean is to the Western literati or the Western public, and on that

question, it didn't seem to me that there was any room for compromise. I mean I had hoped that the book would be, and I had intended to write the book which would reach as deeply as I possibly could into the culture, the traditions, the legends, and folktales and the world view, not of the middle-class Jamaican who readers usually encounter in novels about Jamaica, but of the masses and that it would be quite uncompromising in its use of this material because I believed that that material could be used in as accurate a literary approximation of it as possible and still end up with a very readable, accessible work. I wanted the book not to be a book *about* Jamaica; I wanted it to be a *Jamaican* book, a product and an artefact of the culture itself, and I'm confident now that I've finished it that I succeeded in doing that, I'm very happy about it.

DANCE: Had you planned prior to this to include the glossary or did this grow out of this debate?

THELWELL: Well, it grew out of some of the debates we had, and I said 'Well one thing we could do is publish a glossary of terms from the Jamaican dialect which are not English words, not English terms, and would not be accessible to an American reader or a Western reader,' so that was a sort of additional argument to the publishers to be able to maintain what I considered to be the authenticity of the book. But what it turned out to be is a political event which kind of pleases me, because what I was able to do in the glossary is trace the African derivations of a lot of these terms, so instead of a simple thing telling you what the meaning is, you will learn, when you look at the glossary, something of the history of the words, where they come from, and how their meanings have changed. And then you also get a sense therefore of the real African origins of Jamaican mass culture.

DANCE: OK. Tell me something about the folk aspects of this work, for example the Rhygin songs. Is there a cycle of songs about him? You quote verses occasionally.

THELWELL: No. No, what there is – I don't know if this is what you might be talking about: there is a section I call 'Grapevine Version' or something like that, and it's people talking about Rhygin after he has become famous for this, you know, for this encounter with the police, and what I was trying to do – I was trying to do two things: I was trying to show the hold that he had taken on the popular imagination and I was repeating some of the speculations and attributes which were attributed to him, you know, he had a very powerful obeah, or he was, you know, a legendary figure. I mean a body of legends started to grow around the character. But the form in which I've put it is really based on the Yoruba praise songs, where they're kind of poems, highly stylised language in which praises of the Orishas – Shango or Ogun – might be sung, you know the Yoruba songs of praise for the folk heroes, for the legends, and it was really based on that, and I just invented that; it was an attempt to use again a traditional African form in literature.

DANCE: OK. When you were talking then, Michael, I'm led to ask you one question which I think will clear up something that I don't think you're implying, but it *might* be assumed that you are: you never attempt, do you, to impose Africanisms upon Caribbean culture where they aren't really there, do you? [Pause] Do you understand why I'm asking the question?

THELWELL: I understand the question you're asking. I use those Yoruba praise songs as the form for a commentary in the little section on Rhygin, as an African form which I've imposed on the book, but so far as the events which take place in the novel, as far as the cultural events, the expressions of African culture that you see there, they're either things that I personally witnessed or they are things that I've read about, and overwhelmingly they're things that I've witnessed or heard about or been told about. But you know if anybody accuses one of doing that, they'd have to be particularly ignorant, because there is no question that while Europe rules in the Caribbean, Africa governs. The lifestyles and the cultural styles of the Jamaican peasant are profoundly African. One doesn't have to impose Africanisms on it; it is profoundly African. One of the things that happened is that in my study of traditional African culture and particularly my study of the writings of Chinua Achebe (for whom I have the greatest admiration, love and respect. I think he is the most significant Black writer that has come along, since the beginning, the most significant Black writer), but from my study of traditional African culture what happened was that I was able to recognise as Africanisms things which I had just taken for granted as the lifestyle of Jamaican people.

DANCE: Yes, but they're there. That's the point I want to make.

THELWELL: Precisely.

DANCE: All right. Is the problem story still popular in Jamaica?

THELWELL: I don't know. I haven't been to a Nine Night in twenty years.

DANCE: But twenty years ago you used to hear those problem tales like this?

THELWELL: Right.

DANCE: Is that one that you recount in the book one that you heard in Jamaica?

THELWELL: I elaborate on it a great deal. It's based on one that I heard. And it's based on one that I read in an African collection, and what happened is that in reading (and I remember that it was in a collection of folktales from Angola, I think it's called *Yes and No Dilemma Tales* [Alta Jablow, *Yes and No: The Intimate Folklore of Africa: Dilemma Tales, Proverbs, Stories of Love and Adult Riddles*, Connecticutt, Greenwood Press, 1973]) but as I read that I realised that I had heard a truncated version of it in Jamaica and a much changed version, so for the purposes of the book I simply restored it to its fuller context.

DANCE: In the novel Ivan becomes a different person after he returns home. Tell me something about what his return home means.

THELWELL: Well, that's fairly explicit, you know. I saw the events of that character's life as portrayed in the movie as a skeleton, a very strong and firm skeleton, on which I could rest the whole body of an argument having to do with the evolution of Jamaican society or the devolution of it, whatever the case might be. That is to say the urbanisation, which is such a blight on the society, and the destruction of the peasant culture because of the development and modernisation and so forth; and since that was one of the things I really wanted to deal with very centrally in the book, using the story of this man as an excuse to do so, I was very careful to add to the movie the first hundred and fifty pages which evoked peasant life in a hillside community in the Jamaican countryside – not I hope simply to describe the behaviour of people in their day-to-day lives, but to show that it was informed by a certain kind of vision. And a certain set of values, a certain kind of stability and a certain dignity and sensitivity which becomes totally scrambled and destroyed in a very predatory, jungle-like situation which obtains in the cities; and it is a profound kind of difference – it's a difference between an individualistic, predatory, materialistic, incoherent, desperate kind of existence, which is of course the urban existence and the rural existence in which is a certain organic relationship to the land and to each other and to a sense of tradition, and which while people may not, you know, have had a great deal of material comforts, they were certainly self-sufficient in anything that they basically needed, and it was a very healthy existence from my recollection as a small kid among the peasants in the country of Jamaica. And the destruction of that – so that I was at some pains in the first part of the book to try to establish that, and that when he returns home, it was devastating – not only [because] the older generation was dead, the generation that represents that tradition in fact, but progress has come to the community. Hippies are living, you know, in the homestead, the old homestead; the family plot of his own family, the family home of his own family, is completely overgrown and gone back to jungle; and I experienced something like that once when I went back to Jamaica. Even if you don't think about, you know, the importance of that ancestral home while you're not there, to come and see it completely changed, to see it gone simply back to jungle; it is a very crippling thing and so it seemed to me a device, or a decision in the book – his coming home to find that happening – to find condominiums built up where a fisherman's beach used to be, to find hotels taking over the beaches, to find that the basis of people's existence has now changed and they are now dependent on these forces coming from outside – that the countryside had been impoverished, spiritually and materially by development; and when that happens to him, for the first time he loses his moral base and he's truly alienated, truly alienated and that makes possible the things which then happen to him, and which he is capable of doing when he goes back to Kingston. What I hope is hidden in that is a kind of statement about the kind of urban violence which has been plaguing Jamaica [so] much in recent years, the origins of it and the basis of it.

DANCE: May I go back to the thing you said just before this. It seems to me that when he returns you give him two alternatives – you suggest that [the experience] destroyed the moral structure and then he proceeds on, towards what we would call a life of crime – killing and that sort of thing. But it seems to me at first there's another alternative when he tries to recapture the essence of that life with the young boy by telling him stories and that sort of thing. That's not given as an alternative reaction to…

THELWELL: That's not really an alternative. That is an act of desperation and nostalgia, of personal comfort. The alternatives that he faces when he goes back: it's simply that he's got, you know, two alternatives – one is to make it in that jungle, which is the city, or to be destroyed by it; since he no longer thinks that he has a refuge in the country to go back to, he is determined that his entire existence is now going to have to be an urban one. He's got to make it there. And what we see is a perversion of some of the kind of independence and self-reliance and self-respect that he developed as a kid in those hills, and what it becomes is a desperate attempt of, 'Well I'm not going to be defeated, I'm certainly not going to be defeated. I will do whatever is necessary.' There's one level at which that might be considered heroic: his determination not to be overwhelmed by the forces which surround him; and there's another level at which it is really desperation, and he will do anything; he becomes capable of a kind of violence and predatory behaviour which I would argue is not basically a part of his culture, not basically a part of his personality; it's a distortion of that culture. That is what I'm attempting to establish in that section.

DANCE: Do you attempt in the book to illustrate to us who the main villain is in the perversion of this culture?

THELWELL: It's not a question of *who*; it's question of *what*. And there is no main villain. I mean that is the sadness. On the one hand, certain historical decisions about the path of development which were taken by the Jamaican leadership is responsible. On the other hand, the pressures of population are going to force people out of the country anyway. I mean, as the population steadily expands, for economic reasons there is an escalation of population pressures, of the absence of resources for development, the absence of the kind of money for really building the infrastructure that the country needs. At the same time that the population becomes younger and more numerous, I think there is a disintegration of Third World cultures, Third World societies, and that's not true only of Jamaica, but Jamaica because of its size, it's so small that you can probably see it more clearly there than you can see it in other countries. I see the future for the Third World over the next fifty years as being one filled with incredible dislocation, incredible waste and destruction of human life, of human personality, incredible dangers for bizarre political kinds of alternatives; you know the Third World faces, particularly the African world, the post-colonial world of Africa, faces some overwhelming kinds of problems, some overwhelming tough, difficult, sometimes almost apparently insoluble problems, and it's going to require a hell of a lot of luck and a hell of a lot of resourcefulness and courage and determination too on the part of the people in leadership in these nations if they're going to survive the next fifty years and start to plan a future, and move towards a future which will be somehow more acceptable and – so there's a whole confluence of historical pressures, only one of which, as for example the selfish, narrow-minded and shortsighted attitude of the middle classes in these countries, and that's only one of the problems so that, you know, who *is* the villain? The villain is history.

DANCE: Could you tell me what you consider the four or five most important books that have come out of the Caribbean area.

THELWELL: I prefer not to do that and to answer that question in a much more general way. There are some books which I respect very much and which I think are important books, but I think that Caribbean writing, Caribbean literature, faces, has faced for a long time, which is not unlike the situation that African literature is in or was in, has been in; and that is most of the legal definitions and most of the arsenal of terms and forms which the writer receives comes to him from the West, and in fact the notion of a writer as a career is a Western notion – there ain't no such notion in Africa. There are oral historians and there are story-tellers and all that kind of stuff, but the writer is not an African notion, nor is the novel, even though there are certain antecedents and equivalents of the novel in traditional African culture. The novel is a Western form. Most writers tend to be people who are traditionally educated; there are very few writers taken very seriously who are not traditionally educated. One of them that I can think of who wrote *My Life in the Bush of Ghosts* and *The Palm-Wine Drinkard* is that Yoruba writer, Amos Tutuola, whose sensibilities and whose perception of literature is still very much based on the oral form, but most of the time when you have writers in the modern world they're Western educated people. The consequence of that is that they tend to be in a kind of provincial or colonial complex, they tend to embrace very quickly the fashionable material coming from Europe – existentialism, alienation and all that kind of stuff, and tend to address their writing towards what the West calls in its smugness the community of educated people. What they really mean is that if they're doing that and you're a Black writer, a Caribbean writer, an African writer, you're really addressing the Western literati, you're addressing the literary editor of the *New York Times*, and the *Times* of London and *Partisan Review*, and so forth and so on. The most important Caribbean books are the ones that have recognised this and have consciously set themselves to correct that – works that try to use the experience and culture of the people and try to create the form of literature which is an expression of Caribbean culture and experience. The most important African writers are the ones that do that, and the most important Afro-American writers are the ones who sense that this kind of cultural imperialism has defined to a large extent all the Afro-American literature, most of the Afro-American literature, that we have. What do I mean by that? I mean the stuff that got published, the stuff that got praised, the stuff that didn't die, so that just by virtue of the white folks controlling the presses and the publishing houses, they are tending to define what the body of Afro-American literature is like. The important books are the ones that understand that and try to correct it, try to reflect in the literature the values and the forms and the style, which come out of the community.

DANCE: You can't tell me a few works that have most effectively done that? Or you won't?

THELWELL: I won't – nor will I tell you the ones which patently have not done that; for it seems to me that I've said enough that people can look and see, you know? Well, let me say this: by and large the work of Vic Reid, I think, is very important for precisely those reasons, and Andrew Salkey in his very long career has had a consistent involvement with Jamaican culture, with trying to reflect it accurately and to use it, and to preserve it in literature, so that the careers of these two guys, it seems to me, are the careers of two writers who have what I consider to be a sensible, productive, useful sense of what their roles and responsibilities should be as writers. That's as far as I'm going to go on this.

DANCE: OK. I won't ask any more questions: I'll just ask you…

THELWELL: Hmmn. There's a young Trinidadian writer who has a novel, the manuscript of which I saw, *The Dragon Can't Dance*. And I think his work is absolutely important, very significant, extremely skilful thing. Another reason I liked *The Dragon Can't Dance* is that it involves itself in the culture of the Trinidadian masses, the people who make up Carnival, who dance in the band, and it was very much involved in the life and the problems that they face and how they cope with them: and it seems to me a very mature, very sensible, very powerful book. And so I think there is a tendency in Caribbean writing – there has to be a tendency to affirm some kind of identity, some kind of political identity in the world for the Caribbean nation. It's got to be accompanied, got to be accompanied by a struggle to affirm some kind of literary and cultural identity – and that requires, for the first step, that the Caribbean writer is going to have to have – and a great many of them do this – have to get rid of that provincial attitude they have where they're writing to, they're addressing their works to, and they're trying to impress the European literati – and the unfortunate thing is that you try to impress the European literati by demonstrating to them how well you have mastered the nuances and the forms and the genres and the concerns of Western literature, which may not have doodly squat to do with the forms and the concerns and the values and the attitudes and the problems of the local culture, of the Caribbean culture itself. And that is a form of participation, complicity in cultural terrorism, but most of these writers don't seem to understand that – writers who do this – who shall remain nameless.

DANCE: OK. Is there any issue that we should have touched upon that I have not asked you about that you'd like to comment on?

THELWELL: Hmm. I might say something [more] about one of the things that I have touched upon. I mean I really think that it is a truism that there are times and situations in which writers do themselves and their cultures a service by remaining silent – absolutely. And if you're in a situation where there is not any national publishing house that you have [access] to, which is true of a lot of Caribbean writers, and if you have to depend on Western capitalist firms to publish your work, writers should perhaps ask themselves sometimes, if the only thing I can get published at a given time is something which feeds into the biases and prejudices and attitudes of the West towards the culture, is it really my responsibility as a writer to be writing and publishing in that situation, or should I simply, you know, withhold the stuff or wait until I can write on terms which I consider to be more fair, more desirable, more acceptable towards what my mission as a writer is. Quite clearly there are certain periods in which people shouldn't write, certain conditions under which people should not write and publish if they're serious. I said earlier that I consider myself an activist who writes, rather than a writer with a capital W. There was an incident which might help to explain that. When I was just getting out of college and very much into writing a lot, I was overwhelmingly (as I think anybody Black in this country had to be), overwhelmingly impressed by, appreciative of, the work James Baldwin was doing. I had a great, great, great deal of respect, admiration, gratitude for him and for that body of work he was producing at that time. I had won a few prizes and I had come to the attention of people in the literary establishment – had even acquired for myself an agent. Anyway I found myself in this meeting with a couple of editors, one from a small literary magazine, one an editor for a big national magazine and some other literary people – all white – who were somehow admirers of my work; some of them took credit for having, quote, 'discovered' me. And I found that there was a real agenda, and the agenda, of course, was my career. And people had ideas that I should place stories here, place stories there, what I should do. Everybody was taking a real interest and it was quite flattering until one lady said, she says, 'Oh, no, I'm so certain that, I'm so certain, I feel it so strongly, I just think James Baldwin has' – he had just written, *Blues for Mr. Charlie*, which had not been well received particularly because he said certain things about white folks – I mean it was a lot more aggressive in some statements he said about white people than some of his other works had been. She says, 'That last work of Baldwin's, you know. I think he's just finished, and we're absolutely ready for a new Black writer, and I think you are it.' And the scales fell from my eyes, you know, and I said, 'You are, are you?' And there was some talk about a fellowship for me which would enable me to write a novel. And I went to SNCC and said, this is one of the periods in which I will be active and I will not write, I'm certainly not going to write under those conditions. I think that is very important and I think until Black writers, African writers, Caribbean writers divorce themselves a lot more fully from a certain Western definition of what a writer is and from all the pretentiousness which accompanies that and from all the affectations which accompany that and perhaps start coming together, you know, recognise this problem and start coming together to discuss solutions, and start having serious kinds of dialogues with local governments – and those governments are very, very embattled right now. I mean the overwhelming burden of social and economic problems (which are escalating – every year they get worse as the populations grow) perhaps don't leave them much time or much resources really to consider the creation and assimilation of literature as an important social function. But it seems to me that that discussion has to begin, that discussion has to very seriously begin, so that it can set about in a really deliberate and conscious way the creation of a national literature, and I find it very significant that since the revolution in Cuba made contact with the Western literati and the Western literary establishment very problematic, and you don't get a whole lot of books from the West coming into Cuba, Cuban writing has become much healthier. It has started to examine Cuban themes, Cuban background, Cuban culture, to look at Cuban political development in a way which clearly wasn't possible before the revolution and it is not nearly as colonial in its tone – nowhere as colonial in its tone, nowhere as derivative, nowhere as dependent as most of that Latin American literature which is so widely praised in the West precisely because it patterns itself after and resembles modern Western literature. Because Cuban literature addresses and turns itself inward and starts looking at and developing the historical and cultural experiences of the people in all kinds of clever and imaginative ways, it has taken a quantum leap forward, and I think that we will necessarily experience then the same social and political revolution that took place in Cuba. It seems to me that the Third World has to become more seriously nationalistic in its approach to its literatures. I mean this notion that literature is somehow a universal thing is a myth propagated by the West – which only insures their hegemony. Anytime you see somebody get up and talk to you about universal values and forms of literature, they're really talking about literature which resembles Western literature; and that is the great illusion that I think Black writers, Caribbean, African writers have to disabuse themselves. And that's one of the reasons why I think that the example of Achebe's work is so very, very important – because he has taken the cultural material of traditional Africa and formulated some extraordinarily skilful, extraordinarily resonant, extraordinarily successful novels which are very clearly in their very fibre, in their very language, in their very rhythm, in their very sensibilities, expressions of an African reality; the only thing they owe to the West is that they are novels. The overall form is Western. And I find that to be very, very healthy.

DANCE: OK. Thank you very much.

CONVERSATION WITH

DEREK WALCOTT

DEREK WALCOTT

Derek Alton Walcott was born on January 23, 1930, at Castries, St. Lucia, one of the Windward Islands. After finishing St. Mary's College, Castries, Walcott received a scholarship to the University College of the West Indies in Mona, Kingston, Jamaica. For several years he taught in Jamaica. He has worked as an art critic and book reviewer for the *Trinidad Guardian*, as a feature writer for *Public Opinion*, the organ of the People's National Party in Jamaica, and as artistic director of the Trinidad Theatre Workshop, which he founded in 1959. Recently he has taught at a number of American colleges and universities, including Columbia University, New York University, Yale University, Hollins College, and Harvard University.

Walcott's first volume of poetry, *25 Poems*, was self-published in 1948 when he was only eighteen. Other volumes of poetry include *Epitaph for the Young – a Poem in XII Cantos* (1949); *Poems* (1953); *In a Green Night: Poems 1948-60* (1962); *Selected Poems* (1964); *The Castaway and Other Poems* (1965); *The Gulf and Other Poems* (1965, published as *The Gulf* [1970]); *Another Life* (1973); *Sea Grapes* (1976); *The Star-Apple Kingdom* (1979); *The Fortunate Traveller* (1981); *Derek Walcott: Selected Poetry* (1981); *Midsummer* (1984); *The Arkansas Testament* (1988); *Collected Poems: 1948-1984* (1989); *Collected Poems* (1990); *Omeros* (1990); *Poems 1965-1980* (1992); *Collected Poems, 1948-1984* (1992); *The Bounty* (1997); *Tiepolo's Hound* (2000); and *The Prodigal* (2005). His verse has also been published in a variety of magazines and journals and in numerous anthologies. He reads his poetry on Caedmon's Poets of the West Indies. Other audio-visuals of interest include *Ti Jean and His Brothers* ([videocassette] 1990); *Derek Walcott* ([sound cassette; interview and reading] 1990); *Omeros* ([video cassette; discussion with Walcott and Carolyn Forche] 1990); *Omeros* ([sound cassette of interview by Rebekah Presson] 1990); *Derek Walcott Reads* ([sound cassette] 1994); *Derek Walcott Pantomime* ([video cassette] 1995); and *Walcott on Poetry* (1995).

Much of Walcott's energy has long been devoted to the theatre. His published plays include *Henri Christophe* (1950); *The Sea at Dauphin* (1954; second edition: 1958; included in *Dream on Monkey Mountain and Other Plays* [1970]); *Drums and Colours* (published in *Caribbean Quarterly*, March-June, 1961); *Dream on Monkey Mountain* (1970; first produced in 1967); *Malcauchon, or The Six in the Rain* (1966; published in *Dream*, 1970; first produced in 1959); *Journmard* (1967); *The Charlatan* (1967); *Ti Jean and His Brothers* (published in *Dream*, 1970; first performed in 1958); *The Joker of Seville* (1978; first produced in 1974); *O Babylon* (published in *The Joker of Seville and O Babylon*, 1978); *Rememberance and Pantomime: Two Plays* (1980); *Three Plays: The Last Carnival; Beef No Chicken; A Branch of the Blue Nile* (1986); *The Odyssey: A Stage Version* (1993); *The Haitan Trilogy* (2002); and *Walker and the Ghost Dance* (2002).

Also of interest are *Conversations with Derek Walcott* (1996; ed. William Baer); and his critical essays, particularly 'The Figure of Crusoe', 'What the Twilight Says', and his Nobel speech, *The Antilles: Fragments of Epic Memory* (1992). *What the Twilight Says: Essays* (1998) collected his later essays, as *Critical Perspectives on Derek Walcott* (ed. Robert D. Hamner; 1993) had done with his earlier writing.

Derek Walcott has received numerous honours and awards. In 1957 he was awarded a Rockefeller Foundation grant to study theatre in America. In 1961 he was honoured by the Jamaican Government for his contributions to the West Indian theatre. He has received the Guinness Foundation Award (1962); The Heinemann Award (1966); the Cholmondeley Award (1969); the Obie Award for a Distinguished Foreign Play (for *Dream*, 1971); the Jock Campbell/New Statesman Prize (1974); the Welsh Arts Council's International Writer's Prize (1980); and a MacArthur Award (1981). In 1972 he received an Honorary Doctorate of Letters from the University of the West Indies; in 1979 he became an Honorary Member of the American Academy and Institute of Arts and Letters, and in 1980 he was made a Fellow of the New York University Institute for the Humanities. In 1992, the year after his critically acclaimed epic-length poem *Omeros* was released, Walcott received the Nobel Prize for Literature.

Walcott's poetry and plays have a body of critical analysis, the most notable of which are the following: Edward Baugh, *Derek Walcott* (2006); Paul Breslin, *Nobody's Nation: Reading Derek Walcott* (2001); Stewart Brown, *The Art of Derek Walcott* (1991); Paula Burnett, *Derek Walcott: Politics and Poetry* (2001); Robert D. Hamner, *Derek Walcott* (1993); Robert D. Hamner, *Epic of the Dispossessed: Derek Walcott's* Omeros (1997); Bruce King, *Derek Walcott and West Indian Drama* (1995); Rei Terada, *Derek Walcott's Poetry: American Mimicry* (1992); and John Thieme, *Derek Walcott* (Manchester: Manchester University Press, 1999).

The following interview was conducted at my home in Richmond, Virginia, on the evening of March 3, 1981.

―――――――――――――

DANCE: I'd like to begin by talking about your family. I notice in *Another Life*, which I read as pretty much autobiography, you mention a Black grandfather and a white grandfather. What about your parents? Are they both Black?

WALCOTT: No. My father, who is dead, I did not know at all. He died when I was one (my twin brother and I). And my sister was three, I imagine. Now, once you start to go into ancestry in the Caribbean, you'll likely come across illegitimacy. Right? The further back you go. If you accept that you are one of the old families or something, I mean that's the history of the Caribbean. Now, from what I could tell, my mother, who came from St. Martin… I don't know much about her origins, her ancestry, nor do I know very much actually about my father's. My father's name was Warwick Walcott, my mother's name was Marlin, Alix Marlin. Now I'm not even sure… I know for instance that probably my father's father, my grandfather… the legend about my grandfather I know… Yes, now he allegedly (I don't know how true it is) committed suicide in the house or something.

DANCE: The fire?

WALCOTT: Yes. That's something I heard once or twice, and genuinely neither from curiosity nor from terror of that fact, or anything, I've never really been very interested in it (and I can perhaps explain this), nor have I been very interested in tracing lineage or tracing roots or anything, not because it will lead, culminate in some kind of embarrassment, because there is no one in the Caribbean who, if you take what is considered to be the norm in certain religious, organised societies, that would not come across something that might not be considered by such places to be socially embarrassing. I mean whether it is an indentured Indian family – right? the origins of that kind of family would be in a sense, you know, degrading, coming to the Caribbean; or whether it is a white, you know, descendant of a convict in Barbados, or someone. So all our ancestry is in a sense, bastardy. But it has never been anything that has disturbed me because I think probably quite apart from the social and historical reasons of the thing, the loss of my father, the absence of my father and my mother's strength in bringing us up, precluded any such interest in knowing any more than the fact that my father was dead. So to start from death and to go backwards was not a curiosity for me.

DANCE: OK. But aside from the curiosity, it certainly has had an impact on your writing. I mean there are so many references to the grandfather's dying in the fire and so forth.

WALCOTT: Yes, sure, that's there, but what I'm saying is that there is not in me a *search*, a curiosity about lineage. I mean that is something that one has heard as part of one's family. In other words I don't think of family past my mother, really, and to me this is the same sort of thing, as grotesque as it may sound, but I think it is peculiar in my case because of the fact that my mother lost her husband when he was extremely young and that all I was aware of as a child growing up, and getting into young manhood, secondary school, all that, was my mother's struggle. So that everything was much more immediate and important in terms of survival through her than in any kind of ancestral curiosity about where she came from.

DANCE: I can understand the point you are making, and yet I think one cannot ignore the impact on your writing of racial heritage, and the dual heritage…

WALCOTT: Yeah.

DANCE: And I'm simply trying to get some facts about that. Was your father white or Black?

WALCOTT: No, my father was mixed, but, you know, of a very light…

DANCE: OK. And your mother was…

WALCOTT: And my mother was light-skinned too, you know, and I imagine that her father was white, I think, I'm pretty sure.

DANCE: And you think your father's father was also white.

WALCOTT: Yeah, well I know that my grandfather was white.

DANCE: Your paternal?

WALCOTT: Yes. I imagine my maternal grandfather was also white.

DANCE: Now, in *Another Life* you refer to the white grandfather and the Black grandfather. So that would not be actually the situation in your case?

WALCOTT: Well, Black grandfather. Only maybe a great-grandfather on my mother's side or something, you know, that way.

DANCE: OK, OK.

WALCOTT: Yeah, but I'd like to finish off my point because I don't want to sound like I'm hiding or avoiding any kind of confrontation on that. I really genuinely have felt that it is not a matter of averting your face from the past so much as it is that there is a stronger sense of immediacy… there was a stronger sense of immediacy for me in being in the Caribbean [than anything] which has to do with the idea of ancestry, lineage, history, tradition, and family – right? – that I thought very early was not something that say another kind of writer would be curious about. I mean I felt that from my childhood – not childhood (that's too early) – but I would say from college, and certainly when I was a young master at college, that my strongest sensation was of this beginning – right? – and that the past to me was more of an abstraction than it was a reality.

DANCE: And beginning means your memory beginning with your mother, and…

WALCOTT: No, an immediacy, beginning, in terms of the fact that there were no writers – that I was going to be a writer and that what I was writing when I was putting down the names of things that had never been put down in my island with any intensity, well, as the naming of trees or writing a poem or something – that I had *no* predecessors; and therefore, *family* predecessors – right? – were less important to me than *literary* predecessors, you know?

DANCE: Yes. Well, let me ask you this too. In *Another Life*, there's a sense that you are trying to decide who your predecessors are, and it gets to be racial – or European versus African (versus is probably not a good word), and there's a period when you obviously, like many Black people, mulattoes, wanted to be white.

WALCOTT: Oh, well, that whole experience is another thing, you know. You haven't finished the question, but that's a whole different kind of experience that I can still describe. So you'd better finish the question, and then I will…

DANCE: Well, it seemed to me that there's a connection, because it seemed to me that the family background obviously led to this, and the more immediate the mixture of race, perhaps the more immediate the problem is for you. All of us practically in the Diaspora are mixed, but for many of us it was three, four generations ago. I assume that you might even have known your white grandparents, but that's not true?

WALCOTT: No, no, no. Well, let me see. To try and clarify it. Physically, for instance, when I went to visit my grandmother, who was a very quiet, strong, as was the usual type figure, whose name was Ma'am – she was called that, we all called her that – her daughters were almost white – that is my father's sisters, right? And she lived in a very poor section, sort of a barracks type place, tilted, I mean it leaned, teetering over.

DANCE: This is in St. Lucia?

WALCOTT: Yeah. But near the Cooling Station, near the wharf. Now inside it was fine, but the actual – in fact, that section of the wharf was called the City of Refuge, I remember going there… very pleasantly going there because there were a lot of my aunts, you know, who were very nice, and we'd get comics and stuff like that from America, and I'd go there and read them. Although Ma'am did not talk a lot, you know, you felt a great warmth. You'd be in awe of her, but you felt that… You know she was Black. Right? So I imagine that she must have been perhaps a servant or something. I don't want to get things wrong, for my relatives' sake, but I'm just saying that probably that was what it was. Now I may be wrong, but that's about as far as I know, or knew. But what is more important to me, the same thing that I'm reiterating, is that the curiosity was not there, and I think that I have believed this because I have always been aware from very early of wanting to write, you see, and this absence of a curiosity about… of thinking in a linear way about inheritance is, I think, part of what I am, but it may be that a psychologist could associate that and define it as an absence, a vacuum that is filled by writing or whatever. I feel, for instance, definitely, that the sense of dedication I had from extremely young was a dedication, really, to continue my father's work. This is a fact to me. Now this was such a fierce inheritance to have had as a child. You know my mother was constantly talking about my father. I don't believe in psychic things at all, but I do remember feeling that once I encountered my father on the stair. But this may have been a wish. I didn't see anything, but I felt it there. Now that may have simply been a linear definition given to a presence that was always there in the house. So that was very early for me what history was, I mean linear history, I mean family history; that's about all that it was. When it comes to two things, first of all, the thing, if you wish to talk about it later, about *wanting* to be white or feeling that it would have been better to have been white, which is not quite the same thing, and the other thing of feeling that one was a writer or poet early, that really gave me a great deal of confidence, because I felt in a religious sense that my father's death was an interruption that had to be continued. Right? Because we were Methodists and my mother's constant presentation of my father as… whatever he was… I mean all of the very good things about him. In fact, just this year my mother was staying at my aunt's place in St. Lucia, and my aunt said: 'You know, you keep telling these children about Warwick (which was my father's name) and he's so perfect and so on. He wasn't *that* perfect.' And she was going on like that, you know. She was a very beautiful and, she is an aggressive woman. She *is* aggressive, you know: but full of humour, very vital and so on. But honestly, when she was saying things like, 'He wasn't all the gentleman that you've made him out to be,' one knew, it was simply that whatever faults he had (and my father, in my mother's opinion, was a faultless man, right?) that this was nothing deeper than his sister saying: 'Well, he's not God!' You know what I mean? So, that was my history; that was a sort of a drive for me. I suppose another argument could be, of course, you don't want to look because if you look too deeply you might be ashamed of what you see; but you see, I think shame… is part of a condition inflicted on a colonial society. It's also a condition inflicted (and I'm talking much later) on literature as well, you know, because embarrassment and shame in terms of creativity is what inhibits a lot of people in post-colonial situations to drive themselves to avoid what would be called imitation, to avoid an ambition that seems to be the prerogative of, you know, a superior (allegedly) culture and so on and so on. Shame is not a condition that I've ever felt in terms of my work. What I have, like any child in my colonial condition, watching privileges… watching images, watching the authority of people who were white… and even deeper than that… the images that were impacted on one's mind either from movies or books or whatever was… You know, I would draw white people, right? It would be a long time before I drew or painted Black skins, you know, but that is a total conditioning that I think existed throughout the Caribbean, and I was not peculiar in that kind of situation. I mean that is a condition of colonialism that your mind is made to believe that even physically, even in terms of your hair or your skin, it's a sort of a blight to be Black.

DANCE: You mentioned also a slight disturbance (I don't call it shame) about the fact that the heritage, the literary heritage, is a white heritage, a Western heritage, one which seems a degree alien to you – you're the houseboy in the house of literature. You say when you copy Western ways, 'My voice sounded affected or too raw/ The tongue became burdened…' This quest, I suppose, for what you might call your own language… could you talk a little about that?

WALCOTT: Yeah. I think we're jumping over a phase.

DANCE: OK.

WALCOTT: I think… let us take early childhood because I read a lot. I was a very voracious reader as a child. The fact that my mother was a teacher, the fact that I had terrific teachers in a religious minority who spoke beautifully...

DANCE: By which you mean? Standard English?

WALCOTT: Well, I mean correctly. Yes, I'm not talking about an accent; I'm talking about speaking well, which is something that is inarguable. I mean I don't go for the argument about speaking well is for white people. I mean it's ridiculous... The example I would use is a simple example of the corruption of infancy, which is that the delight that a child has in what he likes – the limitations do not appear until that child begins to enter adolescence – then he becomes aware of social repressions, social barriers, whatever, that say to you either, one, you do not have enough money or you are not the right colour. But the intensity of feeling, of delight in what one loves as a child remains underneath all of that, right through one's life. But between that – what in Traherne is called 'the dirty devices of this world' – when you realise, not that your ambitions can't be realised, but that other people don't think that you should have them, that's a different phase. So when I was reading, and enjoying what I was reading, and wanting to write and writing very early, I felt no inhibition at all because, remember, at that age, when you said you were British, and you sung about the empire and you sung about India and Egypt – and on the map of the world at that time, if you looked at it, it was affirmed. It was pink – that was the colour of the empire, or red – and that stretched – because people have forgotten how wide it was. It included Canada, the Caribbean, England, I mean a huge amount of Africa, India, well including Egypt. Egypt was a protectorate when I was a child, the Sudan... I mean this was the world, right? Now when one sang, when millions upon millions of children were singing on Empire Day with one voice all over the world, what may apparently have been ironic later, as a post-judgement – postmortem of the irony, the truth is that there was a sharing, really, that the Indian child singing 'Rule Britannia' and the one in Canada and the one in New Zealand, and the one in Africa, and the one in Australia, and the one in the Sudan, and so on... It was more than simply an irony of things because in a way that empire was not only... The easy thing to say is that it was keeping people in their place. Right? That's the easy thing to say. It was also teaching; it was giving as much as it was – I mean not as much as it was taking – but it was also giving. And what it was giving was, it was giving law, it was giving literature, it was giving modes of conduct and so on. Now that may sound very stupid to say, but one would talk in a language, whose literature was yours; you knew that Shakespeare belonged to you as much as anyone else and so on and so on, and so therefore that whole globe was glowing from that colour, of the children singing, or the person singing, you know, 'Britannia, save your son; I'm a British citizen' *until* the world broke up and *until* these citizens began to go into the Mother Country and realise that they weren't. And that was the feeling, you know. So the accessibility of one to a literature, to Dickens or to whoever, had nothing to do with your skin, with your colour, because you were taught Dickens or you were taught Shakespeare, or whoever you were taught, as if it were *your* property, right? You were taught in English, you were an English citizen, you know, and therefore it was your privilege. It was part of your heritage. Right? The ironies come later, but that's there, and I think that that made a generation of writers, people of my age, between forty and fifty: and of course, the best, the most explicit argument of that is CLR James's *Beyond a Boundary*, in which what he is saying is, 'When I read Arnold, I was an Englishman.' Right? Now, the sort of Marxist argument about this could easily be made that, of course, you were exploited, you were made to become, think you were one. But the point is not that we were made to think we were. We *were*. Right? And nothing interfered with the delight (Right?) of knowing through literature, which is a phantasm to someone from that distance, the real world of Dickens or of Shakespeare, or whatever. Right? And this is still true that there's no ambiguity in James in being a Marxist and also being a Victorian. And this is the strength of James, that he has both minds. You know?

DANCE: When we are tracing that development, which we started to do, when does it begin?

WALCOTT: Well, you would have to take the period right after the War. During... *Well*, there's a war! I mean the War brought the world together. The War brought the empire together. I mean we sent people from the colonies to die, you know, fighting for Britain, or fighting, if you wish, for world democracy or for freedom. Or whatever. And we had fighter pilots; we had monuments to people who died fighting, people who volunteered to fight. Boys went out to die, and so on. Now the intensity of that war, the dramatisation of the war between freedom and tyranny, theoretically – [the] brutality of the Japanese and Germans as then presented, was an even stronger fusion of people all over the world. Right? So you had people who were in the services who went to draft, and so on. Well I was too young for that, but certainly I was part of that generation of people who had always been in between wars, but who were fiercely anti-Fascist, anti-Nazi, and believed in the valour of the British armies, because we had people in those armies, and so on and so on. So from childhood, say, up to about – the War began in '39 and ended in '45 – one is now fifteen... sixteen... seventeen. Following the War now, with these old ironies afterwards, when a little later you see the reconciliations beginning, you know, the Germany that you thought was a savage whatever, or the Japanese who you thought were yellow bastards, and so on. Much later, when the enemies now become friends (right?) or partners then – but I guess that's true of anybody who had been through those devotions and found them reversed, and so on. But say now, to sixteen or seventeen: I mean the strength is still there within you, of the values, the British values or the values of your own country, its laws, its culture, and so on, even as a colony; it's like someone in the provinces of Rome defending Rome against the barbarians. I mean you identify with Rome as opposed to the barbarians, and the Germans, Hitler the barbarian, and Tojo, or Hirohito, the barbarian. So that takes you pretty deep into adolescence – seventeen, eighteen, and so on. All right. But you see, there were other things you were aware of within your own society that were unjust, or silly, or superstitious, because I came from a minority, from a Methodist minority in a Catholic society, and so that was another war going on, and since Britain principally is a Protestant country, I suppose there was a fierce identification with Britain as opposed to the fact that there were *French* priests, *French* Creole, you know, *French* peasant priests. So all of that intensified the affiliation, but also made you more of an outcast, an exile, someone outside the Roman Catholic culture. So you were a Protestant, in a minority, in a small island which was French, and in a way, you felt a little more British than the people around you.

DANCE: OK. Let me... I keep seeming to harp on the racial issues, but...

WALCOTT: I know. I didn't answer the question completely. As to *when* one became aware... there's no moment that you can say you became aware of anything, you know, of being Black or being colonial, or being white, because you knew what was going on. I mean you knew about lynching, you knew about… well, America was a horrendous place in those terms…

DANCE: Well, rather than use the word aware, may I use one of your phrases in the 'Prologue' to *Dream on Monkey Mountain*. You say: 'Once we have lost we our wish to be white, we develop a longing to become black' [*Dream*, p.20]. Did you ever develop that longing to become Black?

WALCOTT: No. This is all very subtle to explain, very, very subtle. The longing to become Black is a way… it's a political kind of thing to say, you know… This was actually written at a point, at a peak in the Black Power movement in which one could say unless people were blue-black, they were not Negroes or Black or African. But one sees that the Revolution, as translated in the tropics (and misinterpreted there) became a reverse thing. Just as you would go in one direction by thinking out from Black to white, then the other direction took place of intensifying from light to Black, which is the exact thing, just reversed. So that is also prejudice – reversed prejudice, and that's what that statement means. So that it can become a career, you know. I mean there's a phrase which I've always enjoyed, which is somebody saying, 'You're a disgrace to the Negro profession.' Right? Now that phrase at that particular time, you know, would have been a very dangerous thing to say, but there *were* professional Blacks – even some of the writers. This over-assertion that would happen on the part of a lot of writers at that point, which was in a way a chicken sort of thing of protecting themselves, you know, saying, 'Well, look, I'm very Black' and so on. 'Watch out. I'm OK.' A lot of it was there. I can tell you a moment that I was writing about in a book, the prose book, I remember during the Black Power movement in Trinidad in which a lot of these people were out in the Square talking, with berets and leather jackets… Right? In black! On hot days, addressing people in that outfit! Right? Now, OK. That maybe something they chose to endure because they could identify with the uniform, and so on, but I remember being at the edge of the Square when there was a lot of rhetoric going on about 'Black is beautiful', and 'Power'. And when that first began, when you heard those shouts around, it was moving, because what you were seeing was really the beginning of a revolution, one would hope, that was based on economic justice. Right? Then, of course, it very rapidly became misinterpreted; it deteriorated into who was blacker in skin than the other. Right? And at some point, during this thing in the Square, I remember being on the curb, and I was crossing over, and this man began to talk. And there was just this reaction, there was this feeling in me; and I said to myself, 'Hey, wait a minute, you know, I'm red. My children… one of my kids is very light-skinned, and so on. And what is this guy saying? I mean, is he saying that this child of mine (who's very pale, you know, and has reddish hair, and so on), is he saying that she's not in his movement?' And at that point, I said: 'Now, wait, this is not for me, you know, because I don't care what sect, what race you belong to; any threat to my house is a threat!' So that part of it is also there, but finally on this point… in St. Lucia, I would say from very early, from the time that I began to move around the countryside (and that was very early) I would say in my teens, twelve, thirteen, whatever, I mean really going out to the country and travelling, the Africanness (which I didn't name, which nobody named) was so *there* in the country that I have never ever been able to understand what was the need to import it, aesthetically or as

a movement or as a piece of writing or any kind of theory. I mean I lived in it; I mean
it was there. And I have tried to write this too. There is a line in *Another Life* in which
I say, 'those who explain to the peasant why he is African.' I mean the reality – as if
some… someone, some political person or political kind of writer went up into the
heights of… you know, Dennery or somewhere up in St. Lucia, and, first of all, began
to talk in English to that person who is talking Creole and said to him, 'You are an
African. Do you realise that?' The first barrier would be the man's language, which
would be English. Right? So the guy who can't understand English completely,
although he could understand that sentence… you know, you can meet people… I
mean, some time ago I met people who could not speak English in St. Lucia, and
certainly others speak it badly, but I know I met a couple of people, one guy who could
not speak English.

DANCE: Let me ask you some more about that, because you referred particularly
to writers who make that trip back to Africa in this conversation and also in the
prologue. You said, more specifically, 'Some of our poets have pretended that
journey.' Were you thinking about Brathwaite?

WALCOTT: Well, there was a point when things were being dramatised between
myself and Eddie Brathwaite as being, you know, choose one or the other; take your
pick. And there were many points in Eddie's polemics that irritated me because they
implicated me, you know, and I wasn't very fond of the idea of this Bajan (you know,
this is territory talk) talking about Africa and so on. Now it's more involved than that
because Eddie *was* in Africa, lived in Africa and so on, But it was becoming a polemical
division and whatever exchange went on, I felt I should not have been in a position
to have to defend myself, you know. One resents being put in a defensive position.
On the other hand, on a larger basis, I am *very* annoyed about nostalgia as a political
platform because it creates inertia. I was trying to say to somebody last night that the
best thing you can do to a slave is to remind him of what it was like back in his home
country. Because you create a longing; you create a depression; you create inertia; you
create passivity. If the slave says, 'Look; this is my place as much as it is yours,' then
you're in trouble, right? You know? The other thing, even though it's induced by…
by the soothsayer, by the poet, by anyone that says, 'Let us long for Canaan,' or
whatever, 'By the rivers of Babylon we wept, then we remembered Zion', and so on.
That can go on – unless that turns into a very assertive thing that says, 'This is going
to be claimed' (right?) and it becomes active – then it's worthwhile. Otherwise the
other thing of, this sort of simmering pastoral longing. In these things nobody is ever
anything less than a hunter or king, you know, something princely, in that vision.

DANCE: OK. Let me ask you this. That journey back to roots becomes largely
symbolic, with writers in particular. Do you take the journey back to England, looking
for home?

WALCOTT: Not really.

DANCE: Well, you ride on a train there and you think of your grandfather and you
say once 'I am half-home' [*The Gulf*, p.21].

WALCOTT: That's true because half of me *is* England and half of me is… You're
saying that in England there is a sort of quest for… But there isn't. I don't think that
was expressed as a quest… As a matter of fact, right now I have been thinking that
maybe that's a part of my own mature that needs to be explored. What is there in me

that radically has some English source, and why shouldn't that be looked at? In fact, my presence in England – I've only been in England, really, three or four times, very briefly – so there has never been a rooted, pivotal kind of thing, beginning as a quest looking out, you know, leading from one spot, outward, you know.

DANCE: I'm not talking about in actuality, and I wouldn't think you'd even have to make the physical journey to… to feel that there is a quest for home in England, in Africa, wherever.

WALCOTT: I don't know. Well, this is a little important. I think this idea of home… [long pause] I don't know. I… I don't know. Perhaps my work can be looked at like that. I don't feel that I have ever felt less than that the Caribbean is home. I think the questions have been: the arrival – how did one get here? Where did one come from in a broader geographic sense and not so much biographical. But the assertions that I have tried to make, I think, from… from… young have been that *this* is home.

DANCE: OK. I keep persisting with things. There are many lines in your poetry that suggest, even though you are very much at home in the Caribbean, that you become, as a mature person, a stranger attempting to return home. You say one time, 'it is harder/ to be a prodigal than a stranger' [*Another Life*, p.150], for example, which suggests that there is something in your travels that has alienated you to a degree in the same way that those who have lived abroad for a longer period of time…

WALCOTT: Yeah, perhaps even more deeply, but you see there is not any difference between say, Thomas Wolfe saying you can't go home again (he is not saying that there is no home) and Frost saying that 'Home is the place [where], when you [have to] go there, They have to take you in.' You know, it's the same… I mean the home is there. The person entering the home, and if you use this in the whole sense of the Caribbean and the whole sense of one island (Right? Perhaps?) that whatever has caused this alienation can develop for all sorts of reasons. It can develop from the fact that the more you, yourself, become in a broad way, educated or even if you want to use the word… well, not famous, that's not such a strong word, a good word. But I mean… In a way, the penalty is that the more you identify, the deeper you alienate, in a sense.

DANCE: The more you identify with outside forces or…

WALCOTT: No, no, with your *own* people in the Caribbean or anywhere. I mean, if Wolfe writes about his towns in the [South] truly, then the truth is going to alienate. But it is the intensity of his love and concern and honesty about Carolina that makes the alienation. In a way this happened to Naipaul at the worst. I mean that the profundity of his concern has alienated him even more, so there is, you know, there is a kind of penalty that goes with that, and so this sort of homelessness at home is very strong in the Caribbean writer for very many reasons. One of them is the fact that you are not really a functioning writer in a place that doesn't have a publishing house, that doesn't have X or Y or a theatre, that doesn't have proper theatres and stuff, so the more you work at it, the heavier the penalty – or realising that you're moving away towards what you think it should be. I think that there was a very Wordsworthian and Romantic, Shelleyan and all of that (Marxist if you wish) social vision – the whole vision of the Caribbean is not a purely political one. The islands *are* paradisiacal, you know, they *are* that. The poverty in it, set in a paradisiacal situation, almost acquires some of that [Romantic vision] – which is a very, very strange thing to say. When I used to paint (I thought I would be a painter) I would not paint a brick house on a hillside. What I would paint was a shack on a hillside, and somehow those shacks organically came out of that landscape, they were right against that landscape and the concrete blocks were wrong. Now, concrete blocks are richer, safer, whatever, and so on. So, in any formed culture, the architecture is organic to the topography so that the thing would look right from where it comes out of and there is a beauty in that. Otherwise, one would not be drawn to representing. Now what one says is, if you apply certain outside standards, and this is not a theory of poverty, like, you know, an Indian mystic theory of poverty or something theory of poverty, but there *is* something – I heard a man give a talk once, a Latin American, talking about poverty as a philosophical, even a sociological concept. Now that's not so ridiculous as it may sound. Because the other direction, the material direction in which dependency is part of the economic philosophy of the Third World, and because of dependency, exploitation and the multiplication of poverty by ghettoes and stuff, right, is really more degrading than, say, that peasant's shack, self-sufficient within his own garden. And this is very dated to people whose economic programmes encompass cities and large programmes and rockets and stuff, you know. So, in terms of the economic reality, the aesthetic and economic reality of the Caribbean, what it looks like to distort it into something, into plazas or into shopping centres and malls and highways and so on is a brutalisation of the sensibility, of the simplicity of the kind of life that is led there. It makes, for instance, the worst aspects of Puerto Rico or St. Thomas and so on; it gives this air of being… the Midwest, you know, a Midwestern town and so on, and these are the sort of things that are defined obviously as progress. Right? Now, what I'm saying is that we haven't brought, we haven't evolved, really, a life, a way of life, of thinking about life, that is still its own. It has always been modelled on one thing or the other, you know, I think we've had a history of substitutions and excuses. Right? We had the reality of the empire; we had the fall of the empire, the illusion of independence – because it is an illusion. It's an economic illusion – independence. And in between that, aesthetically, we have had the other kind of mental slavery, which is Africa; which is the nostalgia of re-enslaving ourselves to our pastoral dreams, without the reality of being where we are, So, always in the Caribbean we keep looking for large, big brothers, big ideas that will make us feel a little more important, and never relate to our own scale of things.

DANCE: All right. Well in terms of this sense of ourselves and who we are, I suppose that's a major theme you're dealing with in *Dream on Monkey Mountain*.

WALCOTT: Yes.

DANCE: And one thing that interests me is that Makak's negative view of himself is, as one would realise, the result of his acceptance of white Western values; but then it's the white woman who encourages him to a sense of racial identity: 'She say I should not live so any more, here in the forest, frighten of people because I think I ugly. She say I come from the family of lions and kings' [*Dream*, p.236]. Why do you have the Black man's sense of self restored by…

WALCOTT: The white image?

DANCE: Yes.

WALCOTT: Right. Because the white image is several things. The white image is, for instance, the muse. Right? You don't change the colour of the Muse. If, for instance, the Virgin Mary is Jewish (OK, let's say, you know, here's a Jewish girl who is the mother of God). The secondary thing to do is to wish that she were Black. That's the second kind of intelligence...

DANCE: But isn't it possible to envision a Black Muse?

WALCOTT: No, because the Muse as created... No, no, there's no need to give the Muse any particular colour...

DANCE: But you do very clearly. Excuse me.

WALCOTT: That's what I'm saying... The idea of substituting, say, a Black Jesus for Jesus, right, is to me an inferior spirituality because you can go *through* Jesus... you can go *through* the Muse and you can go *through* – both in terms of time and in terms of transparency, you can go *through* that image. And I made it deliberately that image because, like any journey, that image has its traps, right? Now it would be obvious if it were a Black girl... which he [Makak] would *not* have... You see part of the condition that is there in my character is that the image that he would consider to be ideal would be white. The association of what the images of myths, of the Virgin, of the Muse, of some pin-up that he might have pinned on his shack, would be a white image. Now for him to go *through* that, to have it Black, would be an immediate, you know, summary, you know, of... 'What would that be!' You know, I think it is the same parallel as a writer in language, in that the self-deceit of a lot of Black writers is to try to invent and to defy the sound of their own speech by restricting themselves to a sound that they considered to be primarily and only Black (Right?), whereas the obvious thing is you don't deny – I'm not saying algebra is white, but if you think of algebra as white, you will be in a lot of trouble as a mathematician, right? And if you think of yourself as a Black mathematician, you're going to be in trouble, because things are going to come up. Because then you get down to the absurdity of paper being white, and of ink being black, and so forth. And you'll get to a Genet kind of comic reversal where you say everything will become black. Now what Genet means is, yes, it will become black because if you think of it as black, then it is black. Right? It is yours. Right? Snow will be black, everything will be black, and so on. All right? But to make that journey – the quest that he goes on is no different from a knightly quest. Right? The knight, you know, on the medieval journey is the same sort of thing. The person who leads, the quest object, is the one who leads the knight through the labours, through dragons, and through challenges, and out of that there is supposed to be, finally, a consummation. Right? The person is joined, the longed for object, the consummation takes place in the arrival. All right?

DANCE: Uhn-huhn.

WALCOTT: Now, what happens in the play is that in the end of it she is executed, and this is the point – that the purgation, the ritual, exorcism, the ritual execution is that moment when in language a writer says, 'Look, don't call me a Black writer because I know what you mean. Right? I am a Black writer. I am a writer who is Black, but don't call me that and don't make me begin to think like that because you'll have me thinking like you.' Right? So that whole journey, that transparency of going *through*, not only *through* in terms of the transparency of the object, but through it because she is also the moon, so the whole cycle of moonlight 'til sunlight to dawn is also the journey. And when he severs himself from her, when we sever ourselves from that mirror, from that image of ourselves that we thought we saw, when we have done that, then we are free human beings. And that is what the journey means.

DANCE: And it's not a purgation of that *other* that is dangerous?

WALCOTT: It is a ridding oneself of all of those poisons that are put there, purely by association, purely by, if you wish, an imperialist kind of condition in which every image is idealised, every language is idealised, as being the right one, the white one, and so on. And that that severance that… that brings liberation [is the one] that says, 'Yes,' you know. And the beginning of another journey happens, just a very simple journey of continuing to be who you are, that's all. You know, the object that is longed for, right, that he travels *through* to arrive *at*, is the one that finally, in a way, betrays him, but frees him. Right? It is like a man following the moon, believing that he will get there, and, you know, the next thing that happens is that the sun comes up, and the sun is a stronger light than the moon, so the realisation is stronger.

DANCE: It seems to me, Derek, and I may be reading this wrong, but the important thing is not that she frees him, but that he frees himself. Does that make a difference there?

WALCOTT: Yeah, sure, I mean, but how can that be done except it is done in the same undertaking that happens – that any knight in a medieval romance, you know, can only arrive at the maiden by killing dragons. Right? Now those dragons…

DANCE: But this man kills the *maiden*. This is the… it seems to be the crucial…

WALCOTT: Ahhh. That's the whole point, you see. That's the whole point – that the maiden – she says nothing. She never says a word. Right? So this, you know this sacrificial object that she becomes, right, is the thing that liberates him. I mean it seems to me… quite simply as a metaphor that the slave cannot but yearn for the condition of the master… Out of [an envy of his] comfort, out of an envy of his freedom. All right. The pursuit, the following of that, that journey towards that kind of freedom – not of mastery, right, comes at the point, the arrival comes when the slave knows that the master is no better than he. Right? But the master is someone beckoning, in the same way that this woman, this image is beckoning, and the severance happens when out of the nightmarish experience there is a purgation and that nightmarish experience is saying, 'Don't call me a second-rate human being, don't call me an ape, don't call me a Black writer, don't call me a Black dancer, don't give me that image of myself,' because she's a mirror in front of him.

DANCE: I almost hesitate to ask this question, after what you had to say last night about critics reading things into works that quite clearly the author already knew were there, but we aren't often telling the *author* what's there, but trying to help interpret for others. Were you consciously influenced by O'Neill's *Hairy Ape* in this play?

WALCOTT: No.

DANCE: No. Had you read *Hairy Ape?*

WALCOTT: I know it, I know it. No, not at all, I mean I would happily acknowledge it. What *is* the strongest influence – I've written about it – is Japanese theatre, I would think. I had wanted to write this play purely in sounds, if I could have made it, you know, as if the sounds had to be translated, and I think that the brutality of that idea of the grunt, you know, like hearing Japanese subtitles, like Japanese movies and so on, I tried to do this and I think it gave it some force because in the back of my head there was always this contrast between the inarticulate and the eloquent, you know, throughout.

DANCE: Uhn-huhn. Let me ask you about the influence of John Hearne on your work. I notice you acknowledge him in *O Babylon!* and also dedicate a poem to him. Has he been an important influence on your development as a writer or simply someone you admire?

WALCOTT: No, John hasn't been an influence stylistically on me. Not at all. But, as a friend, what he's always been, is someone whose conversation has always been brilliant. I mean his perceptions have always been very tough, very astute, very brilliant: and of course there's a friendship which is an intense thing. And most of the time these dedications are based, not on any debt to his work, but to his mind and his friendship. The fact that John Hearne and I have always admired the same writers for instance would hardly make him influence me. You know, we'd be influenced by the same writers.

DANCE: Yes, OK. I want to ask you about another line from a poem. You write in 'Codicil' (*The Castaway*): 'Schizophrenic, wrenched by two styles,/One a hack's hired prose, I earn/my exile' [p.61]. Are you often conscious of a Western audience that you are particularly directing your work towards?

WALCOTT: Well this was written simply about journalism. I've done a lot of newspaper work in the Caribbean, and it is ultimately a degrading work in the sense that you're poorly paid and then you're writing with little respect for – I think in the world of journalism there's a cynicism that always exists with a writer, that's always there. Then there's another kind of cynicism that one has always fought anyway, which is that as soon as you are a writer – and you *are* a writer – and it is seen that you are a writer, people give you attitudes that you don't have, provoke you into attitudes. I've had this a lot. In my drinking days, I mean, I had an act, in which I would let myself be provoked into all sorts of obstreperous conduct, which was of course what was expected, on the grounds that I was a poet. You see what I mean? So you're really doing a dance, you know, for certain people. Well *that* I learned to stop. So the 'hack's hired prose' thing is simply the torture of writing daily journalism as opposed to poetry – it wasn't aimed at an audience outside of that. I don't like the phrase, 'I earn my exile'; it's a little too pretentious. I think what it is saying is that I have paid my dues... I have done enough now that my [energy], you know, should be going somewhere else because it is really saying, 'this is killing me!'

DANCE: In an interview with Dennis Scott in 1968 you said that you were becoming more serene and that that was having a negative impact on your poetry. You said, 'happiness is not a theme for poetry these days' [*Caribbean Quarterly*, XIV, 78]. And it caused me to think about the tone of your poetry which is pretty despairing, particularly in the earlier works. Would you like to talk a little bit about that? Do you indeed feel that you cannot write when you are happy?

WALCOTT: No, I think when I said 'negative' – I wish I could have said that better because I think I went on to say (and I remember the interview) that the things I wanted to try to celebrate were very simple things, like your wife, your house, light, the moon, stuff like that; and that was hard to do. I mean it's very hard to praise simple things – ordinary objects – it is very hard, because generally it sounds selfish, and happiness is not a thing that is shared; having happiness is common, you know; and by 'negative', I think I must have meant that it was doing something to the vocabulary that may have become so domestic, you know, that ultimately what you would get would be something like *Woman's Home Companion* feelings. But there is a deeper thing than that; I mean… I think… there is a lot in Rilke that has that deep down happiness that is not a selfish happiness; it is… universal, it is subterranean, it is underneath the normal family experience, but to get there I think you have to be a better poet than I was then. The period in my life I was talking about, a lot of things had been resolved for me: I had stopped drinking, I was having a family, I was published, I knew who I was… not knew who I *was*, I knew that I would continue to do what I was, and the joy and happiness and exhilarations of *being* that existed for long stretches in my marriage, the second marriage, was what I wanted to talk about; but you know when you say things like, 'My wife is nice,' or something, you can say it better than that, you know – I think that is what I meant – that the vocabulary of happiness is very difficult to use, but I think that later with the loss of that, I mean this increased intensity, the meaning of that has increased for me.

DANCE: You frequently portray the poet, especially the West Indian poet, as Adam, a new man in a new world giving things their names; and yet most of the time there is not this kind of optimism in your poetry about the poet, who is the damned poet, who is the man destroyed by society, who is unable to find the language that naturally expresses himself. What's your present view of yourself as the West Indian Adam?

WALCOTT: No, I don't accept what you are saying at all.

DANCE: Oh, OK. None of it?

WALCOTT: No, I mean the despair and whatever. Sure. All right. But you see ultimately a work is *made*. Even if you write within the frame of a book, within the two covers of a book, you say, 'This is a despairing book.' The fact is that the book has been made and there is nothing that can be made totally out of an act of despair or a feeling of despair because there would be nothing. Even in Beckett, where the feeling is one of despair, Beckett is consciously trying to make a work of art out of what he is doing, regardless. I mean the thing has shape, it has an intention, you know, it has harmony; therefore it is an art object, whatever its content is. So that even the act of making that poem is an affirmation. Now even if the content appears to be despairing, there is other stuff around it; there is the society. I mean my bitterness about the betrayal of the West Indian people is *very* intense, and I don't want to sound like it's not a political thing. But the thing that is laughable, I imagine, to rationalists is the fact that one refers to the West Indian man or I say the West Indian poet in this part of the world as Adamic in this sense. But you see, physically, it is always renewed when I go back to the Caribbean. I go back to St. Lucia. I know it is home. I prepare myself just looking at it, against all the seductive nostalgia that anybody returning would feel. I look and I see the poverty and I see the condition of the people. It is something that I have known and I see what is true; I see a great improvement in living conditions and so on. And then I come around to some place that I have forgotten, that has changed a lot, or I might recognise a thing, a place or two. Then I come around the corner into the Cul de Sac Valley or into the other place (I can't remember the name now) and then, unrestrainedly, I gasp at the beauty of the place. I mean I do; you just say, 'Jesus!' It doesn't matter how you *want* to feel; this is irresistible! Now, I would much rather feel that than be someone who, say, is an economist who sees a banana plantation and poor people working in the bananas and shacks on the hill… because that I *know*, and… limiting, framing, and saying that *this* is reality… Reality is that these people over here are probably undernourished or backward or whatever and this is the big division between people who look. I am not doing that kind of mystic poverty thing; I am just talking about the exhilaration, the irresistible exhilaration. Even if it sets up its defences, it happens in the beauty of some parts, you know, those places in the Caribbean. Now maybe it would be less if it weren't home, but the fact that it *is* home intensifies it. And the other thing that is also true is that there are so many places that are virginal, really primal, in the Caribbean; that there are so many places in St. Lucia where there has never been a human footprint. I mean, it's true! You can call it 'bush', you can call it whatever you name it, but the fact is that there has never been an imprint of a human being on that soil. This is real. And that if one can lift one's foot up sharply and put it down on that place, the resonances of that are the same as the resonances that it meant for Adam to put his foot down in Eden. Now I'm not saying that the social situation is Edenic – I'm not saying that. But there's no political philosophy that does not start with Utopia – whether it is a Marxist philosophy, it is utopian – whether it is a capitalist, it is utopian, or whether it is anything, it is utopian. So that we can't be denied the right of an utopian vision politically, and in addition to having paradisiacal visions – several parts of the Caribbean – the two seem to me to go together, you know.

DANCE: I want to ask you something about a few people that appear in your poems. Anna, I take it, is a real person, your first love... somebody who still remains a romantic image of... what? the beautiful Caribbean woman? Is she mulatto, white, what?

WALCOTT: No, she's not a white.

DANCE: But very fair, I take it?

WALCOTT: Yeah. Yeah. But that is not the point in the thing. First of all it could have been anybody, I don't think we ever lose our first love. I think, you know, I think it would have been equally important to ask Dante – whether Beatrice was short or tall. I don't think – it's a consequence, the description is a consequence of who she is. It's not a fact that because she was this, one fell in love with her; it isn't that, you know, it's not the thing preceding it that makes it happen, you know.

DANCE: Well, the speaker in the poem frequently talks about his attraction to whiteness and so forth, so that I would think...

WALCOTT: Oh, yeah, but that's not there, that's not there in a – it's not a substitute – it's not a transference from, say, an aesthetic thing, from a painting or from whatever *onto* – it's not a transference from one onto the other. It's a correspondence and not a transference. Right? The fact that this person reminded one of... was a white screen star – but the person that she reminded me most of was Bergman. Right? You know. But that's not *because* Bergman was a white Swedish actress. That's not the point. The point is that this particular person had her own colouring – which is a mixed colouring. Right?

DANCE: Uhn-huhn.

WALCOTT: And the attraction – the love for her – you can't separate it... First of all the direction that you appear to be heading in is that this is an inaccessible – generally the connotation is that this object is inaccessible because it's white or because it's...

DANCE: Well it's inaccessible if it's *really* white. It's accessible if it's black enough to be accessible and yet...

WALCOTT: Well... No, no, no. The ideal is inaccessible, and therefore this person was not inaccessible. Far from that. The person was accessible. I don't mean the person was promiscuous. I mean the person was there, but what was beyond that was an idealisation of that person. Right? And not because of her colour, but because of who she is, because of what she was. So it's not an inevitability that it would have to be a girl of that colour. I mean that's not a *consequence* of it, you know. [Continuing the discussion of *Another Life*, Walcott mentioned his 'rage at the death of Harold Simmons', his friend and mentor who committed suicide on May 6, 1966.]

DANCE: When you say 'rage at the death of Simmons', what would be the rage? I understand the despair, but did you feel there were people responsible for the suicide?

WALCOTT: No, no. I wouldn't blame them for the suicide, but I don't think artists should be in a condition where physically they are reduced to suicide – not that one *has* to kill oneself. But I think conditions should never be such where it is inevitable that a kind of physical despair has to happen – and this has been very possible in the Caribbean. And it's a simple matter of fury... You can't blame the death of anyone on the state. Right? I don't think that it is the responsibility of the artist to [just to] endure. I don't think there's any laurel due to somebody just for surviving. I don't think conditions should be set up to test an artist's endurance. And what is totally infuriating is to see us pattern ourselves on a kind of nineteenth-century concept of the artist as survivor. That a country like Trinidad, particularly, that is so wealthy (people have no idea of how wealthy it is [Note: this was 1981]) has no programme for the arts! You know you go around talking about twenty years... twenty years later, about conditions in Trinidad to encourage simple things like, you know, a dance studio, or a good theatre, or a gallery. When you get older you realise that this is not an abstraction – this is your tax money that is not being used properly.

DANCE: What about the Trinidad Theatre Workshop? Is that subsidised at all by the Government?

WALCOTT: No, never ever. I spent seventeen years of my life trying to... Well, the way we operated was we would do a show, and we'd always be in the deficit at the bank. A lot of it I used was my own money sometimes... And the patronage was very thin. I mean, the people in Trinidad, (I don't want to sound like Naipaul or someone like that – it's not only his privilege to be cynical, I mean) the coarseness that exists – it's a kind of a hearty vulgarity that can exist in people who have money, whom I had to really at times go to and beg, you know, ask for help and so on and be given the equivalent of a tip, or be told by a television station that you have to creep before you can walk and all that kind of business: all these insults and so on are a part of the experience of the Workshop, you know. I suppose that things may appear to be a little better now from my point of view because they aren't as hard now, but I imagine that they are equally hard for the young, given the proportion of their age and what they want and going back twenty years, you know, to what I wanted at that age. So it has not really improved. I think it has remained the same. And it is even more insulting because the money is there.

DANCE: Uhn-huhn. And the Workshop continues even though you're not associated with it.

WALCOTT: Yeah, well right now I'm trying to finish off a play for them.

DANCE: OK. You referred in a poem to 'exiled novelists' who spit on their people and the people applaud and the former oppressors laurel them [*Sea Grapes*, p.88]. Who are these people?

WALCOTT: You're going to ask me if it's Naipaul. [Laughter]

DANCE: Yes. [Laughter]

WALCOTT: Yeah, I don't want to go on about Naipaul now because I'm very tired of the subject now, really. I've given up on him. Not as a writer, you know, because… I find it hard to read his books now because they are too, too poisoned, but yes, it's meant for Vidia, because I think the trap that he has fallen into, which he may not admit to being in, is that what he says, is really, *he* can say it, but… *they* don't dare say it really.

DANCE: They? Oh… the oppressors?

WALCOTT: Yes, yes. What he says simply confirms all the prophesies that were made, say, with the withdrawal of empire or the arrival of independence and so on…

DANCE: Does it disturb you that sometimes people suggest that you and Naipaul are very similar in having a kind of contempt, they suggest (I'm not suggesting that I hold this view), for…

WALCOTT: I suppose the difference is that I'm there. I think the view of Naipaul is that there is no hope, you know, just forget it! And I 'admire' a kind of mind that can dismiss an entire, you know, people – when I say 'admire' I mean that very cynically, obviously – but I think if there is any comparison, that my fury is earned in the sense that I am there – anger turns into contempt very quickly from a distance. Right? And so the further away you go the further you can spit, whereas if you are confronting someone there's more of a struggle, you know.

DANCE: Yes, yes. Are there any things *you'd* like to talk about…

WALCOTT: Last request! [Laughter] No, no, not really.

DANCE: Any West Indian writers whom you'd like to comment on whose work you think is very important?

WALCOTT: No. Well, the situation here now is tough because I don't think there are many novelists, for instance, published. There was a time when people thought there was a West Indian boom – a lot of the writers are still writing. They were young writers. I've always thought that when these writers get into their fifties, certain kinds of writers who remained subdued and somnolent in their work, that there would be another kind of explosion of some kind from these very writers around this time in their fifties and sixties… I think that if they keep writing… the whole traumatic thing between – that middle period for the West Indian writer was a difficult one because the popularity, the idea, waned and they found themselves a little stranded by the critics, who then said, 'What were we making all the fuss about, really?' Nobody's looked back at those books… I really think that we have produced a fantastic number of good short stories – excellent short stories. The poetry – very negligible, I would think. Why that is I don't know, but of course we may be a more physical kind of people than a literary. And the novel I think – you see, sometimes it looks so cunning – with independence an attitude began, I think, that said, 'All right, you're on your own, but you're not so hot.' For instance, Naipaul is the person who is most widely read, the most famous, the most attended-to writer, and… he is treated as a phenomenon, right? I mean somebody who comes out of the bush with a typewriter and a tie, you know what I mean, like… The society produces a writer – a writer

NEW WORLD ADAMS

doesn't just emerge out of a society. But you don't get a situation where people say, 'Hey this guy is – what kind of freak, a *phenomenon* is he?' – an image which Naipaul perpetuates of course, by saying, you know, 'I'm the only kind of one that matters and it's amazing that I've come out of there' – which is total nonsense. They never look around – for instance, the Latin American writers (I'm not saying that they are of the same stature)… I am saying that Naipaul is not a peak with a lot of surrounding foothills. I think for instance James is a phenomenal mind – CLR James.

DANCE: But as a novelist – he has done only one novel.

WALCOTT: Yes as a writer – a man who writes prose. I think *Beyond a Boundary* is a fantastic book, you know, I mean it is elegant, beautiful, a wonderful and exhilarating book. That's terrific! So even if you use Naipaul as a pivotal thing, the work around him – even if you want to think of him as a peak above others who are the foothills and so on – which is not the proportion. The Latin American literature when seen as a whole – I mean there's a Marquez, a Fuentes, a Borges and so forth, but these other writers are not being looked at. But I think they can't be looked down on as being inferior to Naipaul.

DANCE: Naipaul, I take it you're suggesting, has certainly been a bit overly lionised. Are there any writers who simply have not received the kind of recognition that is their due?

WALCOTT: Well, I wouldn't call Naipaul over-lionised. Everything he has gotten he has earned. I mean I wish he would get the Nobel Prize. It would be a great thing for him to have gotten it – a young prize-winner, you know. That would be a thing! What I am saying is that the attention that is paid to Naipaul is not one that is paid to West Indian writing or to the West Indies; it's still a freakish kind of attention, isolated attention, that there can't possibly be anyone with that intelligence and so on. Right now that's the attitude, which is absurd, whereas one could not say that about the Mexican novelists or the Latin American poets.

DANCE: What I am asking you is does the Western literati say, 'Now we've got our West Indian writer with Naipaul,' and do they therefore not recognise any other important talents who are writing today?

WALCOTT: It would have been very easy for Naipaul to point out to people that he is not the only one writing, you know, that's a very simple thing to do. I mean if he chooses not to do that, for whatever reason – he may have contempt for the other writers, which he is entitled to have, but I mean, you know, he has colleagues, he has associates. There was a time when he would say something about West Indian endeavour – a phrase which he would now disparage, you know – in reviewing a book by CLR James. But you see, you can't look on the mind of CLR James also as being an aberration or a phenomenon, you know, I mean the intelligence that one has encountered, in conversation even, in the Caribbean is of an extremely high quality; it is extremely high. And if the conversational quality of people is high, it is just natural that the literature is going to have some quality to it too.

DANCE: OK. Let me ask you about a later generation of writers.

WALCOTT: Yes.

DANCE: The Lovelaces and the Michael Anthonys and so forth. Are some great things going to be happening with these newer writers? Are you as excited about their works as…

WALCOTT: No, I don't like to make that kind of prophesy about people. Now one of the great things about Naipaul obviously is his industry. I don't know how hard a lot of writers in the Caribbean work. I think that (I'm not talking about Earl Lovelace or Michael Anthony), I'm just saying that a lot of writers, especially the poets, for instance… I don't think that writers in the Caribbean (and this may be all over, but let's talk about what I know), that they don't realise that verse is an industry – that the making of verse is as active an industry as somebody going to the office. I'm not saying you have to write every day, but I am saying that that is your craft. And so we get an attitude that is going to expect a poem to emerge suddenly without a practice of the craft… We don't have enough of that attitude of craft of verse. And that has come about because of two possible dangers – race, which is saying that 'I am a Black writer in a Black situation and so on which means that the disciplines that existed before don't apply to me.' That's one. And secondly that nationalism which says that in any small place anybody who publishes a book automatically gets some kind of stature without judgement, and if that person has the least kind of quality in his talent, he can be quite content with limiting his horizon to the immediate approbation around him. And the constant struggle that one has to have in the Caribbean is to keep creating challenges – and this is true of the theatre as well – to keep reminding yourself very hard, that this is not good enough for Paris or for London or for New York, really, and people may say it's following metropolitan standards, but these ultimately are the ones that matter – not in the poetry – I'm not saying you have to go in the same directions – I'm saying that an actor, performing (Right?) is setting himself up in standards that are going to be accepted on stages all over the world, and that we aren't going to become very provincial and say, 'I'm a terrific actor in Trinidad. I'm the best!' and even have the humility about being the best and not keep every day creating a challenge that is going to exhaust him in terms of how much work he has to do to make his craft better. Now this is not saying that these people are imitative of the kind of acting that happens, say, in New York or in London. Because the two South Africans who were in *Sizwe Banzi Is Dead*, and who got, you know, the Toni Awards, and when they asked certain of the actors, 'What do you think of these amateur actors from South Africa?' – two Black actors. And they said they had never seen acting like this, and these were professional actors. It wasn't that they were presenting some kind of spontaneous South African Zulu type of acting that did not have its own fantastic discipline in it, you know, and I guess that whole process of not working hard enough that comes with nationalism is the biggest threat to Caribbean writing.

DANCE: And you don't want to be any more specific about those writers who aren't serious enough about learning their craft?

WALCOTT: No, no. I can just say a couple of things. I think one of the things in the Caribbean is we don't have a publishing house – we don't have our own books published and that is why you never know who is writing. I'm fifty, and there is a generation who is in their late thirties, and then there must be a third generation of people in their twenties, and you worry about, with the situation in publishing as it is, where are they going to get their books done? And that's what we need to have done in the Caribbean, to start to do our own books.

CONVERSATION WITH

SYLVIA WYNTER

Sylvia Wynter was born in Cuba in 1932 to Jamaican parents. After completing her early education in Jamaica, she studied at London University, from which she received the BA and MA degrees. For several years she was a lecturer in the Department of Modem Languages at the University of the West Indies in Kingston. More recently she was Professor of Comparative and Spanish Literature at the University of California at San Diego, and she is currently Chairperson of the African and Afro-American Studies Department and Professor of Spanish at Stanford University.

Ms. Wynter's novel, *The Hills of Hebron: A Jamaican Novel* (1962), focuses on the efforts of a Pocomania-type sect, the New Believers, to establish a religious settlement which they call Hebron. Prevalent in this work are two particular themes which have consistently been of interest to her: the growing awareness of self, specifically the Black's growing awareness of the impact of African influences and traditions; and the strength and endurability of women in relationships with men who attempt to assert their dominance, but who are in actuality weak and impotent.

Several of Ms. Wynter's plays have been produced, including *The University of Hunger* (with Jan Carew), broadcast on the BBC in 1961, televised in 1962 as *The Big Pride*, and performed by the Georgetown Theatre Guild in 1966; *Miracle in Lime Lane* (with Jan Carew), performed in Jamaica in 1962; *Ballad for a Rebellion: Epic Story of Morant Bay Rebellion*, produced in Jamaica in 1965; *Brother Man* (based on Roger Mais's novel), produced in Jamaica in 1965; *Rockstone Anancy: A Magical Morality*, produced in Jamaica in 1970; and *Maskarade*, staged in California in 1994.

A recognised critic of Caribbean literature and a devoted student of the history and culture of the African diaspora, Ms. Wynter has published several significant scholarly and pedagogical pieces: *Do Not Call Us Negroes: How Multicultural Textbooks Perpetuate Racism* (1990); *New Seville [Jamaica], Major Dates, 1509-1536* (1984); and *Jamaica's National Heroes* (1971). Her critical pieces appear in Baugh's *Critics on Caribbean Literature*; John Hearne's *Carifesta Forum: An Anthology of Twenty Caribbean Voices*; Miriam Da Costa's *Blacks in Hispanic Literature: Critical Essays*; and she continues to publish widely in numerous journals. She also contributed to *The Black Feminist Reader* (2000; eds Joy James and T. Denean Sharpley-Whiting).

Also of interest is the cassette recording of one of her lectures, *The Rhetorics of Race and the Politics of Domination* (1983); as well as Anthony Bogue's *Caribbean Reasonings: After Man, Towards the Human: Critical Essays on Sylvia Wynter* (2005).

Ms. Wynter, who is divorced from Guyanese novelist Jan Carew, was, at the time of the interview, living in California with their two sons.

I interviewed Ms. Wynter in Hampton, Virginia on February 21, 1980.

———————————

DANCE: In an essay, 'Reflections on West Indian Writing and Criticism' back in 1968, you wrote, 'I write… to attempt to define what is this thing to be – a Jamaican, a West Indian, an American' [*Jamaica Journal*, II, Dec. 1968]. Would you elaborate on that a little bit?

WYNTER: Well, I told the students today when we were speaking here at this seminar that when I was about seventeen I remember being struck for the first time by the extraordinary role that shades of colour played in the Caribbean, and the way the degrees of colour functioned as a kind of exchange value, just like money. So much so that a professional Black man, for example, would swap [his] education for an uneducated woman of a lighter colour. This seemed to work logically, going beyond subjective choice. So questions about identity became insistent, and I remember writing my first letter to the press on this issue. So I think that the question of identity and how you perceive your identity became very central, and then of course growing up in my childhood, the whole eruption of the social movement of 1938 or 1939 had cast a long shadow, a creative one. For out of that eruption, the labour movements and riots and so on, there was suddenly an awakening to a sense of a group identity in Jamaica. My growing up coincided with the region coming to consciousness. And therefore, when I started writing, I never had any hesitation about what were the questions I wanted to answer. It's always been that in a way, and it's still that to a certain extent.

DANCE: Is it a kind of progression so that first you do indeed define yourself as a Jamaican; then you see yourself in a larger context as a West Indian; and then as an American?

WYNTER: Yes – as an American on the continent, and of course, now, living in the United States, very much in the larger context, as being Black, you see, as being Black and as a part of the African diaspora; and out of all of these, there is the experience of multiple identities that one responds to.

DANCE: Is it significant in this respect that you subtitled your novel *A Jamaican Novel*?

WYNTER: Well, that was rather, that was far more the publishers who did this. It was their title. My title had been quite different. It was called *The End of Exile*. They called it *The Hills of Hebron*. I didn't like that title.

DANCE: Why did you call it *The End of Exile* – because exile is not – well, I started to say it's not a theme in this novel, but what do you mean by exile? Is going to Hebron...

WYNTER: Well, actually I think I had read a poem or something of the writings of Santa Teresa, and I was struck by the phrase where she spoke of 'this welcome hour of the end of exile'. The novel has to do with a community which stops worshipping the dead prophet founder and comes to an awareness of itself. The suggestion was that this worship of a dead past had also been a kind of exile. So here were multiple exiles, and one had to do with exile from a tradition – the tradition of Africa. So although the episode didn't work, the idea of this anthropologist giving this Black carving to the hero, it was intended as another sort of return, a reconnection of a tradition when the community consciously comes to know where it's come from.

DANCE: Do you say it didn't work because you imposed it upon the novel – that it didn't come naturally out of...

WYNTER: I think the idea of the novel was a very good one. I would actually like to use it again. I think the theme was excellent. But I failed with it because I wasn't bold enough to have broken away from the format of the realist novel. The magical realism of say Gabriel Garcia Marquez in Latin America – that's what I should have done with the novel; but at the time, of course, novels like that hadn't been written, so I didn't have it as a model, and I myself was not inventive enough to create such a model.

DANCE: OK. Let me ask you about another statement you made in that same essay, in which you said that literature is not an end in itself but that it should be a means towards 'revolutionary assault' against the sickness of society. Were you attempting to make a 'revolutionary assault' against the sickness of Jamaican society there?

WYNTER: Well, I suppose now I would put it more carefully, especially in the light of events that have occurred in Jamaica, and possibly a statement like that might have been too careless at the time, because the whole question of ends and means… perhaps I would not use it. But I still feel that all social orders are constituted by the meaning systems, by what Cornelius Castoriadis, a French theorist, calls social imaginary significations. Now, I think that what literature actually does… at a certain level is to make these social imaginary significations real, make them visible. That's why we read with such fascination, because these significations we can't see; they're not empirically graspable, but I think that fiction actually enables us to see some of these meanings in which we live enmeshed, embedded, not even aware that they exist. These meanings help us to perceive reality in a certain way and therefore act upon reality in a certain way, and I think literature helps us to grasp these meanings and to be able to help change and transform these meanings when this is necessary.

DANCE: Do you think immediately of any Anglo-Caribbean works that have achieved that or that have come close to that?

WYNTER: I would say that *In the Castle of My Skin* does this magnificently. First of all there had been the riots in the Caribbean in 1938, a rupture with the colonial consciousness, but when Lamming evokes the Empire Day celebrations in the school, what he makes us see is our pre-1938 way of seeing, the way in which our identity at that time was actually coded as British, and how it had been logical that we should feel ourselves British because all the structures coded us to feel that way. He does this in that hilarious scene in which the students discuss the fact that all the flags are up with their red, white, and blue – they want to know whether perhaps Queen Victoria's bloomers were also red, white, and blue too. Here is a parallel with Garcia Marquez's *The Autumn of the Patriarch*, a novel which sends up the whole despotic nationalistic tradition of Latin America. In his novel the dictator's hammock is in the national colours too. The train is in the national colours. The same wrapping-up of despotism in the national flag – or the party colours. With Lamming's novel suddenly all of us were able to see that we had had a British national identity, and that's why we had acted in certain ways: made choices, desired our own subordination.

DANCE: It's interesting that in that novel in sort of, if we may say, the quest for identity, one of his characters expands his quest through his trip to America and comes to some new realisations there, Is that particularly significant? It's perhaps the step that you were talking about earlier.

WYNTER: Yes, and we discussed this again at the talk. That's a very significant scene, because Trumper points out that in the Caribbean at that time (because things *have* changed very much) you were a Caribbean man, or a Barbadian man, or a Jamaican man, and, yes, there was this tremendous colour thing embedded in the society; but you were not *just* Negroes, without the man attached. When you came to America, suddenly you were Negroes, and therefore you come to know the race, to sharply experience being a category excluded from manness. And I'd like to mention that this still happens: that for me as a West Indian, coming to America has been a learning process, in which one aspect of my identity in the Caribbean becomes more dominant in response to the total way in which Blacks are stigmatised in this society. So you shift from a primarily Caribbean identity to a primarily Black identity when you're here in the States.

DANCE: I see. OK. You seem to be very interested in the fact that West Indian literature should reflect the West Indian people, by which I think you perhaps mean a peasant class, and you certainly treat that class in *The Hills of Hebron*. But one thing that interested me there is that in your treatment of that class, you do not do very much in terms of reproducing the dialect. Why was that?

WYNTER: Well, there were a lot of unsolved problems in that novel, because I don't think that one can be… you know, you write a novel, and you should have the time to continue with other novels, which I've just not had for all kinds of reasons – you know, essentially having to make a living, and finding the different ways. Well, I think there are a lot of unsolved questions. One thing unsolved was the problem of an inventive literary use of dialect, because for one thing, I do not have that immaculately sensitive ear that Selvon and Naipaul have. So that was obviously not my strength. So I would say that what I should have done was to do what Lamming did at the beginning of *In the Castle of My Skin*, and just use the Biblical cadences and not attempted the dialect at all. Do what Alejo Carpentier does in *The Kingdom of This World*. In the novel I'm doing, I'm trying to use the cadences of the language, the dialectal forms rather than to try and reproduce the dialect, since I don't think that that's my strength. I haven't got a very good ear.

DANCE: The novel that you're doing to which you refer – can you tell me a little about it?

WYNTER: Well, it's called *The Work*. I did an enormous amount of research on a historical event in Jamaica called the 1865 Rebellion, and I actually wrote a play for it, which was put on; but it was not a good play, because I collected a lot of material, and again I hadn't had the time to find the form. But there were a few good parts. And so I thought what I'd like to do is to try and work on a historical faction, something like *Roots*, including actual documentary material with the fictional story.

DANCE: Will its scope be as broad as *Roots*?

WYNTER: Not quite – because it would deal from post-slavery (1839) up until 1865 when the whole thing breaks, 1866 – it would not be that long.

DANCE: Andrew Salkey told me that you wrote *The Hills of Hebron* in response to *A Quality of Violence*.

WYNTER: No, his was published after mine.

DANCE: Oh really?

WYNTER: Mine was published in '62. When was his published?

DANCE: I was thinking it was earlier than that. [It was published in 1959.]

WYNTER: Really?

DANCE: I may be wrong. I'll have to check.

WYNTER: Please check it for me. But even so, even if it didn't come after – my novel was originally a radio play which we had broadcast, and practically every West Indian writer was in it. Salkey had one of the lead roles. I then rewrote the play into a novel. This play was put on somewhat earlier. We could check the date of the play's broadcast. The irony is that I think *A Quality of Violence* is my least favourite West Indian novel.

DANCE: Really?

WYNTER: Yes. In fact, my own criticism of my own novel is in the areas where I think it falls into the same pseudo-populism as I think Salkey's does. And I'm not being malicious – this is really a critical judgement.

DANCE: Is that what you consider the problem with the novel?

WYNTER: Yes, you see – you listened to Selvon, and there's no distance. One of the dangers I think all of us fall into, including myself, is wanting to write for the people. We tend sometimes to manipulate the people – and I'm no exception to that. You posit the people, and they become manipulated figures. That horrible scene in Salkey about whipping away the drought shows an entire ignorance of you know, the meaning behind the cult religions. I think that some of my book, where it fails, also fails because of an insufficient awareness of the logic of the popular culture we were trying to write about. I still did not know enough. In fact, in my writing now, because I now know so much more, it's like being able to give the structures of meaning that underlie them, you see, to reach down to the symbolic logic that underlies the popular customs. *A Quality of Violence* is melodramatic and pseudo-populist. So are some areas of my novel. But I really didn't write it in response to Andrew, I assure you. You can check the dates. It may be that it's earlier, but I do know that the play – it was written as a play – and this was done by the BBC before I wrote it up into a novel.

DANCE: Yes. OK. Tell me why you have Moses exclaim just before he dies, having offered himself up to be crucified for this Black god, 'God is white after all'? Is that sort of *your* disillusionment…

WYNTER: No, I think that – I don't know what it was I thought then, because it just came that way. It just came. It just seemed very logical. I didn't plan it that way.

DANCE: Such a cruel irony though.

WYNTER: Yes, it just leapt up. I don't think I even planned it. I suppose what I was trying to show or what at the time I felt was that Moses's dream had been a dream of grandeur, but a dream that focused on his own desire for grandeur. His dream was a dream in which he then caught up the others, even to their own detriment. The one part of the book that I'm very proud of still is that incident when he has led them up into Hebron and tells them to burn everything that [they owned in the past], and Miss Gatha conceals this apron from him and she hides it. This is the beginning of her rebellion against him because what he is trying to do is a total imposition of his dream on them, and she rebels against this. I'm proud of that. I look at it and I say, 'But I did that – that was good.' I am not proud of much else. Now Moses had a dream in which the people existed as, in a sense, players in this great dream that he had, and Miss Gatha is the only one who rebels against this. Somebody, by the way, rang me and said did I realise that there were parallels with Jonestown. I hadn't thought about that, but you see now that's the kind of thing I think Moses had, something like Jim Jones, megalomania, and this grandeur. So I made Obadiah, the hero, the exact opposite. He didn't quite come off though, fictionally speaking, not in the way Miss Gatha does –

you know, her hiding away this frilly apron and keeping it, and taking it out and stroking it, whenever this rage built up in her against him.

DANCE: Could you tell me something about historical influences on the characters? Is Bedward...

WYNTER: Yes, of course, it was – the idea was Bedward, and then mixed with the Jordan in Guyana who also actually attempted to crucify himself and in fact Jan Carew uses Jordan's crucifixion in *Black Midas*.

DANCE: Yes. There's a revolutionary character whose name is Bellows who appears periodically in the novel and he suggests Garvey and Bustamante a bit to me. Were they...

WYNTER: Well, he's far more... actually I think even at that time, however vaguely, I was touching on what has become a central concern – the distinction between the Marxist approach to revolution and what I see as a Black approach – some of it is cultural nationalist, but it's not only cultural nationalist, popular, perhaps. I think it's a different approach to a different kind of transformation. As you notice, this chap Bellows comes, and he speaks, but in the end it's Obadiah who somehow carries whatever it is through. It was a vague positing of the distinction, but there was something of Bustamante in it, of the Marxist-populist distinction, but not really sorted out.

DANCE: I'd like for us to talk a little bit about the role of women in Caribbean literature. Would you just comment generally? Who are the outstanding names among women in Caribbean literature, particularly Anglo-Caribbean?

WYNTER: I don't think there are any. I gather there's a young girl called Merle Hodge who has written *Crick Crack Monkey*. I haven't read it as yet. I don't think women have played a large role as yet in fiction. I think there are all kinds of reasons why not. I mean certainly from my perspective, I had no choice after this novel. If I'd stayed in London, I'd have continued writing novels. But once I went back to the Caribbean I had to take a job to support the two children, and then I started to teach. But I think that we're going to have generations of young women now coming up who will be writers because the automatic idea that you get married and so on is somehow, with women's lib and so on, being marginalised. So, I think we're going to start getting some women writers now, full time writers, not occasional like before.

DANCE: Let me ask you about your interest in Jamaican folklore, which is quite obvious as one reads your works. Could you tell me something about how this developed.

WYNTER: Well, I think I was very lucky in my family background in that I was not part of the official middle class, which meant that I wasn't cut away from that surrounding popular culture that was there. Both sets of my grandparents were in the country, and we were sent to the country; and both of them were peasants in the sense that one would have fifty acres of land and one would have, say, like twenty-five. Compared to the surrounding people they were reasonably well off but they were sort of peasant families; and therefore in my childhood I lived in a popular cultural tradition. But my intellectual interest really came from about 1970 when I first did a long article called 'Jonkunnu in Jamaica: Towards the Sociology of the Folk Dance' [*Jamaica Journal*, IV, June 1970] and as I said last night it was a fantastic discovery of a real buried archipelago that was there, another world, imaginative and alive. Since then I have been working and reworking the ideas of the original paper, and I have found parallels here in the United States and all over the Caribbean. Obviously there is an Afro-American culture sphere, and I think it's out of this sphere that jazz and the whole gamut of the reggae and the calypso emerged as new universal popular forms helping to transform the global imaginative landscape.

DANCE: Yes. What about *Rockstone Anancy*? I haven't read that, but one critic says you attempt there a 'new' view of Brer Anancy. What is he talking about? What is the 'new' view?

WYNTER: Well what had happened was that we had only seen the funny side of Anancy as the trickster, but Anancy is a part of Akan folklore, and the other side of him is the god, the trickster god. What I did in this pantomime was to suggest that only the trickster part had come to the Caribbean. The god part had been left in Africa. But when things got bad, the god part came to rescue and purge the trickster part, so that god and trickster were rejoined again.

DANCE: I am struck by the preponderance of selfish, lost, weak male characters in the works of several Caribbean writers such as Salkey and Lamming and Austin Clarke, in particular, but also in a lesser degree in the works of almost all of the male writers. What they do with women varies. Andrew Salkey and George Lamming [sometimes] tend, I think, to romanticise them, and yet I find their women shallow. Could you tell me how generally you perceive the pictures of women projected by Caribbean writers, who are by and large male writers.

WYNTER: Well, the really powerful ones are mothers I think – Lamming's mother in *The Castle*. But apart from John Hearne who deals far more in the middle-class world and therefore deals with women characters as other than mothers, women as wives and lovers, that's been absent. Women are curiously absent in Lamming's novels – women as women – they're just not there. Even in *Natives of My Person*, where they appear, it seems to me that… they are related to the men insofar as the men fail or do not fail to carry out a project. But it's the mother figure that is dominant. I haven't read much of Salkey. I remember one novel he wrote in London, set in London, which I thought responded very much to his own experiences, and I liked that one, but I haven't read any other things of his. Naipaul's women are very well observed, as in *Biswas*. They remind you very much of Tina in 'Brackley and the Bed' by Selvon. By the way, that's an excellent woman character – Tina, in 'Brackley and the Bed' I mean. But if you look at it in terms of the love relations, they just don't exist, somehow.

DANCE: Yes, I really think among the writers that I've read that Austin Clarke creates probably the most fully-rounded…

WYNTER: … Women characters. That's true, that's very true. You're quite right. I hadn't thought of that, because I haven't read very much of him, but I have read a couple of his novels and that's true…

DANCE: I don't know whether you remember Rachel Ascom – you mentioned John Hearne – in his *The Faces of Love*. She's certainly a contemptible bitchy kind of woman, and yet she's extremely powerful. I've not seen any other female who wields that kind of power.

WYNTER: Yes. She's a very good character. There's just – she's almost a stereotype of that mulatto, but I think he brings it off and it's not the stereotype – but it's always on the edge of a Cecille B Demillish, Dorothy Dandridge kind of a thing, but I think he does bring it off actually by some of the complexities, now that I look back upon it from this distance. I think he brings her off.

DANCE: Let me ask you if you would just comment briefly on your assessment of contemporary Caribbean literature. Where is it moving? What new themes are emerging? What are its major concerns? What should be its goals? Any of these areas that you'd like to touch upon.

WYNTER: Well the only thing that I would say that seems to mark a new direction is a novel that I read called *Ikael Torass* [by ND Williams], it uses the Jamaican expression 'to rass'; and it's based on the Rastafarian scene. It's about a young student from somewhere else in the Caribbean who comes to Jamaica and to Mona. The novel deals with, for example, the University march and riot in the 1960s after Rodney was refused readmittance. It deals with that whole generation and the problems at the University and their awakening to political consciousness. This novel begins to deal with problems we never dealt with – the relations of men, and women; and you know they're sort of messed up in all kinds of problems, but I think that's where it's going to go – more focus on the interpersonal relations interlinked with the politics, which I think hadn't been there before.

DANCE: Who do you consider the most important writers on the scene today? Anglo-Caribbean writers?

WYNTER: Lamming, and Selvon, in his way, and Naipaul, although after *Guerrillas* (you know *Guerrillas*?) I detect a note of repetition. They gave it high praise. Yet if you compare *Guerrillas* with Lamming's *Water With Berries*, I'm willing to bet that within twenty-five years *Water With Berries* is going to be a masterpiece and *Guerrillas* will be seen as a good novel, good, competent, very good, very competent – but it's not a great thing, and I think that *Water With Berries* is. I know Harris is considered great; I just cannot read him. I know that there is something quite different about him and quite extraordinary, but I do not feel that it has got gelled together to make a novelist, but this is, as I know, a highly eccentric opinion. What I think is beginning to happen in the world is that increasingly as academia spreads over everything there are some authors that I think are – it's not that they write to be read as texts, but they provide material for critical works.

DANCE: And he is one of those?

WYNTER: I think so, although he doesn't set out to do that. He's a very honest man, and he's very engaged, and he has a quite remarkable mind, but it's as if somewhere, to me, there's something that doesn't really come together, certainly for me. But I think, you know, one has to mention him, but I would say that the new young ones to have come up...for instance in the theatre now, we have someone like Trevor Rhone. Trevor Rhone is obviously very, very gifted. And you're getting people like Thelwell beginning to write short stories and I gather he has just rewritten *The Harder They Come*, and I'd like to see that. So I think that there is a new thing beginning to emerge but it hasn't really emerged as yet.

DANCE: All right. Well, thank you very much.

INDEX

ABOUT THE AUTHOR

Daryl Cumber Dance holds A.B. and M.A. degrees in English from Virginia State University and a Ph.D. in English from the University of Virginia. She is currently Professor of English at Virginia Commonwealth University. She has been awarded two Ford Foundation fellowships, three Southern Fellowship Fund grants, two NEH grants, one Fulbright research grant, and others, and has presented approximately 50 papers at conferences.

Her publications include *Shuckin' and Jivin': Folklore from Contemporary Black Americans* (1978); *Folklore from Contemporary Jamaicans* (1985); *Fifty Caribbean Writers: A Bio-Bibliographical Critical Sourcebook* (1986); *Long Gone: The Mecklenberg Six and the Theme of Escape in Black Folklore* (1987); *Honey Hush! An Anthology of African American Women's Humor* (1998); *The Lineage of Abraham: The Biography of a Free Black Family in Charles City VA* (1998); and *From My People: 400 Years of African American Folklore* (2003)

Edited Stewart Brown
All Are Involved: The Art of Martin Carter
ISBN: 9781900715263; 414pp; 1999; £15.99

This book sets out to celebrate Martin Carter's life and work and to establish a context for reading his poetry. It locates the several facets of Carter's work in the historical and cultural circumstances of his time, in Guyana, in the Caribbean. It includes essays by many leading academics and scholars of Caribbean literature and history. It is distinguished particularly by a collection of responses to Carter's work by other creative writers, both his contemporaries and a younger generation for whom Carter's work and commitment has been a powerful influence on their own thinking and practice. As well as demonstrating the profound respect in which he is held as a writer, what emerges most strongly from this group of essays and poems from his fellow writers is the extent to which he was loved and admired as a man who - despite the turmoil Guyana has experienced over the last fifty years - remained true to his fundamental belief in the dignity of humankind.

Contributors include John Agard, Edward Baugh, Kamau Brathwaite, Stewart Brown, Jan Carew, David Dabydeen, Fred D'Aguiar, Kwame Dawes, Michael Gilkes, Stanley Greaves, Wilson Harris, Roy Heath, Kendel Hippolyte, Louis James, Linton Kwesi Johnson, Eusi Kwayana, George Lamming, Ian McDonald, Mark McWatt, Mervyn Morris, Grace Nichols, Ken Ramchand, Gordon Rohlehr, Rupert Roopnaraine, Andew Salkey and many others.

Niyi Osundare writes in *World Literature Today*: '*All Are Involved* is a difficult book to review. Its contents are so packed, so vital, the statements so well made that paraphrasing them becomes an act of egregious violence. Here is Martin Carter, that "gifted, paradoxical man" (p.45), that "friendly, dreamful, dangerous man" (p.370), analysed, extolled, lavished with the recognition which eluded him in life because of the politics of his poetry, and the poignant truth and moral force of that politics. This book demonstrates how wrong we were to have neglected Carter's voice, how diminished. *All Are Involved* is a treasure so empowering, a tribute we pay through Martin Carter to all that is human in us. It is a most enduring legacy.'

Laurence A. Breiner
Black Yeats: Eric Roach and the Politics of Caribbean Poetry
ISBN: 9781845230470; 312pp; 2008; £16.99

For readers of West Indian literature, a study of Eric Roach requires no justification. He is the most significant poet in the English-speaking Caribbean between Claude McKay (who spent nearly all of his life abroad) and Derek Walcott. Roach began publishing in the late 1930s and continued, with a few interruptions, until 1974, the year of his suicide. His career thus spans an extraordinary period of Anglophone Caribbean history, from the era of violent strikes that led to the formation of most of the region's political parties, through the process of decolonization, the founding and subsequent failure of the Federation of the West Indies (1958-1962), and the coming of Independence in the 1960s. This book presents a critical analysis of all of Roach's published poetry, but it presents that interpretation as part of a broader study of the relations between his poetic activity, the political events he experienced (especially West Indian Federation, Independence, the Black Power movement, the 'February Revolution' of 1970 Trinidad), and the seminal debates about art and culture in which he participated.

By exploring Roach's work within its conditions, this book aims above all to confirm Roach's rightful place among West Indian and metropolitan poets of comparable gifts and accomplishments.

Laurence Breiner is the author of the critically acclaimed *Introduction to West Indian Poetry*.

Edited Lynne Macedo
No Land, No Mother: Essays on David Dabydeen
ISBN: 9781845230203; pp. 236; 2007; £12.99

The essays in this collection focus on the rich dialogue carried out in David Dabydeen's critically acclaimed body of writing. Dialogue across diversity and the simultaneous habitation of multiple arenas are seen as dominant characterics of his work. Essays by Aleid Fokkema, Tobias Döring, Heike Härting and Madina Tlostanova provide rewardingly complex readings of Dabydeen's Turner, locating it within a revived tradition of Caribbean epic (with reference to Walcott, Glissant and Arion), as subverting and appropriating the romantic aesthetics of the sublime and in the connections between the concept of terror in Turner's painting and in Fanon's classic works on colonisation. Lee Jenkins and Pumla Gqola explore Dabydeen's fondness for intertextual reference, his dialogue with canonic authority and ideas about the masculine in his work. Michael Mitchell, Mark Stein, Christine Pagnoulle and Gail Low focus on Dabydeen's more recent fiction, *Disappearance*, *A Harlot's Progress* and *The Counting House*. By dealing with his more recent work and looking more closely at Dabydeen's Indo-Guyanese background, this collection complements the earlier *The Art of David Dabydeen*.

Lynne Macedo currently lectures at the Centre for Caribbean Studies, University of Warwick. She is the author of *Fiction and Film: The Influence of Cinema on Writers in Jamaica and Trinidad*.

Edited Martin Zehnder
Something Rich and Strange: Selected Essays on Samuel Selvon
ISBN: 9781900715737; pp. 252; 2003; £14.99

Critical work on Samuel Selvon has passed through several phases. Initially there was a tendency to treat it as charming, humorous, folksy, naïve and lacking in structure. Then criticism focused on his innovations in the language of narrative and Maureen

Warner-Lewis's essay is one of the most brilliant in this framework, demonstrating just how sophisticated and artful was Selvon's play with language register.

Another tendency was to treat Selvon's work as expressing a West Indianness that subsumed his own Indo-Caribbean origins. Harold Barrett's essay shows by close analysis that Selvon's treatment of Indianness always suggests the necessity for it to become part of the Caribbean whole, but without in any sense becoming subsumed. Major cultural theorists such as Kamau Brathwaite and Antonio Benitez-Rojo have begun to delineate a specifically Caribbean aesthetics, and the essay by John Thieme shows how central Selvon's work is to this project in its use of the archetype of carnival.

More recent postmodernist treatments of Selvon have seized on the ironic play with intertextuality in his later novels in a way which loses sight of underlying patterns of meaning and social commitment. John Stephen Martin's essay is a salutary restatement of Selvon's humanist philosophy. In short, the essays in this collection both advance the depth of appreciation and understanding of Selvon's fiction and present an admirably balanced range of approaches towards it.

Stewart Brown
Tourist, Traveller, Troublemaker: Essays on Poetry
ISBN: 9781845230531; pp. 300; 2007; £16.99

This isn't a conventional book of academic essays, though these pieces on Caribbean, African, British and American poets are always scholarly and intellectually rigorous. They are particularly rewarding as the work of a practicing poet writing about those of his peers whose work he admires. There are essays on major Caribbean figures, on Walcott, Brathwaite and Martin Carter, and on the major African poets Niyi Osundare, Jack Mapanje and Femi Oyebode, but there are also pieces on less well-known poets such as Frank Collymore, Ian McDonald and James Berry that, without any agenda, bring to view work that ought to be taken far more seriously. As the editor of major anthologies of Caribbean poetry, Stewart Brown is more than usually aware of the new directions that Caribbean poetry has taken, and pieces on Olive Senior, Linton Kwesi Johnson and Kwame Dawes indicate some of these.

How other societies are perceived has long been a preoccupation of Stewart Brown's own poetry and critical writing, and essays on the work of poets who have travelled frame this collection. Here he explores his own and other writers' work to make distinctions between the discourses of tourist, traveller and troublemaker. One subtext of the collection is a mistrust of the academic industry of postcolonial criticism. Here it is always the poem that matters (although the essays are alert to social, political and cultural contexts) and the emphasis is on close and sensitive reading rather than theory.

A good many of these essays began as papers for oral delivery. One of their great pleasures is that they retain a flavour of the speaking voice: enthusiastic, generous and respectful of the presence of listeners, and now readers.

Kwame Dawes
Natural Mysticism: Towards a new Reggae Aesthetic
ISBN: 9781900715225; pp. 296; 1999, 2004; £14.99

Kwame Dawes speaks for all those for whom reggae is a major part of life. He describes how reggae has been central to his sense of selfhood, his consciousness of place and society in Jamaica, his development as a writer – and why the singer Ken Boothe should be inseparably connected to his discovery of the erotic.

Natural Mysticism is also a work of acute cultural analysis. Dawes argues that in the rise of roots reggae in the 1970s, Jamaica produced a form which was both wholly of the region and universal in its concerns. He contrasts this with the mainstream of Caribbean literature which, whilst anticolonial in sentiment was frequently conservative and colonial in form. Dawes finds in reggae's international appeal more than just an encouraging example. In the work of artists such as Don Drummond, Bob Marley, Winston Rodney and Lee 'Scratch' Perry, he finds a complex aesthetic whose inner structure points in a genuinely contemporary and postcolonial direction. He identifies this aesthetic as being both original and eclectic, as feeling free to borrow, but transforming what it takes in a subversive way. He sees it as embracing both the traditional and the postmodern, the former in the complex subordination of the lyric, melodic and rhythmic elements to the collective whole, and the latter in the dubmaster's deconstructive play with presences and absences. Above all, he shows that it is an aesthetic which unites body, emotions and intellect and brings into a single focus the political, the spiritual and the erotic.

In constructing this reggae aesthetic, Kwame Dawes both creates a rationale for the development of his own writing and brings a new and original critical method to the discussion of the work of other contemporary Caribbean authors. *Natural Mysticism* has the rare merit of combining rigorous theoretical argument with a personal narrative which is often wickedly funny. Here is a paradigm shifting work of Caribbean cultural and literary criticism with the added bonus of conveying an infectious enthusiasm for reggae which will drive readers back to their own collections or even to go out and extend them!

All Peepal Tree titles are available from our website:
www.peepaltreepress.com; email contact@peepaltreepress.com
Write to or phone us at Peepal Tree Press, 17 Kings Avenue,
Leeds LS6 1QS, UK (Tel +44 113 245 1703)